T0279457

Desire to Serve

The Autobiography of Congresswoman Eddie Bernice Johnson

Eddie Bernice Johnson

As Told To
Cheryl Brown Wattley

UNT Dallas College of Law

University of North Texas Press
Denton, Texas

10 9 8 7 6 5 4 3 2 1

Permissions:
University of North Texas Press
1155 Union Circle #311336
Denton, TX 76203-5017

The paper used in this book meets the minimum requirements of the American
National Standard for Permanence of Paper for Printed Library Materials,
z39.48.1984. Binding materials have been chosen for durability.

Library of Congress Cataloging-in-Publication Data

Names: Johnson, Eddie Bernice, 1934- author. | Wattley, Cheryl Elizabeth
    Brown, 1953- author, editor.
Title: Desire to serve : The Autobiography of Congresswoman Eddie Bernice
    Johnson / Eddie Bernice Johnson; as told to Cheryl Brown Wattley.
Other titles: Autobiography of Congresswoman Eddie Bernice Johnson
Description: Denton, Texas : University of North Texas, [2024] | Includes
    bibliographical references and index.
Identifiers: LCCN 2024009289 (print) | LCCN 2024009290 (ebook) |
    ISBN 9781574419504 (cloth) | ISBN 9781574419597 (ebook)
Subjects: LCSH: Johnson, Eddie Bernice, 1934- | Texas. Legislature. House
    of Representatives--Biography. | Texas. Legislature. Senate--Biography.
    United States. Congress. Senate--Biography. | African American women
    legislators--Texas--Biography. | African American women
    legislators--United States--Biography. | Women
    legislators--Texas--Biography. | Women legislators--
    United States--Biography. | Legislators--Texas--Biography. |
    Legislators--United States--Biography. | Texas--Politics and
    government--1951- | United States--Politics and government--
    20th century. | United States--Politics and government--21st century. |
    Texas--Biography.
Classification: LCC E840.8.J613 A3 2024 (print) | LCC E840.8.J613 (ebook)
LC record available at https://lccn.loc.gov/2024009289
LC ebook record available at https://lccn.loc.gov/2024009290

The electronic edition of this book was made possible by the support of the Vick
Family Foundation. Typeset by vPrompt eServices.

Contents

Contents

Foreword

I f there ever has been a finer person to serve in Texas state government or in the United States Congress than Eddie Bernice Johnson, I do not know who she or he is.

She was the first woman to represent Dallas in both the Texas House and Texas Senate; the first African American female to chair a major Texas House committee, the Labor Committee; the first registered nurse (RN) ever elected to the US Congress; the longest-serving member of the US House of Representatives from Texas; dean of the Texas congressional delegation; and chairwoman of the House Committee on Science, Space and Technology.

She never lost an election in her fifty years of public service. "I worked every day to try to make things better," she once said. "There is no Texan in the history of this state who has worked harder to bring more home to their district."

An example: "My baby from the first day that I got there was the Dallas Area Rapid Transit system (DART)." DART has an annual ridership of 36.9 million. It is the longest light-rail system in the United States, moving 220,000 people a day around Dallas and its twelve surrounding cities (seven hundred square miles of services).

To me she has always been an understated, dedicated, passionate, and courageous fighter for "what's right," whether it was for equal opportunity for the disenfranchised and underrepresented, including job creation and American global competitiveness.

Eddie Bernice is a uniter, not a divider. Much of her success has been in building bipartisan relationships across the aisle with Republicans. "As much as we Democrats sometimes trash Republicans," she said, "they were the same ones who helped me to be successful." As another example of her reaching out to diverse groups, Eddie Bernice created the "Tri-Caucus" that brought together the Congressional Black Caucus, Congressional Hispanic Caucus, and Congressional Asian Pacific Caucus.

She is recognized as one of the most effective legislators in Congress, credited with authoring and coauthoring more than 292 bills passed by the House and Senate and signed into law, including the most significant investment in American science, technology, and innovation in over a decade, the CHIPS and Science Act.

Of very personal interest to me and to millions of others was Eddie Bernice's fierce advocacy of the National Suicide Hotline Improvement Act that was passed and signed into law by President Biden last year. Her persistent and successful leadership led the Federal Communications Commission to establish a three-digit suicide hotline number for the entire nation (988). (I lost two close personal friends, both Texans, to suicide in recent years.)

Having been an assistant to President Johnson for eight years and having served for thirty years as chairman of the LBJ Foundation, I believe I can speak for him with his highest compliment: "Eddie Bernice, I am so VERY proud of you. I give you A plus for all your accomplishments for Texas and for America."

This splendid book tells the spectacular story of her incredible life and times. America is a better place because of Eddie Bernice Johnson.

Tom Johnson,
former chairman, Lyndon B. Johnson Foundation;
former editor and publisher, *Dallas Times Herald*;
former publisher, *Los Angeles Times*;
former CEO, CNN;
former executive assistant to former president Lyndon B. Johnson

Preface by Cheryl Brown Wattley

❝ Eddie Bernice. God love you. You're sitting there, you're ready, you did it all, you moved it." Those were the words spoken by President Joe Biden as he thanked the congressional leadership before a crowd gathered on the South Lawn of the White House for the signing of the CHIPS and Science Act. This shout-out by President Biden underscored something that I have grown to appreciate about Congresswoman Johnson as I have worked with her on this book: she doesn't give up. When she knows that she is working on a righteous cause, she refuses to submit to roadblocks, patiently yet persistently finding another way around. In times of growing acrimony and strident partisanship, she has remained steadfast that legislators must work together, that our governmental institutions depend on the commitment of public servants.

I first met Eddie Bernice Johnson in 1986 when she was running for Texas State Senate. I had recently left the United States Attorney's Office and for the first time in my adult career was able to actively support a candidate in a partisan election. I connected with her campaign, serving as a volunteer and attorney.

One morning when we arrived at her campaign headquarters, we discovered that the building had been burglarized. She walked to the door of her office and immediately noticed that her portable radio had been stolen. It was a radio that she had purchased for her father while he was in the hospital during his final illness. Her face showed the pain that she felt at the theft as it took her to the memories of her father's illness and death. She entered her office, closing the door behind her. A few minutes later she emerged, totally composed, ready to focus on the business of the day. As I watched her, Ernest Hemingway's words "grace under pressure" came to me—words that I continue to associate with her. It is a memory that stays with me, a reminder of the humanness of an icon.

In helping her to write her autobiography, I faced two challenges that I did not fully appreciate when I started: How to present the breadth of a career spanning fifty years and how to spotlight all that she has done when she herself is understated about her accomplishments? In other words, how do I assure justice to Congresswoman Johnson's legacy?

The tributes and accolades after the announcement of her retirement, each event, every speech created a crescendo of praise and gratitude. With each article, magazine profile, or banquet, the pressure to capture the powerful impact of this unassuming woman intensified. The culmination was the installation of her portrait at the Capitol—the first African American and first female to serve as the chair of a House committee.

Questions often overwhelmed me as we worked on this book. Congresswoman Johnson has addressed so many issues. She has championed causes, being steadfast in her consistency. Will we omit something that should have been included? How do I help her capture the work that was required, the skill that was commanded and make it more than just a litany of accomplishments? In what way do we incorporate legislation when she sponsored or cosponsored over thousands of bills and resolutions, hundreds of which were passed into law? How do we demonstrate the work that is required to identify a problem, shape ideas about solutions into finite activities, maneuver through agencies and committees, translate into legislation—usually hundreds of pages in length—and then secure votes to assure passage? How do I help readers appreciate the breadth of the work that she undertook to serve her nation? Will they understand that presenting legislation and projects that needed decades to achieve may require referencing earlier described activities, that not all of her work fit neatly into chronological boxes? How do we create a sense of the woman who not only personally broke so many barriers but also remains a constant voice that those barriers need to be removed, who continued to be integral to critical legislation up to her retirement?

As we were working on the manuscript, celebrity suicides brought a spotlight on mental health issues and became the springboard for news stories, articles, and commercials about the launch of the 988 federal suicide hotline. The media attention underscored the importance of this innovation and the impact of having a simple, easily remembered lifeline. Dial 988 to get connected to a mental health expert anywhere in the country. You can get help.

This accessible resource for mental health assistance was Congresswoman Johnson's idea. She understood the impact of mental health from her days as a psychiatric nurse. She knew that getting help had to be easy. It took years from conception to launch, but it happened.

But every step of the way, Congresswoman Johnson was patient, steadfast, and determined. She crafted the legislation directing the Federal Communications Commission to do a feasibility study for a simplified hotline. She took their favorable assessment as the foundation for legislation implementing the 988 hotline. She pushed for funding to facilitate the beginning of nationwide coordinated mental health services provided through crisis centers. She gave the American public a lifeline for people contemplating suicide. Yet she only spoke of it when I asked her about it. This is a theme of Congresswoman's Johnson's accomplishments: What impacts people? What can be done to help? How do we make that happen?

There are so many things that we take for granted, as if they have always been around, such as not getting fired for missing work to go to jury duty. But it took her recognition of that problem, her development of a solution, and her skill to gather the votes to make this an expected part of Texas life.

When we take time to pause, to learn of her work, we see our lives have been touched by it. We become aware that, as recognized in the Arizona State University News, "it's hard to name a single person who has had a greater impact on U.S. science legislation in the 21st century than U.S. Representative Eddie Bernice Johnson." We appreciate the "real grit to have the cards stacked against you from your identity and still persist in being able to have major deliverables" for the nation.[1]

While we can identify legislation and programs, what may be less obvious is her impact and role in reaching back while reaching out. But for those of us who traveled to DC for the unveiling of her portrait in the Committee Room for Science, Space, and Technology, we were immersed in outpourings of appreciation.

A small group was gathered in her office, visiting, enjoying her great-grandchildren, when Luci Baines Johnson, the youngest daughter of President Lyndon Johnson, walked through the door. She had come to honor the congresswoman. She presented her with a signed copy of President Johnson's memoirs, one that had been a family copy. It had been Luci's desire to do research on the impact of hearing impairment on speech development that had led to her volunteering in then Texas House Representative Johnson's office. Luci referred to that time as "working for Eddie Bernice." The congresswoman called it the foundation of a lifelong friendship with the Johnson family.

As the morning continued, on the monitor playing in the background we heard Speaker Nancy Pelosi announce that she would not seek a party leadership role in the upcoming Congress. Within minutes there were predictions that New York Representative Hakeem Jeffries would be selected to serve as chair of the Democratic Caucus. Congresswoman Johnson had been partially listening to Speaker Pelosi's announcement while talking with us. With the mention of Representative Jeffries's probable selection, she grew quiet. She bowed her head slightly, closing her eyes. After a few seconds, she looked up at us, tears in her eyes, her hand clutched in a fist of victory. "If this happens, if he is selected, then my career is complete. I recognized his talent immediately, and if we've been able to get this party to the place where we can embrace his talent and name him as our chair, then this is a good ending point."

This was not boasting; she wasn't trying to put a spotlight on herself. She was genuinely grateful for having had the opportunity to inspire the next generation, to share the benefit of lessons learned through her journey so that there might continue to be progress. When Chair Jeffries visited Dallas just a few months later, he spoke of her mentorship, her guidance. She was instrumental, he said, in his journey through the House, identifying opportunities for him to have an impact and grow into the leader that he had become.

As she journeyed through her final year in Congress, people spoke of her example and impact on their careers. Her counsel and mentorship had clearly been available to those who chose to receive it. Beto O'Rourke, Texas candidate for governor and US senator, said that she epitomized the three Cs: confidence, control, and command. She was confident in what needed to be done, she knew how to leverage votes to achieve control, and her opinion commanded respect. Congressman Colin Allred spoke of her life, leadership, and legacy, all of which were born out of her love for others and this nation.

We may have a sense of Eddie Bernice Johnson the successful congresswoman. But the stories that we don't often hear about—the solitary train ride from Waco, Texas, to South Bend, Indiana; sitting alone and feeling alone during her early days at the Veterans Administration hospital; the moments that build and test a person's character—are not as known. As one attendee suggested at her final prayer breakfast in Dallas, "This good and faithful servant has earned the right to sit down and rest a little." I doubt that the congresswoman will ever really sit down and rest. And for that, we should all be grateful.

Addendum

On December 31, 2023, while this manuscript was in the peer review process, Congresswoman Johnson passed. She was at home, her son Kirk at her side. While recovering from spinal surgery, she developed an infection that led to a painful second surgery and weeks fighting a relentless infection. A woman who had begun her professional career as a nurse, advocated for affordable and effective health care, developed a system for the delivery of hospice care, and served as a member of Congress is believed to have died because of medical neglect. The sense of loss is exponentially exacerbated by the maddening reality that her death was likely avoidable.

For me it was intensified by the awareness that, although she had read the typed pages, she would never see this book, hold it in her hands, or attend book signings. This had been a project we worked on for years, and we were so close to completion. But it isn't to be.

This is Congresswoman Johnson's book, her words telling the story of her life through her retirement from Congress. She was unpretentious and unassuming even as she recounted the barriers she overcame, the challenges she surmounted. She was even more modest when describing her accomplishments, the legislation that was passed, the funding that was secured. What was important to the congresswoman was the impact that her work had, such as infrastructure improvements that stopped the flooding of south

Dallas residents' homes, the focus on STEM to keep this nation in the forefront of the technology race and provide meaningful economic opportunities for diverse populations, working with nations to support democratic governments. Congresswoman Johnson wanted to focus not on herself but on the work that had been done. She wanted it understood that serving effectively is not easy, but it is most worthwhile.

The tributes, condolences, and expressions of sorrow that flowed in from across the nation and the globe showcased the reach of her service. The respectful accolades and admiring compliments contrast sharply with her unassuming descriptions in this book. Words such as *icon*, *legend*, *warrior*, *trailblazer*, *groundbreaking leader*, *champion*, *statesman*, and *mentor* flowed through the statements—words that Congresswoman Johnson would have never used in describing herself. Instead, as she has done through this autobiography, she would talk about the work.

Proverbs 27:1–3, one of the congresswoman's favorite scriptures, reads, "Let someone else praise you, and not your own mouth; an outsider, and not your own lips." Congresswoman Johnson did not sing her own praises, as shown by the text of this book. But the overflowing tributes attest that there can be no mistaking the powerful impact and valuable contribution of her service. Indeed, her work speaks for her.

May this book also speak for her. I shall be forever grateful and humbled that the congresswoman, EBJ, gave me the privilege and honor of being a part of telling her story.

Preface
by Eddie Bernice Johnson

O ver the years, especially as I contemplated retirement, people would ask whether I had written my autobiography. Such inquiries usually made me wonder, Would people really be interested in my life story? I hadn't started my career trying to make history. I didn't set out to be the "first African American woman who . . ." I was following my heart, my call to serve other people.

But along the way I have had so many blessings. I have met and worked with dynamic, committed visionaries. I have sat at tables of power and influence, able to participate and contribute my thoughts and perspective. I have been able to literally see the fruits of my labors in highways, levees, buildings, clean spaces, breakfasts for children, aid to women across the world, expansion of scientific research and STEM opportunities, space exploration, support for historically Black colleges and universities, and the return of chip manufacturing to the United States.

I have seen and worked with selfless, dedicated public officials and servants. I have been assisted by countless staffers, researchers, policy advisors, and budget analysts, enabling me to better address issues and present solutions.

Yet, sadly, I've also witnessed others whose biases, financial interests, and personal feelings dictated their positions and votes. I have been sickened that some are unable to focus on service, on using their positions to advance opportunities and to provide solutions for the problems still plaguing our nation. The pursuit of power, just for the sake of power, is a betrayal of the trust given to us by voters.

There have been so many moments in my fifty-year career that have caused me to be grateful, so many people who have touched my life and allowed me to be a part of theirs. It is impossible to write of every moment, to mention every person. I have chosen events, activities, and legislation that were important to me in the hopes that I have captured the essence of my career and what has driven me all of these years—the desire to serve.

Chapter 1

Family, My Foundation

My sister, Sallye, and I felt a special honor being the daughters of Edward Johnson, our Little Daddy. He was lovingly called Doc by our mother, Lillie Mae. When she called his name, we could feel her love and respect for him. We learned at a very early age that for Little Daddy, loving his wife and providing for his children was his mission. He would be a leader and example in our city, but it was most important to him that he be the foundation of our family. And he was.

It wasn't easy raising a Black family in Waco in the beginning of the twentieth century. Daddy had to protect his family and inspire his children. He had to protect us from the racial attitudes of the times while teaching us that we could achieve our dreams. He had to show us how to be safe while also showing us that we should have the courage to be bold. He had to teach us that despite the obstacles in our path, we had to do something with our lives. He had to wrap us in his arms and love us so that we would always know that being his daughters made us special. And he did all of these things, and more.

Waco, Texas, is on the Brazos River, halfway between Austin and Dallas. It is the seat of McLennan County and home to Baylor University. For most of its existence, it has been an agricultural town. Waco was a major producer of cotton, growing, ginning, and shipping it internationally. When he was young, Daddy worked at the Waco Cotton Oil Mill.

Growing up in Waco, we learned about the racial hatred that was part of its past. As children we heard about the lynching of Jesse Washington that had occurred just eighteen years before I was born. Washington was only a teenager when he was convicted of rape and murder of a white woman. His trial lasted only an hour. Spectators in the courtroom became an angry mob. The jailers were either unable or unwilling to protect him. He was taken out of the courtroom and into the town square. He was beaten beyond recognition. His fingers, toes, and genitalia were cut off. Coal oil was poured over his body. He was hung from a tree and burned. A mob of nearly fifteen thousand white men, women, and children watched and cheered as his body was raised and lowered for over two hours. To our father, it was important that we know that this brutal attack had happened in the place we called home.

We grew up hearing also about Roy Mitchell. He was beaten, tortured, and threatened that he would be lynched. Not surprisingly, Mitchell finally confessed to a number of crimes. After a trial, he was publicly hanged. A crowd of about five thousand people gathered around to watch. It was one of the last recorded public hangings in Texas.

We knew that white people in authority, such as police officers, could physically harm Black men. One afternoon when we were out for a drive, a white police officer pulled my father's car to the side of the road. Before the officer could even get out of the patrol car, my father got out of the car and stood in front of it. He had his arms folded across his chest, his bearing and posture demanding to know why he was being stopped. My father wouldn't be intimidated when stopped. He wouldn't panic and become timid. He stood there. This startled the officer because my father would not back down. My father seemed confident, but I was frightened. I was afraid that the police officer would shoot him. The officer ultimately just drove away. He didn't give my father a ticket or a warning. He simply left.

We knew about the violence. We knew about the segregation. We knew that whites lived in one area of Waco while African Americans lived in a different area. We knew that there were "colored" and "white" water fountains, even though as a small girl, not understanding the significance of the signs, I drank from both of the fountains, preferring the water from the white fountain because it seemed colder. And, of course, we knew about the separate schools for "colored" children and white children.

But most importantly, we knew that we lived in a home that would be not just our shelter but our refuge. It would be the place where our family would come together.

Our home had a special feeling because my father had built it himself, with his own hands. Located at 1014 Pecan Street, it was originally a two-bedroom wooden house with a distinctive half red brick exterior. Sallye and I originally shared a large bedroom, but my father soon built another bedroom that would be mine. Daddy also added a combination study/library that we called the reading room. There were built-in desks and shelves that created a special space for us to do our schoolwork.

There was a small garden in the back where Daddy would grow corn, green beans, and strawberries. We kept chickens in the backyard. Once we even had a pig. When I was ten years old, my father added an indoor toilet, so we didn't have to go outside to the outhouse. He also built a two-story garage that was separate from the house.

Our home also felt special because of the atmosphere. It was joyful, full of laughter and love. We had family traditions that really helped to shape us as we grew up. We would always eat dinner together. Each night before we could begin eating, Daddy blessed our meal. Mother quoted a scripture. And then Sallye and I each had to recite a Bible verse before we could lift our forks. Eating was important, but giving thanks to God for our blessings was always most important. Dinner always involved conversation. It was a time for Daddy to talk with "his precious little girls." He asked us about our activities and what we had done that day. He would talk to us about the arts, religion, history, politics, farming, health care, and travel. He asked us our thoughts and what we wanted to do with our lives. The topics were wide and varied. But they all had one thing in common: Daddy thought that they would expand our minds and improve our intellect. He had a reason and a purpose for this dinner table conversation—to prepare us to lead lives of meaning and achievement.

On some evenings Daddy would become more animated in his discussions. He would point to his fingers as he talked, ticking off his points. Some nights we were grateful that he only had eight fingers and two thumbs. When making a point, he'd look at a finger, and then looked at one of us, making sure that we understood his argument. He wanted to make certain that we understood each and every point.

Sometimes Daddy would get a little carried away as he talked. On those nights, Little Mother, our name for our mother, would raise her hand and gently say, "That's enough, Doc." And he would stop immediately. Even though Mother would generally be quiet during the dinner discussions, when she spoke, her words were heard.

We'd also have Monday evening family meetings. Daddy would ask us what was on our minds, what was going on in our lives. We weren't viewed as being sassy or disrespectful when we spoke up. He was encouraging us to give our opinions. He'd give us feedback, letting us know that he'd heard what we had said and that it had value.

Daddy was an avid reader. He hadn't attended college because he didn't want to become a teacher or preacher, the two primary professions for college-educated African Americans. But that didn't mean Daddy didn't value education. He was proud that his wife had spent a year in college. He believed that you learned from reading. He read books, national and foreign newspapers, magazines, and encyclopedias. He taught us that you had to be well informed. It was important to him that we understood that knowledge was one of the tools that you needed to sustain your freedom and have opportunities to advance in life.

We had to be ready to pursue those opportunities. Our father believed that we should be fiercely independent. If we wanted or needed something of value, we had to be prepared to go after it. We had to understand that it was up to us to attain our goals. We had to be prepared to reach for our goals, to pay the price for it regardless of the cost or what others thought.

Family and neighbors were a large part of lives growing up. I was named after Eddie, a cousin who died before I was born, and Bernice after my aunt. We were among the very first families in our neighborhood to purchase a black-and-white television. On many evenings neighbors would come to our house to watch TV with us. Mother would serve popcorn and cold drinks. Some evenings were spent listening to music. Everyone in the neighborhood knew that the Johnson girls loved to dance. We'd move like two spinning tops on the dance floor, our mother always close by, watching. My father liked to listen to jazz, especially Count Basie and Jules Bledsoe. My mother preferred gospel. But whatever music was played, whatever TV show was being watched, the Johnson home was a place of refuge. Everyone was—and felt—welcome.

My mother was known for her cooking. She was a master baker. If someone was going to have a special event, they would come to Mother and purchase a custom baked cake or pie, a way that she would bring money into the home. She baked delicious tea cakes, which she would deliver to residents of local nursing homes. She would drive around Waco in her little white Plymouth, visiting the sick or people who were unable to attend church. She would share the gifts of her baking and her time.

My father drove a big, black Buick, a car that symbolized how solid and strong he was. He held a number of jobs to provide for his family, including one at the Veteran's Administration Hospital, where he worked the evening shift as an aide. He ran a side business, moving families and their households throughout the Southwest. He was determined that he would earn enough money to support his family.

Clothes were important to my parents. They wanted us to have the finest clothes that they could afford; they didn't want us going to used clothing stores. Our father told our mother not to purchase us "cheap clothes." Our shoes had to be sturdy, our coats warm. Quality counted. And, of course, we had to have gloves and hats to go with our coats. It may have meant that he had to work several jobs, but my father was going to make sure that his girls looked presentable and respectable when they went out.

But one shopping trip remains with me. My mother and I had walked from East Waco to downtown. It was quite a warm day. I was hot and thirsty and I wanted a drink of water. Inside the store there were two water fountains. I went to one fountain, drank some water. It wasn't cold. It didn't satisfy me. I asked my mother to please help me up, that I wanted to get some water from the other fountain. No one was around, so she lifted me up. But then she quickly and abruptly put me back down. "I saw a lady coming," she said. "This water fountain has a sign that says 'white.' Even though this water's cold, it's not for us." I responded, trying to understand, "You mean white people?" Her answer was simple, short, "Yes."

That was a defining moment for me. I was young but I started to notice things, to become aware that there were restrictions. There were times when I had to sit in the back of the bus, give up my seat to a white person, wait at a food counter until all white patrons were served, or even not be served at all. I knew that we had to show white people that we were people too.

Church was an important part of our life, so going to church every Sunday was natural. Daddy was a deacon in the Toliver Chapel Baptist Church. Mother was a soprano in the choir. We were taught that Sundays should be devoted to worship. We attended morning Sunday school, church service, and after a short return home for dinner, evening service.

The congregation was led by Reverend O. L. Hegman, who believed that the African American church had a role outside of worship services. Reverend Hegman organized the first branch of the National Association for the Advancement of Colored People (NAACP) in Waco. He understood the need for political power and encouraged all of his members to vote and get involved in civic affairs. His wife, Emma, was the first lady of the church and led the Girl's Auxiliary. The focus was on teaching the girls how to carry themselves, to work together as a team, and to respect each other. Most of all, we were being taught what it meant to be a Christian.

If Sallye and I weren't in church on Saturdays, we might go to the movies. We had to go to the Gem Theater, the local segregated movie house. I hated westerns and avoided them at all costs. But space travel and science fiction fascinated me. I would watch those movies and wonder whether such stories would one day be real.

Our parents didn't believe in children being idle. We were immersed in activities through the Girl Scouts and the Camp Fire Girls. Sometimes they would pack us in our father's car and drive to Dallas to see a play or some special entertainer. We would also go to the YWCA, just a stone's throw from our house. We learned to play tennis and participated in other sports and theatrical productions. We became very involved with Y Teens, a program to help young women and girls develop leadership skills. And, with our love of dance, we especially enjoyed the dances that the YWCA sponsored.

During the school year, the dances were held on Friday nights. In the summer there was an extra night of dancing on Wednesdays.

Sallye and I always looked forward to our summers. We would spend them in Brenham, Texas, with our paternal grandparents, Shed and Leola Blount Johnson. We would stay with them for the entire summer until school began. Like our parents, our grandparents spoiled us. We each had our very own bedroom in their home. We spent most mornings and afternoons running through the various orchards that our grandfather owned. He grew peaches, strawberries, watermelon, peanuts, and pears. Sometimes we ate so much that our stomachs would ache. We would help our grandmother with the laundry and other household chores. At night we would sit on the ground, looking up at the dark sky, trying to count the stars and figure out if there really was someone on the moon.

We had so much fun spending summers in Brenham that we fell into the habit of calling our grandparents Momma and Daddy. Being sensitive to the issues that could cause, my grandfather solved the problem. He suggested that we call him Big Daddy and our grandmother as Big Momma. We could then call our parents Little Daddy and Little Mother. We thought that was a great idea, and for the rest of our lives those names stuck.

Sallye was two years older than me, but from the time that I was a child, I wanted to be her equal. When I was five years old, I'd sit with our mother as she helped Sallye with her homework. Sometimes I answered the questions quicker than Sallye did, annoying her to no end. When she took piano lessons, my parents insisted that I go along with her. But I didn't learn to play piano.

We might have been rivals at times, but it was never a mean-spirited rivalry. We weren't belligerent toward each other. Our parents taught us that we were family, that we had a responsibility to care for one another, that we should love one another. And we did.

But I couldn't help being jealous when Sallye started school and I couldn't go. I was so eager to start school, I couldn't wait. I was really upset that Sallye was getting to go while I had to stay home. My parents noticed how upset I was. Maybe they were eager to get me out of the house, if only for five hours each day. Whatever their motivation, my parents altered my application so that I could begin school at East Waco Elementary School before I turned 6 years old.

I had just turned 7 when the Japanese bombed Pearl Harbor. Our father began a campaign in our community to honor Doris "Dorie" Miller, an African American sailor assigned to the kitchen but who manned antiaircraft guns and shot down several Japanese planes. Because of the country's segregation policies for sailors, Miller had not been trained to shoot the ship's guns. But he saved lives that day because of his bravery and courage. He saved a number of his fellow sailors from dying during an oil fire on their ship by carrying them to safety. His parents owned a farm in Waco and everyone, especially our father, was proud of what he had done.

My father let me go with him as he went door to door, soliciting funds to purchase a gift for Mr. Miller. I may have been just a little girl, but I listened attentively at each stop as my father proudly explained the significance of Mr. Miller's actions. He would share how important it was for the Waco community to honor him. He would talk about Dorie and the meaning of what he had done. He was able to raise the money for a gift for Mr. Miller, and in doing so he taught me the power of door-to-door campaigns.

There was a ceremony and reception held at the Earle Street YWCA. My father and I stood near the building, waiting for Mr. Miller to arrive. When he walked up, my father greeted him, introducing me as his partner and telling him that I had walked the neighborhood with him, inviting people to attend the reception. Once inside our father presented Mr. Miller with a lovely silver bracelet with his name engraved on it. It was a gift from his hometown, grateful for his service to our country, proud of his courage in the face of grave danger. It was a special and proud moment for Mr. Miller, the community, and for our father. Dorie Miller was embraced as our hero. And I had been personally introduced to him, the only time that I would be in his presence.

With the beginning of WWII, our father went to work for the United States Defense Department. He was assigned to a facility in Portland, Oregon. Right before Christmas 1942 our father came home to help us pack and get us ready for the trip to the northwestern United States. He and my mother had been making plans for the three Johnson girls to join him in Portland. My younger sister, Lee Helen, had been born in August of that year.

But then he received a letter informing him that he had been drafted. For the first time in my life, I saw my father cry, but not because he didn't want to serve or that he was afraid. He cried because it meant leaving his family behind again. He cried because he did not know what would happen to his girls if he didn't come home. Mother cried too. We had been separated and we were just going to be reunited, but now he was having to leave again. It was the saddest holiday season that the Johnson family had known.

Sallye and I did not know what to think about our father going into the service. Our father gathered the family for a meeting and explained the war to us, and the reason why he was drafted. He told us not to worry and to obey our mother while he was away. But the two of us were somewhat unsettled, feeling the fear and concern of our parents.

In addition to my father, other members of the Johnson family were drafted. My uncles, Oscar and Shed Jr., went to serve in the navy and army, respectively. I'd grown up with them, playing with my cousins. Like my father, they were proud to wear the uniform of our country and to play a role in its defense. But like my sisters and mother, their children and spouses were fearful of what might happen to them.

Our parents devised a plan for the time that the family was going to be separated. I would go to stay with our paternal grandparents, while my sister would live with our maternal grandmother. My mother and baby sister, Lee Helen, went to Florida to be with our father once he had completed his basic training in Great Lakes, Illinois. During his time in the navy, he was able to visit us. He looked so handsome in his blue naval uniform and white cap. I remember that he used to stand so erect with his hands at his sides. We were very proud of him.

While I missed my father terribly while he was away, I enjoyed being with my grandparents and living on their farm. I liked to ask questions and bombarded my grandfather with them. I wanted to know things such as why did strawberries have so much dirt on them? And why did the farm workers have so much soil all over their clothes? My grandfather often laughed at my questions, but he was patient and answered each one of them until my curiosity was satisfied.

When news of the war's end reached Brenham, the citywide sirens were blaring. I remember the sound of those horns. My grandmother ran around the backyard with her hands stretched toward heaven, shouting, "The war is over. The war is over!" I did not know quite what she meant, but I knew that she was happy. I soon learned that our family would be back together. I had missed being one of my father's "precious little girls," and looked forward to the attention and adoration that I knew he would shower on his children.

My father had always made me feel that I was his special little girl. After my baby sister was born, he worried, I think, that I might feel a distance between the two of us. I was used to being the youngest. Now I was eight years old and there was a baby sister. My father made certain that I would know that nothing had changed, that I was still his special little girl.

We were so excited and eager for our father to come home. We had a big celebration to welcome him. We were able to be together again and spent many evenings listening to him tell us stories of his adventures in the navy. He had met many people and traveled to many parts of the country and the world that he had not visited before. He was saddened that his friend, Dorie Miller, had been killed at sea.

Now that he was home from the war, my father resumed his focus on us and our rearing. He wanted us to know that there was life beyond Waco. He wanted us to know that he expected us to help people and make a difference in the lives of others. He closely observed our friends and was very hard on the boys who demonstrated an interest in us. And he didn't hesitate to intervene.

Once, when my sister was in the seventh grade, a math teacher, Reverend Lafayette Chaney, hit her hand with a ruler because she had eaten an orange in class while he was in the hallway. My father was upset when he heard what had happened. He had used his considerable influence in the community to help Reverend Chaney to acquire a church. He'd assisted Reverend Chaney, and now the reverend was hitting his daughter's hand. That didn't sit well with my father. He immediately went to the school to talk with Reverend Chaney and made sure that he would never again hit my sister with a ruler.

My father wasn't a violent man. There was not any concern that he would physically harm Reverend Chaney. He was just making certain that everyone understood that his daughters would only be disciplined by him. No one else would hit his girls. Word of his visit and that message spread quickly through the school. We never had that type of problem again.

Chapter 2

Education Is Preparation

My father wanted us to get a college degree. Living in Waco, it was easy for us to believe that we could get one. Paul Quinn College, an institution of higher learning established by the African Methodist Episcopal church to educate formerly enslaved persons and their descendants, was located in Waco. Paul Quinn was known for its demanding education and well-prepared graduates. Many of the people in our community were associated with Paul Quinn, making it a ready inspiration for pursuing a college degree.

I had attended East Waco School for elementary school. When I was in the eighth grade, I told my father that I wanted to become a doctor. That became my dream. But when I got to high school, my counselor told me that I was too feminine to be a physician. She suggested that I would be better suited for nursing. I didn't question her guidance and focused on becoming a nurse.

I attended the segregated A. J. Moore High School. Named after its founding principal, the first commencement was held in 1896 and celebrated the graduation of five students. By the time I became a high school student, Moore had had only had four principals. Moore's principal during my time, Joseph J. Wilson, set the tone for the school. Dressed in fashionable suits, smartly shined shoes, and wire-rimmed eyeglasses, he led with pride and purpose. He had learned from his father, the previous principal, that setting high standards would challenge everyone to do their best. It did not matter that the superintendent and school board were all white men. He commanded their respect because he knew that he had a mission—to oversee the education of Waco's Black high school students.

Principal Wilson led by example. He was always at student activities and events. With his presence, he pushed us to do our best. He was determined that Moore would be an exemplary school bringing pride to our community. There were about twenty-five teachers at Moore for the first to twelfth grades. Our teachers were members of our community, living in our neighborhoods, worshipping at the same churches, shopping at the same stores. Most significantly, they knew our parents.

Our teachers believed in and encouraged us. They demanded excellence in our studies because they knew the obstacles that we would face. They wanted more for us than society had allowed them. They made sure that we knew about W. E. B. DuBois, Harriet Tubman, Marcus Garvey, Sojourner Truth, Frederick Douglass, Paul Laurence Dunbar, and other people of color who had successfully fought segregation and systemic racism.

But it wasn't just the formal classroom instruction. They were role models. They knew that how they carried and presented themselves would send us a message that school was important. Whether male teachers in shirts and ties or female teachers in dresses or skirts with stockings, they were all professionals. Through their appearance, demeanor, and commitment, they were telling us that we were worthy. Their teaching was an investment in the community and the nation. Their teaching was our inspiration.

Our schoolbooks came from white schools. Markings in the margins, drawings, and handwritten words were constant reminders that we were getting white students' used books. It was so common for pages to be missing that there was a minor celebration when a complete book was found. But Principal Wilson and our teachers would not let us be distracted by the lack of materials. We were not allowed to use the inequalities of the educational materials as excuses for poor performance. We were admonished that we could not "sleep on the educational opportunities" that we had. There were many who had come before us who were not allowed to learn to read, who didn't have the chance to go to school. It was our privilege and duty to learn everything that we could.

In this environment I blossomed as a student. While I had always been a good student, there were opportunities in high school that did not exist in elementary school. I eagerly participated in extracurricular activities, participating in the drill team and playing on the basketball team. I was a member of the Dramatic Art Club, J. A. Kirk Chorus, Book Lovers' Club, National Honor Society, Student Council, library staff, and Elm Wood Y Teens.

My senior year I served as the editor of our yearbook, *The Lion*. On the day that we took pictures for the class yearbook, I impulsively decided that wearing a pair of eyeglasses would be the thing to do. I had not worn glasses before and could see perfectly. A friend let me borrow her glasses. I looked quite serious and studious in my yearbook photo.

Part of our learning experiences included attending outings at Baylor University near downtown Waco. African Americans were not allowed to enroll in or attend classes at Baylor even though Baylor employed people of color for its nonprofessional jobs. We were allowed to go on Baylor's campus to watch plays or attend concerts. We sat in the theater balcony, but we refused to let that segregated seating rob us of the joy of the outing.

We had a nurse at Moore High School, Jean Braithwaite, who everyone called Sis. I knew Sis because she was the daughter of the local Black dentist, Dr. B. T. Braithwaite, who lived a few blocks from our house. I remember seeing her in her white nursing uniform and nurse's cap. Even though she was quiet, her genuine concern for each student earned everyone's respect.

Sis was the first nurse that I remember meeting. I began to speak with her about nursing. I listened to her describe why she'd become a nurse, the types of things that she did, and the experiences that she'd had. I was drawn by what she told me. Not only was she knowledgeable about her field, but you could also tell that she liked what she did. I was very impressed. I liked her style. I also admired that she helped people. I wanted to be like her.

One evening I came across a nursing advertisement in one of the magazines that my father had ordered. It offered a nursing degree for only thirty dollars. I convinced my father to purchase the course for me, telling him that I would become a nurse. Then I could earn money for myself and contribute financially to our family. My father was skeptical, but he was never one to discourage his children from pursuing their dreams, particularly something that they really wanted to accomplish.

When the materials arrived, I discovered that the materials included the test questions and the answers. All I had to do was memorize the answers. I made a perfect score on the examination. I was very excited when the school mailed me my diploma. When it arrived I just knew that I would soon be going to work as a nurse and earning a paycheck.

Not once did my father attempt to discourage me from taking the course. He believed that life was the best teacher. "Now tell me," he said as I proudly displayed the diploma, "what is the first thing that you would do as a nurse when you get to a hospital?" I was speechless. The correspondence course had not taught me anything about actually being a nurse. It had not prepared me for my father's inquiry. "I don't know," I said. With that simple question my father had proven his point: anything worth having is worth putting in the time and effort.

But I did know that pursuing a college education was the best thing I could do if I really wanted to become a nurse, help my family, and keep people in good health. I had spent much of my spare time with Sis in the nurse's office. I asked her questions about nursing and schools that I should consider because there was not an accredited nursing school in Texas that would admit a Black student. I would have to leave Texas. She had studied in Indiana. Maybe I should go there? She gave me a list of schools and suggested that I write them.

I followed that advice. Many of us in my graduating class sought advanced academic training. Most of my classmates went to schools in Texas, but a number of us had to venture outside of Texas and seek universities and colleges in other states. My father and mother were very supportive and proud of me. They told me that my journey as a woman had just commenced.

I could have attended Prairie View University, one of the two historically Black public universities in Texas. But its nursing program did not have national accreditation. The other school for African American students did not offer a nursing program. If I wanted to stay in Texas, I would have to attend an unaccredited nursing school.

That didn't make sense to my father. He told me that applying to Prairie View would limit my career choices and the places where I could work. He was working at the Veteran's Administration Hospital in Waco in the psychiatric unit, so he was dealing with health professionals every day. To him there wasn't any reason for his daughters not to have the fullest of opportunities; the sky was the limit for Sallye and me. My father understood that he had limited opportunities due to the social and economic realities of his time, but he wasn't going to let his girls suffer those limits. He made certain that we were able to set, and attain, the goals that we wanted for ourselves. He gave us the gift of our dreams.

One Saturday my father drove me and a classmate to Dallas to the Baylor Dental School, where we took a national nursing school entrance exam. I had done very well in school, achieving the second highest grade point average in my high school graduating class. I did very well on the test and scored high enough to apply to St. Mary's at Notre Dame in Indiana.

My father or mother opened the envelope that contained my acceptance letter. I was too nervous to open it myself. I stood there, watching as they pulled the letter out of the envelope. I had never received a letter from a university. I was very happy and so excited when I realized that I would soon begin the formal training that would lead to becoming a nurse, a healer just like Sis. I was proud of myself.

I couldn't wait to share the news of my acceptance with Sallye. She was a college student, having first gone to Austin to study at what is now Huston-Tillotson College and then transferring to Paul Quinn. Always one of my boosters, she was very happy. Now the stories that she told me about some of her experiences as a first-year college student had more importance. My memories of going to Austin with my parents to visit Sallye, visiting the campus, and hearing stories of her student life contributed to my excitement about becoming a college student.

Sis was excited that I would be going to St. Mary's. She had attended St. Mary's and was understandably proud of her school. She believed that the school had become even stronger with more college-related courses than when she had attended.

As I prepared to attend St. Mary's, I was beginning to get a sense of just how different life might be for me and the challenges that I would face, even in simple ways, such as what clothes I would need. St. Mary's suggested that new students would need to bring a winter coat. I had never experienced a harsh winter like an Indiana winter, but I knew that I'd better follow that advice. My mother and I went looking for a heavy coat, somewhat difficult to do in a place that did not see cold winters. We were finally able to find such a coat from one of the local Waco stores.

During most of my high school years, I had worked at Piccadilly's, a segregated cafeteria-style restaurant in Waco. It had an all-white clientele, refusing to sell food to African Americans. I cleaned trays, wiped tables, and occasionally served soft drinks to customers. I saved money to help with my college expenses and personal items that I needed for school. Fortunately, I also received an academic scholarship that helped with my expenses.

During my senior year, a family friend working at Bauer McCann, the largest department store in Waco, recruited me to be a candidate for the Ms. Fashionetta contest. This was a competition sponsored by the Alpha Kappa Alpha Sorority, her sorority. I solicited advertisements for the program, raising the most money for the competition. Participating in this AKA activity and meeting the members of the sorority inspired me to want to join. I had a 1½-inch leather belt. On the inside of that belt, I wrote AKA because I knew that I wanted to become a member.

There were other, more serious challenges that I would have to face. First was the question of how I would get to South Bend. We did not have enough money to purchase more than one train ticket. Driving up to South Bend to drop me off and then coming back to Waco would have been costly. In addition, road travel was always challenging because you had to know which service stations sold gasoline to African Americans. Driving would have been too much of an imposition on my family. By this time my younger sister, Lee Helen, was 9, and my baby brother, Carl, was only 6 months old. Such a long road trip would have been extremely difficult for them. The only option was for me to take that train trip alone. I had never traveled anywhere by myself before. We had driven to California to visit my mother's sisters. We regularly traveled to Brenham and Corsicana. But these trips were as a family, riding together in a car.

I couldn't help but be nervous as I anticipated going to South Bend by myself. But once again, my father was my rock. He sat me down and explained all of the things that I would need to do in order to have a safe journey to South Bend. He explained that he had spoken to a local Pullman car porter whom he knew and had told them that his daughter would be traveling alone to Indiana. His friend understood the concerns and fears that my father had about my trip. He would reach out to other porters who worked the Chicago route and make certain that the porters would know who I was and where I was headed. He promised my father that working together, the porters would be my guides and protectors. Under their watchful eyes, no harm would come my way. As he told me of the arrangements he had made, any fears that I had faded away. I had faith in my father. He had, again, taken care of me, and I could be confident that my travels would be safe and without incident.

As each day of summer slowly passed, I became more and more excited. Sometimes I would stand in front of a mirror in our home, smiling, thinking of the day that I would wear a nurse's uniform, just like Sis. I'd remember my paternal grandmother, who died of cancer while living in our Waco home, and wonder if I'd been a nurse how I could have helped her. At St. Mary's I'd be getting the training and knowledge to care for people with health problems. Maybe during my career I'd be able to help end diseases such as cancer. My summer was filled with thoughts of possibilities, dreams, and responsibility.

Everyone was so proud of me, and they let me feel that pride. To my father, his "precious little girl" had transformed into a "special young lady." For my mother, her happiness was burdened with the fear and concern of her young daughter going so far away to school. My family at Moore High School—the instructors, counselor, and principal—told me never to forget that I was representing them as I tackled my studies at one of the country's finest nursing schools.

It was 1952. I was only 17 years old. I'd been accepted to a white nursing school. I'd be studying with white students for the first time in my life. I'd be traveling by myself to Indiana. But I wasn't apprehensive or afraid. I was eager for this new adventure, this next stage of my life. I knew that there would be challenges that I couldn't yet foresee. But I knew that I had to face those challenges and overcome any obstacles.

I had confidence in my future. I was not going to let down my parents and family and all who had believed in me. I knew that I would always remember the lessons I had been taught. I was committed to always conducting myself according to the highest standards. And most of all, I was a Johnson whose foundation was rooted in a father's labors to provide his children with the opportunities that had been denied him. I knew that honoring and treasuring that fatherly gift would always keep me on the right path.

Chapter 3

Becoming a Nurse at St. Mary's

South Bend was exactly 1,123 miles from Waco. My journey began when my father, mother, Helen, and baby brother, Carl, took me to the train station in Waco. I had two suitcases filled with new clothes, three books to read during my trip, and crackers, peanut butter, fruit, and written instructions on how to arrive safely in South Bend.

My parents hugged and kissed me goodbye. My father got on the train to speak with the porters. Then he gave me some final fatherly instructions just before the conductor shouted, "All aboard." And with those words I had to leave my parents and younger siblings and climb up the steps to the train.

I waved to my parents and blew them a kiss. They blew kisses back. We were all excited about my going to school but also deeply saddened by the separation. I could see my mother take her white handkerchief and wipe tears from her eyes. I kept my head turned toward the back of the train so that I could see my parents. As the train gained speed, they became smaller and smaller. Eventually, of course, I couldn't see them anymore. It was so sad I wanted to cry. But I remembered what my father had told me about being strong. Also, I did not want to embarrass myself in front of the ten or so strangers who were sitting with me in the segregated train car.

So I sat there and for some reason I thought of the only cat that I had owned, Jimmy. He was black and white, and during the winter months he kept my feet warm at night by sitting on them. He would wake me in the mornings. He would wait for me to come home from school.

Jimmy usually stayed around the house, but one day he disappeared. I searched for him but could not find him. After a few hours when he hadn't come home, I began to worry. Two days passed before we found Jimmy's body a few yards from our house. Even though we buried him in our backyard, nothing could ease the aching pain in my stomach—a pain that I could still remember, a loss that was so deep that it would keep me from ever wanting another cat.

I was feeling a similar aching pain as I watched my parents disappear from my sight. I tried to distract myself by reading one of the books that I had with me. My eyes would not focus. I tried to find refuge in sleep, but my thoughts would not stop.

Shortly after I boarded the train, one of the Pullman car porters came to my seat and introduced himself. He told me that he knew my father and that my father was counting on them to make my trip pleasant and safe. He asked me if I wanted to rest in one of the private rooms. I said yes, gathered my things, and walked with him to the back of the car. There he opened the door to a private room. I sat there for a while but began to feel uncomfortable and informed the porter that I wanted to return to my original seat. He did not protest. He simply escorted me back to where I had been sitting.

I don't think that he had any untoward intentions. I think he was just trying to be kind. But my father had taught me to be cautious, and I thought it would be prudent to sit where others could see my every move and the moves of everyone around me. We traveled for nearly two hours before I managed to take a nap.

When I awoke I saw the stunning countryside outside my window. There were long patches of prairie and small country towns with signs for gasoline, places to sleep, and food. I wondered what it was like living in some of the places that we passed. We slowed down when we went through small towns. Children and some adults waved at the train and I waved back.

When we reached St. Louis, I had to change trains to get to Chicago. Once I got to Chicago, I had to go to another train station. Following the written instructions that my father had given me, I found a cab and gave the driver the address that my father had written on a piece of paper. I had no idea what I would do if I got lost, or if the driver decided to drive to some distant place with me in his cab.

I was literally traveling on faith. This was the first time that I had traveled by myself. It was so different than our family trips to California. At times during that twenty-eight-hour trip, I recited Bible verses that I had learned in Sunday school. I repeated lyrics from my favorite hymns. I found strength and comfort in those familiar words. I was on my own and determined that I would make it.

When I finally arrived in South Bend, I took a second taxi-cab ride to St. Mary's campus. I had received instructions in the mail, so I knew exactly where to ask the driver to take me. It was dark but a group of nuns was waiting. They helped me with my luggage and showed me to the dormitory where I would be living.

Arriving one day before registration, I beat my roommates to our dorm room. When I opened the door, I discovered a single twin bed and one bunk bed. I decided that I would take the single bed and leave the fight over who would climb toward the ceiling each night to my new roommates, the strangers with whom I would be living.

I knew that there were only a few Black students at St. Mary's. There was only one Black student in the class ahead of me and another Black student in my class. But somehow I just assumed that my roommates would look like me. I really hadn't given much thought to that fact that I had never slept in the same room with a person of another race. But I wasn't alarmed when two white girls appeared the next day and said that they had been assigned to the room. My only thought: they'll have to decide who is going to be on top and who will sleep on the bottom.

I can't remember whether Sue from Illinois or Patricia from South Carolina was the first to arrive. Sue came with her family that I would come to know well, often being an invited guest in their home during vacations and on holidays. Patricia arrived with her older sister, who seemed a bit uncomfortable that one of her sister's roommates was Black. She did not say anything, but having been raised in the segregated south, I knew the facial expression of disapproval.

My parents taught me to treat others fairly and with respect. They said that color was a fiction, and often pointed out that my great-grandmother, Mary, had white skin. My father believed that character was far more significant than color. But that didn't mean that I didn't recognize prejudice and racial attitudes in others.

St. Mary's was not a place where racial prejudice was tolerated. Sister Madeleva Wolff, the third president of the school, was an enlightened woman. She had studied at the University of California–Berkeley, the University of Southern California, and Oxford..She was a scholar of medieval literature, publishing books on Chaucer.

By the time I arrived at the school, Sister Madeleva had been president for over twenty years. She had established the Department of Nursing. She created a theology school for women. She made certain that most of our classes were taught by nuns who would make it very clear that we were special young ladies being prepared for positions of leadership in whatever fields we selected and in whatever parts of the world we chose to live. She was committed to making certain that St. Mary's students were provided a solid educational foundation to become the professionals that we wanted to be. Students were viewed as future leaders, change agents who would make a better world by breaking down barriers that separated people and dedicating themselves to encouraging women and serving the poor.

Her truth included empowering all women. She had admitted the first African American woman to St. Mary's. She made certain that it was a school that attracted students from across the country. Sister Madeleva brought together women from across the country so that we could learn from each other.

My roommates and I quickly settled in as peers, borrowing clothes from each other and sharing items from the care packages that our families sent us. We shared a bathroom in our dorm room. A pattern developed where I would always be the last one to use it at night because I had to fix my hair. I had to roll my hair, pinning it down with bobby pins to keep it straight. It was something that my roommates did not have to spend as much time doing. To me it seemed only fair that they were able to get ready for bed before I did.

My classmates came from places that I had only read about. They were from Central America, South America, Boston, New York, Kentucky, Pennsylvania, and California. I was the only one from Texas in my class. In just a matter of weeks, I became known as Eddie Tex. It was a nickname that stayed with me the entire time that I was in school.

Our school days started at 5:30 a.m. with mass in the chapel. It lasted about an hour, and our first class began at 8:00 a.m. The school day was over at 4:00 p.m. On most nights we studied. Occasionally, there was time to watch television and read books that were outside of our coursework. I also learned to play bridge.

The coursework during our first year was rigorous. We took anatomy, physiology, and chemistry in addition to traditional college courses such as English and math. I took copious notes during classes. We had exams every week.

I thought of my father often. I would hear his voice saying, "I am doing the best I know how to help you with your future, and I hope you can appreciate it enough to give it your very best." He didn't have the opportunity to attend an elite university. He had worked with a construction crew building a highway, earning a dollar a day. He had worked in a cotton mill. He had sacrificed everything for his children, and what he wanted from us was to always do our best. I couldn't let him down.

So each exam, every time that I raised my hand in a classroom to answer a question, I was determined to do my best. In many ways I was still his little girl, even though I was approaching womanhood. I was always aware that my performance represented our family. When my turn came to present in class, I performed as if I had been trained at one of the country's finest boarding schools. All of the practicing at night and the images of perfection in my head paid off. I did as well as anyone in the class.

My favorite course was physiology. I enjoyed it because we had to learn the function of body parts. We learned about muscles, organs, veins, and arteries. I had a small advantage over my peers because I had taken Latin in high school, which helped me with many of the medical terms.

There was a study hall in our dorm. Students who had problems with their studies were assigned to study hall. Because it was near the dorm reference library, we knew that a student was in trouble if we saw her going into the room regularly. If a girl did not consistently maintain good grades, her parents showed up on campus to help pack her belongings and take her home for good. I was not going to be one of those girls.

All of us wanted to do well in school. About twelve of us decided to form a study group. We made up rhymes to help us remember body parts. We created various associations to remind us of difficult words and phrases. While studying late at night we usually dressed in our gowns and pajamas. One evening a nun walked into the study room uninvited and all of us screamed. She was obviously uncomfortable because we were not fully clothed. Some of the girls were only wearing bras, panties, and slips. The nun told us to return to our rooms. The next morning each of us was called into a meeting with Sister Ann Miriam.

I was afraid and thought that I was going to be suspended from school. She told each of us that we needed to be careful about our appearances. She told us that rumors about the social behavior of women would spread quickly in the school. She admonished us to study with our clothes on and to be careful about the company that we kept. At the end of the meeting, I did not know what Sister Ann Mariam was trying to tell us. It was days later that I learned that she was attempting to educate us about lesbian behavior.

We talked about the meeting in our study group. Some of the girls, like me, did not know anything about lesbians. I had never even heard the word. I did recall that there was a female teacher at my high school that dressed like a man and sometimes people laughed behind her back, but I didn't know why.

In our first year we also had a course on social etiquette. A complete dinner table was placed at the front of the classroom, and each student had to select the proper utensils to use. Fortunately, I was not the first student chosen to sit at the table. I watched those who went before me very closely, noting the correct choices and the mistakes.

A part of our coursework in our social service course included designing a family tree so that we knew about our heritages. I consulted with my father to learn even more about my grandparents and great-grandparents. Tracking my ancestors and creating the family tree helped me to better understand the issues of race within my own family. My father was intrigued by this assignment and asked me to send him a copy.

On weekends when many of my fellow students went to dances and parties at Notre Dame, I would find an empty room where I could study without interruption. I didn't feel lonely doing this. I felt that I was doing what I needed to do. I had an obligation to be prepared. I knew that I had to do well. My family and folks in Waco believed in me, so I had to do my part.

I still remember the weekend that I took a bus into town to find a beauty salon and a hair stylist who could style my hair. One of the challenges Black women faced, particularly in the 1950s, was having a hairstyle that was acceptable to white America. I had asked one of the nuns for help in finding a place to get my hair done. She suggested that I ask one of the Black employees, which I did. She told me of a beauty shop on Chapin Street.

When I got to the shop, I asked the stylist to wash and style my hair. She did a very good job. Before I went back to the campus, I found a restaurant to eat dinner. I ate chop suey for the very first time. I did not know what it was, but everyone else was ordering it so I decided to try it. It was a good decision as I discovered that I liked it.

When I returned to campus, my roommates wanted to know what had happened to my hair, which I had been wearing long and curly. They saw the tight curls and believed that I had gotten my hair cut short. I hadn't really anticipated that they would ask questions, but I explained to them what the stylist had done to my hair. I think that it was the first time that they learned about caring for Black hair.

Eventually I joined friends and attended football and basketball games at Notre Dame. We were not members of the all-male cheer squad, but we led most of the yells. We were louder than the official cheerleaders and we always attracted plenty of attention.

We liked going into town to eat, to the dances that the school sponsored on our campus, or the game victory parties that were held at Notre Dame. One night Sue said that she had arranged a date for me. He was a student at Notre Dame, a boy from Louisiana. She said that she told him that I was "colored." Initially, I did not want to go on the date but finally decided to go out with him. Six of us rode in a car to a restaurant. The three boys sat in the front and the three girls in the back. After eating we went dancing and enjoyed ourselves. My date asked me if I would go out with him again, but I simply did not have an interest in dating. I was at school to study, and earning my degree was my primary objective.

When we went to bed that night, Sue and I talked well into the morning. She never asked me about the boy from Notre Dame. I think she knew that I was not overwhelmed by him. She also knew that I had a boyfriend in Waco, Burford Evans, who was in the air force and who had given me his class ring. He wrote me regularly, sending me trinkets from the various places he visited such as Paris and Rome.

We had short breaks during the semester, usually a week to ten days, but Waco was so far away and a train ticket cost too much, so I couldn't go home. My father could not afford the gas for the round trip between Waco and South Bend to bring my family to visit me. So I spent many of the first school breaks alone. The nuns tried to make me feel comfortable, but it was very lonely. There were activities, but I missed my family.

Even though he was miles away, my father kept close tabs on me. He reached out to Mrs. Vern Buchanan, a supervisor at St. Joseph's Hospital, where I began my practical student-nursing work. She was a very dignified lady. I could feel her pride when she spoke of Harriet Tubman, Frederick Douglass, and others in the struggle for equal rights. I think that she liked being in a position of authority, holding a clipboard in her hands as she recorded the activities of those who worked under her supervision. She seemed to be extremely exacting in her work, but she was respected by those who worked for her because she was a professional. All of the students liked her as well. I never heard anyone say anything unpleasant about Mrs. Buchanan.

A terrific cook, on special occasions she invited me to her home to have meals with her family. Sometimes I spent the night sharing her daughter's room. I knew that I was always welcome in her home and that I would be treated like a member of the family. Being in the Buchanan home and having the opportunity to interact with her children was a little like being with my family. But watching them allowed me to appreciate, even more, the value that my parents placed on education. When her daughter got a full-time job at a local store, her mother wanted to celebrate. She gave me the impression that she felt that this job would be the pinnacle of her daughter's professional life. But simply finishing high school would not have been enough in the Johnson household. Graduating from college was the passport to an even greater future, and I thanked God that my parents held the beliefs that they did.

When Thanksgiving arrived, Sue said that her family wanted me to spend the Thanksgiving and Christmas holidays with them in Champaign, Illinois. I was delighted with the idea. They checked with my parents, who agreed that it would be good for me if I spent the holidays with them. Sue's father drove down and picked us up. Compared to the long ride to Waco, the couple of hours that it took us to get to Champaign seemed like nothing.

Her family had a modest home. Mr. Nixon was a manager at a large retail store. Mrs. Nixon was a housewife. They went out of their way to make me feel at home, introducing me to their neighbors and dinner guests. To my pleasant surprise, Sue and her parents did not talk about race while I stayed in their home. I had been a little nervous, wondering whether they were going to question me about life as a Black female. I had always found it to be uncomfortable when I was treated as an oddity. But the Nixons were interested in me as a teenager who was pursuing an education. They seemed to enjoy my focus and maturity. They liked the fact that their daughter and I were not only roommates but also had become close friends.

I had enjoyed the Thanksgiving break with the Nixons, so I was pleased to be able to spend Christmas with them as well. My parents sent a package filled with holiday goodies that I shared with the Nixon family. My mother sent some of her baked goods, which were a huge hit. She also sent a small gift for each member of Sue's family.

I grew closer to Sue and wanted to share some of my secrets with her, some of the experiences that I had had as a young child growing up in the South. But for some reason I did not, and our conversations usually revolved around relatively superficial topics. I often wondered how she would react if I opened up about my life. What if I told her about one of my memories from when I was about 5 years old? My grandfather, Thomas White, my mother's father, was walking home from a grocery store in Waco when a group of white teenagers approached him, savagely beat him, robbed him, and left him on the side of the street. He was rushed to a hospital where he died a few weeks later. No arrests were ever made.

If I shared such experiences, I was not sure if Sue or any of my classmates would, or even could, understand the depth of my hurt and anger. If they didn't understand, I knew that not only would I be disappointed, but it would also be hard to get over that lack of understanding. So I maintained my silence. I kept a part of myself away from them, pushing such memories to the back of my mind. After all, it was not their fault that they might not be able to understand my life experiences. And many of them had befriended me. They had included me, using the nickname that Sue had given me, "Eddie Tex."

My relationship with Pat was so different from my friendship with Sue. Pat never invited me to her parents' home. She never directly asked to borrow my clothes. But she admired the clothes that I wore and commented on them. She would pretend that my clothes belonged to Sue and then ask her if she could borrow them. This happened frequently. We all knew what was going on, but we went along with it and allowed her to get away with it.

Pat was never totally comfortable with me and never really was able to just interact with me as a friend. After a while Pat tried to explain her distance to me. She shared that the only Black person she had ever had a relationship with was the family housekeeper. They had fairly strict rules for the housekeeper; she was to answer the front door to announce visitors, but she was never to enter the house through the front door. The family housekeeper was clearly subservient to the family. Pat struggled with seeing me, an African American woman, as an equal.

I needed to find ways to meet people and develop relationships with other students. I had enjoyed singing in the church choir when I was growing up. I had desperately missed being a vocalist and wanted to sing again. I could achieve both goals by joining the Catholic choir at St. Mary's. Every morning, we would sing at the 5:30 a.m. mass. That experience influenced my decision to change my faith from Baptist to Catholic.

I took instructional classes and read the doctrine. I felt a sense of belonging and was happy about my decision after being baptized. I was somewhat afraid to tell my father. When I finally told him, he said that he was proud of me and reminded me that his great-grandmother was Catholic. Being a practicing Catholic was very different from my prior religious experiences. I began to go to confession on Fridays. I liked having someone I could confide in and trust and not have to worry whether the details of my conversation would be shared with the entire world.

There was only one faculty member who made me feel as though I did not belong at St. Mary's. She was a chemistry instructor who later joined the Holy Cross Order. When she asked the class questions, she always ignored my raised hand. This went on for the entire semester. But I knew immediately what was going on. I was invisible to her. I could perceive that she was intentionally slighting me. But I didn't complain to anyone. I had been taught that you confronted racism by working harder and being better. So that was what I did. Throughout the semester I made certain that I had my work done. I did well in my coursework and homework assignments. But when final grades came out, I discovered that she had only given me a passing grade.

I was very distraught. I knew that I'd been treated unfairly. I knew that this wasn't right. I called my father to tell him that I was unhappy and that I wanted to return home for good. He patiently listened and attempted to calm me down. He said that he would send me a ticket to come home. But instead of helping me to come home for good, my father called a senior nun at St. Mary's and explained my unhappiness. Together they worked out a plan for me to go home to Waco. But he wasn't bringing me home for good; I'd be returning to school after a two-week brief rest.

The very next morning, after speaking with my father, I received a message that the dean of nursing wanted to meet with me. She told me that I was very welcome at the school. But I needed to understand that there were some prejudiced people in the world and that it was up to me whether I would allow their ignorance to deter or prevent me from accomplishing my goals.

My father sent the roundtrip ticket and I made the long ride to Waco. It was my first trip back to Waco since I had left that previous summer.

As I sat on the train, I comforted myself by saying that I would be able to convince him that I needed to stay home. I'd be able to change his mind and not have to return to St. Mary's.

But my return home turned out to be just a visit. My days were filled with friends and supporters who had been invited by my parents to come see and talk with me. They told me they were proud of all that I had accomplished and that they were looking forward to the day when I became a health professional. All of them were so encouraging that I knew that I could not let them down. So after a couple of weeks, I returned to St Mary's to continue my work toward becoming a nurse.

Having completed the classwork required for the first year, it was now time for me to start my clinical work. Over the next two years, all of us would complete four rotations: pediatrics, psychiatric, general medical/surgical, and rural public health. We were assigned to the various rotations at random. For each rotation there might be a different group of students from St. Mary's and, on occasion, nursing students from other schools. As advanced students, we were personally responsible for our transportation to the sites where we did our rotations. The school would provide information as to the various bus routes and estimated length of travel.

My first rotation was my psychiatric nursing rotation. I was supposed to travel to Louisville, Kentucky, to work in the Our Lady of Peace Hospital. But when I arrived at the Terre Haute station, the bus had already departed. I was stranded and alone. I didn't know anyone in Terre Haute to call for help. I had to figure something out because I did not feel safe sitting in the bus station overnight. I walked up to a lady at the ticket counter and asked her whether there was a safe place nearby where I could get a room for the night. She told me that the YWCA was about four to five blocks away. I had grown up a block away from the YWCA in Waco and hoped that the YWCA might have a room for the night. But there was no way that I could carry my two heavy suitcases that far. I found the lockers, removed the items that I needed, and paid a quarter to lock up my suitcases. I walked those blocks to YWCA, not knowing whether they would have a room. Fortunately, I was able to get a room. I had no choice but to pay the four-dollar room fee, even though I was traveling on a rather limited budget. The next morning

I was on my way to Kentucky, relieved that I had been able to navigate having missed my bus.

My psychiatric rotation was fascinating to me. I found it so interesting to try and understand patients' behavior. This rotation would be the basis for my lifelong interest and commitment to be a psychiatric nurse.

After Louisville, I traveled to Anderson, Indiana, for my medical-surgical studies and care rotation. In this rotation I studied with two African American nursing students who were ahead of me at St. Mary's. This was the first time that we'd really had a chance to work together. We became good friends, staying in touch with each other for most of our adult lives.

My pediatric rotation was done at Indiana University medical center in Indianapolis. Because this was a large university hospital, there were nursing students from other schools in our rotation.

Most of my classmates were assigned to do the rural public health rotation in Cicero, Illinois. I had never been there and was looking forward to joining the others, experiencing that new city. But before I could depart, a nun came to my dorm room to tell me that I would not be going to Cicero. There were racial tensions in the city and the school did not want to subject me to that ugliness, she said. Instead, I would have to travel to Jacksonville, Illinois, to do my rural public health rotation. The nuns had decided that would be a safer setting for me. During this rotation, we worked with residents of rural communities to get vaccinated for polio prevention. The Salk polio vaccination had just recently been developed, and we worked to encourage everyone to get the vaccine.

The students on rotation slept in a dormitory, attended classes, and worked on hospital wards. Most of our instructors were nurses, with doctors serving as members of instructional teams. A typical day began on a hospital ward or in the classroom. Like other students I felt very special in my white uniform and cap. We studied various diseases, learned practical things about nursing and about patients, washed bodies and emptied bed pans, and cared for people who could not care for themselves. Taking care of elderly patients reminded me of taking care of my dying grandmother. I felt badly for some of the patients, especially those who were terminally ill. I did well, earning mostly As and occasionally high Bs during most of my rotations.

Time passed quickly. It seemed that we were always traveling. Just as I became accustomed to one hospital setting, it was time to move to another. I liked the independence of making my own travel arrangements and setting my own schedule. I liked getting to know the nurses and doctors who were part of the instructional teams. All of these experiences were a part of getting us acclimated to the real world. The end of rotations marked the completion of the first phase of my nursing training.

My parents drove up from Texas for the diploma ceremony with my younger sister, Lee Helen, and brother, Carl. Daddy had driven the entire route, stopping only for gas and, when they could park at a safe location such as a church, for brief naps. He had not been able to get much sleep. He didn't believe that there would be a motel or hotel that would provide a room for our family.

I was celebrating with friends at Lake Michigan when my parents arrived on campus. My father called Mrs. Buchannan, who was able to make arrangements with one of her neighbors for my family to stay in their home. They left a note for me at the dorm, telling me that they would be staying with a Black family in South Bend. I eagerly called my father, asking him for the address so that I could come see him. But he was so tired, he told me to wait and that they would see me in the morning.

I was so happy that my family had been able to make the trip to see me receive my diploma. It was the first time that my parents had been able to afford to travel to South Bend to be with me. I proudly showed them around the school. I tried to show them everything, where I had studied, the Notre Dame Football stadium, and the beauty shop on Chapin Street—the locations that had been a part of my St. Mary's experience. I eagerly introduced them to my classmates and instructors. I was bringing my two worlds together, my parents and younger siblings, who meant everything to me, and those with whom I had spent the past three years. I wanted my family to meet the people I had told them about.

One evening I suggested that we eat at a restaurant where my friends and I had eaten on numerous occasions. It was in downtown South Bend. It had good food, and I thought that my mother and father would enjoy the atmosphere. We were shown to a table when we walked into the restaurant.

Moments passed and I watched as other families were given menus and served their meals. My parents did not seem to question whether there was something amiss. I knew that there was a problem but was confused because I was a regular patron and had never experienced any problems.

Finally, I called the waiter to our table. To my great surprise and embarrassment, I was told that "Negroes" were not served in the restaurant. I protested, telling the waiter that I was a regular customer. It did not seem to matter. We were denied service while others sat and enjoyed their food. I was in a state of shock as we got up from our seats and left the restaurant. I was outraged and wanted to show my anger. My father grabbed my hand as we walked out of the door and rubbed it. He was calming me as he had so many years ago when I was a small child, those times when I would want to drink the cold water from the whites-only water fountain but had to make do with the tepid, weak stream of the colored water fountain.

My father did not say anything. He was so happy and proud that I was graduating that he would not let anything or anyone spoil our family's sense of victory. Not even the bitterness of racial segregation would rob him of the joy that he had in my graduation. He had planted in me a deep love for education and a sense of purpose. He had guided me throughout my lifetime, teaching me that hard work and determination would ultimately pay off. Not even having to leave a restaurant could steal the success of those teachings. Not even racism would diminish the pride he felt in seeing my love for education and my sense of purpose.

I watched my father closely while we were together in South Bend. I knew that my accomplishment was rooted in the times that he had encouraged me and told me to continue my journey, no matter the depth of the pain that I might encounter. I thought of the ways that he had taught me to learn for myself, the ways that he had taught me to make good decisions.

Once, when I had gone home on a break, I asked my father to teach me how to smoke. He purchased a pack of Camel cigarettes, lit one, and took a drag. He gave it to me and told me to "draw hard." I did and nearly choked myself to death. It was a horrible experience. I threw the pack of cigarettes away and never picked up another one.

On another occasion he produced a glass of homemade wine and instructed Sallye and me to take a sip. I thought it was some of the worst stuff that I had ever tasted. My father was teaching us a lesson. He wouldn't lecture; he would let us make the discoveries on our own, confident that we would make the right decision.

On that August 1955 morning when we received our diplomas, I was filled with appreciation for my father and mother. It had been three years since I arrived at South Bend, and I had learned a lot during that time from the opportunity that they had given me.

I remember it being a lovely morning as we gathered on St. Mary's campus. The graduates were dressed in white uniforms, white hose, and white shoes. We marched down the aisle in alphabetical order and took our seats. When our names were called, we'd rise and walk up to the stage. I could feel my mother and father beaming as I was given my nursing cap and pin. Every step I took that morning, marching in with my seventy-five nursing classmates, walking to and from our seats, was for my parents as much as it was for me. They had done all that they could for me and my siblings. They had made every possible sacrifice. They had devoted their lives to our success.

It was a moment that we had all worked very hard to achieve. My friends and I laughed and cried and proudly marched in unison as we had reached a tremendous milestone in our lives.

Chapter 4

Lessons Learned as a Veterans Administration Nurse

The day after the diploma ceremony, my family and I began our journey home to Waco. I had already registered for the next semester, so I was only going to be home for a few weeks. But I was ready to be home, to see the rest of my family.

After a brief stay, I returned north to Indianapolis, where I had a job at the Indiana University Medical Center, assigned to the La Rue D. Carter Psychiatric Institute. This position would get me experience in psychiatric nursing while allowing me to take courses and study for the national nursing examination.

I didn't originally decide to go into psychiatric nursing. When I entered nursing school, I really thought that I wanted to be a pediatric nurse. There is always something so special about working with children. But during my pediatrics rotation, I had worked with children who were undergoing heart surgery. We would hold them, feed them, and get them ready for this most serious surgery. For the operation itself, we would pack bags of ice against their bodies as part of the procedure. Open-heart surgery was risky and not all of the patients survived it. I realized that I would get too emotionally connected to the children I was treating. I reluctantly acknowledged that it would be too difficult for me to make pediatrics my career.

But I could use my concern and genuine interest in people to help with psychiatric patients. That was the reason that I had sought a placement at the La Rue D. Carter Psychiatric Institute. It was a time when there were not that many African Americans in nursing in hospitals. With this placement I would be in a hospital setting, learning how to interact with patients with psychiatric issues. They still needed regular nursing services; we just had to understand how their mental illness might impact how they would interact with us. We would take our patients to their therapy sessions and generally support them however we could.

Because I was enrolled in classes at Indiana University, I was able to live in one of the dormitories. This was common for St. Mary's students who went to Indianapolis to work at the hospital. There were three other students from St. Mary's living on the same floor.

When I received my first paycheck, I sent my mother and father twenty dollars. It really felt very special to know that I was able to finally give them a financial contribution to their expenses. A week later when my mail arrived, it contained a letter from my parents with a twenty-dollar bill. While they appreciated that I thought of them, they wanted me to know that to them I was still their "little girl" and that as my parents, they were to take care of me.

My loneliness and distance from my family was made easier because of my friendship with Mae Helen. She was two years ahead of me in nursing school and we had worked together during one of our rotations. She was from Anderson, Indiana, and while I was doing my medical-surgical rotation there, I had met her parents and family. Mae Helen had graduated and married an oral surgeon and they had moved to Indianapolis, so I was able to be a frequent guest in their home. On weekends we went to parties, to the movies, and to church.

Being part of their family made my life less lonely. I was still wearing a friendship ring that had been given to me by my high school boyfriend, Burford. We wrote each other regularly and talked about getting married. I had often thought of a career, marriage, and starting a family. My career was beginning, so now I could think about marriage and family. For a number of years, I had collected items for my hope chest. I first acquired some sterling silver; then I added linen and crystal. I did not have a trunk, but I would purchase items for my future marriage and family. At the time I thought that future was with Burford, so dating and going out with anyone else was out of the question.

I took the national nursing exam in the early fall of 1955. Every moment that I was not working or in classes, I studied for the examination. The nursing board was an intense two-day exam that covered the four major rotations: psychiatry, medical/surgical, rural public health, and pediatrics. Each section would be scored separately, and to be successful you had to pass each section. Passing the national exams meant that I would be a registered nurse, able to get a nursing job even if I didn't complete my last semester of studies to obtain my bachelor's degree.

When I received the news in October that I had passed all four sections of the national boards, it was one of the greatest days of my life. I was so excited; only about a third of the exam takers had passed. I called my parents, screaming with delight and happiness. I had passed my very first time. I could pack up and go home; I didn't need to complete that final semester to work as a nurse. I was 20 years old, not even old enough to vote, but I was an RN!

I had decided that I would return to Waco to begin my professional life. I wanted to be home, with my family and friends and the community that I had known growing up. But before I could leave Indiana, I had to travel one more time to South Bend. I wanted to be certain that the courses that I had taken while at Indiana University would be added to my transcript. If I ever decided to complete my bachelor's degree, I wanted all of the credits that I had earned to be recorded. I spent a couple of days in South Bend, telling people good-bye, buying Christmas gifts, and preparing to close out that part of my life.

I eagerly boarded the train for what would be my last ride from South Bend to my home in Waco. My father met me at the station. It was Christmas Eve. It may have been the same station that I had departed from three years earlier with two suitcases, three books, some peanut butter and crackers, and written instructions on how to arrive safely in South Bend, but I was not same person. I was returning as a mature young woman. I had traveled around the north on my own, I had lived and studied with white classmates, and I had earned my RN degree. I had been trained at one of the finest institutions of nursing education in the world. I had started earning my own money and knew that I had a very marketable skill.

But I was still very much my father's daughter. I knew that I had changed from my time in Indiana. I also knew that those changes might make me different than the person that many of my friends and family members remembered, but I was at home and determined to enjoy it. While Waco was vastly different from Indianapolis, Chicago, or Louisville, it was what I knew better than any other place in the world. My family and my roots were there, and that was where I wanted to be also.

In anticipation of coming home, I had applied to the Waco Veteran's Administration Hospital for a job. I was accepted. My father already worked at the VA as a senior aide, so we knew that it would be a good place for me to start my nursing career. During my second day of orientation, my father came to pick me up and proudly told everyone within the sound of his voice that I was his daughter.

Early the next morning the senior nurse called me to the side and informed me that there was a policy that forbade two members of the same family from working at the same VA hospital. She gave me a choice of working at VA hospitals in either Dallas, Marlin, or Temple. The decision was not difficult. When my father and I discussed it, I was firm that I was the new person and the one who should move. This rule was a surprise to him, and he was really disappointed that we would not be working together. But I knew that I had to be the one to leave.

But I also knew that I was not about to choose a town smaller than Waco to start my career, so that eliminated Marlin and Temple. Going to the Dallas hospital also made sense because I knew people in Dallas. My father had a cousin, Mabel White, a realtor in Dallas.

The VA hospital was located on South Lancaster Road in the heart of southern Dallas. It was built on 244 acres of vacant land to serve veterans who lived in Dallas, Fort Worth, and the surrounding areas. Dedicated in October 1940, it was a 265-bed facility consisting of eleven buildings, including a five-story main building, a residence hall for nurses, a dining facility, a garage, and various storage facilities. With two hundred employees, it was a major hospital.

Most of the patients had psychiatric diseases, which matched my interest in psychiatric nursing. Some were also neurological surgical patients. The patients were of varying ages, having served in the Spanish-American War, World Wars I and II, and the Korean War. Even though I had not originally sought to work at the Dallas VA hospital, it was a good option for me to pursue.

I received a letter from the Dallas VA telling me that I had been hired. I was also informed that I would reside in the nursing quarters that were located on the grounds. Everything was in place for me to start my first full-time position and begin my professional career—or so I thought.

My father drove me to Dallas. I was to meet with the chief nurse at 9:00 a.m., so we had to leave very early in the morning to make that four-hour drive. But the ride did not seem that long. I was excited to learn about my assignment and responsibilities of my position. I had always been taught that first impressions were important, so I wore one of my smartest suits, black shoes, and brown hose. I had recently been to the beauty parlor and my hair was neatly styled. I was ready to meet the chief nurse.

My father waited for me in the hospital canteen. We thought that the meeting would not take longer than an hour. Fifteen minutes before the appointment time, I introduced myself to a woman sitting behind a circular desk, telling her that I had an appointment with the chief nurse. She told me to take a seat and that someone would be with me shortly. I sat down, opened a book, and waited patiently.

One hour passed, and then another half hour. Still, no one appeared to see me, no one came to talk to me. No one asked if I wanted a drink of water or whether I was in the wrong part of the hospital. At eleven o'clock I went to the reception desk. I gripped the sides of the desk and emphatically said to the receptionist that my name was Eddie Bernice Johnson, that I was a nurse, and that I had an appointment with the chief nurse.

I could see the blood flowing in the receptionist's face as she turned red. I did not know if she knew what was taking place, but I knew that I was in the right place. I knew that I had an appointment. And I knew that I was being disrespected. She rose from her seat and rushed to the back office without saying anything. I turned and slowly walked back to my seat, angry and upset.

In a matter of moments, an older woman appeared with a slightly bewildered smile on her face. She was the assistant to the chief nurse. She explained to me that they had been waiting for a nurse named Eddie Johnson, thinking that he was a male. They had planned on meeting with me after they had met with him, she said. She then escorted me into the office.

The chief nurse, Emma Pope, greeted me. She seemed somewhat pleasant and apologized profusely for having me wait. She informed me that I did have a job, but that she would have to check on whether there was a room in the nurse's residence for me. She excused herself and left the office. I found it strange that she said that she had to check on the availability of a room because my acceptance letter stated very clearly that I had a room in the nurses' dormitory.

When she returned, she told me that my housing acceptance had been premature, that there was no room in the professional quarters, but that my job was secure. There seemed to be a sense that this situation was comical. The housing problem was rooted in the fact that they thought that "Eddie Johnson" was a male but I had shown up very much a female and they needed housing for a female nurse. Either way, Ms. Pope said that she would remedy the housing mistake by placing me on the payroll immediately and giving me thirty days to find a place to live. "Don't concern yourself with coming to work," she said, "you will get paid as if you were working every day." Because I had been hired by the VA in Waco and was simply being transferred to Dallas, I never worried about not having a job. But I have wondered whether I have been hired if they had known that I was African American before they saw me. I don't believe I would have been.

I filled out the necessary paperwork and thanked her for the time that she had spent with me. I immediately went to the canteen where my father was waiting. Once in the car, I told him what the chief nurse said about housing and her offer to pay me even though I would not be reporting to work. We both began to laugh at the idea of not working but still getting paid. We decided that I'd return to Waco and stay for those thirty days. It was frustrating but not enough for me to consider not going to work at the VA. The VA was still a good place for me to continue my training. It paid more than other nursing positions. And, as African Americans, we confronted obstacles and attitudes all the time. I knew that I couldn't give up and quit, that instead I had to figure out how to make the situation work best for me.

So I took a temporary job at Hillcrest Hospital. For thirty days I worked one job but received two paychecks, courtesy of good old-fashioned racial prejudice. I knew that I would go back in a month to work as a nurse at the VA hospital. It was the best paying nurse's position around. And, sadly, it wasn't that unusual to encounter racial attitudes and discrimination. I just knew that I'd have to deal with it and not let their racism keep me from being successful.

We contacted Mable White and asked her assistance in finding a room that I could rent. There was only one apartment complex in Dallas that rented to African Americans, and Mable told me that I wouldn't want to live there. Because of the racial prejudice that was rampant across the south, Black people were accustomed to finding rooms with other Black families instead of a hotel room or apartment. Mabel had been able to find me a room with Johnnie Mae Mingo, who owned a house with her husband on Caddo Street in the near–North Dallas section of the city. I had the upstairs bedroom, bathroom, and dinette sitting area. It was like having my own apartment in their house. Ironically, because of the hospital's racism, I actually had a better living space than I would have had in the nurses' dormitory. And I did not have to worry about anyone's attitude or bigotry, not wanting to sleep in the same room with me or sharing a bathroom. Instead, I was with people who welcomed me and treated me as a member of the family.

Living with the Mingos turned out to be a wonderful experience. Through them I was introduced to many prominent African American activists whose names are now recorded in Dallas history: Juanita Craft; A. Maceo Smith and his wife, Fannie; and L. A. Bedford Jr. I was also able to meet many African American visitors to Dallas, both in the political and entertainment arenas—people such as Whitney Young, Thurgood Marshall, Vernon Jordan, Maynard Jackson, and Lena Horne.

My first day at work began with another meeting with Chief Nurse Pope. During that meeting she told me that I would be the only Black nurse on the hospital's staff. In fact, she said that I was probably the first African American nurse. It was a cordial but candid conversation. She acknowledged that I was walking into a working environment where people thought I didn't belong, that I couldn't do the work. They were the doubters. They didn't have the training, skills, or experience that I had, but they held on to a false sense of privilege and superiority because they were white. But Ms. Pope was confident that, despite the challenges, given my credentials and my background, I should do very well. She said that I had to stay and work with them, that someone had to be the first.

We both agreed that I would have to work very hard to prove myself. I had known that this would be my reality. All my life I'd had to prove myself to others, especially white folks who would judge me. So Ms. Pope's remarks about proving myself didn't bother me. Her words of encouragement were welcomed even though both of us knew that had the VA hospital known that I was black, I would not have been hired.

Knowing that I'd face animosity and hostility, I felt a sense of apprehension when I started to work. I was not yet 21. I was very small and diminutive in size. Patients would often remark that I looked like a little girl as they questioned whether I knew what I was doing. At times it felt like I was a spectacle, as if I was on an island by myself with everyone watching me.

My fears and apprehension were justified. Most of the nurses were given reasonable working schedules. Not me. My assigned schedule included day work, evening work, and late-night work. On a week's schedule, I'd work two days, 8:00 a.m.–4:00 p.m.; two days, 4:00 p.m.–midnight; and two days, 11:00 p.m.–8:00 a.m. I'd work different shifts, with different personnel and doing different tasks. It was impossible to establish any routine that made any sense.

Chief Nurse Pope was a great supporter. She would tell me that I had to stay, that someone had to go through this experience to make it better for others. She had confidence in my training and abilities. Her encouragement helped me make it through those times when I would start feeling discouraged. Her intervention got my schedule changed so that I was working the shift rotations on a weekly basis, something that was much more manageable. But unfortunately for me, she retired shortly after I began working there.

There were times that my supervisors deliberately held me past the end of my shift. They knew that I took the bus to get to work and home. The hospital was in the south Oak Cliff section of Dallas. I lived in the near–North Dallas area. The last bus that would take me downtown to catch a transfer bus to my house left the hospital at five minutes after midnight. They would purposely hold me over, knowing that I would then have to walk about eight miles, in the dark, through stretches of undeveloped lots. It would take me nearly an hour to get downtown to the station to catch the second bus to get home. Once, after walking downtown, I missed the second bus, which forced me to walk the rest of the way. It was late. I was dressed in my uniform, spending an hour navigating streets that were unfamiliar to me, and walking past strangers. I was afraid, but there was nothing that I could do. I had no choice. If I was to get home, I had to walk.

During the lunch break for my shift, I would sit by myself in the cafeteria while the other nurses would eat together, laugh, and enjoy the break. Not one of them reached out to me. I felt alone. I was alone. But I was not going to allow them or their bigotry to affect me. Their prejudice would not deter me from accomplishing my goal of becoming the very best nurse in the hospital. In fact, their racism strengthened my determination. I knew that I was breaking new ground at the hospital and that every move that I made was being watched very closely. I was very aware that there were people looking for any opportunity to criticize me and have me removed from my position.

I found that many of the nurses were not accustomed to doing detailed work. Some were even ignorant about the most basic nursing procedures. They could not perform the work that a student in her first year of rotation at St. Mary's had learned to do. Many of them had limited training, but they were able to keep their jobs because they had relatives or friends who protected them and overlooked their shortcomings.

One morning when I reported to work, I was told that I had been assigned to another ward. When I questioned why I had been transferred, I was told that a patient had expressed that he had a problem with me. I hadn't yet worked on that ward, so the only basis for the patient to have a complaint was my race. It was so clear to me, but no one else seemed to see it. Racial prejudice was present and manifested itself in many different forms. Once, I was startled when even a Black patient questioned my competency because of my race. Fortunately, those incidents did not dominate my experience at the hospital.

Working with patients was the reason that I had become a nurse. It was important to me that my patients knew that I was giving them the best care that they could get. I was small and looked younger than most of my colleagues, and occasionally patients questioned whether I was a nurse. But when I worked with a patient, many of whom were veterans of World War II and the Korean conflict, I talked with them. I shared what I had learned about nursing with them. I told them that they could confide in me. When I performed a procedure, I explained to him exactly what I was doing. I recognized that for many of them, being in the hospital was a new experience, so I would check on them frequently. Before long, patients appreciated me and began to request my services.

My evaluations at work were exemplary, and eventually I was promoted to serve as the head psychiatric nurse. At the time I was also one of the youngest people ever appointed to be a head nurse. This meant I was responsible for scheduling nurses, overseeing patient assignments, and working to make certain that our patients were being given the best care possible. I also helped write one of the procedure manuals that would be used by the nurses. I was constantly proving myself to be one of the best nurses at the VA.

As a leader I knew that how I presented and carried myself was important. Nursing was very difficult and demanding work. At that time the profession required that we wear immaculate white clothing, white shoes, and white hose, so my appearance had to justify the respect that I demanded. On my days off, I washed and ironed my uniforms, one for each day of the week. When I could afford it, I took them to the Fishburn Laundry to have them cleaned and starched. Nursing attire was a signature, a sign of the value we gave to our patients. It was a sign of our pride in being a nurse.

While I was a head nurse, I started a day treatment psychiatric service at the hospital. This center provided services to our veterans who came to the hospital for therapy sessions. These patients lived at home and came to the hospital for therapy sessions, to learn to manage their illness, and for activities such as ceramics and woodwork.

Word of my performance, my interaction with patients, quietly spread throughout the hospital, particularly among the doctors and African American aides, mostly college-educated men, who assisted the clinicians. Some were teachers by education and training, but the Dallas Independent School District had a rule that spouses could not work in the district. Black male aides could make as much money as a teacher, so they came to the VA to work. Some of the aides and their families provided social outlets for me. I was not a member of a sorority, which would have connected me to members of my age group. It was the friendship of aides and their families that helped me to become comfortable in Dallas.

On a personal level, things did not improve much for me in the very early days at the hospital. There were still flagrant signs of racial prejudice exhibited by my coworkers. Once, I grew tired of the treatment at the hospital and applied to a graduate program in New York City. I was accepted and informed the chief nurse that I was leaving. She had become somewhat of an ally and pleaded with me to stay. I told her that I would consider her request, but only if I was transferred to a ward where the racial climate was less hostile. She agreed to the transfer, and before long I was working on the eye, ear, nose, and throat ward. I was treated more fairly there, and I decided that I would not leave Dallas for New York.

On the new ward I met Doris Jones, the first white nurse to make an effort to befriend me. Many considered her a grouch. She had been an army nurse before coming to the VA hospital, and she didn't really try to fit in. She was strictly business and wanted the best for her patients. I appreciated her commitment to our patients and found her to be very kind.

The two of us bonded quickly. One June 19 she brought doughnuts to the ward and announced that she wanted to share them in celebration of Juneteenth. She knew that was the date that African Americans in Texas celebrated receiving formal notice that the Emancipation Proclamation had been signed by President Abraham Lincoln.

The doctors in the hospital were friendlier than the nurses. Most of them were at the VA for special training. I was able to talk with many of them regarding the types of medicine that they were learning. For the most part, they seemed to appreciate my attention to detail and the manner in which I prepared patients.

Even though I was a registered nurse, I still intended to get my degree. During my first year at the hospital, I had been unable to take any courses because of the irregularities of my work schedule. Once I was in the eye, ear, nose, and throat ward, I was able to start taking classes toward the completion of my bachelor's degree. I took courses at Texas Woman's University and what was then North Texas State University. Both universities offered courses at the local Methodist hospital in Dallas, so I was able to continue my coursework through their programs.

Although things were better, I continued to protest whenever I witnessed injustices and to record my observations in my notebook. I reported that when I had questioned why a male nurse with similar duties made more money, I was told that he was a man and had a family to support. I typed my handwritten notes and sent them to the regional headquarters in St. Louis, hopeful that senior administrators would be more sensitive to the needs and concerns of minorities and, upon reading my notes, would make changes.

Even with those hopes, I was pleasantly surprised when one day I was called to the office of the hospital's chief administrator. After an exchange of pleasantries, he told me that the correspondence that I had sent to St. Louis had been shared with administrators in Dallas. The chief administrator asked if there was anything that he could do to make things better. I told him that there needed to be improvements, that people of color were not being treated fairly. I assured him that I was willing to work with anyone who wanted to help change the working environment. The administrator agreed that changes needed to be made in the hospital. He asked that in the future I share my grievances with him rather than reaching out to his superiors.

He respected me and my work habits. He knew that I was fully committed to nursing. He knew that I always agreed to assist when the hospital asked for volunteers to do screenings in various parts of the city. In one instance I was the only nurse to volunteer. It was a glaucoma screening in an all-white section of Dallas. I was asked not to attend because there was concern about how I, as a Black nurse, would be received. The screening had to be canceled because no one else had volunteered.

One of my closest allies at the hospital was a young man by the name of Alberto Gonzales. He was a Mexican aide who was upset by the treatment of minority aides. He also documented incidents in a notebook and shared them with me. Alberto had a car and occasionally gave me a ride home. As he drove we talked about the need for more minority leadership at the hospital. Alberto shared my concerns for social justice. A bond was created that would last through my political career.

I was eventually contacted by an administrator with the Dallas office of the VA, Tom Gaubert Sr. He came to my house to talk with me about the situation at the hospital. He listened to my descriptions of the problems, the way that the Black employees were treated. I was assured that he would investigate my complaints and that changes would be made.

I had always known that it was important to speak up about injustice and unfairness. But I didn't always believe that officials would listen and try to change things. This experience taught me that I had to always try to point out the problems, even if I couldn't be sure who would listen. If my voice was loud and clear enough, then it would be heard.

Chapter 5

Becoming an Activist

I had not lived in Dallas before and was eager to explore its downtown department stores, the primary shopping area before shopping centers were built. The three leading downtown stores at the time were A. Harris, Volk Brothers, and Neiman Marcus. When I received my first paycheck, I went shopping. I had been a student with limited resources, and now I was earning a salary that allowed me to purchase items that I had only been able admire in store windows. I was excited and eager to go shopping.

But I was shocked when I went to the stores. African American patrons could not try on clothing or hats. We could spend our money, make purchases, but we could not try on anything to make certain that it fit or to see how it looked. I had never encountered anything like this in Waco, a much smaller, seemingly more provincial city. Waco stores didn't discriminate.

But each of the downtown Dallas stores had similar policies regarding customers of color. In one store a salesclerk actually selected the clothing that she thought I might want to purchase. In another a clerk presented me with a cloth napkin to place over my hair. If I refused to use it, I would be unable to purchase a hat, she said.

Even the restaurants discriminated. They had different menus for Black and white patrons. The menus for Black customers would have higher prices for the food items than the menus given to white diners.

These policies were insulting. They were not right. I had worked as hard as any white person for a paycheck and my money equaled theirs, but I was treated differently. I did not like it. And there was something that could, and would, be done about those policies.

I also looked for chances to meet people. Having grown up understanding the value of the YWCA, I volunteered at the branch near Washington Street. There I met interesting people, thinkers with ideas who were interested in social change. I worked with a group of women, using the YWCA as the central organizing place. The Open Accommodations Committee was made up of fourteen women, seven Black and seven white, including Jewish women and a Greek woman. We were an inclusive group. I worked with Yvonne Ewell, Imelda Brooks, Mary Lou Kirven, Liz Jackson, Ovetta Rousseau, Mae Sanger, Hermaine Tobolowsky, Adlene Harrison, Bau Weisbrod, and others to develop and implement a strategy to have these policies changed. We would meet at homes all over the city. One time I was driving through North Dallas to attend a meeting. The police stopped me when I pulled up to the house and asked me where I was going. They walked me to the door of the house, standing with me until someone came to the door and confirmed that I was supposed to be there.

This group was the impetus for the creation of another organization, Fifty Sensitive Black Women. Imelda Brooks, Yvonne Ewell, Marian Dilliard, and I were among the leaders of the group. We met regularly, sometimes two or three times each week. Together we decided that we would launch a boycott of the stores that had discriminatory policies. We claimed that we were fifty women strong, although our actual number was lower because we knew that the name gave an appearance of strength.

We were determined. We were assertive. We had recruited other women to join us. We asked other women not to shop at the offending stores and made it known to those who continued to shop that we believed that their behavior was unacceptable. We even suggested that there would be consequences if they kept shopping at stores that disrespected African Americans. But the threat of consequences had been a bluff. There really wasn't any retaliatory action we could take, but we wanted people to know that we were serious about the boycott.

We approached a local African American newspaper publisher, Tony Davis, to assist us with our boycott. He told us that he could help by having a photographer take pictures of Black women walking into the stores that were the target of our boycott. We knew then that we had our consequence. When photos of Black shoppers going into boycotted stores started appearing in his newspaper, the *Dallas Weekly*, there was no ignoring the boycott.

It took six months, but victory came when Stanley Marcus, one of the leading merchants in the city, announced that the policies of his store, Neiman Marcus, would no longer prohibit Black shoppers from trying on clothing before they made a purchase. It was a significant victory.

Interestingly, most of the women who engineered the boycott were not natives of Dallas. We were from smaller towns and often viewed as outsiders by some Dallas natives. We brought our experiences from those other cities, including the social practices and the relationships between the races. Those experiences gave us a basis to judge the practices that we were encountering in Dallas. We could more clearly see what was wrong with the Dallas social systems.

There had not been any major acts of civil disobedience or massive demonstrations in Dallas like those that had occurred in Detroit, New York, Newark, Baltimore, and Chicago. Whenever there was turbulence caused by the Black community, a group of white business owners met with their Black clergy allies and things were calmed down.

At that time the Dallas City Council members were elected at-large. The first Black man to run for city council was Maynard Jackson Sr., pastor of New Hope Church and father of Maynard Jackson Jr., who would become the first Black mayor of Atlanta. Dallas was southern apartheid, not unlike the system of government in South Africa that kept the races apart and prevented social and economic progress. Jackson lost the election. Eventually there was a Black candidate who did win, but he had been selected by the white power structure and put forth as a candidate.

As I compared Waco and Dallas, I saw interaction between the races in my hometown was much more common. I remembered having white guests in our home. A few of our neighbors were from other races and we interacted socially with them. But it wasn't that way in Dallas; most Black and white people kept their distances from one another. People lived in different and distinct worlds.

Much of the leadership in the Black community in Dallas came from other cities. Zan Holmes, a noted preacher, was from Waco, as was State Representative Joseph Lockridge. George Allen, who served four terms on the Dallas City Council, was from New Orleans. They were among those who held the reins of leadership and pushed for better treatment for African Americans. It may have appeared that many Blacks in Dallas were content with the way things were, but the truth is that there were constant efforts by African Americans to fight for political and social gains.

My involvement with the American Nurses Association is another example of how Blacks—this time nurses—created vehicles for change. It was through this organization, which met at the VA, Baylor, or Parkland Hospitals, that I met Mrs. Mary Walton, an older African American nurse who served in the military. She convened meetings of Black nurses in her home. There were about six of us who met regularly, using the time together to fellowship and talk about our workplace experiences. These meetings provided us with a support system, encouraging and empowering each of us to withstand the pressures and inequities and to be advocates for change. Fighting against inequality can be draining and you need a space to get recharged, to be refueled. Our meetings gave us that space.

I got involved in civic activities because I felt that I could help change society. I had been taught to play a role in improving the quality of life that people lived. I was not comfortable with being a professional with means, while others had very little. But I was not protesting and fighting just for myself. While my natural focus was the treatment of African Americans, I believed that everyone should be treated fairly and equally. I knew that I would spend the rest of my life, regardless of what job I had, working for change.

Chapter 6

The Road to
My First Primary

A. Maceo Smith was a proud member of the Alpha Phi Alpha fraternity. I had gotten to know him through the Mingo family with whom I lived. One time he invited me to attend a party. When I mentioned to one of the aides at the hospital that I would be going to an Alphas' party, he told me that he would arrange to introduce me to a DISD school teacher, Lacy Johnson. Lacy was the math teacher at Booker T. Washington High School, the high school for Black students that was located near my home on Caddo Street. Lacy, who had been born in Ardmore, Oklahoma, had lived in several places before moving to Dallas. His father, Reverend D. Edwin Johnson; his mother, Ida Mae Johnson; and he were all graduates of Bishop College, the historically Black college located in Marshall, Texas. Reverend Johnson was an influential figure in the Baptist church community in Dallas. He was also politically active. The first time that I met Dr. Martin Luther King Jr. was in Reverend Johnson's home.

Lacy and I had similar interests, and we began to date regularly. Because theaters and social venues were segregated, most Black social life revolved around visiting friends. We would also travel to Waco for Lacy to meet my family. After five months of seeing one another, Lacy proposed marriage and I accepted.

At the time I was a member at Holy Cross Catholic Church, having become a practicing Catholic at St. Mary's. I believed in the mission of Holy Cross. I enjoyed being a part of the church and believed in its doctrine. Being Catholic was an important part of my life, even though I had been raised in the Baptist church where my parents were always very active members. I felt a deep sense of commitment to my God, my church, and to members of the congregation and took my religious responsibilities seriously. When I could not get a ride to Holy Cross, I would get there using the bus. Because it was on my bus route home, I often went to evening services directly from work, when my shift allowed.

I was excited about getting married. Lacy, although he was Baptist and the son of a Baptist pastor, honored my wish to get married in the Catholic church. As I thought about the wedding, I knew there were numerous guests I wanted to invite, including church members. And of course my family, who had been so supportive, would be there. I would imagine the look on my father's face as I walked down the aisle while he stood at the altar with Lacy and Monsignor O'Brian.

Lacy and I took marital instruction from Monsignor O'Brian at the church. Then the day came that I had to approach Monsignor O'Brian about the wedding date. I had always liked him as a priest. He looked so stately in his clerical robes, regal as he conducted communion and gave his homilies. I thought he spoke to Christ as a partner in the faith, and not simply as a worshiper, like me. I believed that he was wedded to the cross, and that he believed in what was written in the Bible.

I dressed in one of my finest suits, one that I had worn to mass on numerous occasions, to meet with the monsignor. I was so excited to talk with him about my wedding day, one of the most special days of my young life. We would set the date and schedule the wedding. Life was good.

When I got to his office, his secretary told me to have a seat, that he would be right with me. I sat down and waited. Then I was told to go into his office. When I walked into his office, it was clear that he had just completed a phone call. The look on his face was one that I had not seen before. I thought that perhaps he was ill, so I asked how he was feeling. He replied that he was doing "just fine." I then asked him which dates were available for our wedding. He looked at me sadly and told me that I could not get married at Holy Cross. There had never been a "Negro wedding" in the church, and he did not want to upset some of the members.

I began to breathe deeply. I was saddened and enraged. It was not what I had expected to hear. I was not prepared for what he told me. My eyes searched the room and I looked at various religious symbols on the walls, including one of the crucifixion with blood flowing from the body of Jesus. I couldn't speak. I just sat there silent. "There is a Negro Catholic Church in South Dallas, St. Anthony's Church, where you can be married. I am sorry," he said. "We have never had a Negro wedding here," he repeated.

"I am sorry too," I said before reaching for my purse and walking out of his office. I do not remember if I spoke to his secretary. I walked directly from the church to the bus stop.

Once the bus arrived, I took a seat near the front. I sat alone and looked out the window, watching people and lights as we passed. Darkness had come, and it seemed as if I was taking the longest bus ride of my life. I was greatly disappointed with Monsignor O'Brian, Holy Cross, and the Catholic Church. My spirit was nearly crushed. By the time that I arrived at my room, I had decided that I would never return to the place where I had proudly worshiped.

I never did go back to a Catholic church. In fact, it would be months before I even went to a Baptist church.

On July 5, 1956, Lacy and I were married in his parents' home. Reverend Johnson, Lacy's father, presided over the ceremony. Sallye stood with me. A fraternity brother served as Lacy's best man. The hurt and disappointment of not having my wedding in the Catholic Church was forgotten as we stood surrounded by our parents, siblings, and family.

One positive consequence came from Monsignor's refusal to allow me to get married at Holy Cross Church: we saved money. By having the small ceremony at the Johnson home, we did not spend as much. Lacy and I took the money that we had saved and used it to buy a home.

We moved into our house in south Dallas, on Birmingham Street. It was a two bedroom, with a living room, dining room, and an enclosed back porch. We spent that summer painting, refinishing cabinets, making the house ours. It was to this home that we brought our son, Kirk, who was born in 1958.

I took maternity leave from the VA when Kirk was born. But after a short time, I went to work part-time at St. Paul Hospital. Working at that hospital, I learned that they did not have a standardized nurse's procedure manual. I observed that nurses had their own ways of approaching services and activities, which could put the hospital at risk. I went to the VA hospital, got a copy of the nursing procedure manual, and brought it back to the nursing administration at St. Paul. We talked about possibilities for creating nursing protocols and improving procedures at the hospital.

In January 1960 Lacy and I moved into a new home. I had returned to work full-time at the VA hospital. We became one of the first Black families to integrate the Oak Cliff neighborhood adjacent to the public Cedar Crest Golf Course. It had been a white neighborhood, with a number of empty lots for new construction. Within five years the neighborhood became home to a number of Black professional families: Dickie Foster, owner and publisher of the *Dallas Post-Tribune* newspaper; C. B. Bunkley, an attorney, and his wife; Dr. Emmett Conrad and his wife; Harvey Boykin, businessman; Burl Ridge; and several school principals, teachers, and administrators lived in this neighborhood. We quickly knew that this home would be where we would live and raise Kirk.

It was important to me that the residents in this neighborhood join their talents and skills to promote and support the interests of African Americans. We organized the Cedar Crest Civic Club, which became one of the most active neighborhood associations. Living in a neighborhood next to the public golf course, it was important to make sure that the Black residents could play on the course. I played golf, so I would regularly play at the Cedar Crest Golf Course.

The presidential campaigns by Richard Nixon and John Kennedy also took place in 1960. This was the first presidential election in which I was eligible to vote. I had not turned 21 until December 1956, after the Eisenhower/Stevenson election. But if I had any illusions about voting, the harsh reality of having to pay a poll tax was a stark reminder of the laws designed to impede African Americans from voting.

I had been taking courses at Texas Woman's University and University of North Texas toward finishing my degree. I firmly believed that education was vital to personal growth, and I knew that I needed to finish my degree. In 1967 I decided that it was time to focus on completing my degree. With support from Lacy and his mother, I essentially moved to Fort Worth for a semester to attend Texas Christian University. Taking a full course load, I stayed in Fort Worth during the week and came home on weekends. I completed the requirements and on a hot, summer day in 1967, I marched in the Texas Christian University graduation exercises and received my Bachelor of Science degree.

Later that year, one of our neighbors, Dr. Emmett Conrad, ran for a seat on the Dallas school board. I supported his candidacy and became involved in his campaign. I walked through various neighborhoods, Kirk at my side, and knocked on doors, telling prospective voters why Dr. Conrad should be elected and leaving behind campaign materials. This was a nonpartisan race, so I could openly support and campaign for a candidate. I was still working for the VA hospital and as a federal employee was under the restrictions of the Hatch Act.

During this time I became even more heavily involved with community organizations. I joined the Dallas chapter of the National Council of Negro Women (NCNW), an organization founded by Mary McLeod Bethune, to promote the interests of and opportunities for African American women. Although the membership of NCNW tended to be older Black women, it was very comfortable for me because I had grown up hanging around my mother and her friends.

I also became very active in the Progressive Voter's League (PVL). The PVL was one of the oldest Black political organizations. For years it had been involved in fights against restrictions on voting, such as the poll tax. When I joined the PVL, its target objectives were the election of an African American to the state legislature and Dallas City Council. Attorney L. A. Bedford, a Dallas native who went to Brooklyn Law School because a Black person could not get a legal education in Texas, recommended Joseph Lockridge as a candidate for the state House. With the support of the PVL and other organizations, Lockridge defeated his white opponent and became the first African American from Dallas elected to the Texas House since Reconstruction.

In the 1970 race for the United States Senate, I was a supporter of the liberal incumbent, Senator Ralph Yarborough. Yarbrough had attended West Point for a year, returning to Texas to complete his education. He later served in the Texas National Guard, worked in Germany, and was elected to the US Senate in 1957. Most important to me, he had voted for the Civil Rights Act of 1964 and the Voting Rights Act of 1965. He was highly regarded in both Texas and Washington, DC. Senator Yarborough was a splendid politician, a great humanitarian, and an ally of minorities. He had been an advocate for higher education for poor people, fighter for veterans' rights, and a distinguished senator. Despite these things, he was defeated in the primary by former United States House representative Lloyd Bentsen, a wealthy businessman.

George H. W. Bush was Bentsen's opponent in the general election. The early polls showed Bentsen trailing Bush. Bentsen desperately needed the support and assistance of African Americans to win the election. He came to me seeking my support. I decided that Bentsen would be a good senator and decided to work with his campaign. I placed his campaign signs in my yard and began to distribute his campaign materials in communities where I had previously campaigned or had contacts. I went door to door asking voters to back him. I reached out to other leaders and persons of influence to support his candidacy. At the campaign's request, I even recorded a radio commercial endorsing his candidacy. Bentsen won overwhelmingly over Bush, who had criticized the civil rights legislation. My support and active participation in the Bentsen campaign gave me even greater visibility and stature.

Two years earlier, May 1968, Joseph E. Lockridge, the candidate recommended by L. A. Bedford and supported by the PVL, had died in a tragic plane crash. Ben Barnes, the speaker of the Texas House, praised Lockridge, saying, "I know of no man who did more to promote equality than Joe Lockridge." Lockridge's death had left a vacancy in the North Texas delegation.

Reverend Zan Holmes, also from Waco and a longtime friend, was selected to replace him. He had gained stature in the Methodist Church. As the pastor of the Warren Avenue Methodist Church, Reverend Holmes had allowed various community organizations to use their building for meetings. Precinct chairs would meet at the church. He was supported by African

Americans and white leaders. After serving two terms in the state house, Reverend Holmes suggested that I consider running for the Texas House. He told me that my election to the Texas Legislature was crucial to the progress of African Americans in Dallas and throughout the state, appealing to my commitment to social advancement.

But at the time I was a divorced mother with a young child. In 1970, after almost thirteen years of marriage, I had reluctantly filed for a divorce. Like many couples, there were simply some issues that we could not move beyond. It wasn't acrimonious. In fact, as life progressed, Lacy supported my campaigns and my work. We remained friendly up to his death.

As I contemplated running for office, I had to be realistic that I was a single parent. I had to focus on the fact that I was the primary breadwinner. I would have to quit my job if elected. I couldn't figure out how I could support my son as a single parent. So I resisted the suggestion. The very idea made me nervous.

Shortly afterward, during a community meeting, Reverend Holmes took the floor and announced that I would be a candidate for a seat in the Texas Legislature. He said that the community needed quality public servants and that I was prepared to serve. There were other influential people who said that I should consider becoming an elected official. A. Maceo Smith, whom I had met through the Mingos; C. B. Bunkley, a neighbor and NAACP attorney; Dr. Emmett Conrad, the school board trustee and his wife, Eleanor; Reverend Scott, pastor of St. John's Baptist Church, my new church home; Sim Stokes, a former Dallas Cowboy; and others encouraged me to run.

I received support from prominent white citizens as well. Earle Cabell and his wife encouraged me to run. I had supported him when he ran for mayor and in his 1964 race for Congress. I had even hosted a reception for him in my Oak Cliff home. Having the support of the Cabell family meant that I would also get the support of many of his powerful colleagues who influenced Dallas politics.

When I asked my son about the race, he said that it was something that I should do. Stokes became my campaign manager. I had met him while working with civic organizations in support of single-member districts. We had walked door to door trying to educate voters about the importance of single-member districts and the lawsuits that had been filed to achieve that governance structure.

Ambivalent about becoming an elected official, I still had not filed my official candidate's declaration by the final day to file. I was at home helping Kirk with his homework when Stokes called and said that if I wanted to run, I had to be at the Democratic headquarters by 6:00 p.m. It was 5:30 p.m. when I jumped in my car to rush downtown, leaving Kirk at home. The traffic was extremely heavy and I did not arrive until almost 6:00 p.m. I parked my car and ran the final block to the headquarters. Stokes was there and had completed the candidate's declaration form. All I had to do was sign my name. If he had not filled out the form, I would have missed the deadline and would not have become a candidate.

Even then, I did not have the required fifty-dollar filing fee. The election official gave me thirty days to pay it. When I returned home, I found Kirk sitting in the living room. I began to think about what I had just done. With all of my doubts, a voice inside of me kept saying, "Do it." My son smiled when he learned that I had declared my candidacy.

My family was very surprised by my decision to seek elected office, but they were also supportive and helpful. My father, as he always did, asked questions to make certain that I had thought of the ramifications of my decision. I admitted that I didn't fully know what I was getting into but that Reverend Holmes had encouraged me to accept this opportunity. My father knew Reverend Holmes and respected his opinion that I would be a strong candidate capable of winning the election.

My sisters, Sallye and Lee Helen, were supportive but reminded me of a long-held dream—to join the Alpha Kappa Alpha Sorority (AKA). I had known since my senior year in high school when I wrote AKA in my belt that this was the sorority I wanted to join. But St. Mary's did not have any Black sororities. I had been ineligible for the graduate program until I received my degree from Texas Christian University. Sallye and Lee Helen, already members of AKA, urged me to join before being elected to office or otherwise, they predicted, I would never have the time. I would be giving up on this dream. So I went through instruction while preparing for the election, being happily inducted into the Alpha Kappa Alpha Sorority in 1973.

I also knew that I had to find other employment if I was going to become an elected official. Government regulations would not allow me to work at the VA hospital and serve in the legislature. One of my supporters knew Stanley Marcus, an owner of the Neiman Marcus Department Store. She approached him about giving me a job so that I could run. He knew about my activities in North Dallas and my efforts to bridge gaps between different people. A meeting was arranged. He liked my politics and admired the work that I had done at the VA hospital and in the community.

Stanley Marcus remembered me from the boycott of the store. Yvonne Ewell and I had met with him at that time, and I had shared my experiences growing up in Waco and my surprise at the restrictions and slights encountered while shopping in Dallas. I had told him of my experience when I was buying an outfit for a wedding and wanted to try on a hat. The salesclerk had insisted that I cover my hair with a piece of paper before allowing me to try it on. The embarrassment and humiliation of that moment had stayed with me.

As I met again with Mr. Marcus, I was fairly certain that he remembered that first meeting. But we talked about the opportunity before me. Understanding that I could not run for office and remain employed by the VA, he offered me a job. I left my position at the VA hospital the Friday after the filing deadline. That Monday I started at Neiman Marcus in administration. With that I did not have to worry about how I was going to take care of my son. My position at the department store focused on personnel issues, health policies, and labeling. I knew that I wanted to learn the retail business and the philosophy that made it successful. I knew that Neiman Marcus would allow me to do my job as a legislator, but I also wanted to contribute to the store.

My campaign budget for my first election was five thousand dollars. I had three opponents in the primary election: two white men and a Black man, Berlaind Brashear, a practicing attorney. Berlaind and I made it to a runoff.

There was one problem that I had that wasn't shared by Brashear. There were two men in the community whose names were Eddie Johnson. I had to include my middle name, Bernice, on my campaign literature so that there would not be any confusion. Pink, brown, and white were the colors that I used on my campaign literature and signs to be certain that my materials were distinctive.

Brashear's campaign platform was brief and insulting. During forums and interviews he said that he was a native of Dallas, had trained as a lawyer, and had worked to get off welfare. He said that a woman was unprepared for the environment in the Texas Legislature. His theme was "Let a man do a man's job. Let lawyers make your laws." He continued to say that we were competing for a "man's job." With that he expected voters to send him to Austin.

My response during our debates was simple. I told voters that no one cared that I was a woman when I worked to create single-member districts, raised money for the heart fund, fought for equal public accommodation laws, helped to reveal that certain Dallas restaurants charged Black customers more than they charged whites, worked to improve our schools, and labored to improve conditions for working people. I promised voters that if they sent me to Austin, no one would work as hard as I would to represent them and their interests.

Then the race got even uglier when Brashear made a false statement that was printed in one of the local newspapers, stating that I was having an affair with Stanley Marcus. I was shocked and embarrassed. Marcus laughed and told me to ignore it. "It is the nature of the game you're in," he said.

I walked the streets of the district each and every day during the period leading up to the election, going to forty homes a day, urging voters to send me to Austin. Often Kirk was at my side. He helped me make campaign signs and place them in yards. Once during the campaign, he said that he would study cooking so that he could prepare our meals since I would be busy representing the electorate.

One of the key people that I met during my primary campaign was a North Texas Hispanic leader, Francisco F. "Pancho" Medrano Sr. I quickly came to deeply respect his opinion. In fact, much of what I learned about electoral politics, I learned through him. He opened his home to me, and I was a frequent dinner guest, talking politics and social issues at the table. Medrano had been involved in union activities through his membership in the United Auto Workers. He had confronted racial prejudice in the union, fought against the poll tax, worked with Dr. Martin Luther King Jr., and befriended Rosa Parks and Cesar Chavez. He had assisted with John F. Kennedy's presidential campaign. Medrano took me to the union halls and introduced me as a person worthy of their votes. He walked neighborhoods with me, telling people that he supported me. He made certain that I was introduced to political leaders.

I also received considerable support and encouragement from members of a number of community groups: the Seven Women's Group, the National Council of Negro Women, the Greek Women's Council, the National Council of Jewish Women, Jack and Jill Inc., the YWCA, and the Business and Professional Women's Group. Either I had been a member of each organization or my work had touched them in some way. Highly influential members of the clergy, including Reverend S. M. Wright of the People's Missionary Baptist Church, supported me. Reverend Caesar Clark, the esteemed pastor of Good Street Baptist Church, made a radio endorsement for my campaign.

My opponent had far more money than I did. He probably outspent me five to one. He could afford to hire professional staff, while I relied on volunteers. The contributions of my campaign volunteers were invaluable. One of them, Dr. Dan Weiser, a statistician, worked for Mobil Oil. A Rice University graduate, he contributed his considerable talents to my campaign during evenings and on the weekends. His was one of the most brilliant analytical minds in North Texas. A member of the PVL, he mapped out the district, showed me where voters resided, and suggested strategies for gaining their support.

Women of all ages who had worked with me on civic issues helped me to walk neighborhoods and distribute campaign literature. Women who I worked with to open the Women's Center in the Zale Building assisted with my campaign. A member of the Zale family sponsored my very first fundraiser. Judge Sarah T. Hughes, who had administered the oath of office to Lyndon B. Johnson after President Kennedy's assassination, actively supported my bid for office.

The primary battle against Brashear had been ugly, but I cruised to victory on June 2, 1972. Winning that primary also meant that I had won the seat, because there was not a Republican candidate for this seat. I was on my way to the Texas House.

Chapter 7

The Beginning of My Rise in the Democratic Party

My victory in the June 1972 Democratic primary was the catalyst for another important nomination. After the primary results, my name was placed in nomination to run for vice-chairman of the Texas State Democratic Convention. This was my first state convention, and I wasn't even certain what the vice-chairman's responsibilities were. But it would be the first time that an African American was elected to this position.

Encouraged by a sizeable group of people, including Pancho Medrano, who believed that I should run for the position, I allowed my name to be put into nomination. I was going up against Roy Orr, the incumbent state vice-chairman and a powerful member of the Dallas County Commissioner's Court. He was also the State Democratic Executive Committee chairman.

Medrano and other supporters convinced me that I could win the state convention election. Women were rarely represented in positions of leadership in state politics. My election would be significant. But my nomination also drew a surprise supporter from the floor. A white female delegate wearing a George Wallace hat urged the convention to vote for me. She said that she might be "cutting her own throat" but that she thought it was important for the convention to be unified.

Her statement underscored the stark contrast of the highly visible delegates supporting presidential candidate George Wallace, the former Alabama governor and staunch segregationist, and the possibility of my being elected vice-chairman of the convention. A straw vote on presidential preference had given Wallace 33 percent of the state delegates against McGovern and Humphrey. Wallace had the highest margin.

There were thousands of people in the auditorium at the state convention. Roy Orr, with the backing of the nominee for governor, Dolph Briscoe, was confident of victory, thinking that there was little chance that I would beat him.

Medrano, with unequaled passion, was the first of many to nominate me, speaking in English and Spanish. A tedious roll-call vote lasted nearly two hours. As the votes were being tabulated and the count being reported, a voice shouted "that did it" as a county delegation reported its votes putting me over the necessary numbers. Delegates were chanting, "No more Orr," and "Good-bye Orr, we're glad to see you go." When my victory was announced, my supporters almost drowned out the announcement with their cheers. I had soundly defeated Orr. Dolph Briscoe, despite his endorsement of Orr, attributed my victory to a "completely open and fair convention."[1]

I slowly made my way through crowds of delegates to the front of the convention. I was pulled onto the stage by a group of supporters including Sissy Farenthold, a leading feminist, to speak to the thousands of delegates. Almost everyone rose to applaud. I had never spoken to so many people. I had written a few notes while the votes were being tabulated, but I hadn't prepared a full speech. I felt a little numb as I walked onto the stage and looked out. Everywhere I looked, there were people. Calling my election "the first step toward real Democratic justice in Texas," I thanked everyone for this honor. Saying "this is just the beginning and that we can do it together," I committed myself to the work necessary to justify their votes. My election had "given me faith in the Democratic party."

The *Dallas Morning* News carried the news of my victory on the front page with the headline "Democrats Drop Orr for Johnson." Other newspapers called it a "rebuff" of Dolph Briscoe.[2] It was an astounding upset.

This new position propelled me onto the national stage. I was elected to the Democratic National Convention as a Humphrey delegate and was appointed to serve on the Credentials Committee. I attended my first Democratic National Convention later that summer in Miami. In just a matter of months, I had become an elected official and a participant in national politics. In fact, former United States senator Ralph Yarborough commented on my "rapid rise" in Texas politics, comparing it to Mirabeau B. Lamar, a former president of the Republic of Texas.

George McGovern received the Democratic nomination for president on July 12, 1972. Although I had attended the convention as a Humphrey delegate, I threw myself wholeheartedly into the McGovern campaign. Bill Clinton, then a recent Yale Law School graduate, had returned to Arkansas to lead McGovern's campaign in that state. We worked together on the McGovern for President campaign, believing that a strong McGovern showing in our states would help the national campaign. We traveled throughout Texas in an effort to get McGovern elected. Working with Clinton on that campaign, I was able to see his political skills and talents. I believed then that he was destined to become a national leader.

The McGovern campaign also gave me the opportunity to work with Willie Brown, a native Texan. He had already moved to California, where he had become active in politics, but he came to Texas to help the campaign. He would later become a prominent elected official in California and was another outstanding political mind, a master politician.

One of the specific activities that I was involved with for this campaign was hosting a luncheon for Mrs. Eleanor McGovern when she was scheduled to come to Dallas for a speaking engagement. I met with party stalwarts to ask for their support. Most of them had been backing Vice President Humphrey and declined an invitation to participate in any event that supported McGovern. I did not know what to do and went to see Stanley Marcus, telling him of my dilemma. Without my asking he offered to sponsor the luncheon for Mrs. McGovern. He said that he would be in attendance and that he did not care who knew it.

While McGovern lost the election, working with that campaign was my first exposure to a national election effort, but it definitely would not be my last. It was the same election day that saw me receive the majority votes to win the Texas House seat. My family had driven up from Waco on election day to help with the final moments of campaigning. They were with me as I celebrated my first general election victory.

With the election results began the work of preparing to take office. This was the first state election that had single-member house districts. All of the African American candidates won their elections. Including me there were four women elected to the house: Senfronia Thompson, also a Black woman; Kay Bailey of Houston; and Sarah Weddington of Austin.

I had always believed that success came with preparation and organization, particularly if one wanted to accomplish goals and objectives. Being a legislator was serious business, and I knew that I could not simply show up in Austin and expect the mountains to move because I had arrived. It was time to get down to business.

Figure 1. Eddie Johnson in her high school cap and gown, "To Mom and Dad." Courtesy of the Johnson family.

Journalism

This group is responsible for the Moore Highlight, a by-monthly publication and a weekly News Letter with Eddie Johnson and Ruth Wells, editors respectively. They sell the school to the public through an interpretative view of school life. Miss N. R. Cobb, instructor.

National Honor Society

The Kirk-Wilson Chapter of the National Honor Society serves as an inspiration for higher scholarship and leadership. Highlighting its activities with an "Honors Day Program" Bobbie Robinson heads the chapter with Miss N. R. Cobb, Sponsor.

Figure 2. Page from 1952 A. J. Moore High School Yearbook. *Journalism group, far right, seated at table,* Eddie Johnson; *National Honor Society, second person, far right,* Eddie Johnson. Courtesy of Waco Independent School District.

Figure 3. Eddie Johnson in nursing uniform. Courtesy of the Johnson family.

Figure 4. Eddie, Lacy, and infant son, Kirk, Johnson, spring 1958.
Courtesy of the Johnson family.

Figure 5. Family gathering at Rev. D. Edwin and Ida Mae Johnson's home. *Second boy from left, seated on floor*, Kirk Johnson; *standing, last row, fourth from the left*, Lacy Johnson; *leaning on back of sofa, sixth from the left*, Eddie Johnson. Courtesy of the Johnson family.

Figure 6. Eddie, Lacy, and Kirk, 1963. Courtesy of the Johnson family.

Figure 7. Founding Members of the Texas Black Legislative Caucus. *First row, left to right*: Eddie Bernice Johnson, G. J. Sutton, Senfronia Thompson, Mickey Leland; *second row, left to right*: first man not a founder, Sam Hudson, Paul Ragsdale, Anthony Hall, Craig Washington, last man not a founder. Courtesy of the Texas House of Representatives.

Figure 8. Eddie Bernice Johnson voting on the floor of the Texas House. Courtesy of the Texas House of Representatives.

Figure 9. Eddie Bernice Johnson, floor of Texas House of Representatives. Courtesy of the Texas House of Representatives.

Figure 10. George Foreman, Texas Rep. Eddie Bernice, and Kirk Johnson. Courtesy of the Johnson family.

Figure 11. Eddie Bernice Johnson is sworn in by US District Court Judge Sarah T. Hughes as regional director for HEW, 1977. *Left to right*: Secretary Joseph Califano, Judge Hughes, Eddie Bernice Johnson, Kirk Johnson. Courtesy of Larry Provart / *Dallas Morning News*.

Figure 12. State Senator Eddie Bernice Johnson holds up voter intimidation sign during state supreme court confirmation hearings, February 26, 1996. Courtesy of Texas Senate Media Services.

Figure 13. State Senator Eddie Bernice Johnson standing in Texas State Senate. Courtesy of Texas Senate Media Services.

Figure 14. State senator Eddie Bernice Johnson voting in Texas State Senate. Courtesy of Texas Senate Media Services.

Figure 15. State senator Eddie Bernice Johnson with State senator Craig Washington. Courtesy of Texas Senate Media Services.

Figure 16. Family gathering to celebrate Mrs. Lilie Mae White Johnson as Woman of the Year. *Left to right*: Carolyn (holding daughter, Kanisha) and Carl Johnson (son, Karlton, in front row, center); Lee Helen; Eddie Bernice; Edward Johnson (father); Lillie Mae Johnson (mother); Sallye Johnson Moore (sister), her daughter-in-law, Juna, and son, Gregory; Kirk Johnson. Courtesy of the Johnson family.

Figure 17. Congresswoman-elect Johnson with daughter-in-law Sondra Johnson and grandsons, the evening before congressional swearing-in. Courtesy of Official House Photographer–House Creative Services.

Figure 18. President Bill Clinton with Sallye Moore (sister) and Congresswoman Johnson. Courtesy of Official House Photographer–House Creative Services.

Figure 19. Congresswoman Johnson and her mother, Lillie Mae Johnson, at the Thirtieth Congressional District Office. Courtesy of the Johnson family.

Figure 20. Congresswoman Johnson and members of the Congressional Black Caucus meet with President George W. Bush. *Left to right*: Congresswoman Eddie Bernice Johnson, President George W. Bush, Congressman Elijah Cummings, and Congressman Bobby Rush. Courtesy of Agence France-Presse.

Figure 21. Congresswoman Johnson campaigns on behalf of Ron Kirk, first black candidate for United States Senate in Texas. Courtesy of the Johnson family.

Figure 22. *Left to right*: Kirk Johnson, Congresswoman Johnson, and former president Clinton at Congressional Black Caucus banquet, 2002. Courtesy of Johnson family.

Figure 23. Congresswoman Johnson speaks to A World of Women for World Peace conference, 2002. Courtesy of Official House Photographer–House Creative Services.

Figure 24. Ceremonial swearing in. *Left to right*: Speaker of the House John Boehner, Sallye Johnson Moore (sister), Congresswoman Johnson, Lee Helen Johnson (sister). Courtesy of Official House Photographer–House Creative Services.

Figure 25. Members of the Alpha Kappa Alpha Sorority visit the
Capitol. *Front row, eighth from left, in pantsuit,* Eddie Bernice Johnson.
Courtesy of Official House Photographer–House Creative Services.

Figure 26. Congresswoman Johnson walking down steps of Air Force One arriving for a memorial service honoring slain law enforcement officers. *Bottom to top*: First Lady Michelle Obama, President Barack Obama, Congresswoman Johnson, Congresswoman Nancy Pelosi, Senator Ted Cruz, and Congressman Marc Veasey. Courtesy of Ashley Landis / *Dallas Morning News*.

Figure 27. New Frontiers Congressional Gold Medal Ceremony honoring Apollo 11 astronauts and first American to orbit Earth. *Left to right*: Senator John Glenn, Buzz Aldrin, Congresswoman Johnson, Michael Collins, Neil Armstrong, and NASA Administrator Charles Bolden. Courtesy of Official House Photographer–House Creative Services.

Figure 28. Ribbon cutting at UNT Dallas for the grand opening of the first residence hall. *Front row, left to right*: Michael Williams, distinguished leader in residence; Texas state senator Royce West, Congresswoman Johnson, UNT chancellor Lee Jackson, UNT Dallas president Bob Mong, Dallas City Councilman Tennell Atkins. Courtesy of David Woo / *Dallas Morning News.*

Figure 29. Congresswoman Johnson with other members of the Congressional Black Caucus paying respects to Rep. Elijah J. Cummings, the first African American to lie in state in the Capitol. Courtesy of Official House Photographer–House Creative Services.

Figure 30. Congresswoman Eddie Bernice Johnson at the dedication of the Eddie Bernice Johnson Elementary School. Courtesy of Vernon Bryant / *Dallas Morning News*.

Figure 31. The Links, Inc., visit the Capitol. *Front row, fourth from the right*, Congresswoman Johnson. Courtesy of Official House Photographer–House Creative Services.

Figure 32. Congresswoman Eddie Bernice Johnson at the renaming of Union Station. Courtesy of Cheryl B. Wattley.

Figure 33. President Joe Biden fist-bumps Congresswoman Johnson during his entrance into a joint session of Congress. Courtesy of Official House Photographer-House Creative Services.

Figure 34. House passes America Competes Act. *At podium,*
Congresswoman Johnson. Courtesy of Official House Photographer–
House Creative Services.

Figure 35. Congresswoman Eddie Bernice Johnson stands behind
President Joe Biden as he signs the CHIPS bill, which includes the
Eddie Bernice Johnson Inclusion across the Nation of Communities of
Learners of Underrepresented Discoverers in Engineering and Science
(INCLUDES) Initiative. Courtesy of UPI/Newscom.

Chapter 8

Serving as a Representative in the Texas House (1973–1977)

Representative-Elect Johnson

After my victory I was thrilled and exhausted. But I knew that I had to spend the weeks leading up to taking the oath of office to prepare. As I anticipated being a legislator, I knew that if we were going to be effective as legislators, we had to be able to galvanize support from throughout the state among Black community groups, civic leaders, members of churches, and their pastors. While we were the largest class of African American legislators, we were all from larger urban areas. We had to reach out to Black voters in smaller cities, small towns, and rural areas, even if they were not from our electoral districts. We needed to have those connections and relationships so that there might be avenues to influence and put pressure on their elected representatives.

I decided to write a letter to each African American member who had been elected, inviting them to my home in Dallas for a meeting to consider establishing an organization that would collectively represent us and the interests of people who voted us into office. Each of my new colleagues felt that a meeting was a good idea. When we met in December of 1972, everyone agreed that we needed an organization, like the Congressional Black Caucus, to allow us to speak with a unified voice.

That winter the Texas Legislative Black Caucus was born. We wrote a mission statement, elected officers, and assigned duties to specific individuals. The founding members were Houston legislators Anthony Hall, Mickey Leland, Senfronia Thompson, and Craig Washington; Dallas members Sam Hudson III, Paul Ragsdale, and me; and San Antonio representative G. J. Sutton, who was elected chairman. He was from a politically prominent family. His younger brother, Percy, would later become a major figure in New York City politics.

As a group we identified our priorities. We decided that we would work closely with the NAACP. We would support increased funding for the state's Black colleges. We reached a consensus that we needed to take a hard look at the Texas prison system. And we would address the numerous other problems that affected African Americans and other disenfranchised people in Texas.

Our group was an impressive collection of people, some of the finest legal and political minds in Texas. Each had a legacy of leadership in his or her community, often working alone or with few allies and resources. I felt a sense of relief and wonderment that I had a family of like-minded elected officials who had spent most of their lives working for others. Now we were a small army, a force that would stand together no matter the challenges. I was certain that we would make a difference as members of the Sixty-Third Texas Legislature.

I got the delegate list from the Texas Democratic Party. We identified the African American delegates and sent letters to them. We wrote Black elected officials, representatives of local chapters of the NAACP, pastors of African American churches, and many others inviting them to meet in Austin. We let them know that we were looking at creating a statewide organization.

About fifty leaders came to our first meeting in Austin. The attendees were some of the most committed activists in Texas. We discussed issues such as public education, economic development, and political empowerment for minorities. This opportunity for concerned activists to meet and interact with Black legislators led to new connections and lines of communication.

From this meeting it was decided to proceed with formalizing the Texas Legislative Black Caucus. In fact, we had talked with Joe Reid, an organizer of an Alabama statewide organization of Black teachers, and obtained a copy of their bylaws to be used as a guide. It was the first time that such an organization had been established in our state.

Establishing the caucus was important for a number of reasons. We were committed to the growth of Black political power in Texas and knew that we had the opportunity to continue the increase in the numbers of African American elected officials. If we were effective legislators, understanding the issues and meeting the needs of the people of Texas, we would have demonstrated the value of a diverse legislature. If we identified and nurtured talented young people, there would be even more individuals interested in serving as legislators. Achieving these things was uniquely our opportunity and our challenge.

Since there were so few of us in elected office compared to our white counterparts, it was important that we have contacts and relationships across the state to help us gather information and ammunition to support our legislative initiatives. Caucus members also acted as our representatives across Texas. They followed their legislators' event calendars and activities, sharing that information with other caucus members, such that members in El Paso, for instance, were able to stay in regular communication with their counterparts in Galveston, San Antonio, and East Texas. Through this communication, elected officials were kept current on the latest issues, statements, and positions taken by representatives across the state.

We intentionally worked closely with young people, particularly those who showed promise and interest in social, economic, and political issues. Our recognition of the importance of developing leadership for the future was confirmed when a number of young people came to me asking if they could join our group. We embraced them with open arms. We paid membership dues for those without a source of income.

I served as the first president of the caucus. I accepted this responsibility not because of a personal need to run things but because my colleagues viewed me as the person best to guide and build the organization. I had an unwavering conviction that the caucus would help us to be better positioned to serve the state. That conviction directed my decisions. My confidence has been proven to be justified as the Texas Black Legislative Caucus, now known as the

Coalition of Black Democrats, became instrumental in yielding significant legislative accomplishments. We had laid the foundational cornerstone.

Representative Eddie Bernice Johnson, Sixty-Third Session

When I took the oath of office on January 3, 1973, for the Sixty-Third Texas Legislative Session, I became the first Black woman elected to the state legislature in North Texas and the first Black woman elected to any public office in Dallas. As I stood there, I recalled the things that my father had told me about being prepared for the future, accomplishing goals that others might think that I could not reach, and always doing my best. These memories were with me as I raised my hand and took the oath of office.

I did not know where life would take me, but I knew that I had to keep going to accomplish the things that had eluded women and racial minorities. During the campaign I had not been particularly focused on the historic nature of my candidacy. But knowing that I was the first Black woman from my district to take this oath made me feel an even deeper sense of obligation to be an agent for meaningful change. I knew that there was still so much more to do, so many mountains to climb and battles to fight. But I knew that I was not alone in this journey; not only were my son, Kirk, and my family with me, the other members of the Texas Legislative Black Caucus would be behind me.

During the very first week that Kirk and I were in Austin, former president Lyndon Johnson made a visit to the Texas Capitol. President Johnson had returned home to the Hill Country, near Austin, after deciding not to run for a second term as president. There was a long line of people waiting to take pictures with the former president, and Kirk asked if he could get his picture taken. The line was too long, we'll see him another time, I said.

President Johnson died of a massive heart attack the following week. Kirk and I attended his funeral, ironically on Kirk's birthday, and visited with the Johnson family. It rained as if the sky itself was grieving. We went to the burial site and spent time with Lady Bird and her daughters after the ceremony. Dignitaries from throughout the country were there. It was a very moving and solemn experience. It was also a time when I wished I had listened to my son.

As I began my first session, I was keenly aware that I had two important responsibilities: always being a supportive and loving mother and being the very best legislator that I could. I had found us an apartment on the north side of town and a high school for Kirk, Reagan High. I made arrangements for him to come to the capitol after school. Kirk adapted to our new life, even chasing Mickey Leland around the offices as if they were brothers.

But I also made a commitment that Kirk would maintain his Dallas friendships. We would regularly drive to Dallas on weekends, stopping in Waco to see my parents. I'd give them a grocery list and they'd do the shopping so I could pick up the groceries on my return to Austin. This was their way of helping me to balance all that was going on in my life.

While in Dallas we would go to our regular church, St. John Missionary Baptist Church. Kirk participated in the church activities, was a Boy Scout, and was a member of Jack and Jill, a national African American organization. He loved bowling. Just like for any other working mother, it was not easy, but it was necessary.

In the beginning the working hours were very long and the learning curve was steep. Over the first weeks, I had to learn the intricacies of the legislative process. There was not any official orientation program or training. While we had the benefit of guidance from former Black legislators, all of the sitting Black legislators were new. We had to learn the process for moving a bill through committees and subcommittees. We had to use the language and terminology of legislation. But most importantly, we had to learn the most effective approaches for garnering support and building coalitions to secure the needed votes for the passage of bills.

But first I had to set up a legislative office, something that was new to me. Fortunately, there were Black people working in the capitol postal office who were extremely helpful to me and the other newly elected African American legislators. They told us what supplies we needed and helped us to organize our offices. We could sense that they were proud of us and wanted to assist us; they wanted us to be successful.

There were a number of issues that I wanted to address in Austin even though our legislative session met for only five months, from January 9 to May 28, 1973. Maternity leave for teachers, adequate funding for minority academic institutions, feeding programs for poor schoolchildren, minority business development, financial parity for women, and prison reform were priorities for me. To be able to focus on these issues, I knew that it was important for me to assemble a talented staff and to build close relationships with key colleagues. I was fortunate to recruit talented, dedicated people to work in my Dallas and Austin offices. My Austin office staff concentrated on matters that affected state policies.

One Austin staffer was Gary Bledsoe, a third-year student at the University of Texas. He came to the office after class, made phone calls, did research, and performed other tasks. Bledsoe was a political science major. His honor's thesis was an analysis of the Texas House members' personalities and the issues that they addressed. He had interviewed nearly every member of the legislature regarding their political views, legislative interests, and voting records. Bledsoe shared that information with me. He was, in essence, an informal think tank that provided me with information on how to approach various members.

My district office, located in Dallas, had primary responsibility for managing activities in the district, connections with constituents, and goings-on in Dallas. Staying in touch with my constituents was important to me, so I held community meetings. Each month we'd pick a different location—a community center, church, or library. My district office promoted these meetings, working with precinct chairs to make certain that they helped to announce the date and location. This was my opportunity to tell the voters what was happening in Austin and hear their concerns and interests.

Another activity that I started early in my first term was to regularly bring groups of district residents to Austin. Active precinct chairs, ministers, volunteers, and anyone interested in government were encouraged to visit. They came on buses that my office organized. Some of them had never visited the capitol. I wanted them to have the opportunity to become familiar with state government and how it operated. As taxpayers, they deserved that and more.

The overwhelming majority of the members in the Texas House were lawyers, but that did not make them better prepared to serve than me. When I needed insight from a legal perspective, I turned to Craig Washington, a highly regarded lawyer from Houston. He was also a member of the Texas Legislative Black Caucus.

Barbara Jordan and I were close associates, although by the time I arrived in Austin, she had been elected to the United States House of Representatives, becoming the first Black woman from the south to serve in Congress. However, I was still able to call her whenever I needed advice. A graduate of Texas Southern University and Boston University Law School, Congresswoman Jordan had served in the Texas Senate from 1967 until 1973. On June 10, 1972, she served as Texas "Governor for a Day."[1]

I was also able to get legal information and analysis from Jim Mattox, who was also elected in 1972, to represent the east Dallas–Oak Lawn district. A graduate of Southern Methodist University law school, he was progressive and passionate about social change. In the early days, Jim and I met for breakfast each morning, either in the house cafeteria or in a restaurant near the capitol. We used the time to study proposed legislation. There were literally dozens of bills that had been proposed, covering a full range of issues. Because we were new to the legislative process, we had to work diligently to review all of the proposed bills as well as create strategies for our issues. I found Jim to be a unique legislator, both in his vision and in his willingness to stand with and for the powerless.

I was uncertain as to how the incumbent members of the legislature would react to me and my colleagues. Many of the legislators were descendants of soldiers who had fought for the Confederacy during the Civil War and seemed to hold on to Confederate ideals and principles. The newly elected members were also keenly aware that before our arrival in Austin, the legislature and state government had been a good old boys' club run by and for the benefit of white men. Even most of the senior administrators were friends of elected officials, holding positions because of their connections and not necessarily their qualifications. Some of their thoughts regarding matters of race and gender were profoundly prehistoric. The presence of the largest group yet of Black and progressive legislators would significantly challenge those dynamics.

In my mind people had to put the past behind them and concentrate on the future. I understood that the very state that I had sworn to represent had policies and practices in place that were in direct contravention to the interests of racial minorities and women. I did not know for certain how I would change things, but I knew that change had to come. Our mission as legislators should be the creation of a new Texas that would benefit people of all colors, faiths, and ancestral backgrounds.

I had never been one to view the world through the lens of color. I had always judged people by what they carried in their hearts, not the pigment of their skin. There were many white legislators who believed in equality; some of them became important allies of mine.

I also knew that I could not enter the legislature using only my voice as a weapon, but that I had to use my head. I knew that I had to appeal to the hearts and minds of people. I wanted to be able to sit down with any member of the legislature, no matter their beliefs, and meet them on common ground.

This was my thinking on the day I took my first oath of office and when I made an enthusiastic endorsement speech for Marion Price Daniel Jr. After the spring 1972 Democratic primary, Daniel had started actively campaigning to become Speaker of the House. A descendant of Sam Houston, he knew politics well because his father, Marion Price Daniel Sr., had served as governor in the midfifties. He promised that he would only serve one term as Speaker—an important commitment. He had been a member of the "Dirty Thirty," a reformist group within the Democratic party created in response to the corruption revealed by the Sharpstown Stock Fraud Scandal. I believed that he wanted change.

Labor unions backed his selection as Speaker. He was also endorsed by influential Democrats such as Reverend Zan Wesley Holmes. The Black legislators had decided to support his candidacy, and he was elected to be the Speaker of the House.

But my optimism about meeting people on common ground wasn't always justified. Within weeks Paul Ragsdale, Sam Hudson, Chris Semos, and I had concluded that a new state agency with authority to investigate and enforce laws prohibiting discrimination in employment, housing, and public accommodations was needed.

I had been approached by women who complained about the treatment of females in the Texas comptroller's office. The comptroller was Robert

Calvert. I was somewhat surprised when they came to me instead of one of the white female representatives, especially Kay Bailey Hutchinson, but I was honored that they trusted and believed in me. Seven women provided affidavits. One woman alleged that men were hired to do the same work but were given different titles so that they could be paid more. Another woman alleged that lists of eligible candidates were segregated based upon gender. Among other insults they experienced, women in the office were called "girlies" by male administrators.[2]

After an investigation I discovered that not only were their complaints merited, but there was also racial discrimination in hiring. Women made up over 40 percent of those employed in state agencies, but in Calvert's comptroller's office, women comprised only 37 percent, and most of those were clerical or maid positions. Out of more than one thousand employees in the comptroller's office, only eight were African Americans.[3] Along with Representatives Paul Ragsdale and Ben Reyes, I conducted public hearings with state agency representatives to investigate employment practices. Comptroller Calvert appeared, as did the Department of Public Safety director and the chancellor for the University of Texas. Based on those hearings, I, joined by Paul Ragsdale, filed a legal complaint with the Equal Employment Opportunity Commission (EEOC) alleging racial and gender discrimination in the comptroller's hiring and treatment of employees.

When I spoke at the press conference announcing our filing of complaints with the EEOC, I spoke as someone who had experienced discrimination, both as an African American and as a woman. I declared that the time had come for discrimination against women to be no longer tolerated. I then said that changes needed to be made in the comptroller's office.

The EEOC validated our complaints in its finding of discrimination based on gender. It found that many of the comptroller's female clerical employees possessed qualifications superior to male employees in nonclerical positions. It confirmed that there were no female tax collectors. It further found evidence that there was discrimination against women in its pregnancy policy.[4] After the EEOC sent me the letter finding discrimination, I released that information. In response to a reporter's question about the EEOC finding, Calvert said she's "a nigger woman who doesn't know what she's talking about." He went on further to say that he would never hire a woman tax collector because he couldn't send her to a "nigger or Mexican neighborhood" to collect taxes.[5]

Calling me a "nigger woman" got Calvert statewide, national, and international attention. Members of the legislature said that they were embarrassed that a state official would refer to a member of the House in such a manner. I was incensed at his comment. I understood that Calvert was in his 80s and ill-prepared for the new political and social realities in Texas. His behavior and comments reflected a culture that he had embraced all his life. But that didn't make his comments and attitudes acceptable. It didn't make his words any less objectionable. More importantly, they confirmed that he would not voluntarily change his employment practices. I had to act.

I held a press conference announcing that I had prepared a letter to Governor Briscoe requesting a special session to consider articles of impeachment if Calvert did not resign or end the discriminatory hiring practices. I also requested that the governor block any further expenditures from the comptroller's office and for a criminal investigation because the state spending bills prohibited discrimination. I made it clear that my action was not based on his insulting racist comments about me. My action was needed because Calvert's hiring practices had violated the law. He had unlawfully discriminated against more than 65 percent of the population of the state—women, Mexican Americans, and African Americans. I vowed that I would not be distracted by his racial slurs, his use of the word "nigger," or calling African Americans "darkies." I was determined to end sexism and racism in Texas.[6]

Colleagues in the house quickly called for Calvert to apologize to me. Others called for his resignation. But Calvert was adamant that he would not resign but rather he would seek another four-year term.[7] Knowing that Calvert would be up for reelection, I had personally recruited a former member of the legislature, Bob Bullock, to run against him. By the time the EEOC sent me the letter of its findings, Bullock's campaign was well underway and going strong. This controversy and focus on Calvert's racial slurs only strengthened Bullock's candidacy.

Calvert, whose signature was on the state's currency, could see the political handwriting on the wall. He came to the floor of the Texas House and said that he was prepared to work with me to bring about changes in his office. Then he walked across the floor and told me that he would withdraw from the race and retire at the end of his term.

There were many times when I was angry and wanted to explode. But I had learned years earlier that ugly confrontations were rarely productive and could cause irreparable damage to relationships. I knew that to be successful and have an impact I had to work with all types of people, even if I thought that their thinking was simpleminded. Being an effective legislator was about getting votes so that the issues that you cared about, and that helped your constituents, became legislation. So my philosophy was to work with all people, even if I passionately disliked them.

Committee Work

By statute the Texas Legislature meets every other year, during the odd-numbered years, beginning the second Tuesday of January. The Texas Constitution limits the term to a maximum of 140 days. But the legislators work even when they are not in session. We hold hearings, meet with constituents, and conduct committee work.

That first session I served on a number of regular House Committees: House Calendars; Constitutional Convention Planning; and Human Resources, including subcommittees on Mental Health and Mental Retardation (MHMR) and Public Health; and State Affairs, including chairing the Subcommittee on Law Enforcement Education, Training, and Standards. I was also appointed to special committees on Prison Reform and Reorganization and Modernization of Public Education. I was especially pleased to have been appointed to the Prison Reform Committee because the Texas Black Caucus had identified prison reform as a priority issue.

Prison Reform: The Path to Sweeping Change

The Texas Legislative Black Caucus had decided to focus on the treatment of African American and Hispanic prisoners in Texas prisons. I had received letters from inmates and their relatives telling me about horrific conditions in penal institutions. I was passionate about assisting inmates and their families.

I was the mother of a son, and I could only imagine the pain that gripped the hearts of those whose children were incarcerated in institutions located great distances from anyone they knew or could trust.

I shared the letters with Craig and Mickey. We decided that we would make unannounced visits to prisons to investigate. The conditions described in those letters were awful. There was horrific overcrowding, which posed significant safety threats and violence. There were descriptions of incidents of brutality with vivid descriptions of the injuries suffered by the inmates. There were reports of inmates, with limited or no medical training, performing medical procedures on other inmates. The infirmaries were in poor shape and there was a lack of medical services in general. Some of the inmates who were ill went without medical treatment. Inmates with serious medical conditions often died before they were released. If a family did not claim the body of a deceased inmate, the remains were sometimes thrown in a river located near an institution.

Extreme understaffing led to frighteningly dangerous guard-to-inmate ratios. Poorly trained prison guards encouraged the use of "building tenders," a term used to describe inmates who were given authority over others. The tenders were allowed to physically attack other inmates, demand sexual favors, and threaten other inmates. It appeared that in some institutions the building tenders actually ran the prisons. There was not an effective system for punishment and guards used the building tenders to impose summary discipline.

It was obvious to us that something needed to be done. The state wasn't simply warehousing men and women; it was operating facilities that encouraged brutality, violence, and neglect. The way the prisons were being run was illegal and immoral. And the prisons clearly weren't preparing inmates for release; they weren't even keeping them safe while incarcerated.

The headquarters for the state prison system was in Huntsville, Texas. It was placed there during Reconstruction when a Black member of the legislature, Richard Johnson, thought that it would bring economic development to the district that he represented. Most of the Texas prisons were in remote rural areas and were essentially run by residents of that county and surrounding communities, frequently employing members of the same families, neighbors, or friends. There was little to no emphasis on recruiting diverse guards.

The first Black prison guard in the Texas system, Ralph Mayes, was not hired until 1964. The treatment that he received from other guards was such that he left his position after only six months. When Mayes walked into the area where prison guards ate their meals, the other guards would immediately get up and walk away. We knew this history when we decided to personally visit various institutions.

When my colleagues and I arrived at an institution, we identified ourselves as state legislators and asked to see the warden or chief administrator. We would tell them that we had received information that we were trying to verify. We generally had cordial meetings. But we were repeatedly told by wardens and other prison officials that they were not aware of any major problems in the institutions they operated—denials that we did not believe. We knew that there were problems. So they were either trying to conceal the truth or they were woefully ignorant. Either way, it was a problem.

We told the wardens that we wanted to meet with inmates. We especially wanted to meet with inmates who had written to us with complaints. Sometimes guards would try to be present during our conversations, but we would ask them to leave the room. The inmates were always fearful of retaliation—a fear that we understood. We assured them that we wouldn't do anything to jeopardize their safety. We also encouraged them to reach out to us again if there was any retaliation.

Prisoners were often beaten by guards or the building tenders. The worst beatings occurred at the Retrieve Unit and came to be known as the Father's Day Massacre. On June 18, 1973, ten inmates were beaten by prison officials.[8] No one was killed, but a number of inmates were badly injured. Prisoners wrote to us about the incident. On July 11 Mickey and I visited the Retrieve Unit. The warden was surprised by the visit and tried to be cordial. Despite assurances that things were being handled, we insisted that we be allowed to see the inmates who had been beaten.

We met with each prisoner who had been beaten. They told us that they had refused to go to the fields on Sunday, June 17, to pick corn and had then been put in isolation cells. According to the inmates, the next day they were beaten in their cells and forced to run through a line of five to eight guards armed with ax handles, baseball bats, and rubber hoses to get to the fields to pick corn.[9] We saw the bruises and cuts from those beatings. I particularly remember one elderly inmate. He had a large lump on his shoulder, having been hit by a stick or something; it was badly bruised. I was alarmed by the extent of the bruising, so I asked that he be given medical attention. He was taken to a doctor, and it was determined that the lump was actually a tumor that needed to be surgically removed.

Not surprisingly, prison officials justified the use of force against the inmates, calling it necessary force to stop a "mutinous situation." The officials' stance prompted Mickey and me to urge a legislative review of the beatings. We knew that it would take such an official act to investigate not just this incident but all the problems plaguing our prison system.

We also realized that another action that we could take was to arrange transportation for family members to visit their incarcerated loved ones. Inmates had written about the lack of visitors and the added burden of loneliness. We arranged for charter buses to transport family members and friends to the different sections of the state to prison locations. We charged a nominal fee to cover the costs of the charter. We advertised on radio, making announcements of the weekends that we would be going to different institutions. At times, the bus would depart at 3:00 or 4:00 a.m. in order to travel the vast distances to the remote prisons. For many of my constituents, these buses were the only way that they were able to visit their loved ones.

These family visits became an important aspect of prison life. Inmates looked forward to seeing people who cared about them and their welfare and who wanted to maintain a connection with them. Seeing their spouses, children, and parents reminded them of the outside world and added a new dimension to their prison life. Those visits were positive motivation for them to follow the rules and not lose their visitation privileges. They also gave the inmates incentive to plan and prepare for the time when they would be released, to participate in job training and rehabilitation programs. Regular family visits positively impact inmate morale and discipline such that even the prison officials welcomed this service.

Our visits to the prisons and our inquiries about inmate care apparently troubled certain prison officials. Once after I had come home from a prison visit, a Dallas police officer warned me that I was being watched. He told me that Craig, Mickey, and I should be careful because dossiers were being kept on our activities. He suggested that I write down the names of all prison officials that we met with and leave the list in a safe place.

I listened to that warning. I reached out to Dallas police administration to see whether they were aware of any problems. From that point to the present, Dallas police have provided me with security. I have been very fortunate that Dallas police officer Arthur Busby accepted the role of watching out for me, even during my time in Congress.

It was obvious that prison authorities were not going to make changes without court intervention. William J. Estelle was a prototypical state administrator. He did not want to rock the boat and parroted much of what we had been told by wardens in prisons that we had visited. A lack of diversity among prison personnel was not an issue that concerned Estelle. While he said that he wanted to see improvements, he took little action toward achieving them.

A 29-year-old inmate, David Ruiz, had written me a letter complaining of the prison conditions. It had been hard to find someone willing to be a plaintiff in a lawsuit because of possible retaliation. But Ruiz agreed, and in June 1972 he filed a handwritten petition alleging that his constitutional rights had been violated. Attorneys from the NAACP Legal Defense and Educational Fund in San Francisco (including William Bennett Turner, a Texan) agreed to represent him. Turner had earlier represented another Texas inmate suing the state over its solitary confinement practices.

The lawsuit was filed against the Texas Department of Corrections and its director, William J. Estelle. The suit alleged that conditions in Texas prisons constituted "cruel and unusual punishment" in violation of the Eighth Amendment to the US Constitution. At the time that the legal action commenced, the state had eighteen prisons holding more than twenty-five thousand inmates. The Ruiz suit presented the concerns that we had been hearing about and looking into: poor health care, inadequately trained medical personnel, poor safety standards, arbitrary disciplinary procedures, and severe overcrowding.[10]

The case was assigned to United States District Court Judge William Wayne Justice, sitting in Tyler, Texas. He was considered one of the fairest judges in the state. Only two years earlier, he had ordered the Texas Education Agency, the governing body for public schools, to desegregate school districts under its jurisdiction.

While Ruiz's suit was pending, a special joint House and Senate committee was created. This was the type of legislative investigation that Mickey and I had urged. I was appointed to this committee that conducted a two-year study of "needed reforms in the Texas system of imprisonment."[11] Our first meeting was in August 1973, at which time Mickey Leland and I reported to the committee what we had learned about the beatings of inmates during the Father's Day Massacre. We told them of our visits to the prisons and shared the information provided by inmates and their families.

The Joint Committee held sixteen public hearings throughout the latter half of 1973 and 1974. We held hearings at prisons, receiving testimony from inmates. Remarkably, shortly after we were appointed, eleven inmates, naked because they were walking back from the showers, were beaten by approximately eighty to a hundred officers and inmate-guards with knives, iron pipes, and blackjacks because they were supposedly talking too much in line. We had to intervene to ensure that the inmates were given medical attention to treat their injuries.

Our staff did extensive research interviewing inmates and Texas Department of Corrections employees. They spoke with employees of state and federal agencies involved in prison oversight. We received input from the Citizens' Advisory Committee. The working papers were over one thousand pages. In December 1974 we submitted our far-reaching report to the incoming members of the Sixty-Fourth Legislature. Our report was deemed the "most comprehensive study yet accomplished on the Texas penal system."[12]

After almost two years of study, the Joint Committee unanimously approved a comprehensive prison reform package that stressed rehabilitation.

We made over 150 recommendations on twenty topics. Among the recommendations, we encouraged the institution of a community-based correctional program, a statewide probation program, and pretrial diversion as an alternative to incarceration. We also made recommendations targeted at the Department of Corrections, including placing inmates at prisons closest to their home, instituting mental health and psychiatric evaluations at the Diagnostic Center, and ending discrimination in treatment of inmates and employment of personnel. We also encouraged the legislature to review statutes that denied professional licenses based upon convictions and to enact an expunction statute that would remove civil disabilities and make records of conviction confidential if the former inmate maintained a clear record. A far-reaching recommendation that I had proposed was adopted by the Joint Committee—that "the legislature shall compel the Texas Department of Corrections to forever end discrimination based on religion, race, nationality or sex in the treatment of inmates and its employment practices."[13]

The recommendations set forth in the Joint Committee report, if followed, would have had a favorable impact on the prison system in Texas. If they had been implemented, they would have allowed the legislature to be in the front of effecting the changes and improvements.

While the Joint Committee was doing its work, Judge Justice consolidated Ruiz's case with seven other cases filed by Texas inmates. He ultimately certified the case as a class action suit. Finally, in March 1978, after years of legal proceedings, the trial began. I spent hours on the witness stand, detailing the conditions that Craig, Mickey, and I had personally witnessed, as well as the legislative oversight of the prisons. There were 159 days of trial proceedings lasting for nearly a year. Nearly four hundred witnesses were called. Approximately 1,565 exhibits had been entered into evidence. Based upon the testimony and evidence, Judge Justice ruled in favor of Ruiz and the Texas inmates. Their constitutional rights had been violated. Based upon his findings, sweeping changes were ordered.[14]

But the Texas Legislature did not act upon the recommendations made by the Joint Committee. Instead, Judge Justice's rulings and orders would direct the actions that the state needed to take. It would take almost thirty years of federal judicial oversight to bring about change in the Texas penal system. His ruling in this case and others led me to give remarks in the *Congressional Record* upon his death honoring his life and work. On October 20, 2009, I expressed my incredible gratitude for his decisions and sacrifices, which had helped carry Texas into the modern era, knowing that our observations and reports of horrific prison conditions and unlawful practices had contributed to major prison reform.

Helping Texas's Children

During the Sixty-Third Legislature, there were several investigations relating to the care of Texas children. I was honored to be involved in this committee work that would touch on the lives of our children.

In the spring of 1973, the House passed a special resolution establishing a task force to conduct an interim study directed toward a complete reorganization and modernization of state agencies administering education in Texas.[15] I was eager to be a part of this task force because I knew the importance of education. The "Committee of 24" was divided into subcommittees, and I served on the subcommittee focusing on financing public schools. The resolution also provided that a report be prepared for the incoming Sixty-Fourth Legislature. To address our mandate, we held meetings in 1974 throughout the state. We heard from educators, businessmen, administrators of local and state education, policy planners, and concerned citizens because we knew that the education of our children needed all of these perspectives. We developed a comprehensive set of proposals because we wanted to assure the quality of education for future generations and improve educational administration.

In July Speaker Daniel charged the Human Resources Committee to do a thorough study of all childcare, education and guidance facilities as well as all laws and regulations relating to those entities. Just a few weeks earlier, the owner of a private childcare facility had been indicted for the murder of one of the children in his care. An investigation by one of the human resources subcommittees determined that there was a pattern of objectionable conduct at the facility and irregularities in the licensure of that facility. More significantly, it found that there were irregularities in many private childcare facilities and questions about the effectiveness of the Department of Public Welfare's oversight.[16]

As part of this comprehensive review of facilities impacting children, we also looked at facilities operated by the Texas Department of MHMR. Mickey and I made unannounced visits to several residential facilities. I was appalled at the conditions in which these young people were kept; the rooms were filthy, and the children were strapped into wheelchairs with no meaningful activities. We learned that the medical records for patients at one of the residential treatment centers were incomplete, that the facility was not in compliance with fire and safety standards, and that it used nonlicensed persons to serve as psychologists.

During this same time, there were other reports about substandard conditions in institutions operated by the Texas Department of MHMR. Representatives of a nonprofit organization, Free the Slow, alleged that residents were being used as guinea pigs to test new drugs.[17] There were also allegations that some of the conditions and practices were alleged to have caused the death of almost forty residents. A special subcommittee of the Human Resources Committee was created. I was named to serve as vice-chairman of that subcommittee.

Despite the seriousness of the allegations, we were slow getting started. In fact, in early November I had to publicly ask that the Speaker extend the deadline for submission of our report because the chairman, Dave Allred from Wichita Falls, had neither called a meeting nor returned my calls or acknowledged my letters.[18] It is not my nature to publicly expose a colleague, but another child had died. Our charge was to find out why children were dying in the Texas MHMR facilities. We were doing nothing, and to me that was unacceptable. If it took a public light being shined on our inaction, then I would shine that light.

Shortly after my comments, we began the investigation. We held a public meeting where a number of parents with children at the Austin State School, representatives of Associations for Retarded Citizens, and other individuals associated with programs for residents in state facilities testified. The commissioner, assistant commissioner, and board members for the Department of MHMR also appeared.

On November 12, 1974, we issued our report. We found many deficiencies in the delivery of services to children. The quality of care in large institutions was frequently substandard and sometimes inhumane.[19] There was a crisis, a crisis that had been caused by the legislature's refusal to candidly identify the problems or to do anything to remedy them. We called upon all Texans, all citizens of the state and the government, to make a commitment to the well-being of its children to ensure their development into healthy, productive adults.

Prairie View and Historically Black Colleges and Universities

An issue that was extremely important to the Texas Black Caucus and to the people we represented was the improvement of historically Black colleges and universities (HBCUs) in Texas. Having grown up in Texas, I knew that Prairie View A&M University, established during Reconstruction, was the first Texas university for African Americans. Like many educational institutions segregated under the myth of "separate but equal," Prairie View had never been provided the financial resources that were regularly allocated to the white state institutions. As a result, Prairie View was not accredited until 1959.

On March 12, 1973, I was appointed by the Speaker to a special Committee on Prairie View A&M College Administration with the defined mission of conducting an investigation. Shortly after our arrival in Austin, the Black Caucus had been confronted with allegations of financial irregularities at Prairie View. The best way to address those claims, the caucus believed, was to propose a resolution that a twelve-person committee review and investigate Prairie View's operations. That committee would study the financial affairs and general operating procedures, employment policies, student activities, academic curriculum, and any other matters deemed important. I tried to assure everyone that the investigation was not a personal matter but based upon calls that I had received from students, alumni, and others that the college president was receiving kickbacks from teachers. Viewed from this perspective, the alumni association ultimately supported the passage of the resolution, recognizing that the investigation would quell the adverse publicity surrounding the university. This committee was the result of that resolution.[20]

Craig Washington was appointed to serve as the chair. Sam Hudson, Paul Ragsdale, G. J. Sutton, Mickey Leland, and Senfronia Thompson were also assigned to this committee. Within days of our appointment, a grand jury for Waller County, where Prairie View is located, issued warrants for the arrest of some of our legislative aides, including my aide, Jo Baylor. This action caused quite a stir. Under Texas law grand juries have the authority to issue arrest warrants for potential witnesses who reside outside of the county. The grand jury was reportedly trying to get information about the allegations of financial wrongdoing. We had to scramble but we were able to get the warrants withdrawn. But the entire incident showed the tensions surrounding our investigation of Prairie View.

We held public hearings from the fall of 1974 through January of 1975. One specific accusation was that the president had been accepting kickbacks from the teachers he had hired. We determined early in the investigation that those allegations were unsupported and that the president was due an apology. Notwithstanding this conclusion, it was recommended that a new president, a distinguished progressive Black educator, should be appointed.

But we also learned that Prairie View had been systematically shortchanged in the biennial appropriations. My colleague Representative Senfronia Thompson recounted her experience as a student at Prairie View. She told us that they taught swimming, but that there was no swimming pool. Students laid on the floor and imitated kicking and paddling. Horseback riding was also offered but there weren't any horses. Such memories spurred our review of the physical plant, finances, and curriculum. We found that the facilities at Prairie View's campus could not begin to compare with facilities at Texas A&M. In fact, the dean of students called any such comparison depressing. Representative Paul Ragsdale called the buildings dilapidated, noting that no other state school was as bad as Prairie View.

Although the committee expired when the Sixty-Fourth Legislature opened, subcommittees had prepared sections of a draft report. To address the precarious funding situation, it was recommended that Prairie View be allocated 20 percent of the proceeds from the A&M system school bonds. This approach would begin to provide secure funding, something that had not existed. In fact, we learned that funds designated for Prairie View had been diverted and used to support other educational programs. The founding of the University of Texas Medical School in Galveston was funded by monies originally allocated to Prairie View. Those funds were never restored.

These findings confirmed the propriety of our focus on the need for increased funding for Texas Southern University and Prairie View A&M University in the sixty-third legislative appropriations. We were able to secure an extra $7.5 million in funding: $4.5 million for Texas Southern and $3 million for Prairie View.

Interim Subcommittee on Law Enforcement Education, Training, and Standards

In the fall of 1972, Dallas experienced four fatal shootings by police within a five-week period. I had personally witnessed a police shooting at a shopping center. These shootings had led to protest marches, rallies, and a threatened city boycott. Reverend Ralph Abernathy from the Southern Christian Leadership Conference led a mass demonstration.

A biracial committee, the Greater Dallas Community Relations Commission, held hearings to investigate the shootings. The then Dallas police chief also appointed a committee to study the shootings. The police report specifically asked for improvement in police training, equipment, communications, policy, procedure, and law. Troubled by the shootings in Dallas and the number of complaints received by caucus members about police brutality, I decided that something needed to be done.

In early May 1973, I offered a House Simple Resolution that the House Committee on State Affairs do an interim study of law enforcement training programs specifically including sociological training in community relations. The report was to be made to the Sixty-Fourth Legislature in its regular session. This resolution was considered by the State Affairs Committee and unanimously voted favorably out of committee.[21] Following the sixty-third regular session, Speaker Daniel directed the formation of a special committee. I was appointed to serve as chair of the Social Services

Committee's subcommittee on Law Enforcement Education, Training, and Standards. We were authorized to do an interim study of law enforcement education and standards by a subcommittee of the State Affairs Committee.[22]

We held public hearings in Dallas, Houston, and Austin. As we conducted those hearings, I assured everyone that we weren't there to just complain and be critical but that we were doing an in-depth study of law enforcement. Law enforcement officials from local police departments, sheriff's departments, and the Department of Public Safety, as well as representatives of community and civil rights groups, testified. We received sworn testimony from over thirty witnesses. In addition to that testimony, the committee members and staff reviewed studies and reports about law enforcement standards and goals.

Recognizing that the problems in law enforcement were vast, diverse, and complex, the subcommittee encouraged the legislature to move in a positive fashion to assure effective law enforcement. Knowing that each police agency had to conduct its own recruitment program, we suggested that smaller communities unable to afford full-time recruiters combine recruitment efforts with neighboring agencies. Employment, assignment, and promotion of ethnic minority officers, particularly for jurisdictions with a substantial minority population, was a priority recommendation. Noting that the attitude of officers contributes to their effectiveness, we urged a requirement that candidates have psychological evaluations before they were licensed to carry guns and police communities.

The subcommittee also recommended that the police training curriculum should be reviewed with attention directed to psychology and sociology as it relates to the role of police, police-community relations, and sensitivity training. To achieve these training goals, we proposed that there be detailed monitoring of the training provided by the Texas Commission on Law Enforcement Officer Standards and Education. We also supported the establishment of a centralized police training academy. It was clear to us that increased educational standards and educational incentive programs were important steps to achieving more effective law enforcement.

Finally, we addressed the issue of funding the improvement of training programs. We affirmed our belief that it was the state's responsibility to provide leadership in criminal justice administration by providing adequate funds. Although we had spent over a year doing our research, we recognized that the establishment of minimum standards was a complex problem. But we were convinced that having minimum standards was a significant step toward improvement of police relations and the criminal justice system.[23]

The legislature moved quickly to implement some of our recommendations. On June 19, 1975, Governor Briscoe signed a bill requiring the Commission on Law Enforcement Officer Standards and Education to make reports to the governor and the legislature on the minimum standards of qualifications of law enforcement officers, minimum courses of training, and procedures for the certification of law enforcement officers and instructors. The commission was to create the required reporting forms, which were to be completed by the chief administrative officer of every law enforcement agency.[24] Two years later, on May 4, 1977, Governor Briscoe signed another bill addressing funding of the Commission on Law Enforcement Officer Standards and Education. This law authorized the designation of a portion of court costs assessed against persons convicted of crimes to be put into a fund to be used by the commission.[25]

As we had stated in our interim report, criminal justice administration and crime reduction are primarily the responsibility of state and local government. Our recommendations and the subsequent legislation reflected the leadership role that the state has with respect to criminal justice.

House Study Group

At the end of the regular session in May 1973, the Democratic legislators realized that we needed to become better organized and structured to advance our legislative agenda. The sheer volume of bills that we had to read, evaluate, and assess demanded that we have resources to assist in synthesizing the need for the bill and its potential effectiveness. We also understood that although the dates of actual legislative session were established by law, our work would continue throughout our two-year appointment through special sessions, committees, and task force assignments. The end of the session did not mean that we were on vacation.

We had also watched the political battles over the constitutional convention, which was to rewrite the 1876 Constitution. It was clear that we had to become more skilled and adroit at using the power of a coalition. One of Jim Mattox's interns in that first legislative session, Les Weisbrod, proposed the creation of a policy study group.

I had known Les since he was a young boy. His father, Harry Weisbrod, was politically active in progressive politics in Dallas. I was a frequent dinner guest in the Weisbrod home. Harry, originally from New York, was also my accountant. He had relocated to Texas when his wife, Bea, a native of Dallas, insisted that life would be better for the family in her home state. Les, who was then a student at Claremont Men's College, approached Mattox about organizing a Texas version of the Congressional Democratic Study Group. While in school he had studied a California policy group, reviewed their materials, and established a model that we could adopt in Austin.

In January 1975, steps were taken to establish the study group. Representatives who were identified as liberal, labor friendly, or moderate were invited to an exploratory meeting. Mattox reached out to a number of representatives to join him in extending the invitation. I gladly agreed to be a part of this organizing effort.

The House Study Group operated as a think tank, analyzing legislative proposals and suggesting legislative initiatives. Because this was the age before computers, doing research meant hours in a library, tracking down sources and identifying materials. In contrast to the previous session, we now had a mechanism to conduct legislative analysis in a manner that gave us the data and information necessary to oppose or support bills. Through the study group, we developed talking points and arguments that helped us to defeat bills that were not in the best interests of our constituents or that were self-serving for various legislators.

Members of the House Study Group met for weekly presentations and discussions about upcoming legislation. The organization also published a very valuable weekly bulletin and a daily analysis of legislation that was introduced in the House. These meetings allowed us to collaboratively scrutinize the precise wording of proposed drafts to assure that the results of our negotiations were being captured.

Because we recognized the significance and importance of the House Study Group, sixty-five members of the legislature financed this independent legislative research activity. When Weisbrod graduated from college, he became the executive director of the House Study Group and hired a staff of eleven aides, including two lawyers. It became the principal research arm that liberal and progressive legislators relied on for guidance because the legislative research staff provided by the state was often extremely conservative, hostile, and dismissive of new ideas. Its work helped us to defeat bills or matters that served narrow special interests and quickly attracted the wrath of conservative lawmakers.

The House Study Group became an integral tool for the Texas Legislative Black Caucus. Until that time we did not have adequate resources to conduct the necessary research and data analysis. But with the assistance of the study group, we had the tools to make our passion and commitment even more powerful.

Constitutional Convention

One of the items on the 1972 ballot was a proposal for a constitutional convention to revise the Texas Constitution. That proposal passed. There would be a convention in 1974 to consider the revisions. This would be the first time that the Texas Constitution, originally passed in 1876, would be comprehensively reviewed.

I was appointed to serve on the Joint Constitutional Convention Planning Committee, the only woman and only person of color. Because it was important that the House and Senate cooperate in planning the convention, there were five senators and fifteen representatives on the committee. We were charged to prepare recommendations for the rules, organization, and staffing of the convention, and methods of presenting proposals to voters.

I worked on the Public Information Subcommittee. It was important that there be public education and information as the convention proceeded. The voters would ultimately decide whether the revised constitution would be adopted. We recommended that there be a director of public information with appropriate administrative staff to provide daily press briefings; prepare written brochures, handouts, and slide shows; organize a speakers' bureau; establish a visitors' center; and many more information related duties and activities.

My Second Term: Sixty-Fourth Session

The year 1974 was another election year. The Dallas Democratic Party was actively looking for more women to run for office. I was the only woman in the Dallas County's eighteen-member state House delegation. At the same time, I was being urged to consider running for the state Senate or the Fifth Congressional District. My work and dedication had been recognized, and it was acknowledged that I had proved myself as an able legislator.

But I knew that I would not run for any office that I could not win. I looked at the boundaries of the districts, the voting patterns, and potential opponents. I decided that I could best serve my constituents by building on the work that I had done during my first term. I would run for reelection for the House.

Politics, like life, is not all black or white. I could decide to run for reelection, but I also had to consider the impact that it had on my son, Kirk. Even though I worked diligently for my constituents, there were people who used every opportunity that they could to slight me, even destroy me. The phone at home rang day and night. Kirk would go to bed and I would stay up until two and three in the morning, working on various proposals, reading materials. It was a lonely life. My son, who had always been observant, began to detest politics. He often wondered why I gave so much to others while receiving so little in return. But he continued to support me and did not complain about the long hours that I spent away from our home.

My most difficult time as a mother came just before the start of Kirk's senior year at Reagan High School in Austin. Kirk told me that he wanted to return to Dallas and complete his senior year at Bishop Dunne. While I could agree with his returning to Dallas, I wanted him to stay with a member of the family, a cousin, who I knew would look after him. But Kirk did not want to stay with a family member. In fact, he wanted to reside in our home by himself. The very thought of that horrified me. I discussed it with my father, who sided with his grandson. He said that when he was 16 years of age, he left home and began a life on his own. My dad assured me that Kirk would not disappoint me. I simply had to give him an opportunity to become a man. My father gently reminded me that I was only 17 when I had left home to study nursing. And he pointed out, I had done rather well for myself. He also pointed out that Kirk would not be totally on his own or unsupervised during the five months that I was in Austin for the legislative session. My cousin, Bernice Hodge, lived a few blocks from our house. She would be there for him and could help if an emergency arose. Kirk's paternal grandmother, Mrs. Ida Johnson, lived within walking distance, and there were other neighbors I could count on to ensure that he was safe.

Although I was still nervous and anxious about the idea, I agreed to allow him to live in our house by himself. Of course, I called him each day while we were apart, sometimes two and three times. At night we talked about his schoolwork, what was going on in his world, and generally stayed in touch. Long-distance phone calls were not free. Having these frequent and extended conversations took their toll on our family budget, but it was a necessary cost for a mother away from her only son.

I returned to Austin by myself. As much as I missed Kirk, being alone allowed me to be even more focused.

At the beginning of the Sixty-Fourth Legislature in January 1975, there was a scramble to see who would succeed Price Daniel as the next Speaker. My first preference was Representative Fred Head, a lawyer and courtly southern gentleman who, as head of the House Education Committee, had agreed with the Black Caucus that Texas should allocate adequate funding to support predominantly Black schools. While he represented a somewhat conservative district in Athens, he was a member of the reform-minded Dirty Thirty and had gained significant support from African Americans in East Texas. We had many meetings with Head discussing issues and his view of opportunities for Black leadership. He had joined us when we went to investigate polling places in East Texas that were reporting problems. Because I admired his courage and his politics, I committed to him early in the Speaker selection process.

Carl Parker, a liberal legislator from Port Arthur, was seeking the Speaker position. Politically, Parker was close to Fred Head. But he took Black elected officials for granted, apparently believing that he would automatically get our support. Because the Speaker determines committee assignments, we asked him about leadership positions for caucus members. He had a "you owe it to me" attitude and acted insulted that we would negotiate before giving him our support.

Another candidate, Bill W. Clayton, a moderate conservative from West Texas, was approachable, straightforward, and honest. When we visited with him, we found him open and forthcoming about what he would do regarding the issues on our agenda. In response to whether he would appoint caucus members to leadership positions, he said that he would certainly consider giving us opportunities.

The Speaker race was somewhat vicious, with name calling and rumors printed in the press, most of them directed at Head, who was the front-runner. The insults and innuendo overwhelmed him, causing his withdrawal from the race even though many of his supporters urged him to remain a candidate.

With Head's withdrawal, the Speaker's race was between Parker and Clayton. The Legislative Black Caucus, which had been divided between Head and Parker, decided to come together to support Clayton. When evaluating potential Speaker candidates, it was important to support a candidate with whom you could have disagreements on issues but who would not use those differences as a platform to be vindictive or malicious. Clayton was a man of his word. He was someone we could all get behind. He was someone who would hear and respect the caucus. When the time came to select committee chairs, Clayton named Craig Washington to serve as the chairperson of the Criminal Justice Jurisprudence Committee. Mickey Leland was appointed to the Appropriations Committee. These were two very significant committee assignments.

Speaker Clayton phoned me asking that I chair the Labor Committee. I told him that I did not have any particular interest in labor issues and was not closely connected with organized labor groups. He insisted that I take the post, telling me that he had made phone calls inquiring about my political judgment and that he wanted to see me in a position of leadership. I continued to decline the position, but he kept pushing. I finally told Clayton to give me the night to think about it. He agreed, saying that we would talk again in the morning. After speaking with Clayton, I phoned Zan Holmes and Dan Weiser, telling them of my predicament. They both said that I should give serious consideration to taking the post. Weiser assured me that I could learn the issues and be able to help develop solutions.

I talked with Clayton the next morning. He told me that the other leadership positions had been filled, and that the labor committee chairmanship was the only position that remained. He said that he desperately wanted a woman to lead the Labor Committee, that everyone he had talked to had agreed that I was the best possible person, and that I was industrious and would do a great job. Even knowing that I would be in new territory, I told him that I would take the appointment and would do my best as chairwoman.

These appointments made headlines. It was the first time in the history of the state that a woman had been named to head a major legislative committee. The appointments were also seen as a sign that African Americans were now major players in Austin.[26]

I knew little about labor issues. As soon as the announcement of my appointment was made, labor leaders were in my office telling me who to hire as staff and what issues the committee should consider. I purposefully did not review any of the resumes that were given to me. I wanted to set my own agenda and did not want people working for me who owed their jobs to others. I had always been independent and decided that I would remain that way.

Chairwoman Johnson, House Committee on Labor

The Texas Department of Labor has jurisdiction over the administration and enforcement of thirteen laws reaching across various subjects. It oversees laws governing labor, such as prevailing wage standards, safety rules and regulations, health conditions, child labor; employment agencies; working conditions; auctioneering; boiler inspection; boxing and wrestling; and mobile homes. Speaker Clayton charged the committee with (1) reviewing all laws affecting the Department of Labor and Standards to assure consistent, complementary statutory provisions; (2) studying and appraising the unemployment and placement services and unemployment compensation services; and (3) surveying the retirement benefits and pension plans of employers in the state. To accomplish these tasks, the committee was divided into corresponding subcommittees.[27]

Speaker Clayton had appointed committee members who were mostly sympathetic to labor supporters. The labor lobby itself was well organized and diligent. Many of its leaders had come from the ranks of working people, and they did not have any problems standing up for their beliefs. Union membership had grown slowly in Texas and peaked during the early 1960s when approximately four hundred thousand workers were members of organized labor. Most unions were organized by the AFL-CIO, although some were associated with other national unions or Texas-based entities. The unions were a potent force that used effective lobbying techniques. Politicians respected them because they were active in elections and kept track of who voted for and against their issues.

One of my first tasks was to hire staff to assist us in carrying out the charge. I hired a staff consisting of a legal counsel, a committee clerk, a research assistant, and a typist. Even though there was a separate physical office for Labor Committee, I primarily operated out of my legislative office.

It was critical that I quickly master issues such as fair wages, labor law, and unemployment compensation. My only prior experience with unions had been at the VA hospital, where I had helped to organize the first employee union, even though I could not become a member because of my position as a nursing supervisor.

While much of the work of a committee chair was conducted with fellow legislators, I believed in citizen involvement in government. I wanted to hear from voters and learn their perspectives on labor and business issues. I regularly held conferences on labor and small business in Austin and throughout the state. I invited business owners to attend and asked that they share their ideas with me and members of my committee. Hispanic and Black entrepreneurs were frequently present at hearings. I wanted to be certain that our committee also held public hearings as we fulfilled our charge.

In addition to the work required by the Speaker's charge, we had to review and consider proposed legislation that fell under our jurisdiction and that was directed to us by the Speaker. We held sixteen weekly meetings from the beginning of February to early May. During those meetings we would commonly have witnesses appear either in support of or opposition to a pending bill. Some persons became frequent speakers, such as Harry Hubbard, president of the AFL-CIO, or Jackie W. St. Clair, commissioner of the Department of Labor and Standards.

One of the bills I sponsored has become engrained in our laws relating to judicial proceedings. I introduced the bill because of a case of a Dallas Black woman who had lost her job for serving a few days on a jury. Once I filed the bill, I learned of other similar cases. It struck me that firing Black employees for doing jury service was designed to discourage African American participation on juries. My bill was designed to protect employees from being terminated due to their jury service. To emphasize my point, in my public comments sponsoring its passage, I criticized such employers, calling them Scrooges. The bill received an editorial endorsement from the *Fort Worth Star-Telegram* and was signed into law by Governor Dolph Briscoe on April 30, 1975.[28]

Another bill that I sponsored was reported out of committee but was not calendared. That bill would have clearly declared that pregnant women qualified for unemployment compensation if they were able and available to work. Pregnant women were being denied unemployment benefits under an approach that ruled pregnant woman were unavailable to work.[29] Our committee also considered a bill that related to the licensing of labor agents, people who employ workers to provide services to a third party. Along with an identical bill in the Senate, it would require a background investigation and a licensing exam. There were also requirements that workers had to be paid promptly and given notices about compensation rates, written in both English and Spanish. The bill was aimed at protecting "much exploited" migrant farm laborers. The governor signed this legislation into law on May 13, 1975.[30]

We also considered a bill introduced by Rep. Craig Washington to establish a Texas Fair Employment Practices Commission.[31] At that time there was not a state agency specifically designed to enforce antidiscrimination in employment on the basis of race, color, religion, sex, age, or national origin. As noted in the House Study Group report, this bill paralleled the federal EEOC and would oversee state agency compliance with affirmative action plans.[32] It was favorably voted out of committee and despite efforts to table it, passed the House. The bill then went to the Senate, where it died in the Committee on Human Resources. It would not be until 1983 that the legislature would create the Texas Commission on Human Rights Act to enforce the antidiscrimination employment policies of the 1964 Civil Rights Act.

Employee Payment of Fees to Labor Unions

One controversial bill that came before my committee dealt with the question of whether employers and unions could contract to require employees who had chosen not to join the union to nonetheless pay fees to the union. Texas policy clearly protected a worker's right to decide to join or not join a union. Under this bill employees who chose not to join a union could still be required to pay a fee equal to dues to the union.

Because all employees would share in the benefits negotiated by the union, it seemed to me only fair that they should share in the expenses. Once again, the House Study Group had provided a valuable assessment of the bill. If the majority of the employees voted to have a union, that union was required by federal law to represent all of the employees. The issue of right to work and unions had been hotly debated during the state constitutional convention, but given the composition of the legislature, it was tabled on the floor. This bill suffered the same fate as it was tabled in the House.[33]

The Mobile Home Bill

Another very controversial matter was a bill that protected Texas consumers who resided in mobile homes. A sizeable number of Texans, over one million, lived in mobile homes, the second-most popular form of housing in the state. An investigation of the industry had concluded that residents were not being treated fairly, that industry standards were substandard, and that many of the home warranties that had been issued were deficient. Some unscrupulous mobile home dealers would close their business when buyers complained that the units were defective. Consumers had little or no recourse when they sought improvements.

The intent of the legislation was to improve standards in the mobile home industry and provide consumers with effective avenues for recourse. The law, fueled in part by the belief that some members of the mobile home industry were unprincipled and dishonest, mandated that mobile home industry standards in Texas be consistent with national standards established by Congress when it passed the Federal Housing and Community Development Act in 1974.

The bill proposed a mobile home standards code that reached both mobile home manufacturers and dealers. Oversight was placed with the Texas Department of Labor and Standards. The department was charged with regulating requirements for the installation of electrical systems, heating and plumbing systems, and construction and spacing of mobile homes. Tie-down mechanisms were especially important because Texas ranked number one in the nation in injuries and damage due to winds. Enforcement was strengthened by the authority to inspect, or have local government officials inspect, mobile home construction and parks to ensure compliance with the legislation.

Manufacturers had to establish quality control standards for their facilities prior to their being certified by the state. Any mobile home that did not receive a state-issued seal of approval could not be sold. Dealers of used mobile homes also had to bring their products up to state standards and were barred from selling a used mobile home unless it passed state standards. Manufacturers and mobile home dealers were required to pay fees for acceptability certificates and seals of approval.

Additionally, the bill required manufacturers, salesmen, and dealers of mobile homes to file performance bonds on an annual basis. The bonds were designed for use in cases in which consumers alleged and proved liability against members of the mobile home manufacturing and sales communities. The mobile home manufacturers and dealers were not in favor of the legislation, which they made known in the capitol. Indeed, the House Study Group memorandum noted that the mobile home industry was "strongly opposed" to the bill and that the lobbyists were predicting that it would drive many mobile home manufacturers and dealers out of business. Industry representatives descended on Austin like vultures.[34]

Once the law was signed and became effective on June 20, 1975, I was asked to speak to the Texas attorney general, requesting a delay in the law's implementation. They were complaining that the bond require- ments would put dealers and manufacturers out of business. I told them that I was not in favor of any delays. One of the dealer-representatives actually threatened me during a phone call, stating that the industry would not make any financial contributions to my campaign during the next election cycle. I told him that I had checked my financial records and that they had not contributed to me in the past, and that what they did or did not do in the future would be of no consequence to me. I informed him that my vote was not for sale, and that he and his associates could keep their money. That was the end of that.

There were a few mobile home parks in my district. I had visited those residents during my campaign, encouraging them to register to vote. But those parks were well maintained. No one shared any complaints with me. But I knew that in our rural areas, compliance with health and safety needs was harder to achieve. While there was not a large number of people in my district living in mobile homes, I thought my support of the legislation was important because the measure helped citizens throughout Texas.

When I first took my oath of office, I had pledged to work on behalf of all Texans, not just those who lived in my district. If my view of public service had been narrow, I would not have been concerned about families that resided in mobile homes. Their welfare, however, was important to me, as was that of the urban dwellers in my district. My concept of a stable and compassionate society was one in which everyone was treated fairly. We were all members of the human family and deserved to be treated with dignity and grace.

Unemployment Compensation

Unemployment compensation was another contentious issue. Nationally, unemployment rates had been soaring to levels higher than in the preced- ing thirteen years. A major unemployment bill was introduced in the House and assigned to my committee. The proposed bill would change the method of calculating unemployment benefits, increasing maximum benefits to 66⅓ percent of the statewide average weekly wage; change eligibility requirements; allow benefits to persons who voluntarily left employment due to a move necessitated by a spouse's change of employment; and provide for prompt payment of benefits.[35]

The House Study Group provided a review of the proposed statute. It noted that the advantage of the percentage approach to determining unemployment benefits would account for the upswings in the amount needed to live without requiring repeated legislation. The prompt payment of benefits had been required by recent court decisions. Their report also pointed out that employers might become reluctant to hire military spouses if the employer was to be required to pay unemployment benefits for such spouses who must leave employment due to a military reassignment.[36]

We held a hearing in mid-February. Administrators from the TEC and a member of the United Auto Workers union appeared and spoke in support of the bill. A representative of the Texas Manufacturers Association appeared to oppose the bill. To promote further consideration of the bill, a subcommittee was created to conduct further review of the bill.

Both labor and the business lobby were all over us, arguing the pros and cons of the bill. Labor supported the bill and management was against it, arguing that if unemployment compensation rose, it would affect their bottom lines and profitability. As a committee, we debated the bill thoroughly. As chair, I allowed each member of the committee to have their say. I was not a heavy-handed type of leader. Ultimately the bill, which was a good compromise, did get out of our committee, but it died on the House floor. It was tabled by a record vote of "71 ayes and 69 nos." Two votes kept the bill from proceeding.[37] Some labor leaders held the failure to get those two votes against me, suggesting that I did not fight hard enough for their position.

Regardless of such criticism, I took my work very seriously. The Labor Committee had reviewed statutes, rules, regulations, and operations that touched on many aspects of our citizens' lives. Our work impacted the quality of life in Texas. I had done my homework, learning the issues and arguments surrounding every area that each subcommittee had considered. While subcommittees authored the proposed recommendations, it was my responsibility as chairman to guide the committee's review and deliberation of those recommendations.

My colleagues respected me and my judgment. There were those who doubted me in the beginning who later said that they were impressed with my leadership, and that I had gained their confidence and trust. We did a lot for labor while I chaired the committee, and I made many friends in the labor community. Indeed, it was this time as chair of the Labor Committee that I included as one of the most rewarding experiences of my legislative career when I resigned from the House.

Completing the Speaker's Charge

Some of the bills that we considered in our committee related to topics that were part of the Speaker's charge. But we still needed to specifically study the topics presented in the charge. Over the next year, the subcommittees held six public and formal hearings.

Department of Labor: After surveying the Department of Labor's work, we determined to review certain specific areas. We looked at private employment agencies, public pension systems, the Prevailing Wage and Payment of Wage statutes administered by the TEC, and the Unemployment Compensation Act.

Private employment agencies: A private employment agency is anyone who attempts to find employees for an employer. While employment agents had been regulated since 1923, employment agencies were not regulated until 1949. Over the years requirements had been established setting forth the qualifications.

Just a few years before our review, the legislature had created a Private Employment Agencies Regulatory Board. We believed that structural changes were needed for the board to represent the interests of consumers and employers more effectively. The board needed to be empowered to impose fines and to revoke the licenses of repeat offenders.

We also recommended that all agents be required to be licensed to add a level of professionalism. The committee had conducted a survey and found that the majority of consumer complaints were based upon actions by the counselors. Licensing would be a focus on the moral character of the agent applicants.[38] That survey also found consumer complaints about misrepresentations about potential jobs or the amount of the fees that would be assessed. If an applicant accepted the job and then discovered the duties were not as anticipated and quit, the employee was liable for the full placement fee. To protect against such applicant exploitation, we recommended that agencies be required to provide applicants with written job descriptions before sending them out on job interviews. This procedure would allow the applicant to determine whether the agency was sending them out for interviews that were desired opportunities.

Our review of the Minimum Wage Act brought us to review the TEC. We were concerned about the commission's efforts with respect to its affirmative action plan. Women and minorities were overrepresented in the lower paying clerical jobs within the commission. Our review identified serious weaknesses in the commission's staffing patterns for female and minority employees.[39] As a result of our investigation, the Labor Committee began working with the commission to address these deficiencies. We provided the commission with lists of minority organizations and colleges for recruitment efforts. We identified media outlets to be used to promote employment opportunities.

The charge to survey private and public retirement and pension plans required a focus on the adequate funding of plans and management of pension funds for private, state, and municipal employees. A variety of governing statutes and constitutional provisions governed these pension plans. Reviewing private pension plans included an additional wrinkle because Congress had recently passed the Employee Retirement Income Security Act (ERISA) governing private pension plans, thereby limiting state authority. We recognized that as a state we wanted to provide public employees with the best benefit structure possible while protecting taxpayers from an unreasonable tax burden. We were also mindful of a bill pending before Congress that would lead to federal oversight of public pension funds, much like ERISA governed private plans. Consistent with our stated goals, we recommended that all state and local plans utilize investment guidelines to best protect and manage the fund income. We also recommended further study of specialized pension plans for police, firefighters, and other municipal employees because those plans were governed by more generalized statutes. The requirements for those statutes were not as rigorous for administration, record keeping, or fund management.[40]

My Other Committee Assignments

Even though I was chair of the Labor Committee, I also had the responsibility to serve on a number of other House committees. That work was also important to me because it gave me the opportunity to address other needs and concerns in Texas. And there were occasions when I sponsored legislation that was considered by committees other than the ones on which I served.

Social Services Committee

My experience as a psychiatric nurse allowed me to identify the need for standardized requirements for professions who provide mental health care. I knew that there needed to be standards to protect the public from being treated by untrained or inadequately trained and unethical practitioners. On January 22, 1975, I introduced a bill to create a State Board of Examiners in Social Psychotherapy. This bill created requirements relating to education, internship, ethics, and professional behavior of mental health practitioners. It established enforcement procedures, including the imposition of civil penalties. The bill was passed by the House and Senate and signed by Governor Briscoe on June 21, 1975, and with that action the State Board of Examiners in Social Psychotherapy was created.[41]

　　Through this committee I was also able to continue addressing issues with the Texas Department of Corrections. There was a history of inmate job assignments based upon race. To stop that practice, I sponsored a bill that prohibited the department and director from discriminating against a prisoner on the basis of sex, race, color, creed, or national origin. This bill passed and became effective in late September 1975.

Special Committee on Drug Abuse Education

I was also appointed to the Committee on Drug Abuse Education. We heard testimony from experts in the treatment field, law enforcement, educators, and concerned parents. The committee found that there was evidence that hard drugs were related to soaring crime rates in Texas and the nation. We concluded that it was important that there be increased awareness of drug abuse and that there be a determined effort to fight drug abuse.

Corrections Subcommittee

Prison reform continued to be a pressing concern. The previous session I had served on the Joint Committee on Prison Reform. Our work was an unprecedented review of the Texas Department of Corrections. But our recommendations had not been well received. The House passed the directive for the department to begin community-based corrections programs, but the Senate did not concur.

This time there was a crisis because the prisons had reached capacity. If the inmate population continued to grow at the same rate, the prisons would become overcrowded. Following public hearings, the subcommittee determined that this problem could be addressed by the construction of more units, creation of a statewide probation program, and increased parole opportunities. We made recommendations that each of these options should be pursued.

Fixing Homes and Feeding Hungry School Children

During this term there were two important bills that I authored that had nothing to do with my committee assignments. Housing conditions are directly related to the health and well-being of a community. Blighted residential neighborhoods can breed disease, crime, and misery. They demand disproportionate public funds for health and social services, police protection, and property clearance.

Recognizing the critical need to address such conditions and to institute measures to prevent deterioration of housing stock, I authored a bill for the creation, administration, and financing of a housing rehabilitation program.[42] Entitled the Texas Housing Rehabilitation Act, it empowered the Texas Department of Community Affairs to make loans and other actions appropriate to prevent neighborhoods from becoming slums. It also established a Housing Rehabilitation Loan Fund to be used to finance loans for home repair and rehabilitation.

Talking with residents in my district, I realized that the plight of children who began the school day hungry because they came from families that could not afford to feed them needed to be addressed. Nationally recognized studies showed that students performed better if they received proper nutrition before they went to school. It was also concluded that poor behavior was associated with an empty stomach. The negative consequences flowing from students not having breakfast concerned me greatly.

To fulfill my responsibilities, I often read late at night and early in the morning. I researched federal legislation and policies that had not been adopted by Texas and considered whether they would improve conditions in our state. I learned that in 1966 the US Congress passed the Child Nutrition Act, which provided nutritious meals—breakfast and lunch—for low-income public-school students. It was an essential part of President Johnson's "war on poverty" program. In late 1975 Congress passed the School Lunch and Child Nutrition Act, which made the free breakfast program permanent.

The need for such food programs was obvious. In the early 1970s, to avoid desegregation orders, many white families had withdrawn their children from public schools to send them to private institutions. As a result, the percentage of students in public schools from families needing assistance had grown significantly.

As I envisioned it, the goal of a breakfast feeding program in Texas would be to protect the health of children and to foster their ability to learn. It would allow them to start the school day on a full stomach, which had been proven to improve learning and lessen discipline problems. It would also ease the pain and guilt of parents who knew that their children went to school without a meal because they could not afford to provide one.

But not everyone saw the need to feed our schoolchildren. There were some who argued that such a program would be too costly, that many schools did not have the facilities to prepare meals, and that it was the responsibility of parents to feed their children. Yet I had witnessed the sorrow on the faces of children, of all colors, who had not eaten before they arrived at school. I had listened to stories told by their teachers, who frequently used their personal resources to purchase food for children. I knew parents were having to choose between paying the rent and buying groceries. Something had to be done.

In the spring of 1977, I introduced House Bill 136, which would require all school districts with a student body that had at least 10 percent of its students eligible for free or reduced-price breakfasts under the Child Nutrition Act of 1966 to offer to those students a free or reduced-price breakfast meeting the nutritional standards required under the national program.[43] At the time only 193 of Texas school districts provided break-fast. Even my hometown of Waco did not provide free or reduced-price breakfasts. Under the 10 percent requirement of the bill, more than one thousand school districts would be serving breakfast to needy children.

I knew that I needed an ally in the Senate to carry the bill there. I reached out to Carlos Truan, who had spent eight years in the House and had been recently elected to the Senate. We had worked on a number of projects together. He had been on the Labor Committee that I had chaired. A Democratic legislator from Corpus Christi, Senator Truan had grown up poor, living in federal housing projects and working several jobs to help support his single mother and his siblings. He would have been a student helped by the breakfast program, so I believed that he would be empathetic to the need to feed our schoolchildren. Senator Truan had also been active in sponsoring legislation prohibiting discrimination and promoting opportunity. Through his efforts the Texas Human Relations Commission was created. He had successfully sponsored the Texas Bilingual Education Act and had worked with Black legislators to address problems that impacted Black, brown, and poor people. He would be a perfect ally in the Senate.

We worked on the legislation together and found allies in both legislative chambers. Senator Truan sponsored the companion bill, S.B. 1073, which was identical to H.B. 136.[44] But we had to compromise to get the bill approved. My original proposed legislation would apply to school districts if 10 percent of their students met the federal food eligibility standards.

To secure passage the bill was amended to raise the percentage to 25 percent. I had to also agree to postpone the effective date for one year to allow school districts more time to prepare to provide the breakfasts.

I had learned that compromise and negotiation were often central to getting bills passed. Being obstinate and immovable wouldn't have achieved my objective: to feed hungry children. Of course, I still believed that even more school districts should offer this program, but an unwillingness to compromise would have meant that the bill would fail and no school district would be required to provide free breakfast. It was better to accomplish something rather than lose everything, an insight that would become even more poignant in my latter years in the United States Congress.

On May 2, 1977, I appeared before the House Committee on Public Education to present the bill. Also speaking on behalf of the bill were Julia Brantley, director of Food Service for the Dallas Independent School District, and Diana Camacho, a nutritionist from Austin. The bill passed out of committee on a six to three vote.[45]

Passage through the Senate was more heated. It came up for full Senate approval just days before the legislative session would expire. On Saturday, May 28, 1977, Senator William Moore from Bryan angrily opposed the bill, even appearing to threaten a filibuster. When his proposed amendments, which would have watered down the bill, were tabled due to his mistaken support of the motion to table, he challenged Senator Truan by saying, "Why don't you speak up like a man?" implying that Senator Truan's speech was not clear.[46] But despite such animosity, just two days later, Senator Truan, as I knew he would, successfully shepherded the bill to approval on the last day of the session. The bill was signed into law on June 16, 1977, becoming a part of the Texas Education Code.[47]

Unfortunately, I was not totally surprised when school districts resisted the mandate that free breakfasts be provided to needy children. Lubbock Representative Joe Robbins announced an intention to introduce a bill reversing the statute and making participation in the breakfast program again voluntary.[48]

Garland and Lubbock Independent School Districts actually filed suit in federal court seeking a declaratory judgment that the statute was unconstitutional.[49] The school districts argued that the state could not require them to provide breakfast, that it was up to each school district to determine whether the children would be fed. In an opinion upholding the law, the Fifth Circuit noted that Congress's particular concern was that as many poor children as possible be served free or reduced-price breakfasts. Speaking directly about the statute that had resulted from my bill, the court said that the Texas statute had tried to bring Congress's plan to fruition and that it had been faithful to Congress's intentions. Even then the Garland Independent School District pursued litigation filing a petition for the United States Supreme Court to hear their case. That petition was denied.[50]

It was this piece of legislation that, in interviews after I announced my retirement from elected office almost forty-five years later, I identified as one of the accomplishments of which I was most proud.[51] Not only had we acted within our authority, but we had also acted in the interests of millions of Texas's children who needed our help.

Chapter 9

Being a Federal Official

Director of Region VI, Department of Health, Education, and Welfare

On Friday, September 30, 1977, I resigned my position in the Texas House of Representatives after serving two and a half terms. When I ran for my third term in the House, I had no idea that my path and my future would take another direction in just a short while.

Several months earlier, my friend and fellow legislator, Jim Mattox, had approached me and said that it was time for me to make some money for a change. I was startled and had no idea what he was talking about. A legislator's salary was $7,200, as we were considered part-time legislators because we were only in session for 140 days out of a two-year term. It didn't matter that the work was really full-time because issues arose daily and people continued to seek you out. It may have been a part-time job but it was a full-time obligation.

I had never really thought about the salary. My focus was on serving my constituents and my state. I was comfortable with my station in life, supported by my income as a manager at one of the country's finest department stores. In contrast to many of my colleagues, I was not independently wealthy or working as a lawyer or banker. But suggestions that I become an attorney or a lobbyist did not interest me. I was doing what I wanted to do, and I was able to care of myself and my son, Kirk. So Jim's comment took me quite by surprise.

One morning after that curious remark, while I was sitting at my desk on the House floor, I received a phone call from Robert S. Strauss. Having worked with Bob in local and statewide political campaigns, I admired him for his fairness, decency, and brilliance. A native of West Texas and graduate of the University of Texas Law School, he had worked for the Federal Bureau of Investigation before establishing what would become one of the most prominent law firms, Akin, Gump, Strauss, Hauer, and Feld. In 1973 Strauss became chairman of the Democratic National Committee, a position he held for three years. When Jimmy Carter became the Democratic party presidential nominee, Strauss served as his campaign chairman. After the election, President Carter appointed Strauss to serve in his cabinet as the special trade representative.[1] Strauss was unquestionably a man of influence.

When the conversation began that morning, I thought it was going to center around a piece of legislation or activities of certain elected officials whom we both knew. Instead, Strauss said, "Don't say anything to anyone, but you are under consideration for a position in the Carter administration." I was floored. It had come out of the blue. I had not asked for a job or for any political favors, but according to Strauss, all I had to do was pass a security clearance. He told me that the FBI would be looking into my background. As the conversation ended, he left me with one admonition: don't say a word to anyone about what we had talked about. Still stunned, I agreed that I would keep my mouth shut and simply wait for things to evolve.

Shortly after that conversation, the state director of the Texas Health and Human Services told me that he was leaving state government to take the exact same job that Strauss had told me about. He said he had been informed by US Senator Bentsen that he was being considered for that position. I listened to him brag without any comment. As Strauss had instructed, I didn't say anything.

I thought the FBI would be calling a couple of people for its security check. But I soon learned that they were interviewing just about everyone

I knew. The FBI talked to people I had worked with at the hospital, my neighbors, my colleagues, and even members of my church. Mickey Leland called and said that he had been interviewed by federal agents who wanted to know things about my character and habits, whether I hosted a lot of parties, and if he knew of any skeletons in my background. Mickey laughingly said that he had told the FBI, "She works all the time. I wish she would host a lot of parties." That comment was just like Mickey.

The position for which I was being considered was regional director in the Department of Health, Education, and Welfare (HEW). If selected, I would have oversight over HEW offices in five states: Texas, Oklahoma, Arkansas, Louisiana, and New Mexico. The department's objective was to protect the health of American citizens and provide them with basic human services, a focus that would be strengthened by President Carter's decision to remove education from the department and create a separate Education Department. I had seen the impact of my work and legislative initiatives on Texas's social issues and services for its citizens. Being regional director would give me an even greater ability to continue to improve the lives of people. This position would be a significant challenge and an outstanding opportunity.

HEW was headed by Joseph Anthony Califano Jr., an activist liberal lawyer and graduate of Harvard Law School. A former special assistant to President Lyndon B. Johnson, he had played a crucial role in the passage of the Voting Rights Act of 1965. After leaving the Johnson administration, he joined the powerful Washington law firm of Arnold & Porter. His appointment as secretary of HEW positioned him as President Carter's senior domestic policy advisor on economic and domestic issues, causing many to view him as the deputy president for Domestic Affairs.

I flew to Washington to meet with Secretary Califano. We had never met, but I had read so much about him and knew of his accomplishments. I knew it would be an honor to work under his leadership. We talked about social policy, the new administration, and various changes that needed to be made in the country. The Carter campaign had promised the electorate social change, and the secretary was looking for people who were change agents. We talked about his relationships with former president Lyndon Johnson and Robert Strauss, both of whom I knew and admired. He asked about my work and activities as a member of the Texas House. His questions showed that he was looking for someone with administrative skills and a familiarity with legislative process. I was confident that I had the experience and abilities. I knew that I could do a good job if I was selected.

While I was in DC being interviewed for this position, I was saddened by the news that Edward Marcus, of the Neiman Marcus family, had passed. He had run the catalog division at Neiman Marcus and befriended me when I started working at the store. He and his wife had hosted me at their home for dinner, providing invaluable guidance and counsel. While Stanley Marcus had offered me the job, it was Edward who had advised me and made me an integral part of the store's professional staff. His passing, at this time of my own professional advancement, reinforced for me the importance of mentorship.

After that meeting and the background check, I was offered the position. In announcing my selection, Secretary Califano called my experience in the legislature and my years of nursing a background well suited for the position.[2] With this appointment I became the first woman and first African American to hold this position. With Kirk on one side, Secretary Califano on the other, and in front of my parents, siblings, and hundreds of HEW employees, United States District Court Judge Sarah T. Hughes administered the oath. I solemnly swore to support and defend the Constitution of the United States, an oath that I would repeat on a number of occasions over my lifetime. I was committed to serving this nation and its people.

I was now a federal official with a major federal government department, earning $47,500 a year. My regional office, located in downtown Dallas, gave me a good base for traveling throughout my region and overseeing its seven thousand HEW employees.[3] As the regional director, I was to implement the master plan for the region by gaining the commitment of the governors and elected officials of the states within the district. Secretary Califano had identified two national major social problems: escalating hospital costs and programs constituting the welfare system. As I would point out in speeches, the health care industry lacked consumer choice, cost reduction incentives, and competition. In particular, hospital costs were increasing faster than the rate of inflation.

Another crisis that the department was addressing was teenage pregnancy. The health risks for both the teenage mother and her baby led to significant complications, including increased fatality rates for the mother and infant. The lack of adequate prenatal care all too frequently led to a higher incidence of prematurity and low birth weight. The societal consequences of teenage pregnancies were measured by the high school dropout rates, the high rates of unemployment, and needs for welfare assistance. We oversaw the Adolescent Pregnancy Program to assist local communities for programming to encourage prevention of unwanted teenage pregnancies. But it was clear that the epidemic of unwanted teenage pregnancies required the leadership of parents, schools, and the community. In my speeches, presentations, and articles, I would repeat the message that it would take everyone working together to address this problem.

My position brought me many opportunities to speak to groups and appear on panels. After being honored as the Professional Nurse of the Year by the Texas Nurses' Association in 1978,[4] I addressed them the next year, talking on the future of the government's role in health care. In addition to presentations before civic groups across Region VI, I also traveled back to South Bend to Notre Dame to talk about federal spending on health-related issues in urban areas.[5]

This focus on health care costs led to an initiative to identify sources of fraud, abuse, and error. Medicare overpayments were ripe for abuse. In my region we obtained the largest single recoupment of money to that date, the repayment of almost $600,000 from the Ville Platte Medical Center in Louisiana.[6]

Expansion of health care services prompted review of rural health clinics. State laws requiring "over the shoulder" supervision of nurses and physician's assistants inhibited the growth of such clinics. These restrictive requirements, as I frequently testified, impeded the effectiveness of the Rural Health Clinic Service Act in Texas. This was a significant impact because 173 counties were fully medically underserved, with 55 counties being partially medically underserved.[7] Health care costs were also impacted by unnecessary surgeries. We instituted a program that encouraged patients to seek out second opinions before any nonemergency surgery. With Medicare and Medicaid paying up to 80 percent of the costs of the second opinions, unneeded surgeries could be reduced.[8]

Another component of the master plan was Head Start, a key program within HEW. Created as part of President Johnson's War on Poverty, Head Start was designed to break the cycle of poverty by providing disadvantaged preschool children with comprehensive programing and active parental involvement. Culturally responsive programming was also a key aspect. During the Carter administration funding for Head Start almost doubled. We also implemented bilingual and bicultural programming in about twenty-one states, including states in my region. The responsibility to ensure proper allocation of funds to areas most in need and the implementation of the bilingual and bicultural programming rested, to a significant degree, on the regional directors.

As part of that responsibility, I traveled frequently to Louisiana. Congresswoman Lindy Boggs, a former history teacher, was an ardent supporter of Head Start, committed to strengthening the program for the benefit of Louisiana's children. She had become a member of the House in 1973, when her husband, Hale, was killed in a plane crash. A year later, she was elected overwhelmingly with nearly 80 percent of the vote.[9] She was a key ally as I promoted our programs.

In the spring of 1979, Califano traveled to Dallas. He and Barefoot Sanders, then active in Democratic politics, came to my office. We talked about the possibility of Carter nominating Sanders for a federal district judge. Then the conversation turned to me. Califano advised me that if I wanted to advance in politics and within the Democratic party that I would need to obtain some experience in Washington. We discussed an appointment as assistant to the director of Public Health. A few days later, Califano called me and offered me that position. Mindful of his counsel that working in DC in a significant government position would enhance my future career opportunities, I accepted the position.

Assistant to the Director of Public Health

In mid-July 1979, President Carter decided that he needed to replace several Cabinet secretaries, including Secretary Califano. The day Secretary Califano departed, Patricia Harris was nominated to be secretary of HEW.

She had been appointed the first African American woman to serve as an ambassador for the United States, representing our country in Luxembourg during the Johnson administration. President Carter had earlier appointed her as secretary of the Department of Housing and Urban Development.

It was most exciting to have such an accomplished Black woman heading the department. There was such a feeling of intense pride among Blacks and women who worked at HEW. We knew that Secretary Harris was a brilliant lawyer, earning her law degree from George Washington University after graduating summa cum laude from Howard University. She had worked for the Justice Department during the Kennedy administration, where she and Attorney General Robert F. Kennedy had become colleagues and good friends. She had been actively involved in President Johnson's 1964 presidential campaign, seconding his nomination at the Democratic National Convention. As a significant player in the DNC, Harris was named to the party's credentials committee in 1973. To have her lead our department was a signal that even though President Carter had campaigned on separating out education and creating a new Department of Education, he valued the work that we were doing for the citizens of this nation.

With Secretary Harris's appointment, it wasn't clear to me whether I would be continuing in my new position. I had just moved to DC and hadn't even been on the job a week. Would she want to appoint someone of her own choosing to this position? I needed to learn my fate, so a meeting with Secretary Harris was needed.

I wanted to work under her leadership because she was inspiring. I saw the respect she commanded, carrying herself with dignity and inviting conversation with an engaging smile. To me she was unquestionably intelligent, distinguished, sharp, and focused. But I knew that it was her decision whether I would be on her team.

I met with Secretary Harris. Even though she did a department reorganization, she left me in my position. She recognized that my experience as a nurse was a unique qualification in Washington.

My new job responsibilities included supervising field research throughout the United States. As the department identified its priorities and developed program ideas, it was necessary to have and review research and data. I was responsible for overseeing the various HEW research projects that were being conducted throughout the United States.

I commuted to my office in the Humphrey Building in downtown Washington, DC. It was not lost on me that I had an office in a building named for Vice President Hubert Humphrey, for whom I had been a delegate to the Democratic National Committee. The beginning of my national political career was connected to him.

But I found living in Washington, DC, to be very different from Austin or Dallas. In fact, it was unlike any city where I had ever lived. It had an international flavor and was filled with some of the finest minds in the world. It attracted talent from every part of the globe. It was not uncommon to be in a meeting with a Nobel Prize laureate, a Pulitzer Prize winner, or a Rhodes Scholar. People argued politics, economic policies, currency manipulation, and international relations. But some considered themselves experts on every topic, even though they had just studied materials the night before. They still argued their points as if they held doctoral degrees, refusing to give an inch even when they knew they were wrong. I had never experienced such an unwelcoming environment. Many of the people who I met were not genuinely interested in making lasting, constructive working relationships. Their major interest was in how they could use you or your connections to get the next job or win the next contract. It was a dog-eat-dog environment, and if you were not careful, they would use you as quickly and as brutally as they could, and then be finished with you.

I lived alone in a townhouse in Bethesda. Kirk was at the University of Northern Iowa. Some of my best moments came during our daily phone calls. He visited me during school breaks and holidays. As always, it was a joy to be with him. My connection with my son became even more important in the context of the superficial personal relationships that characterized DC. I was still somewhat shy and found it difficult to fully embrace the Washington social scene. I had several good friends, however, who were members of Congress, including Mickey Leland, who I knew from the Texas Legislature before his election to the seat that had been held by Barbara Jordan. Mickey had not changed much since the days when we were in the Texas House. He was still passionate about public health and food security issues. We still talked often about issues and what we could do to affect policy in Congress and the administration. More than anyone, he was my entrée into Washington power circles.

I knew that I had to develop working relationships. The Congressional Black Caucus (CBC) had been the model for our creation of the Texas Legislative Black Caucus. It was only natural that I would be drawn to the CBC. Now it would become one of the foundations of my introduction to Washington.

Created in 1971, the CBC was founded by thirteen African American representatives, at that time the largest number of Black representatives. Representative Charles Diggs of Michigan was selected to serve as the inaugural chair. When I arrived in Washington, Representative Cardiss Collins of Illinois served in that position. She quickly became a friend, providing counsel and guidance, helping me to adjust to Washington. She had become a member in 1973 after winning a special election to replace her husband, Representative George Collins, who had died the year before in a United Airlines crash. An accountant, she was the first woman to chair the Manpower and Housing Subcommittee of the House Government Operations Committee and to be named Democratic whip-at-large in the House.

Even with her achievements, she was not pretentious. In fact, she reminded me of a kind schoolteacher. She had a welcoming demeanor, sporting stylish glasses and white pearl necklaces. A gracious host, she had a smile that genuinely brightened up a room. Representative Collins also stood firm for women's rights. Among the many things that she did was help to change Medicaid regulations so that the government would cover the cost of postmastectomy breast prosthesis for women.

In addition to Representatives Leland and Collins, there were other members of the CBC who I came to know. I had the opportunity to work closely with New York representatives Shirley Chisholm and Charles Rangel; Missouri representative Bill Clay Sr.; California representatives Ron Dellums and Augustus Hawkins; Michigan representative Charles Diggs; Ohio representative Louis B. Stokes; and District of Columbia representative Walter E. Fauntroy. They were all very accomplished elected officials, committed to using their talents to make government work for all of the nation's citizens.

And as I worked with them and listened to discussions of issues and solutions, I knew that I was observing committed legislators. I watched them work diligently to develop strategies and proposals. I saw their service to their constituents and the nation. I was proud and inspired by the work that I saw being done.

Chapter 10

Return to Dallas

Starting a New Career

It was refreshing to return to Dallas once my years in the Carter administration ended. After years as a government official, I decided to get involved in business. For two years I worked as a consultant for Sammons Corporation, a diversified conglomerate that managed nearly fifty companies ranging from commercial printing to hotels and telecommunications. Cable was in its infancy, when companies were looking for government licenses to expand cable access to cities and neighborhoods. My work with the CBC was viewed as a strength, as I had developed relationships with representatives from major urban areas.

But one of my strongest memories of working with Sammons reinforced the importance of always remembering that employees are people first. My father became very ill and had to be hospitalized. The president of Sammons became aware of my father's illness. He told me to go back to the hospital, to be with my father. Because of his understanding, I was able to sit by my father's side during his last days. And as I sat there, I decided that I wanted to get back into nursing, to return to what I saw as a calling.

After my father passed, a friend who I had worked with on women's issues, Hermine Tobolowsky, reached out to me. She was on the board of the Visiting Nurses' Association (VNA). Over lunch she explained to me that the VNA was looking to expand its geographic service and that my experience doing field research as the public health director would be invaluable in that effort. I pursued that opportunity, accepting an offer as vice president of the VNA.

At that time the VNA provided direct nursing care as a home health agency. In 1978 it formally transitioned into hospice care, one of the first entities to have such a focus. We did a nineteen-county survey of the causes of death, trying to identify the most common health circumstances contributing to fatalities. This information enabled us to set up different modalities dependent upon the unique characteristics of their county.

But the survey also allowed us to identify sources of danger to community health. For example, the presence of a cement plant in West Dallas was the cause of significant lung and breathing disorders for residents in that community. Identification of the impact that the plant was having on the health and well-being of residents ultimately led to its relocation to a more rural area with a dispersed population. During my time with the VNA, I remained politically active, serving as an advisor, not as a candidate. I returned to my life as a community activist concerned with issues such as education, housing, health care, and minority business development. In everything that I did, I brought with me the lessons and experiences of my work in the Texas Legislature and Washington, DC.

While working with the VNA, I also incorporated my own business consulting firm, Eddie Bernice Johnson and Associates. My primary focus was assisting businesses trying to expand into the Dallas/Fort Worth market. My firm helped with business plans, financial statements, and growth analysis. The consulting business also provided a mechanism for me to personally pursue business opportunities. DFW Airport had been operating for about ten years, but airport concession opportunities were just being made available to businesspeople of color. Joining with several other Black businessmen, I obtained a business interest in two stores at the airport.

A project that I put my heart into was Sunbelt National Bank, organized by a group of prominent African Americans. Dr. Ben Clark, a podiatrist;

Reverend Caesar Clark, pastor of the one-hundred-year-old Good Street Baptist Church; Comer Cottrell, founder and owner of Pro-Line Corporation; Albert Record, owner of Record's Barbecue; others; and I came together to organize a minority-owned bank in Dallas. We believed that individual and community wealth building would benefit from a minority-owned bank.

Dallas had a long and strong history of redlining. Banks refused to provide loans for residents in certain neighborhoods, particularly south of downtown Dallas. Home ownership, a primary source of individual wealth, was particularly impacted by this practice. Sunbelt National Bank would not only be a source of pride but it could also provide those loans while attracting business and capital to the Oak Cliff area of Dallas, an area that had been impacted by redlining.

I became a member of the board of directors. In fact, Senator Lloyd Bentsen, a member of the Senate Banking Committee, had encouraged my participation in this endeavor. Building the bank from the ground up, we received significant community support with many individual account holders. Sunbelt was very much a community-focused bank. Comprehensive training seminars to help minority women own businesses were held at the bank. Working with the Small Business Administration, the Service Corps of Retired Executives, Management Training Specialists, and others, the bank provided counseling and services to community members.

But the bank that had been started with such hope and promise ultimately failed. We had raised $1.7 million in capital and acquired $12.5 million in assets. We survived questionable loans to directors and administrators made without the consent of the full board. We had secured an additional infusion of $1.4 million in loan loss reserves. We had hired a new president, a Black woman who had been an examiner with the comptroller of the currency, to campaign for more corporate business to join Aetna, Avon, McDonald's, Kraft, and Sara Lee as bank customers. But we could not survive a national bank crisis that caused its successive correspondent banks—First National Bank, Mercantile Bank, and Republic Bank—to close. In February 1987 Sunbelt became the fifth bank to be closed that year.

The bank closing was devastating to me. When it was all over, I and the other board members were left to pay the government a significant sum of money to reimburse the FDIC. But it wasn't just the financial consequences that were upsetting. I was disappointed that we had not been able to achieve the economic impact that we had intended. An institution that was to be a symbol of pride and financial success had become yet another unfortunate sign of failure. And that would always be regrettable.

Shortly after I had returned home, I was appointed as vice chairperson to the city of Dallas's Health and Human Services Commission. Under the leadership of the chairperson, Hortense Sanger, we held regular meetings during which citizens made their health concerns known. Leaders in the sizeable and increasingly politically influential gay community, such as Bill Nelson, appeared frequently at commission hearings to spotlight a virus that was plaguing mostly white males, Acquired Immune Deficiency Syndrome, or AIDS. The virus, which could be transferred through unprotected sex, was rapidly spreading in the gay community. They sought the commission's help in educating the public about this new health threat. But some commission and community members believed that the virus was only a threat to the gay community, and as a result, they were indifferent. There were even some who said that the disease was a self-inflicted curse. But as a nurse I knew that a virus did not discriminate based on color or sexual orientation.

Nelson, a young political activist, was perhaps the most outspoken and certainly the most persistent. He urged testing. He encouraged the creation of feeding programs to assist AIDS victims who lacked funds. He organized major fundraisers for organizations that assisted victims of the disease. Nelson encouraged elected officials to pass laws prohibiting discrimination against people with AIDS, something that I would later do as a legislator, both in Texas and nationally. Nelson was so effective in his demands that enhanced health care be provided to people who were affected by the disease that I later sponsored a Senate resolution that he be commended for his public service.[1]

Others who appeared before the commission pleaded that we do something before they became ill and died. It was obvious that we had a serious health problem on our hands. We had to start developing plans to fight the disease and promote individual testing. When AIDS began spreading outside of the gay community, we were more prepared to respond because gay rights advocates such as Bill Nelson had educated us and demanded action. At his urging I had started holding meetings with health professionals who were treating people with the virus.

Taking the discussion of AIDS out of the context of the gay community was prompted by a fundraiser organized by Caroline Hunt Schoelkopf, daughter of oil man H. L. Hunt and developer of the Crescent Hotel. Her actions sent the message that talking about AIDS was acceptable, supporting our efforts to reach a broader Dallas audience.

I met with a group of Black ministers who knew very little about the virus. Many people in the community confused the disease with cancer. There was much education that needed to be done. As a public health advocate, I recognized that citizens should be grateful to the leaders of the gay community for their courage in sounding the alarm about HIV/AIDS. Had they not come forward, our community would have been even more blindsided by the disease. It would have become an even more devastating public health disaster, particularly for minorities.

Return to Austin

As I worked with the VNA and served on this commission, political doors were opening. In 1986 there was an opportunity to elect an African American to the Texas Senate from Dallas. In the decade that I had been out of elected office, I had learned that my satisfaction came from getting things for people. I wasn't certain that politics was the best way for me to help people. I did know, however, that it was important to have the right person in the seat.

I immediately thought of Jesse Oliver, an accomplished lawyer. I called him and suggested that he consider running for the seat. I told him that he would have my full support, and that I would help him raise campaign funds. Oliver said that he was going through a difficult divorce and was building a law practice. Thanking me for thinking of him, he declined and committed to supporting the candidate that I backed. I was disappointed that Oliver did not want to get into the race. The Senate only had thirty-one members, and we really needed someone with his intellect and skills to represent us. I knew that Jesse Oliver would do well in Austin, but he had decided against it.

Dr. Jesse Jones, a professor at Bishop College, announced that he would seek the seat. But there was not much support for his candidacy and, frankly, I did not think that he was prepared to go to Austin as a legislator. I continued to search for a candidate, someone who could aggressively represent the people of our district and survive the sometimes-vicious environment of the Texas State Senate. Soon phone calls came like tidal waves. Members of the clergy visited my home urging me to run for the Senate seat. Members of churches, community workers, city and state officer holders, and people on the street approached me about running, as did relatives of the inmates I had assisted. Women with whom I worked at the Women's Center were also insistent that I run.

There were things that I had to consider. I would again have to live on a Texas legislator's salary. There was constant travel between Dallas and Austin while the legislature was in session. But I did see it as another opportunity to assist people and to make history. Barbara Jordan was the first Black female to serve in the Texas Senate, and I could become the second. I went into deep prayer and consulted with family members and close advisors before deciding to seek the position.

Shortly after my announcement that I would run for the Senate, and to my great surprise, Jesse Oliver announced that he would seek the seat. When I approached him and asked him why he was running he said that he had changed his mind. I did not ask him about his previously stated deterrents, his divorce and law practice. I told him that I had no intention of backing out of the race and that I hoped that we would have a fair and honorable campaign. He said he agreed and wished me well. I went home that night, knowing that the voters would be faced with a choice between one candidate named Eddie and two named Jesse.

Among the first people I consulted was Dr. Dan Weiser, who had helped me with my election strategy for my first run for the Texas House by mapping out the district to identify strong voter potential. He supported my candidacy and analyzed the senatorial district, once again showing me where the votes were located, mapping out neighborhoods much like a general preparing for battle. I did not have as much money as my announced opponents, but I knew I could reach the voters if I went directly to them, told them of my record and why

I wanted to represent them in Austin. I knew that voters wanted to see candidates in the flesh. They wanted to hear your views, shake your hand, and look in your eyes to see if you were sincere or if you just wanted the title and status.

I took to the streets, walking each day and knocking on doors in the neighborhoods that Dan had identified. We knew that I needed every single vote I could get, and I was committed to pursuing them. A different group of women, mostly white, walked with me. With a driver to take us to different neighborhoods, members of my team and I would get out, knock on doors, ring doorbells, and work our way down the block. We covered eight or ten blocks each evening. When residents answered their doors, I introduced myself and whoever might be with me. I greeted them, explained to them why I was running, and gave them a bit of my history. If they were not at home or did not answer the door, I left a leaflet detailing my positions on issues that affected their lives.

In my earlier elections, my son and other volunteers had created index cards containing names of voters, their addresses, and phone numbers. We found those index cards in the garage. We had gotten to know people very well, their first names, children, and churches. We phoned, informing them that I was running for the senate seat and that I needed their support. Many of them remembered the things that I had done as their representative and asked how they could support my candidacy.

There was still a bit of parochialism in Dallas. I encountered it on several occasions. The son of a prominent Black physician accused me of being an outsider. He and a number of others said that someone from Dallas, not Waco, should hold the senate seat. But I was not deterred. I had served the people of Dallas as well as I could, often to my personal and financial detriment. I was not going to allow the pettiness of a few keep me from serving.

Labor's leadership did not support me, but many labor union members were on my side. Solid support came from women in groups such as Jack and Jill, the PVL, and the Dallas Women's Center. Cheryl Wattley, a well-respected Dallas lawyer, was central to my campaign. She used her personal and legal skills to assist me.

Actually, I was an underdog in the race. People expected Jesse Oliver to win. He was a lawyer and had access to large sums of money. But I was confident that I was the better candidate and would serve the people in Austin better than Jesse. But I soon learned that we had different ideas about what was a fair campaign. Before Oliver entered the race, I arranged with a realtor to lease a highly visible building with frontage on I-35 to use as my campaign headquarters. Before I could sign the lease, Oliver approached the realtor and asked for the same building, offering him $1,100.00 for the space. That was $750.00 more than I had offered. I knew then that the war was on. I told the realtor that I would match the offer. That made things financially difficult for me, but I was not going to let Oliver believe that he could push me around. I was not going to let him take a space that I had identified and secured for the benefit of my campaign.

I was able to finance my campaign with the assistance of the women's groups that had supported me in the past, neighborhood associations, and individuals such as Les Weisbrod, the organizer of the liberal House Study Group who had become a successful attorney in Dallas. He was crucial in helping me raise funds, soliciting other lawyers and people in his personal circle. He also offered crucial advice concerning how I should conduct the race.

As with any political race, raising money to fund the campaign is critical. Prior to my position at HEW, I had been appointed to the board of directors of the Texas Christian University, where I had received my BS in nursing. Because of the possibility of a conflict of interest as the regional director of HEW with an educational institution, I had resigned my seat on the board. But while on the board, I had worked with Roger Meier, owner of a high-end automobile dealership. I reached out to Roger and told him that I was running for the Texas Senate. Roger supported my candidacy and offered to help me financially. He and his family hosted my largest fundraiser, yielding nearly fifty thousand dollars for my campaign.

The race was intense. There were numerous political forums and debates. During most of the political forums the two Jesses argued and fought one another. I only had to stand by and watch them. Before long, it appeared that the two of them had grown to hate one another.

I told audiences that they were looking at three of the most qualified people in the city of Dallas. I acknowledged that each of us was sincere about wanting to serve the public. But there was one significant difference,

I would say. I had been asked to run because my record in Austin had proved that I would serve the district. Neither Jesse could match that record. I was able to build upon my relationships with precinct chairs, the people who are the front line to voters. One chair in particular, Frances Dirks, with whom I spoke almost nightly, was a very active supporter. She shared my opinion that Oliver was more of a threat to my candidacy than Jones. We would often discuss points and strategies that would benefit my campaign.

Election day arrived and the outcome was still uncertain. I spent the early evening with my supporters at my headquarters waiting for the results. When the news finally came, Jesse Oliver had come in first and I was second. But he had not won a majority, so there had to be a runoff.

Oliver became cocky and was confident that he would beat me in a runoff election. I went to Jesse Jones and asked him to endorse me. He gave me his support. I went to community groups and local leaders, continuing to work as hard as I could, walking and talking. This time I had only one Jesse to defeat. When Dan looked at the votes, he predicted that Oliver and I would each get about 50 percent of the vote in Dallas. The battleground, he said, would be in the city of Grand Prairie, a suburb west of Dallas.

That proved to be the best news I could have been given because I had a secret weapon. My sister, Sallye, the same one that I annoyed as a little girl, had been a much-admired teacher and administrator in the Grand Prairie Independent School District for more than twenty-five years. She convinced her neighbors to place my campaign signs on their lawns. She organized teams of former students to distribute my campaign literature that clearly highlighted that Sallye and I were sisters.

While Oliver continued to ignore Grand Prairie, Sallye and her legion of volunteers actively worked the city. My campaign ran a full-page advertisement in a Grand Prairie newspaper. The ad featured a picture of our family, including my widowed mother, who was living with my sister and her husband, Vandine, and me. At the top of the ad was a statement from Sallye saying, "Vote for my sister, Eddie Bernice Johnson. She will serve you well." People became excited about voting for Sallye Moore's sister. Perhaps, some even joked, more than a few believed that they were voting for their former teacher.

When the vote count came in on election night, we had evenly split Dallas, but I had beat him soundly in Grand Prairie. He had not understood a basic rule of politics: go after votes wherever they are located. He had overlooked the voters in Grand Prairie.

Campaign money alone cannot offset reaching out and touching the hearts of voters. The key to victory was, and still is, passion and hard work. That is what my supporters understood. That is why we walked nearly every block in the district, and that is why, having been asked by the people to run, I was elected to the Texas Senate. Oliver was so bewildered that he did not call to congratulate me on my victory and refused to concede. So I called him and said, "Jesse, let's work together. I know that is something that you want to do."

For several days I made calls and visits, thanking people for supporting my bid for office. With this campaign victory, I could not help but be humbled by the belief that they had in me even though I had been away from Dallas politics for nine years. I was also overcome with gratitude for the friendship and sincerity of those who helped me raise funds, such as Roger Meiers. These conversations made me begin to contemplate my return to Austin, where I also still had many friends. I was once again looking forward to serving my constituents.

Winning the Democratic nomination positioned me for the November election. But I took nothing for granted. The *Dallas Morning News* endorsed me saying, "Her 30 years of community involvement make her imminently qualified to provide the representations that the district deserves."[2] My two former opponents acknowledged that I had toiled tirelessly for the people of our city.

The work paid off. I won the general election, becoming the first African American state senator from North Texas. I was delighted. I was challenged. And I was humbled because I kept my sight on all of the work that had to be done. I was returning to Austin.

Chapter 11

Texas State Senator Eddie Bernice Johnson (1987–1993)

Beginning Work as a Senator

The 1986 election saw William Clements come back as governor when he beat the Democratic incumbent, Mark White. Having served as governor from 1979 to 1983, he had lost the 1982 election to White. In the years between his terms as governor, Clements had served as the chairman of the board of trustees of Southern Methodist University, the institution where a decade earlier I had obtained my master's degree in public administration.

Outgoing Governor Mark White addressed the Seventieth Texas Legislature as the end of his term approached. Covering many of the issues facing Texas on January 14, 1987, certain words were, to me, particularly poignant: "Where there is no vision, there is no future. . . . Building the future has to be a constant, steady, daily process going all the time. . . . Quality education and economic development are one in the same, not separate undertakings."[1]

This was a difficult time for Texas and its lawmakers. The state was faced with a deep economic recession and increasing debt. The largest tax increases in the state's history were enacted, and the largest number of constitutional amendments proposed. Clements concentrated on job

creation, recruitment of out-of-state corporations to Texas, and diversifica-
tion of the state's economy.

The presiding officer of the Senate was Lt. Gov. Bill Hobby, who had held
this same office when I had first become a member of the legislature. We had
worked well together during my time in the House and respected one another.
Hobby had chaired the Hobby-Clayton Commission, which resulted in the Texas
Sunset Act, a commission charged with reviewing state agencies every twelve
years to determine if they should be continued or abolished. That measure led
to significant economic and administrative improvements in the operation of
state government. A visionary, Hobby led initiatives that resulted in progress
in a number of areas, including health care, prison conditions, mental health
programs, state mental institutions, and water resources.

The Texas Senate had long been a male-dominated citadel. The only
female members of the body during the seventieth legislative session were
Cyndi Krier, the first Republican female senator elected from Bexar County;
Judith Zaffirini, an educator from Laredo; and me. An attorney, Krier
was first elected to the senate in 1984, running on the ticket that included
President Ronald Reagan and Vice President George H. W. Bush. Krier was
concerned with child abuse and domestic violence. She sponsored bills that
changed state policies regarding those issues. A member of the Education and
Natural Resources Committees, she was also a strident supporter of business
development, advocating tax incentives for business owners who invested in
enterprise zones.

A fellow Democrat, Zaffirini represented a Senate district that stretched
across twenty counties, reaching from the Rio Grande to the Colorado
River. It was her first term in the Senate as well. She, too, had been forced
into a runoff election. And her victory was also historic as she was the first
Hispanic woman elected to the Texas Senate. She was active in state and
national Democratic Party politics, her interests reflecting her experience
as a teacher in public schools and universities. Her primary focuses were
education reform, job creation, health care, and election of more women to
public office. These similar interests made us natural allies.

There were twenty-five Democrats and five Republicans in the Senate.
Craig Washington, who had served with me in the House, was the only other

African American in the chamber, having been elected to the Senate in 1983 from a Houston district. The majority of the senators represented major urban centers such as Austin, Houston, San Antonio, El Paso, and Dallas. The others were from smaller regions throughout the state.

The Seventieth Legislature was called into session on January 13, 1987, and met until June of the same year. It was the busiest session in the history of the state legislature. Members introduced 4,179 pieces of legislation.[2] There were 1,185 bills passed and signed into law by the governor, including legislation that dealt with open housing, renter's rights, judicial reform, and assistance to Black farmers and small-business owners.

One of my proudest moments came when Senator Don Henderson and I managed an effort to support restrictions on investment in South Africa and Namibia. Those two countries were led by oppressive all-white minority governments based on a system of apartheid. The legislature was considering a constitutional amendment to create a Texas Growth Fund that would direct investment of state retirement funds. We worked in support of H.J.R. 5, which included a provision that prohibited investment with a business unless it submitted an affidavit that it did not have any direct financial investment in or with South Africa or Namibia.[3] After passing the Senate on a 29–0 vote, the constitutional amendment was put on the November 1988 ballot, winning 65 percent approval of the voters.[4]

I admired Nelson Mandela and the many others who fought for democracy in South Africa. With the sizeable retirement funds to be invested, excluding businesses with financial ties to South Africa and Namibia was an important declaration of Texan support for their crusade.

Senate Committee on Health and Human Services: CPS

Lt. Gov. Hobby charged the Senate Committee on Health and Human Services to do a study of the Child Protective Services (CPS) program. We were to review agency procedures, qualifications and training of employees, and the handling of incoming reports of child abuse and neglect. We conducted days of hearings in Houston, Dallas, El Paso, and San Antonio. Over three hundred witnesses testified. Hundreds of others submitted written statements, met privately with committee staff, or contacted the committee by telephone.[5] It was clear that the operations and effectiveness of the CPS struck the heart of Texans across the state.

What we heard was alarming and consistent. We were told by people from across the state that everyday cases of child abuse that had been confirmed were closed, leaving children in dangerous situations because there were not enough staff to monitor or assist the families. In Harris County hundreds of incoming reports were not investigated. CPS employees, including frontline workers, reached out to the committee, telling of their extreme frustration with agency management. The caseloads were unmanageable. Paperwork requirements increased work responsibilities. Opportunities for promotion were limited. There was inadequate management and insufficient resources. The foster care system was woefully lacking. Decisions to remove a child from a dangerous home were impeded because there was no suitable alternative placement. Foster parents reported retaliation for advocating for services or openly discussing or complaining about problems with the agency.

The information that we obtained led us to conclude that the problems in the CPS program were immense. We created a list of more than thirty recommendations to lead the push to caring for our children. What we had heard was not just a call for increased funding. It was a cry for the commitment of the legislature, Board of Human Services, administrators, judges, attorneys, doctors, teachers, child advocates, and citizens to meet our obligations to the state's children.

Joint Interim Committee on Affordable Housing, Texas Fair Housing Act

Lt. Gov. Hobby also appointed me to serve on the Joint Interim Committee on Affordable Housing. Inadequate housing affects us all because it impacts the costs of local government, human services programs, economic revitalization, and what happens to our cities and neighborhoods. Recognizing this impact, Lt. Gov. Hobby charged us to examine the problems of affordable housing for low- and moderate-income persons. We held hearings for nine months and heard from 160 witnesses. Our hearings confirmed what many of us knew: there was a serious need for affordable housing, many families lived in substandard housing, and the lack of housing led to homelessness. And, regrettably, Texas lagged behind other states in developing programs to tackle this problem.[6]

We developed twenty-seven recommendations to address affordable housing, homelessness, and discrimination in housing.[7] We recommended that statewide coordination of federal programs to address affordable housing be effected through the establishment of a Housing Resource Center. The center would assist in the development of community credit corporations, lenders, and developers; provide technical assistance to those providing affordable homes; and support self-help programs for residents of public housing to transition into rentals or homeownership. We also made a variety of recommendations for financing and investment in affordable housing development and acquisition. Recognizing that helping families maintain a residence was critical to the prevention of homelessness, we recommended the development of statewide programs. Enactment of a state fair housing law was deemed necessary. A state law would lead to more effective, quicker action on discrimination claims.

This work on the Interim Joint Task Force confirmed what I had already known and led me to introduce Senate Bill No. 75 in the seventy-first legislative session.[8] This bill, titled the Texas Fair Housing Act, prohibited a refusal to sell or rent to any person because of race, color, religion, sex, handicap, familial status, or national origin. Housing discrimination had especially been a major problem for racial minorities in Texas. Many neighborhoods and apartments were segregated, and when minorities moved into white communities, they were faced with extreme hostility from residents and community organizations.

While a federal housing law had been passed earlier, there were no enforcement provisions in it, so landlords continued to discriminate against people of color without fear of consequences. Title VIII of the 1968 Civil Rights Act dealing with housing discrimination was signed by President Johnson on April 11, 1968, just seven days after Dr. Martin Luther King Jr. was assassinated in Memphis, Tennessee. The statute prohibited housing discrimination in the sale, rental, or financing of housing based on race, national origin, or religion. It provided redress for victims of housing discrimination and penalized individuals and institutions found guilty of discriminatory practices.

In the wake of the federal law, many states enacted their own fair housing laws in an effort to prohibit racial discrimination in housing. Texas—which had a long and morally degrading history of racial steering, intimidation of potential buyers, and violence against minorities that relocated in white neighborhoods— had not been among them. I knew that it was time for Texas to enact a statute that would allow people to live in communities of their choice without fear of rejection by home builders or apartment owners.

Racial steering had also been a common practice in many of our cities, while in rural areas the Ku Klux Klan intimidated minority residents who ventured into previously white neighborhoods. Minority homeowners had crosses burned on their lawns and were physically beaten and verbally abused. The practice of redlining by financial institutions, restricting access for people of color to loans for home purchases to designated geographical areas, was common throughout the state. I knew that the housing bill had to be structured so that various components of the housing community would support it. I met with brokers, builders, rental agents, apartment developers, members of homeowner associations, and housing developers. I shared with them the mountain of evidence detailing the existence and impact of racial discrimination. While I appealed to their humanity, I knew that it was their economic interests that would be compelling. Equal opportunity in housing would create additional revenue and growth for their businesses.

Armed with stacks of housing discrimination complaints, I met individually with colleagues, sharing with them some of the horror stories that I heard from taxpayers who were denied access to housing simply because of skin color. I had examples of white housing "testers" who visited certain housing developments or apartment dwellings, asking to purchase or rent, and being accommodated without any problems. But when a Black or brown "tester" went to the same communities, they were told that the house had been sold or that there were no vacancies in an apartment complex, even though newspapers advertised availability.

But I also had my own story to share. During private meetings and in committee, I shared with my colleagues my personal experiences with housing discrimination, what it was like knowing that there were certain areas of a city where you could not live. I tried to convey to them the hurt that discrimination caused. Many of them were empathetic. These visits allowed me to build coalitions that I knew the bill needed if it were to pass. I frequently met with legislative staff to make certain that the bill was well drafted and would not face any unforeseen hurdles. I worked with colleagues in the House for a parallel House bill.

With everything in place, I introduced the bill on December 21, 1988, four days before Christmas. It was titled the Texas Fair Housing Act.[9] Its stated purpose was to create fair-housing practices throughout the state and to prevent discrimination on the basis of race, national origin, religious beliefs, or color. It empowered the Texas Commission on Human Rights to investigate allegations of discrimination in housing, issue subpoenas, and refer cases to the attorney general's office to institute civil enforcement proceedings. The bill received the support of the Texas Association of Realtors, Texas Association of Builders, the Texas Bankers Association, Texas Apartment Association, Texas Alliance for the Mentally Ill, and AARP.[10] There was no testimony in opposition to the bill. My strategy of gaining the support of impacted businesses before introducing the bill had worked.

The Senate approved the bill on May 29, 1989. Two days later the House concurred. Governor Clements signed the legislation on June 16, and it became effective state law on January 1, 1990. The Texas Fair Housing Act became one of the strongest such pieces of legislation in the country. It placed those who had practiced discrimination, or intended to do so, on notice that state officials and agencies frowned on discrimination in housing and would not tolerate its presence or its practice.

But my concerns about affordable housing extended beyond a nondiscriminatory opportunity to gain housing; it also needed to be decent and habitable. During my first term I introduced a bill that allowed cities to repair single-family homes and duplexes to minimum standards at city expense. The costs of those repairs would be paid by the property owner.

If the owner did not pay the city, a lien could be imposed on the property. This legislation was important because at that time a city could only bulldoze the property, put a "red tag" on the door, or simply allow the building to continue to deteriorate.[11] None of those options promoted restoration of much-needed habitable housing.

In 1989 I sponsored and secured the passage of a bill empowering tenants to address landlords' failure to repair conditions that materially affected their health and safety. An earlier statute provided for legal remedies, but they had proved to be expensive, time-consuming, and intimidating. My bill addressed those problems by providing a simplified mechanism for tenants when a landlord refused to repair such conditions.[12] Recognizing the growing involvement of government in providing affordable housing, in 1991 I sponsored a bill that would allow a political subdivision to acquire and convey property for such housing. This bill was necessary because the property could not be obtained through eminent domain.[13] Because affordable housing was so needed, it was important that we create opportunities for more such housing.

Chair, Special Advisory Committee on Creation and Expansion of Minority and Women-Owned Business Ownership Opportunities

Fighting discrimination and assuring full participation of African Americans was always part of my work. During my first term in the Senate, I sponsored and secured the passage of a statute recognizing that home-rule municipalities with a population greater than nine hundred thousand could adopt a program designated to reasonably increase minority- and women-owned business participation in public contract awards.[14] This bill made it clear that such programs did not constitute discrimination and were lawful.

Serving as chair of the Special Advisory Committee gave me the opportunity to build upon that sponsorship and continue to focus on how to remedy the effects of past and present, public and private discrimination that had so impacted our state. We held eight public hearings, receiving written and oral testimony. The same complaints were voiced at each hearing:

lack of access to capital, financing, and bonding; onerous state contracting procedures; underutilization of minority- and women-owned businesses; complicated certification processes; and a good-old-boy attitude to contract awards. Based upon our review, we recommended that the state establish a goal-based procurement program that would encourage and reflect minority- and women-owned businesses. We also recommended a variety of strategies to increase resources and guidance designed to support such businesses. The work of this Special Advisory Committee and its recommendations provided the foundation for governmental initiatives backing minority- and women-owned businesses.

But my work advocating for minority participation was not restricted to formal committee assignments. When nominations for state appointments were made, I'd raise challenges to assure that minority candidates had been considered. I posed questions when nominations were made for the University of Texas and Texas A&M Board of Regents. When contracts and special programs, such as the building of the Super Collider came up, I was constantly urging for participation of minority- and women-owned businesses.

In February 1987 I sponsored the state statute to make Dr. Martin Luther King Jr.'s birthday a legal holiday in the state of Texas.[15] While Congress had finally recognized Dr. King's birthday as a holiday years earlier, the state had not done so. This bill allowed state employees to select the King holiday as one of their days off with pay. This was extremely important to me, as I would not likely have been elected to public office had not Dr. King and other leaders fought for the passage of the Civil Rights Act of 1964 and the Voting Rights Act of 1965, which President Johnson signed into law.

School Finance

In 1984 school funding became a targeted issue when the Mexican American Legal Defense and Educational Fund representing school districts with lower property tax revenue filed a lawsuit against the state. In *Edgewood v. Kirby*, those districts claimed that school funding should be restructured to provide more funding for less wealthy school districts. Because the amount spent per student can make a difference in the quality of education afforded, the plaintiffs claimed that this caused unequal educational opportunities in violation of the Texas Constitution. The state was required to provide an efficient and free public school system. The Texas Supreme Court ultimately ruled that the school finance system was unconstitutional.[16]

In early 1991 the legislature was given until April 1 to provide a new, equitable funding proposal or suffer a cutoff of state funds to public schools. A court-appointed master had developed a financing plan that was called Robin Hood because it shifted funds from richer school districts to poorer ones. The legislature repeatedly passed funding bills in response to the lawsuit. But it would not be until 1993 that a funding bill would be found acceptable to the court. But the children of Texas benefited from this continued attention to providing them the opportunity for a quality public education.

Prekindergarten Programs

It is well recognized that it is important to reach young children early, especially those with low proficiency in English or who are from low-income families. School districts were required to provide prekindergarten programs. The federal program Head Start, various state-funded programs, and privately funded programs all strove to improve learning opportunities for young children. But those programs were fragmented and contradictory.

I sponsored a bill that would require coordination between the state agencies, Head Start, and other early childhood programs. All pre-K programs had to meet the childcare licensing standards. They also were to investigate the possibility of coordinating with Head Start programs or existing licensed childcare facilities. State agencies were to monitor and evaluate the pre-K programs to assure developmental appropriateness. It was important that we provide our youngest schoolchildren with an environment that enabled them to learn and begin their educational experience.[17]

A closely related concern for educating Texas children was the shortage of teachers. Having authored the resolution for the creation of a Special Advisory Committee on Bishop College, I was appointed to chair that committee. We were charged to study the feasibility of creating a state institution on the site of the former Bishop College Campus located in southern Dallas.[18] Bishop College was a historically Black college created in 1881 in Marshall, Texas. In the early 1960s, the college was moved to Dallas, but due to financial problems, the college was closed in 1988. Development of a state educational institution on this campus would have a positive impact on development in the southern sector.

We held hearings in Dallas and Fort Worth. Over fifty witnesses testified, including alumni, former faculty, staff, and students of Bishop College. We heard from numerous witnesses about education, employment, and socioeconomic trends. Educational experts from the Texas Education Association, TEC, Texas Higher Education Coordinating Board, North Texas Commission, Dallas Citizens Council, Dallas Independent School District, Legislative Budget Board, and the Texas Legislative Council testified before the committee. Through our hearings we learned about the potential student pool, explored possible sources of funding, became familiar with the legislative process to establish a four-year institution, and learned about the approximately $30 million financial impact that Bishop College had had on Dallas County. As a result of our hearings and research, we recommended that a state institution be created that would emphasize recruiting outstanding students to the teaching profession. There was a recognized need for additional teachers, especially minorities, such that a college focused on teacher training located in southern Dallas would address this need. In fact, the University of Texas, Texas Southern University, and Texas A&M University all expressed an interest in serving as the parent institution for this new school.[19]

While this report did not lead to the purchase of the former Bishop College campus, it put a focus on the viability of a state institution in southern Dallas. Our report had spotlighted the fact that this was the largest quadrant of Dallas without an institution of higher learning. It was also the area of Dallas with the largest concentrations of minorities. Years later, the legislature approved the establishment of University of North Texas, Dallas, just miles down the same road from the Bishop campus. Our study and information provided the initial justification for that new university.

Battered Woman Syndrome: Legal Defense

The problems with spousal abuse are well-known. When I proposed the legislation for Texas, a battered-woman defense to murder could only be raised in seven states. My House colleague Rep. Juan Hinojosa, chair of the House Jurisprudence Committee, held a hearing at the Texas women's prison, Mountain View. Women who had been convicted of murder provided testimony about the abuse that they had suffered and how it led to the crimes that they had committed. Such testimony, recurring news stories about abused women killing their abusers, and conversations with Senator Craig Washington, compelled me to be a part of this legislation.

The statute allowed a woman being prosecuted for murder or manslaughter and raising an issue of self-defense to introduce evidence of prior acts of family violence. The statute expressly authorized the admission of expert testimony about the effect of that prior family violence on the defendant's state of mind at the time of the offense. This statute was critical because it made it clear that women who had been the victims of abuse were entitled to be judged in the full context of what had been done to them.[20] To me in order for a jury to judge whether the defendant was reasonable in being afraid for their life, the jury should know the history of what had been done to them.

But this statute was opposed. It was argued that there was inadequate clinical psychological evidence to demonstrate that the past abuse was connected to the act of violence. In fact, there were court proceedings in which so-called experts testified that certain socioeconomic backgrounds accepted and expected abuse such that abuse would not be a traumatic experience. Fortunately, the legislature saw beyond such arguments. On May 1, 1991, Governor Clements signed the bill into law. Victims of abuse could now have evidence of past incidents of domestic violence introduced before a jury determining whether they were acting in self-defense in cases of murder or manslaughter.

When a Giant Went Missing

One of the worst days of my life occurred on August 7, 1989, when my close friend and former colleague in the Texas House, Congressman Mickey

Leland, perished in a plane crash. He was on a humanitarian mission in Ethiopia delivering supplies.

We had started in the House the same year, growing together as elected officials. We shared the vision for the Texas Legislative Black Caucus. We shared a bond, commitment to service, and were dedicated to creating positive social change in the world. We listened to each other, respecting the other's opinions. We had labored for countless hours together, tackling issues for the benefit of Texas citizens. Mickey, Craig, Bennie Reyes (a Hispanic legislator from Houston), and myself met regularly, brainstorming, trying to develop plans to improve minority schools. We talked, reviewed data, and identified potential resources, the meetings running late into the night. Mickey and I had gone to the Texas prisons together, making unannounced visits. We shared a determination that Texas inmates would be treated humanely and with respect.

When I heard the news, I was flooded with memories. Mickey with his enormous afro haircut. The platform shoes that he would sometimes wear. His fearlessness and boldness in approaching anyone who might be able to help advance his issues. And his stories, such as the one about a legislator from Tyler who asked him to trim his huge afro and his beard. Mickey promptly led him to a room with pictures of former House Speakers and pointing to the ones with beards, asked, "Would you tell those cats what you just told *me*?" The legislator, admonished, replied, "I guess you made your point."

I remembered when he reached out to Frank Erwin Jr., an influential Democrat and member of the University of Texas System Board of Regents. We were trying to draw attention to the funding disparities between the white and Black educational institutions. Mickey learned that Erwin frequented a club on Red River Street in downtown Austin. So Mickey started going to that club. While there he'd visit with Erwin, eventually bringing up the need for additional financial support for Black universities and colleges. As a graduate of Texas Southern University, Mickey gave Erwin firsthand accounts of the impact of the funding inadequacies. Through these conversations, not only did Mickey educate Erwin about the problems confronted by HBCUs, but they also became friends. Erwin listened and realized that the funding situation needed to be addressed. He used his political stature and, before long, we began to see increased funding for HBCUs.

Mickey was a people person. He knew people from every walk of life. One of his friends was Houston native George Foreman, the Olympic heavyweight boxing gold medal winner. Mickey took me to my first professional fight, where we sat in ringside seats. Foreman had arranged accommodations for Mickey, Craig, and me at the Hilton and for us to attend the prefight parties. It was something new for me. Celebrities were all over the place. I met the queen of soul, Aretha Franklin and was introduced to Don King, the promoter known by his signature hairstyle.

Even when he left the Texas House in 1979 to take the congressional seat that had been held by retiring Congresswoman Barbara Jordan, we had remained close friends. We continued to talk about issues and explore how they might be addressed on the state and national level. When he fought for sanctions against the apartheid government in South Africa, he got me involved in the South African divestiture movement.

One time Mickey saw my name printed in an advertisement in the *New York Times* supporting Israel. He called to chastise me. I suggested that he visit Israel with some of his Jewish friends. He had done this and his views had changed dramatically. From this experience, he established a program that sent African American teenagers from inner-city neighborhoods in Houston to Israel for two months, where they studied Jewish culture and the history of Israel. Mickey was dedicated to improving relations between African and Jewish Americans. He once cycled through Israel. Quoting the Talmud, he was fond of saying, "If you save one life, you save the world."

Mickey had also traveled to Vietnam and Cuba to bring about understanding among people, and to do whatever good he could. In Cuba he was successful in gaining the freedom of three political prisoners and members of their families. In Vietnam he was able to locate three children whose father, a Vietnamese citizen, had fled that country and relocated in Houston.

But global hunger became his focal issue. He had first visited Africa in 1972 to spend three weeks in Tanzania. But he became so captivated by the country and its people that he remained there for three months. His family did not hear from him and there were rumors that he had been killed. But he had become so engrossed in the problems that he had witnessed and so challenged to think of ways that he could help that he forgot everything else. That was Mickey.

He often said that his efforts to end global hunger began on a trip that he made to Sudan. During the trip he witnessed a very young girl die from starvation while she struggled to speak with him. She looked as though she was 80 years old, barely more than a skeleton, "with a thin layer of brown skin and just a faint breath of life." Her death changed his life, Mickey said. As a congressman, Mickey worked to create the House Select Committee on Hunger. He founded a number of programs designed to attack the famine that engulfed Sudan and Ethiopia during the early 1980s. In 1985 he helped to pass a $784 million bill to fight famine in Africa.[21]

I was attending a national conference of state legislators in Oklahoma City when I learned that his plane was missing. I immediately called his wife, Allison, in Houston. We cried and talked several times each day for the five days US Air Force pilots searched for any sign of Mickey and members of his staff. Not once did we give up hope that he would be found alive and that he would soon be back on his way home to Texas. Neither Allison, who was pregnant with twins, nor I could imagine a world without Mickey.

Our dear friend Bennie Reyes flew to Ethiopia to assist in the search. He was accompanied by New York congressman Gary Ackerman, who served with Mickey in the House. Rodney Ellis, who later became a member of the Texas Senate, had served as Mickey's chief of staff in Congress and had shared an apartment with him for a time, flew to Washington to wait for word. Ellis conducted daily press briefings in Mickey's congressional office and organized a prayer vigil. He was the first person to notify Allison and Mickey's mother, Alice, that the plane was missing. He had been scheduled to be on the trip with Mickey but decided not to travel to East Africa at the last minute.

Allison called me on a Sunday, telling me that the wreckage of the plane had been found. When it was finally located, it was determined that the plane had crashed about 300 feet below the peak of a 4,300-foot mountain. Rescuers said that it appeared the pilot was following the pathway of a river.[22] Mickey was 44 years old and had served with distinction in Congress for ten years.

News of the plane crash stunned Congress, people in Texas, and those throughout the world who had come to know him. President George H. W. Bush said, "Congressman Leland was engaged in a noble cause: trying to feed the hungry."[23] Members of Congress gave expressions of sympathy on the floor of the House. The Speaker, Tom Foley said, "None of us will forget the dedication and commitment that took Mickey and his colleagues on the trip. His mission was fraught with danger."[24] A *New York Times* editorial said he paid with his life because he tried to be his "brother's keeper."[25] A headline in an Associated Press article read "U.S. Rep. Mickey Leland, Lawmaker: Champion of the Hungry."[26]

The day before Mickey's service, nearly three thousand people packed the gymnasium at Texas Southern University, Mickey's alma mater. He had secured funding for Texas Southern while a member of the Texas legislature. The Houston Endowment donated $1 million to establish the Mickey Leland Center on World Hunger and Peace.

The service to celebrate his life and his work was held at St. Anne's Catholic Church in Houston. It was attended by dignitaries from Washington and Texas, ordinary citizens, and even those who had never met him but had heard of his political and social contributions. The entire CBC was present, as were members of the Texas Congressional Delegation. Congressman Ron Dellums, Mickey's closest friend in Washington, delivered a moving tribute to his fallen friend.

A separate memorial service was held in Washington. Vice President Dan Quayle spoke. Ambassadors, members of Congress, and representatives from the executive branch and the judiciary were present to celebrate Mickey's life. A fund was established to ensure that the Leland children—Jarrett, who was 3 years old and the yet-to-be-born twins—would have their college expenses covered.

The services were emotionally draining. We were burdened by the question of why Mickey had been taken in the prime of his life when there was so much more that he would have done to improve the human condition.

There was no telling how far Mickey, with his winning ways, his political wit, and his burning passion, would have gone in public life. While elated that we had known and worked with him, we were despondent that he had been taken from us. For me, it felt like I had lost a younger brother.

Redistricting: The Struggle for Equal Representation

Throughout Texas history congressional redistricting has been a painful and stinging issue for minorities. Even at the height of the 1960s civil rights movement, Texas did not have any African Americans in Congress, despite a sizeable Black population.

In 1987 the majority of African Americans elected to the US House of Representatives were from major metropolitan areas such as New York City, Los Angeles, Baltimore, Chicago, St. Louis, Detroit, Cleveland, and Houston. The issue of a minority-held congressional seat in North Texas was raised constantly in meetings by my constituents. They wanted to know why Dallas was not able to have a minority representative and believed that Congress was at a disadvantage not having a minority member from North Texas. We also believed that Congress was incomplete as long as there was not a minority voice from North Texas and understood that democracy works best when the opinions and experiences of a variety of voices are expressed at the seat of power. I knew that the issue would not go away and believed that something had to be done about it. Quite frankly, the issue was not only about color but also about fairness, equal opportunity, and having a seat in a chamber where major decisions are made about people's lives. We had been overlooked and cheated out of representation during the 1981 reapportionment.

Under our federal Constitution, every decade there is a census counting the people living in the United States. With this updated population data, governmental units, municipalities, counties, and states draw the boundaries that will define their representative districts. In North Texas, where my Senate district was located, the 1990 census documented the significant growth in Black and Hispanic voters, sufficient to justify representation in Congress. North Texas had never been represented by a minority. The strategy of the state legislature had been to pack Black and brown people into state and congressional districts where they would be outnumbered by whites. A minority candidate had no realistic chance of winning a congressional seat.

In February of 1991, the Census Bureau informed Texas officials that the state was entitled to three additional seats because its population had grown to nearly 17 million people. Before the population growth, the state had twenty-seven members in the House of Representatives. Nineteen of the congressional seats were held by Democrats and the remaining eight were in the hands of Republicans. With this population growth, Texas would add three congressional seats, one each in Dallas and Harris Counties and one in South Texas.[27]

Lt. Gov. Bullock appointed me to serve as chair of the sixteen-member Special Subcommittee on Congressional Districts. I had already served on the joint state House and Senate redistricting committee that had held fourteen meetings across the state. I knew that this upcoming redistricting effort would be more complicated than ever. There was the continued threat of state and federal legal challenges. Under the Voting Rights Act, any plan would have to be reviewed by the US Department of Justice. The widespread use of computers to calculate demographic impact on district lines enabled more individuals and groups to become engaged in developing competing plans. And changing any district lines to remedy African Americans' disenfranchisement in terms of representation in Congress would hurt Democratic incumbents.

The minority population in Dallas had historically been represented in Congress by members such as Dale Milford and Martin Frost. Congressman Frost was elected in 1979, becoming only the second Jewish person elected to Congress from North Texas. He grew up in Fort Worth, but a large portion of his congressional district was in Dallas, where significant numbers of racial minorities lived. In fact, without the minority vote, Frost would not have remained in Congress as long as he did.

A former newspaper reporter, Frost cultivated allies in the media. When I returned to the legislature in 1987, Frost had been a member of the House of Representatives for ten years. Considered a moderate Democrat, Frost became a prolific fundraiser. It was rumored that he would become the first Jewish Speaker of the House of Representatives. That certainly seemed to be his ambition. While friendly toward minorities, Frost seemed to do very little to advance our interests. It appeared that he was more focused on his personal rise in the Democratic Party than on issues that affected the lives of Black and brown people. Many minority citizens were unhappy with his leadership, but at the time he seemed the best that we could get.

From the outset the topic of redistricting and creating a minority district in North Texas drew intense attention. Former US Speaker of the House Jim Wright openly called for protection of Frost and John Bryant's congressional seats when the efforts to create a minority district were begun.[28] That plea offended me. I publicly asked what Representatives Frost and Bryant had accomplished that could not have been done by a minority representative.[29]

Redistricting is always complicated. All the congressional districts are to have a comparably sized population. When there are population shifts from rural counties to urban counties, the rural district lines have to be extended to pull in more people to reach the requisite population size. That reality can cause a significant shift in the geographic area included in a district. In addition to the targeted population size, racial demographics impact a district's configuration. Districts have to be drawn to avoid "overpacking" or concentrations of ethnic groups. At the same time, the lines cannot dilute the impact of minority voters. And incumbency is always at the forefront of redistricting concerns. Elected officials rarely endorse a redistricting map that materially changes the configuration of their district and changes their voter constituency. They want to keep the voters who elected them to office. For Frost and John Bryant, the new lines were of concern.

In 1982 Governor Clements had favored a plan that would have created a minority district because it would have also converted Frost's district into a Republican stronghold. The legislature had passed a map that preserved Frost, Mattox, and Bryant's districts by denying a minority district.

The minority vote would not be divided this cycle. Not on my watch. It was time for there to be a minority district in North Texas.

But Frost, chairman of a committee formed by the state's congressional delegation to formulate its own plan, vigorously opposed any reduction of minority voters from his district. Frost's chief concern was that minority voters, who had repeatedly supported him, would be removed from his district, and that he would then have to attract voters in a district that was largely white. That was something that he was not confident that he could do.

He called me repeatedly, trying to pressure me not to change his district lines. During lunch in Dallas, he questioned me like I was on the witness stand during a trial, insisting that I tell him how the lines would be redrawn. My answer that I did not know because the plan would be decided by the committee process did not satisfy him. I assured him that we would be honorable and prudent about our decision and that I would do all that I could to protect his seat. But my words did not ease his fears. The environment became increasingly hostile as he, in effect, tried to bully me into a position that preserved the minority voters in his district. I was told that he even called Lt. Gov. Bob Bullock on his fishing trip, demanding that he instruct me to protect his seat. Bullock, whom I had supported when he ran for lieutenant governor and with whom I had a good working relationship, called me and said, "Eddie Bernice, don't you even talk to that son of a bitch."

His surrogates pressured Governor Ann Richards. Word came from the governor's office that she would not sign any plan that injured him. Rumors began to circulate that I was determined to harm him. At one point a local journalist in Dallas who was friendly with Frost approached me and said that Dallas voters would suffer if Frost was not protected in the redistricting process. The political environment became like a war zone. There were constant accusations, character assassinations, and heated debates that went beyond civility. I even received a telephone call telling me to look out my window to see the man standing across the street with a gun, watching my movements. I was being threatened over redistricting.

While the atmosphere was insane, not everyone seemed to have lost their minds. I received constant encouragement from my former Texas House colleague Jim Mattox, who had won a congressional seat in 1976 when President Carter was elected. Mattox had resigned his congressional seat in 1983 to run for Texas attorney general. I have always believed that one of the reasons he resigned was his belief that one of the North Texas congressional seats should have been held by a racial minority. Mattox was supportive, encouraging me to follow my conscience and the requirements of the law. He also suggested that I consider becoming a candidate once the process was completed—a suggestion that was complimentary but wholly premature.

Senator Chet Brooks was on the subcommittee and was also an important ally. He had been a supporter of equal representation dating back to the time when I first arrived in Austin. He knew that the crucial work in redrawing district lines would occur in the subcommittee. He understood the importance of creating minority districts to comply with the law. Known as the Dean of the Senate, Senator Brooks also chaired the Committee of the Whole, which included all thirty-one members of the Senate. His support of any bill would be critical.

Members of the Texas Black Caucus were assigned various roles during the process. Some were asked to lobby sympathetic white members, gaining their support for a plan that would create districts in which minorities stood a chance of winning. Others were asked to contact influential officials of the NAACP who lived in parts of Texas represented by undecided lawmakers. The officials were provided with census data and asked to apply whatever pressure they could to advance our position. I spoke often with my colleagues in the Hispanic community. Senators Frank Tejeda, my vice-chair, and Gonzalo Barrientos were supporters of the bill. Gene Green, a white legislator from Harris County, also played an invaluable role in assisting us.

Senator Ellis, the only other African American in the Senate, and I took daily one-hour walks in the early mornings. We spent that time discussing how to get our colleagues to agree to the creation of three minority-opportunity seats. One morning we were so engaged we lost track of time and walked for ninety minutes. At that point we were so tired that we had to phone members of our staffs, asking them to come get us and bring plenty of drinking water. That was just how intense and consuming our conversations would be.

Because congressional redistricting impacted both Republicans and Democrats, Joe Barton, a Republican congressman for the Sixth District reached out to me on behalf of the Republican Congressional delegation. I knew Barton because he had played football with my brother, Carl, while they were both high school students in Waco. The congressman and I developed a complimentary approach: fairness. It was only fair that a minority opportunity seat be created. It was also only right that Republicans be treated fairly.

Congressman Craig Washington, who had gone to Washington after Mickey Leland's tragic death, was asked by Democratic members of the Texas congressional delegation to protect their interests in Austin during redistricting. He had been involved in previous redistricting challenges in the legislature and understood both the complicated process we were dealing with and the issues that were at stake. Years earlier he had sued the city of Houston to create single-member districts for its city council and school board elections. His advice and expertise were invaluable.

Washington worked closely with Senator Ellis and me. While he was present to protect his colleagues' seats, he also had a vested interest in seeing that minorities in Texas had the opportunity to elect members of Congress who represented their interests. He was highly supportive of a minority-opportunity seat in North Texas, specifically Dallas.

Washington said that I should seriously consider running. He said members of the Texas congressional delegation were looking for a "well-prepared, knowledgeable and industrious" candidate to join them in Congress once elected. They had concluded that I was that person, he said. While I was flattered by that confidence, I knew that the decision regarding who went to Washington once a seat was created was in the hands of voters. Despite reports that I had decided to run for the seat, I believed that my job, at the moment, was to make the seat a reality and give the voters a chance to choose a candidate who they thought would best represent their interests.

It would take two special sessions of the legislature to pass the redistricting bill. We had created three new congressional districts, including a new district for North Texas that included parts of Dallas, Tarrant, and Collin Counties. We had created two seats, one in South Texas and one in the Houston area, designed to elect a Hispanic. We had also preserved the seats of Congressmen Frost, John Bryant, and Pete Geren. We had drawn districts that received preclearance from the Justice Department.

District Thirty had been created. The original compact district that I had proposed was gone and a new district had been developed, one whose shape reflected the collision of the incumbents' concerns with the competing commitment of a district with a 50 percent African American population. The district lines had been drawn to include their residences, causing unusual bulges in boundary lines, which created an irregular, sprawling district that would be vulnerable to legal attacks.

Of course, there were critics who suggested that I had carved out a congressional seat for myself. When I was elected to the Senate, I had no intention of running for a higher office. I believed that issues that concerned my constituents, such as housing, business opportunities, education, health care, and judicial reform, were best addressed on the state level. I had lived in Washington and was not particularly fond of that city. When the redistricting process began, it still was not my intention to go to Washington. During the subcommittee process, my focus was always on being fair to all parties. At the same time, I was cognizant of the historic underrepresentation of minorities. It was time for that to change. After all, African Americans are taxpaying citizens and deserved to be treated fairly.

I was very proud of what we accomplished as a legislature. There were many white members who supported our arguments for the new districts. Many of them knew that, if necessary, I was prepared to go to federal court to make my claim that minorities in Texas were underrepresented in Congress. And I did defend our map in federal court, testifying in *Terrazas v. Slagle*.[30] There would be lawsuits about the district challenging our map all the way to the Supreme Court. Ultimately, accommodating the interests of the incumbents in the context of our commitment to a majority African American district minority had caused an irregular, meandering district that would be rejected by the Supreme Court.[31]

The day that Governor Richards signed the bill, I knew that great leaders such as NAACP organizer Antonio Maceo Smith, who had died in 1977, were smiling down on our state from heaven. The day that they had fought for had finally arrived. That evening when I returned my home, before I made a single phone call, I fell to my knees and thanked God for allowing me to participate in this momentous event. I had been used as a vessel. I was humbled and eternally grateful.

Chapter 12

District Thirty's First Congressional Representative

During the redistricting process, there had been intense pressure and support for me to declare my candidacy for the congressional seat. I made it clear to all who asked that I would consider making a run, but that I would not make a formal announcement until I learned the sentiment of voters in the district. They were the people who would make the final decision.

Those who urged me to run said that they wanted someone who could go to Washington and not be intimidated. They spoke about my testimony in federal court concerning racism in Dallas city government, my unwillingness to compromise simply because others seemed too powerful. They wanted a fighter, someone they could trust. I was that person, they said. There were phone calls from members of the Texas congressional delegation, elected officials in Dallas and Fort Worth, members of the clergy and the business community, community leaders, and many others. The *Dallas Morning News* wrote, "Eddie Bernice Johnson was instrumental in winning a monumental victory for Dallas blacks when she got the legislature to finally agree to a 50 percent minority district in Dallas County."[1] I was "tough, true and unswervingly devoted to [my] principles, . . . one of the Legislature's strongest supporters of fair treatment for minorities and women."[2]

In October of 1991, from the flag room of Dallas City Hall, I became the first candidate to officially announce for the race. A historic candidacy, it would be a partnership between voters and someone who had served their interests, I said.

It was rumored that State Representative Fred Blair and Dallas County Commissioner John Wiley Price would enter the race, but they didn't. Instead, Dallas businessman and former Dallas planning commissioner Adolph Hauntz opposed me in the Democratic primary. He was most known for his work with the Dallas Merchants and Concessionaires Association and its work on zoning issues impacting liquor store owners. The *Fort Worth Star-Telegram* endorsed me for the Democratic primary, writing that while I had received mixed reviews from other publications, it was endorsing me "on the basis of long legislative experience, acquaintance within both the Dallas African-American community and the business community and her commitment to pursuing economic development and job training for areas facing inner-city blight."[3] Hauntz's candidacy did not pose much of a challenge as I won with nearly 93 percent of the vote.

In the general election, I faced Republican nominee Lucy Cain. A former Democrat who had recently switched to the Republican Party, the *Fort Worth Star-Telegram* had dubbed her the "Republican sacrificial lamb."[4] I heard that Cain had said that she hoped that the fact that she was also a Black woman would have a disconcerting psychological effect on me. I never understood this strategy and I doubted that it would make a difference. And it didn't. I used the strategy that had been successful in my state races, focusing on voter registration drives, frequent fundraisers, and get-out-the-vote activities. I won with 72 percent of the vote, becoming the first African American from North Texas and the first nurse to serve in Congress.

My good friend Bill Clinton was the presidential candidate, heading the Democratic slate. I had known Bill from our work together on the McGovern campaign. When he ran for governor in Arkansas, at his request I campaigned for him. During that gubernatorial race, I had met and become very friendly with his mother, Daisy, because both of us were nurses. When Clinton came to Texas for his presidential campaign, I accompanied him on some of his appearances. We went to East Texas, where I watched him mesmerize and inspire the audience. Even though he lost the state, Clinton did carry East Texas.

Election night was pure jubilation. The campaign had been like a movement, including people of all colors and faiths. While I was delighted, I was also very humbled because I could not lose sight of the fact that there was lots of work to do.

The weeks prior to my official swearing-in ceremony in Washington were hectic. I had to figure out where to live. Because I'd lived in DC before, I generally knew some areas. But the House sent out a list of apartment buildings that were recommended to facilitate finding housing. I was fortunate to decide upon the second apartment that I saw. It would be my DC home for four years.

I also had to set up a district office. It was a new district and had never had an office before. I looked at the boundaries of the district, north to Plano, west to Fort Worth, all of downtown Dallas. I knew that I wanted the office to be accessible to constituents from all of the diverse sections of the district. Most importantly, it had to have free, convenient parking. I finally decided upon the Uptown/McKinney Avenue area. In fact, I would office in this part of Dallas for over seventeen years.

But a district office is more than physical space. It is the people who staff that office, who represent you when you're away, who make the district office work. I knew that I needed personnel to cover several areas. I needed someone to do outreach, to learn the programs and projects that were providing services that could help my constituents, to represent me at community events and hearings so that I could have information about goings on. I needed a case worker to help people who came to my office seeking assistance, veterans needing help with benefits, seniors on Social Security who ran into issues, and people with housing or utility needs. The case manager would be tasked with identifying resources for individuals seeking our assistance. I also needed someone to be the program planner, to arrange town halls for constituent meetings when I was home. The planner would be responsible for identifying any special presentations or information-gathering sessions that might be needed so that I always had my constituents' input on critical issues. Being accessible to my constituents, being knowledgeable about their concerns and issues, and staying connected to my district would be central to any work that I would do as a congresswoman.

Fortunately, I had had the foresight to set up a blind trust after I won the primary, anticipating that I would win over the Republican candidate. At the advice of my counsel, my business interests had been transferred to the blind trust. This arrangement would prevent any conflicts of interest as I would not be involved in any of the business decisions. Instituting the blind trust was certainly fortuitous and wise, especially as I was ultimately appointed to the Public Works and Transportation Committee. But as I was preparing to be sworn in, it was good to know that the blind trust was something that had already been addressed.

In addition to planning for the swearing in, I had to attend a two-week orientation for incoming members of Congress. There were 110 new members of the House, the most since 1948, comprising almost 25 percent of the body. The first session was held in DC after which we traveled by bus to the Kennedy School at Harvard University.

It was a very profound and detailed orientation with much attention given to the procedural rules of the House and the ethical standards to which representatives had to adhere. We had workshops and sessions with cabinet members from different administrations and congressional leaders. I met Madeline Albright and Susan Rice when they made presentations on foreign relations. But the nuts and bolts were also addressed, such as the administrative offices that make Congress run. Details like mail rooms and the use of the franking privileges were covered because we'd be sending out hundreds of mailings a day.

Office assignments were also part of going to Congress. There are three buildings used for House offices: Longworth, Rayburn, and Cannon. The offices are assigned to incoming members by a lottery system. I pulled number 320 out of 435. I was assigned an office in the Longworth Building, where I would remain for eighteen years.

The most significant challenge that I faced in establishing my office was to identify staffers. A couple of my staffers from Texas accompanied me to DC, but the environment and setting was so different that they eventually decided to return to Texas. While there were many who were experienced in working in federal agencies, there were markedly few people with experience in working with elected officials. There were especially few minority staffers. Staffers also assist with tracking the bills that are being introduced, reviewing daily update sheets of who has filed a bill and what the bill covers. Having people around you who are knowledgeable and experienced was important for many reasons, especially for the management of the budget. Oftentimes, people skilled in the financial aspects of the congressional office will work with more than one member.

As we approached my swearing in, hundreds of people made plans to travel there with me. Dallas Democrats chartered a jet to facilitate the attendance of friends and supporters. I was excited that so many would be present but especially pleased that my family was able to attend. I was especially proud that Kirk and my two grandsons, Kirk II and David, then four and two, would be with me.

When I got the chance to catch my breath and pause, it did not seem real. I could not believe that it was happening. It had been a long time since that first trip from Waco to South Bend to begin my studies to become a nurse.

At noon, on Tuesday, January 5, 1993, I gathered with over one hundred newly elected members and three hundred returning congresspersons for the convening of the 103rd Congress. It was a joyous yet solemn occasion— joyous because children and grandchildren were on the House floor and other family members were in the gallery (there was gesturing and waving between the members and the gallery, generally a forbidden action) and solemn because the proceedings incorporated the traditions that honor the constitutional mandate to convene Congress. Precedent established the order of events. The clerk of the House officially called us to order. The chaplain's prayer challenged us to be worthy of this "high calling," mindful of the opportunities that we would have to do acts of justice and deeds of compassion.[5] Everyone in the chamber, elected officials and family members, then rose for the Pledge of Allegiance. Then came the moment that I would for the first time record my presence as a representative elect.

With representatives marked as present, a quorum was announced and the Speaker of the House, Tom Foley, was elected. It was the first time in twelve years that Democrats held both the White House and Congress.

Robert Michel, the Republican minority leader, acknowledged that the new class of representatives was a commitment to renewal, a pledge to reform, and a promise of hope for the House. Michel called upon the entire House— all leadership and all members—to do their best to restore American peoples' confidence in their legislative branch.[6] As a freshman congresswoman, I was pleased to hear his words committing to working together.

Speaker Foley also remarked that this was the largest freshmen class since World War II. To him it was a signal that the American people were impatient with Congress. There hadn't been action on the deficit, economic system, health care, educational opportunity, infrastructure, crime, or drugs. This gave us, he said, a great challenge and a great opportunity.[7] And with that call to action, the oath of office was administered to the members. I rose, raised my right hand, and swore to support and defend the Constitution of the United States. With those words, I was sworn in as the first congressional representative from District Thirty in Texas. I was a member of the 103rd Congress.

My two grandsons, Kirk and David, were with me on the floor of the House, sitting next to Cardiss Collins. It was important to me that they be by my side because my motivation has always been trying to make things better for the next generation. They embodied all the people who would be impacted by my work.

There were two other administrations of the oath of office that day. The next one was organized by the CBC. Third Circuit Court of Appeals judge A. Leon Higginbotham Jr., a well-respected jurist and civil rights activist, administered the oath. This administration of the oath was particularly poignant to me because it stood as a symbol of the struggles for equality, the battles for voting rights, and the determination of African Americans to fully participate in this nation.

The final swearing in took place that afternoon with the members of the Texas delegation. At that time the dean of the delegation, Rep. Jack Brooks of Beaumont, administered the oath. Although I had taken oaths as an elected state official and appointed federal official, this one was different. I knew that it was history making. North Texas had never had an African American voice in Congress before. I felt the responsibility, but I also felt the honor and privilege of service.

Chapter 13

My First Decade as a Congresswoman (1992–2002)

My Beginning

Once the elation of being sworn in had passed, it was time to settle down to work. It is often difficult to fully describe the work of a congressman. We are appointed to committees and subcommittees that consider legislation, conduct hearings, and oversee investigations. We work with various federal agencies in connection with our committee assignments but also in relation to the needs of our constituents. We sponsor legislation that may or may not relate to our committee assignments. We reach out to our colleagues, seeking their support of various bills, negotiating wording and concerns to secure their vote. Because we can vote on every bill that comes before the House, we must read and study all proposed legislation to be able to exercise our best judgment in deciding how to vote.

A natural resource for me in the transition to serving in the House was the CBC. I had worked with several members during my days with the Carter administration. I sought advice from Congressmen Bill Clay, Louis Stokes, Charlie Rangel, and Julian Dixon. I also benefited from my friendships with Alma Rangel, whom I knew through Alpha Kappa Alpha sorority and the LINKS; Jeanette "Jay" Stokes, whom I met through Jack and Jill, Inc.; and Cardiss Collins, whom I knew from my Washington days.

As the weeks passed, it seemed to me that the inclusion of new members into the CBC was complicated due to geographical and generational differences. Many of the new members were from the South and had agendas that they wanted to immediately prioritize. It was as if they expected the senior members of the caucus to abandon either their approach or their concerns to accommodate the newly elected members.

My way of working with people was different. To me it was important to learn from those who had been on the front line in the House promoting the caucus agenda. The senior members of the CBC were from other parts of the country and had been identifying and addressing issues and problems for years. So I sat down with them, listening and eager to learn—an approach that was respected and appreciated by my senior colleagues.

But things weren't always smooth and easy. As a new member of the CBC, I was told by our chairman to remain silent during our first meeting in the White House with the president. During that visit, President Clinton addressed me directly, asking, "Eddie Bernice, what do you think about that particular policy?" Of course, I was not going to remain silent, and I gave him my very best answer.

Many of the people in the meeting were unaware that President Clinton and I had known each other for decades. They did not know that we had campaigned together for George McGovern or that I had gone to Arkansas to help with his gubernatorial campaign. They didn't know that I had taken Candidate Clinton to East Texas as part of his presidential campaign. They did not know of the friendship and the mutual respect that we held, and so they were surprised when President Clinton addressed me directly, soliciting my opinion.

The chairman, obviously shocked, confronted me outside the White House. He urged me to be more circumspect in meetings with the president. I told him in no uncertain terms that I was going to speak my mind whenever I thought it was necessary, and that ended that. I had stood my ground in fighting vicious racists in the South and I wasn't going to stop standing my ground. I let the chairman know that I would fight him, too, if he wanted to engage me in battle.

Ironically, by standing up for myself, I showed that even though I believed in getting along, I also wasn't going to be pushed around. I did know when to be firm. My approach and demeanor were respected by members of the CBC, as demonstrated by my election and appointment as CBC whip within my first term in Congress. My next term I would serve as secretary, ultimately becoming the chair of the caucus in 2002, during my second decade in Congress.

Getting Committee Assignments

I had strongly wanted to become a member of either the Ways and Means or the Energy and Commerce Committees because those two were the panels that would consider national health care, something that I believed our nation desperately needed. The insurance companies were running the health care industry. Unless one was employed by a major company, it was nearly impossible to get comprehensive and affordable health care coverage. Even the hospitals were being dictated to by insurance companies.

I quickly discovered that my preferences were very difficult committee assignments for first-term members to obtain. California congressman George Brown, a fierce proponent of voting rights for minorities and a member of Congress since 1963, wrote me a letter inviting me to join the Committee on Science, Space, and Technology. Congressman Jack Brooks, the most senior member of the Texas delegation, encouraged that committee membership. The chairman told me that he was looking for innovative people with new ideas. He said that much of the nation's future revolved around science, particularly space exploration and research. The Dallas–Fort Worth area was home to defense contractors that would be on the forefront of technological advances. I didn't foresee at that time just how much this committee assignment would position me to guide decisions that would positively impact North Texas.

Lobbyists and leaders from Texas urged me to join the Public Works and Transportation Committee. The anticipated North Texas population growth would require federal funding for roads, highways, rapid transit, high speed rail, and infrastructure. They said that I was needed as an advocate for our highways and interstate roads.

Both DFW Airport and Love Field were in my congressional district. The chief executive officers of two major airlines, American and Southwest, joined the chorus of those who contacted me, urging that I join the Transportation Committee. They argued that my voice would be crucial to the growth of commercial aviation in Texas and beyond. They pointed to areas of the country that had experienced significant job growth and business development. Transportation was crucial to that growth, they said. I had tremendous respect for all of those who urged me to consider the seat and decided to take the assignment on the Transportation Committee.

These opportunities compelled me to do my best to represent my district. The reading materials required to serve well on the committee were voluminous. There were committee reports, legislative proposals, reports from municipalities in my district, industry publications, and demographic analyses. There were questions that I had to be able to answer, such as, How do floodplains work? How do you project population growth patterns to predict highway needs? How do you make public transportation attractive to communities that are so accustomed to single-vehicle travel? What strategies can I use to bring differing sides together? What is needed to make certain our airports can handle future travel demands? I had to develop an understanding of the industry operations to know the concerns and considerations, ask the necessary questions, approach the proper officials and experts, and get the information to develop answers and formulate plans. There was always something to learn or strategize. I was determined to be one of the best freshman members, especially on the committee, and to help North Texas meet its transportation needs, even if it meant that I did not get to go to sleep until two or three in the morning.

The breadth of issues brought before these committees required a steep learning curve. From building major urban airports to assessing whether defibrillators should be required on airplanes, providing grant authorizations for states using a .08 percent blood alcohol limit for intoxication standards, authorizing war risk insurance for commercial airlines ferrying troops in connection with war efforts, highway development, and water aquifers, the Transportation Committee addresses all of those issues. Appropriation of funds and prioritization of programs were critical components of our responsibilities.

Similarly, the Science, Space, and Technology Committee is responsible for wide-ranging concerns, especially with the technology advances of the past decades. With origins dating back to the Sputnik era, it oversees all energy research, development, and demonstration; astronautic research and development, including resources, personnel, equipment, and facilities; civil aviation; environmental research and development; marine research; and commercial application of energy and scientific technology. We work closely with the National Aeronautics and Space Administration (NASA), National Weather Service, National Science Foundation (NSF), National Institute of Sciences, National Institute of Standards and Technology, and the National Space Council. We oversee environmental, marine, civil aviation, and federal nonmilitary research and development, science scholarships, and other activities relating to scientific research and technology development. I served on this committee throughout my tenure in office. My years of service ultimately positioned me to serve as the ranking member and chairman.

Being on these committees allowed me to be a part of the amazing growth and changes of the past three decades, but it all began with these initial appointments. Other members choose to switch between committees. I chose to stay on these committees, a decision that allowed me to earn seniority and leadership status and to make a meaningful impact.

My First Legislative Initiatives

Two of my first legislative initiatives focused on honoring the work of African Americans from North Dallas who had made a difference in our country. I introduced a bill to waive the time limits to allow the posthumous award of the Congressional Medal of Honor to Doris Miller. I remembered the pride we had felt in learning of his heroism and walking with my father to gather money to purchase a gift, and the joy in meeting him. I knew that he deserved the Medal of Honor, a belief held by the more than sixty members who supported the bill as cosponsors. The bill was referred to the Department of Defense for comment.

I reintroduced the bill again in subsequent terms. Each time, the bill was referred to the Department of Defense, the House Committee on Armed Services, and/or the House Subcommittee on Military Personnel. Each time, the bill did not progress out of committee. During these years a great deal of research was done. I was told that shortly after World War II, when Miller was first considered for the Congressional Medal of Honor, the secretary of the navy under President Roosevelt reportedly said, "Don't give that nigger that award" because he thought that it would tear up the navy—words that would bind future considerations.

A destroyer, a supercarrier, and the Veterans Affairs Medical Facility in Waco have been named after him. He has been included in the Distinguished Sailors postal stamp collection. In 2020, for the last time, I introduced a bill to waive the statute of limitations, expressly noting that fifteen sailors had been awarded that honor for similar actions during the Pearl Harbor attack, none of whom were African Americans. And, again, the bill did not pass. The inability to get the Congressional Medal of Honor for Doris Miller is one of my greatest disappointments of my years in Congress.

The other bill was to designate one of the federal buildings in Dallas the A. Maceo Smith Federal Building. I knew that Smith's work with the NAACP and his fight for civil rights had impacted Dallas. He was deserving of this honor. This bill passed easily and was signed into law on February 16, 1994.

I joined the late representative John Lewis in his sponsorship of H.R. 877 authorizing the establishment of the National African American Museum within the Smithsonian Institute.[1] I noted with pride that the bill was first introduced by my good friend the late representative Mickey Leland. As I said on the floor, this museum would be a tribute to him. It would also honor and recognize the often-overlooked contributions of African Americans to our country. It would gain visibility as an important segment of the Smithsonian Institution and would document the many accomplishments of leaders such as the great humanitarian Mother Hale, Ida B. Wells, Harriet Tubman, Langston Hughes, and Thurgood Marshall.[2]

The bill's findings recognized the deficiency in the presentation and preservation of African American art, literature, history, and culture.

It recognized the inadequate attention to the experiences of African Americans in slavery, in freedom, and in the continued struggle to be treated with human dignity and achieve full recognition as citizens. This museum would address those inadequacies by housing exhibits, supporting scholarship, and promoting educational programs. This bill passed the House, but it would be ten years before the Senate acted favorably on the legislation. President George W. Bush signed the bill on December 16, 2003, bringing about the creation of the National Museum of African American History and Culture.[3]

Also in recognition of influential African Americans, during this session I cosponsored the King Holiday and Service Act of 1994. This legislation provided authorizations for the Martin Luther King Jr. Federal Holiday Commission and encouraged inclusion of service activities in the celebration of Dr. King's life. It became law on August 23, 1994.[4]

I also signed as a cosponsor of a joint resolution to authorize the Alpha Phi Alpha Fraternity to establish a memorial to Dr. Martin Luther King Jr. in the District of Columbia.[5] All fundraising and expenses were to be borne by the fraternity. The next term Congress passed the Omnibus Parks and Public Lands Management Act of 1996, which included the authorization for the creation of the King memorial in Washington, DC, by the fraternity.[6]

South Africa's transition from apartheid to democracy continued to be important to me. I was a cosponsor for the South African Democratic Transition Support Act of 1993.[7] This bill repealed the antiapartheid sanctions that had helped bring about reforms and had facilitated the establishment of a nonracial government. Sanctions were replaced with assistance focusing on capacity building and supporting activities to promote human rights, democratization, and a civil society.

In my first term, I sponsored or cosponsored almost four hundred bills and resolutions that were referred to various subcommittees. Reflecting my interest in health, I supported the Breast and Cervical Cancer Information Act of 1993,[8] the Women's Midlife Health Resources Act, the Osteoporosis Risk Reduction Act of 1994,[9] the Mammography Access Tax Credit Act of 1993,[10] the Equal Access to Annual Mammography Screening Act of 1993,[11]

the Medicaid Mammography Coverage Act of 1993,[12] the Freedom of
Choice Act of 1993,[13] the Federal Prohibition of Female Genital Mutilation
Act of 1993,[14] the Access to Obstetric Care Act of 1993,[15] the Lupus
Research Amendments of 1993,[16] the Comprehensive HIV Prevention Act
of 1993,[17] the Reproductive Health Equity Act,[18] and the Ryan White CARE
Reauthorization Act of 1994,[19] among many others.

An important bill that I cosponsored was the Family and Medical Leave
Act of 1993. This bill, which was signed and became law on February 5, 1993,
requires employers to provide eligible employees with unpaid, job-protected
leave for up to twelve weeks for personal or family needs. If health insurance
is provided, it must be continued during the leave period.[20] This legislation
has enabled tens of millions of employees to attend to children and family
without loss of their insurance.

Issues relating to women and children were also a priority for me.
I cosponsored the Violence Against Women Act[21] and the National Domestic
Violence Hotline Act of 1993.[22] Both of these acts were ultimately included
within the Violent Crime Control and Law Enforcement Act of 1994. The Child
Abuse Accountability Act, which I also cosponsored, passed that session,
permitting the garnishment of federal employee's annuities for payment of
damages to victims of emotional, sexual, or physical child abuse.[23]

I was focused on transportation and traditional infrastructure, but
I always recognized that economic issues were also a pressing concern.
That is why I became a cosponsor with then representative Bernie Sanders
for the Jobs and Investment Act of 1994.[24] This bill proposed increased
funding for physical capital investment in highways and mass transit,
airports and railroads, and water and sewage treatment facilities. Dallas was
facing extreme challenges with its interstate highway system, especially the
I-35/I-30 exchange known as the "mixmaster" that was used by nearly a
half million commuters each workday. However, at the time there were
incomplete access ramps, which required drivers to exit and use city streets
to enter the highway. The city of Dallas in its Thoroughfare Plan had
specifically identified a need to provide direct connections between I-30
West and I-35E (south).[25] Expanding these funding opportunities would
position Dallas to seek federal funding assistance for this project. But this

bill also extended to capital investment for job training and educational programs. It sought to provide community economic empowerment by making credit and credit-related services available to low-income families not adequately served by traditional lending institutions. The legislation was referred to committee but did not advance.

Issues pertaining to civil rights were always important to me. I had lived under segregation and had experienced the challenge of breaking racial barriers. I was determined that these advances would not be compromised and that we could continue marching toward equality. That commitment drew me to be a cosponsor of the Civil Rights Procedures Protection Act of 1994.[26] This bill sought to remove mandatory arbitration to unlawful employment claims based upon discrimination. It was referred to two House committees and two House subcommittees but did not advance.

As a legislator I knew that it was important to introduce bills even though they might not pass. Doing so brings attention to the issues and educates members to the need and rationale for the action. Even if there would not be enough votes to pass the bill, I always believed that it was my responsibility to keep the concerns before the House.

NAFTA: The Battle for Free Trade

Without a doubt one of the most significant votes of my first year in Congress was in support of the North American Free Trade Agreement (NAFTA). The original agreement had been signed by President George H. W. Bush in December of 1992, just a month before he left office. However, Congress had not yet ratified the agreement.

NAFTA was designed to combine Canada, Mexico, and the United States into a single economic market consisting of nearly 400 million people, making it, at that time, the largest trading bloc in the world. Barriers on goods, services, and commercial investments between the three countries would be eliminated. There were protections for intellectual property, copyrights, patents, and trade secrets.

But there were concerns about NAFTA's impact. There were fears that NAFTA would negatively impact American workers because companies would relocate to Mexico to take advantage of lower labor costs. In fact Ross Perot, a Dallas business executive whom I knew, had campaigned against NAFTA when he was an independent presidential candidate. He predicted that there would be a "giant sucking sound" as United States companies fled to Mexico.[27] There were also predictions that wages in the United States would become depressed as industries competed against a Mexican work force.

President Clinton addressed those fears and concerns. During the campaign he told voters that he would back it only if it included additional provisions that protected both the environment and organized labor. Trade Ambassador Mickey Kantor, who had managed President Clinton's bid for the White House, was charged with renegotiating labor and environmental agreements with Mexico and Canada to make the agreement more palatable to members of Congress with strong ties to labor and environmental interests. In August 1993 Kantor informed the president that he had successfully reached side agreements with Mexico concerning enforcement of labor and environmental laws. Limitations on agricultural imports and the creation of a North American Development Bank designed to assist Hispanic American farmers living in border states were also added.

On November 4, 1993, the North American Free Trade Agreement Implementation Act was introduced into the House by the powerful chair of the House Ways and Means Committee, Dan Rostenkowski.[28] Texas had always benefited from trade between Mexico and the United States. Business leaders in the state argued that NAFTA would increase growth and would raise the importance of the Texas transportation system, highways, and railroads. I believed that these were highly important issues that had to be considered. If the majority of the trade between Mexico and Texas was transported on Texas highways, that could only benefit our state's economy.

Passage in the Senate was considered likely. It was in the House where the measure appeared to be in trouble. Good people were on both sides of the issue, as was often the case. Most of those supporting NAFTA were Republicans, as business interests overwhelmingly favored the agreement. Much of organized labor was opposed to NAFTA. Their position was that American companies would abandon our country and relocate south of the border. Labor had always been a vigorous supporter of Democratic positions, but they were at odds with the president on NAFTA. The president dispatched key members of his administration to explain the benefits of NAFTA to members of Congress who had not reached a position. Among those who represented the president were Vice President Al Gore and Treasury Secretary Lloyd Bentsen, a Texan.

Another step taken by the president was to name former Chicago mayor William Daley chairman of the administration's task force on NAFTA. Daley had strong connections with labor and was well respected in Washington. At the press conference announcing Daley's appointment, the president said that he believed that the agreement would create a brighter future for the American worker, American industry, and the American economy.

Placing Daley in charge of the NAFTA campaign was one of the wisest moves that the president made. Daley, whose father, Richard J. Daley, had been mayor of Chicago, was an anchor of a midwestern political dynasty. Daley proved to be the consummate politician. He knew how to work with people, treating them fairly and listening to their concerns. He understood how to navigate sensitive political issues. He knew how to explain an issue and talk with people. He traveled the country, including my district, making presentations at town halls. He helped with a White House ceremony that featured three former presidents, Carter, Ford, and Bush. Daley provided what the administration needed—a point person to explain the reasons that NAFTA was in the country's interest.

Perot continued his opposition to NAFTA. He purchased television time that disparaged the agreement. He said that the American economy would experience insecurity if the measure was implemented. He was instrumental in the creation of United We Stand, an organization that encouraged volunteers to phone congressional offices to vent their outrage about NAFTA. They were joined by union members, environmentalists, and human rights activists.

I knew Ross Perot. He came to see me at my DC office. We spoke about NAFTA and shared our differences. He said that he did not intend to pressure me into opposing the law, but that he wanted me to be aware of his concerns.

Many in the business community saw the advantages of NAFTA. Jim Robinson, the CEO of American Express, urged members of the powerful Business Roundtable, an organization of CEOs of leading companies, to back the agreement. It placed advertisements in major newspapers. Its members were encouraged to visit their representatives, to make phone calls and write letters. Legislators who had received campaign contributions were specifically targeted.[29] Environmentalists, usually a reliable ally of Democrats, were also against NAFTA. They argued that because Mexico did not have strident antipollution standards in place, it would become a haven for companies that wanted to escape US environmental standards.

There were marked differences in the House. Torn between their proclivities toward free trade and job losses in this country, there were many Democratic members who wished that the president would put aside his interest in the free trade agreement. They were not persuaded when the president said that while he was governor of Arkansas there were similar dire predictions that some companies would close and relocate, and just as these dire predictions had come to nothing, he did not believe that NAFTA would result in droves of American companies leaving.

The principal opponent in the House was Majority Whip David Bonier from Michigan. He believed that members of the CBC, progressive Democrats, and first-term members would readily join him in the fight against NAFTA. He approached me and suggested that I vote against it. Labor unions were very influential in Michigan, and Bonier could not risk going against them. He also pursued Democrats from states with large agricultural interests, such as Florida and California, suggesting that farmers in their states would lose business to Mexican farmers if NAFTA became law. Minority Whip Newt Gingrich was charged with galvanizing Republican votes in the House for NAFTA. Gingrich told the president and Daley that he had 120 Republican votes, and that their side would have to produce 100 votes to ratify the agreement.

On the Senate side, New Jersey senator Bill Bradley was the most outspoken proponent of NAFTA. He encouraged his fellow senators to lobby members of the House to vote for the agreement and personally made phone calls to House members. The former presidents also lobbied members of the House. I received phone calls from the White House. I also received many phone calls from powerful members of the business community in my district urging me to vote for NAFTA, saying that it would help our local economy, produce jobs, and stimulate economic activity in Texas.

The final blow struck against the anti-NAFTA forces came during a nationally televised debate between Vice President Gore and Perot. They debated on the *Larry King Live* program just eight days before the House vote.[30] Perot performed poorly. The broadcast was a clear victory for the administration.

I was convinced that NAFTA was in the best long-term economic interests of the country. I had spent nine months researching and investigating the bill. I talked to constituents, labor representatives, small business owners, large business representatives and environmentalists. I was repeatedly told that NAFTA would create jobs.[31] I knew that agricultural interests in Texas, particularly in the southern portion of the state, would benefit from the elimination of the high Mexican tariffs on their products that made it virtually impossible for them to compete with Mexican farmers. The free trade agreement was a win for my state.

The House debate began on November 17, 1993. It lasted nearly eleven hours. When the final vote was taken, 234 members had voted for the measure and 200 had voted against it. I was one of 102 Democrats who joined 132 Republicans to pass the agreement. The Senate vote of 61 to 38 took place on November 21.[32]

President Clinton and his aides had built a broad coalition across party lines in order to pass NAFTA. He had not been in office a complete year, but he demonstrated that he knew how to negotiate and garner support. He wrote to me shortly after the NAFTA vote and, as always, began his letter with, "Dear Eddie Bernice." While he was acknowledging my support of the agreement, he knew that I understood that he would have to work hard to win back the support of the labor unions. Sometimes in politics making the right decision is not popular, but elected officials must base their votes on what they determine is in the best interests of their district. The Clinton presidency had, in my mind, started out with great promise and accomplishment. The successful ratification of NAFTA reflected President Clinton's skill as a negotiator and communicator. It also confirmed his understanding of the role of the United States in a global economy. The passion, intellect, and optimism that I had recognized more than twenty years earlier were now being shared with the world.

Because of the work that we had done together since working on the McGovern campaign and the mutual respect that we had built, I was a frequent guest at the White House during state dinners and other occasions. I traveled with the president to Africa and to other parts of the world. He solicited my opinion and support regarding trade policy issues with China, Africa, Europe, and South America. Aware of my background in nursing, he wanted to know my opinion regarding national health care insurance.

President Clinton truly believed in working with all elected officials. He valued bipartisanship, but he was not afraid to tackle the issues that impacted the lives of the majority of the American people. It was a time of low unemployment, low inflation, dropping crime rates, and high home ownership. Not only did he balance the budget, but a budget surplus was achieved. The lives of the citizens were his focus as he pursued legislation impacting education, medical leave, crime, and environmental protection.

There were several controversial bills that were considered by the 103rd Congress. One bill that was approved and signed into law by President Clinton was the Violent Crime Control and Law Enforcement Act. This bill tasked various federal agencies with a role in addressing crime in this country.

Violent Crime Control and Law Enforcement Act of 1994

The early 1990s had seen an increase in the crime rate. A growing percentage of Americans were afraid to walk at night. Gangs were rampant. There was a crime wave, especially in communities of color. States had enacted laws imposing mandatory minimum sentences and "three strike" laws. Use of drugs, especially crack cocaine, had devastated communities. The Violent Crime Control and Law Enforcement Act of 1994 proposed a "stick and carrot" approach. There were punitive measures, such as extending the death penalty to more federal crimes, including drug crimes; increasing sentences; and supporting life imprisonment for a third felony offense. And it banned assault-type weapons.

But it also used a carrot approach, providing funding and grants for state development of programs. It created the Violence Against Women Act, focusing on victims of domestic violence and providing funding for battered women's shelters and assistance to victims of sexual assault. There were grant opportunities for rape prevention and education projects. It called for a competitive grants program to establish a national domestic abuse hotline. The statute withheld grant money from states unless they created registries of sexually violent offenders and prosecuted those convicted of such offenses who failed to register. It also advanced victim input by allowing victims to speak at sentencing hearings.

Funding was allocated for after-school, weekend, and summer programs for at-risk youth. These programs included both in-school and after-school programs. Monies were authorized for local entities to stimulate business and employment opportunities for low-income, unemployed, and underemployed individuals. There was a competitive grant program for organizations to provide residential services to youth who had dropped out of school or who were involved in the juvenile justice system. There was also funding for recreational facilities and services for at-risk youth.

Other measures focused upon law enforcement. Grants were provided for state programs to upgrade criminal history records and support community policing initiatives; increase DNA identification capacity and competitive funding to support continued education of police officers; and support the creation of drug courts to provide supervision and specialized services for offenders with potential for rehabilitation. Funds were also allocated for prison drug treatment programs and for the construction of correctional facilities. The law allowed state agencies to seek funding for construction of boot camps, alternatives to incarceration, and for prison construction designed to incarcerate violent offenders.

I believed at the time, and do even now, that this comprehensive approach was needed to address the impact of crime on our nation. The majority of the members of the CBC voted in favor of the bill. African American pastors signed a letter urging passage of the bill. African American elected officials, including mayors, applauded the approach taken by the bill.

Since the passage of the Crime Control Act, many of the positive advances that we now take for granted, such as victim input at sentencing, drug courts, DNA identification, and the focus on violence against women, have become integral parts of our criminal justice system. But there has also been a most regrettable consequence of this statute: mass incarceration. The grant incentives enabled states to build correctional facilities, boot camps, and alternative facilities but also resulted in the construction of more prisons. States eagerly sought those funds because such institutions often provide a major source of employment, especially in areas of lower population. This prison construction boom dramatically increased rates of incarceration because the prisons had to be filled. With increased penalties, states extended prison terms and grew the prison population, disproportionately impacting people of color and fueling racial disparity within the criminal justice system.

Was the resulting overincarceration a failure inherent in the statute or in the implementation of the programs? What if there had been more construction of boot camps, lower-security facilities, and the development of alternatives to incarceration instead of traditional prisons? Would there still have been the same problem of overincarceration? What if states had brought the innovation captured in approaches such as drug courts and programs for at-risk youth to the development of other, similar programs? Why did the focus on the preventative and rehabilitative approaches get lost in increased sentences and expanded offenses?

The Violent Crime Control and Law Enforcement Act of 1994, passed in the context of the rising crime rates, was a considered effort to address the problem. But we need to ask the questions that, when answered, can help us to move forward with an approach to criminal justice that strengthens the focus on prevention and rehabilitation.

Such a focus on rehabilitation presented itself in the 2018 FIRST STEP Act (Formerly Incarcerated Reenter Society Transformed Safely Transitioning Every Person Act). The debate around that statute recognized that over 90 percent of all inmates are released. As I said on the floor, we had to improve the reintegration of incarcerated individuals into their communities and reduce recidivism. The statute made improvements to the criminal justice system, allowing more discretion in sentencing, limiting mandatory sentencing minimums, and providing federal inmates the opportunity to earn federal time credit for participation in rehabilitation programming. It had taken almost fifteen years, but Congress was finally focused on taking steps to encouraging rehabilitation programming in prisons.

Health Security Act

Health care reform was another central focus for President Clinton and one that had been a large part of his campaign. A task force with First Lady Hillary Clinton as the chair was established early in his administration. It was intended to create a plan for a comprehensive health care system. An interdepartmental working group was also created to gather information and formulate ideas to be presented to the task force.

As a former nurse, I was obviously very aware of and concerned about health care in this country. During my time with HEW, I had seen health care costs rise and the hardship that this caused people. I knew that our health care system was broken for many of our citizens. Parkland Hospital, the public hospital in Dallas, was serving the majority of the uninsured patients in my district. We needed to find a way to provide health care to people who could not afford the rising costs of medical assistance.

Anticipating Republican opposition, President Clinton gave an address to a joint session of Congress about his vision for health care reform on September 22, 1993. He spoke of the work that the task force had done and the thousands of interviews that had been conducted with citizens, doctors, nurses, pharmacists, insurance company representatives, hospital administrators, and business representatives. He called upon Congress to pass a system of universal, comprehensive health care. As I listened to the president that evening, I knew that what he was saying about our health care system was correct. It was broken and Congress needed to fix it.

I signed as a cosponsor of H.R. 3600, the Health Security Act, when it was introduced on November 20, 1993. This legislation was designed to ensure individual and family health care by containing the rate of growth of health care costs, promoting responsible health insurance practices, and promoting choice in health care. The fact that it was over a thousand pages symbolized the complexity of the issues that were being addressed.

As a former hospital nurse, I was one of the few health care professionals in the Congress. Because of my experience, I was appointed to serve on a special ad hoc subcommittee that conducted information-gathering meetings and hearings to support the task force.

The need for universal health care was easily demonstrated, especially the devastating impact of hospital costs upon middle-class families. But there was strong Republican opposition to a comprehensive health care reform bill, joined by health care organizations and the health insurance industry. The appointment of First Lady Hillary Clinton to chair the task force troubled many, even Democrats. While the position of First Lady does not have any written job description, many believed that it should not include the power or influence of a task force chairman.

Despite repeated versions, many amendments, voluminous testimony, and many supporters, the Health Security Act could never garner sufficient approval to bring it to a vote. On September 26, 1994, the bill was declared dead after failed efforts at compromise.

The CBC had actively supported health care reform. Studies had concluded that African Americans and other minorities were disproportionately affected by the health inequalities that existed in our country. Some of the most pressing health care challenges such as diabetes, obesity, cancer, infant mortality, mental illness, and heart disease were at epidemic levels in underserved communities. Minorities and poor whites were more likely to be uninsured than most Americans. Our citizens, including children, were dying from preventable diseases, and we knew that access to proper health care could save many of them. We were determined to continue to press the issue of universal health insurance, making it an item of extreme importance in the national debate.

Although the failure to pass the Health Security Act was disappointing because it could have positively impacted so many Americans, the focus had been put on the health care industry. Over the years there would be repeated efforts to pass health care reform, until finally under the Obama administration we passed the Affordable Care Act. The success of that day more than made up for this earlier disappointment.

Time for Reelection: It Happens Every Two Years

It seems that during every congressional election there are calls for term limits, advancing arguments that elected officials should only be able to serve a defined number of terms. I've always believed that voters had the opportunity to limit a member's terms every two years. If the constituents are dissatisfied with the representative's service, they support and elect another candidate. It is the Constitution's mechanism for limiting the number of terms a person serves in Congress.

There were many bills that I introduced or cosponsored that did not get passed into law. Those bills involved issues that were of concern to my constituents and needed a national focus. But you have to be able to gain enough votes to pass a bill. While you appeal to common interests and shared concerns to garner the necessary votes, having a good relationship allows for meaningful dialogue.

Although I had come of age in the segregated South and had been forced to pay a poll tax the first time that I voted, I never judged or disliked people because of the color of their skin. I view the world as a grand mosaic in which God made many people with various backgrounds and different beliefs and value systems. To me the world would have been a rather boring place if everyone was and thought the same.

I try to understand the origins of a person's actions. From my perspective the Texas state official who called me a "nigger woman" did not hate me; he didn't know me. He simply could not understand me and my experiences. In an odd way, I felt sorry for him. He was a victim of the shallow cocoon in which he lived and that had framed his life. Interestingly, he and I became somewhat friendly as he struggled to understand my concerns and adapt to the changing realities that confronted him. In fact, he made a personal visit to my office to tell me that he had decided to retire from state government.

From my very first involvement in public life, I have included all types of people in my universe. I embraced those who held ideas and beliefs similar to mine as well as those whose beliefs I considered extreme. I welcomed those who spoke languages I did not understand and whose cultural practices were foreign to me.

I have always lived under constraints. I was a woman and a racial minority in a society dominated by white men. During my first year in Congress, I was the only woman in the Texas delegation. I knew that reaching out to others was necessary if I wanted to accomplish things for those I represented.

Some people go to Congress thinking that they were sent there only to represent voters in their districts. In my mind this is a narrow way of looking at government. I believe that those of us sent to Washington to represent our constituents have a larger responsibility. We are sent to represent the interests of all people in the United States.

Some members never try to get to know others. They sit in committee rooms where the real work of the body is done and never get to know more than the names of their colleagues. This unfamiliarity with others is one of the reasons that Congress has become such a partisan entity. Being a member of Congress is an opportunity to learn about others, not simply through congressional niceties but rather through the building of relationships with people from various backgrounds, cultures, and communities. To build those relationships I have actively aligned myself with caucuses, joining the CBC when I first arrived in Congress.

During my first term, I reached out to Representatives Norman Mineta of California and Patsy Mink of Hawaii to encourage the creation of a caucus that addressed issues that affected Americans of Asian and Pacific Island ancestry. My district included significant populations of immigrants, including Koreans, Taiwanese, Pakistanis, Turks, and East Indians. Belonging to such a caucus would help me to better represent them. Another organization that I joined my first year in Congress was the Congressional Caucus for Women's Issues. Comprised of Republican and Democratic members committed to issues such as equal pay, tougher child support laws, and equal educational opportunities for younger women, its support was crucial to the passage of such legislation as the Violence Against Women Act, the Family and Medical Leave Act, the Women's Business Ownership Act, the Child Support Enforcement Act, and the Pregnancy Discrimination Act.

Over the years I joined many other caucuses addressing issues important to my constituency: the Homelessness Caucus, the LGBT Equality Caucus, the Military Mental Health Caucus, the Caucus on Foster Youth, the Caucus on Urban Regional Studies, the Progressive Caucus, the Voting Rights Caucus, the Mental Health Caucus, the Semiconductor Caucus, and the High Speed and Intercity Passenger Rail Caucus. Other caucus memberships revolved around relations with other countries. But all of the caucuses shared a common role: they provided opportunities to collaborate with other members of the House.

Working with those across the aisle is critical to being able to get things done for the people who elected me to serve them. To do that you have to win friends, get them to believe in you, and gain their support. People were more likely to agree or negotiate with those whom they liked, rather than those they held in contempt.

For most of my years, I have served in a Republican-majority House. For only four of my fifteen terms in office was there a Democratic Speaker of the House. To get anything accomplished required support of Republican members. In my early years, working with Republican members of the Texas delegation yielded supportive relationships. Congressman Tom Delay and I had worked together when we were in the Texas Legislature, a connection that remained strong as he served as the House majority leader from 2003 to 2005. We often talked during the weekly Texas Congressional Delegation meetings. He provided advice and support that proved crucial in securing funding for many of my transportation projects. Despite political differences, particularly around redistricting, he was there for me when I needed him. I never hesitated to call him a friend.

Another Republican North Texas colleague, Joe Barton, and I worked on a number of projects together. During my early days in Congress, I sought his support on bills that I sponsored. When the Dallas Cowboys were building their new stadium in Arlington, Congressman Barton and I worked together with the team's owner, Jerry Jones, on infrastructure and flooding issues.

One of my very special friends on the other side of the aisle was Congressman Ralph Hall, the dean of the Texas delegation, first elected to Congress in 1980. A former member of the Texas Legislature, Congressman Hall was a Democrat but later became a Republican. I was the first member of Congress to phone him when he announced that he was switching parties. I told him that his decision would not affect our working and professional relationship and that nothing had changed except party labels. When he chaired the House Committee on Science, Space, and Technology, I was the ranking Democrat. We worked to add jobs at the Johnson Space Center in Houston. For two years we sat next to each other during committee meetings and often participated in congressional hearings in various parts of the country. We were able to get things done that were critical to the country's needs.

Sometimes, though, reaching across the aisle was futile, even within the Texas delegation. For example, Congressman Lamar Smith from San Antonio, onetime chairman of the Science, Space, and Technology Committee, went out of his way to make things difficult for those who did not share his political beliefs. A member of the House since 1987, Congressman Smith and I confronted each other on just about every issue that came before our committee. My worst personal experience in Congress was trying to work with him. After several attempts to work with him, I understood my colleagues' warnings that he was difficult. There wasn't even simple collegiality. When we found ourselves on the same airplane, there would be total silence between us.

Our differences reached the proverbial boiling point in late 2015 when he was the chair of the Committee on Science, Space, and Technology and I was the ranking member. We had made three written requests to the National Oceanic and Atmospheric Administration (NOAA) for information relating to a peer-reviewed study about climate change. NOAA had responded and identified publicly available locations where the information could be accessed. Chairman Smith never articulated a legitimate need for additional documentation. But he unilaterally issued a subpoena to the NOAA administrator compelling the production of all documents and communications between employees and scientists relating to the climate change studies. This subpoena was designed to harass climate scientists as part of an effort to support climate change deniers. Just two years earlier, Chairman Smith had used a similar tactic to access health studies to provide the tobacco industry ammunition to attack research about the harmful effects of cigarette smoking. He had also forced the NSF to provide sensitive details on research grants. These requests were never tied to any allegation of misconduct or fraud.

It was sickeningly clear to me that he was abusing his power as chair of this committee to attack the nation's premier research scientists. I wrote him a letter as ranking member strongly asserting that his actions were bringing disrepute to the committee and the leaders who had come before him. While I and the other Democratic members stood ready to work on legitimate matters of oversight, we would not be complicit in the illegitimate harassment of our nation's research scientists.

While I always tried to reach across the aisle, there has not always been a spirit of bipartisanship. The Contract with America orchestrated by Newt Gingrich and Dick Armey was introduced to the public just a few weeks before the 1994 midterm congressional elections. With this rallying cry and the election of a Republican majority in the House and the Senate for the first time in forty years, the atmosphere in the House changed. They advanced their agenda of money for defense and tax cuts for corporations and the wealthy with an air of self-righteousness and smugness that now hung over Congress and infected negotiations and debates.

I had always been able to at least have respectful dialogue and had never refused to work with someone simply because they were a member of the opposite party. But sometimes refusal to reach across the aisle becomes a tactic, in effect a weapon in a dangerous game of chicken. That was the tactic used by Republicans in pushing the so-called Contract with America in 1995. As I said then during a debate that threatened the shutdown of government unless there were cuts in Medicare, Medicaid, and educational spending, "It is not fair. It is not right. It is not according to anyone's procedure. It is heavy-handed. It is insulting and it is ignoring the wishes of the American people." The seeds of divisiveness and acrimony that were planted and nurtured during the intervening years gave rise to Donald Trump.

But getting reelected is not solely dependent upon the bipartisan work done in Washington. Your constituents have to know that you are working on their behalf. You need to be accessible to them and need to assist them with problems, provide information about federal programs that might be beneficial. My district office was the front line of access for my constituents. I've been fortunate to have hard-working, dedicated staffers who understood the importance of giving service. But it isn't enough to have others working on your behalf; you must establish your own presence. The people whose vote I needed for reelection needed to know me, to see me walking in the grocery store, living in their community.

I came home almost every weekend. On Saturdays there were frequently events to which I'd been invited or town halls that I convened. Sundays were usually church services and yet other activities. And there was family to see; my mother and sister lived nearby while Kirk and his wife had moved to Austin. Maintaining relationships in Texas was as important as building bridges in Congress.

Haiti

One of the crises that confronted the Clinton administration from its beginning was Haiti. It also marked my first entrée into foreign issues as a congresswoman.

In 1990 Father Jean-Bertrand Aristide, a Catholic priest, won 67 percent of the popular vote, becoming the country's first democratically elected president. But a coup in September 1991 led by the military and elite families overthrew his government. The French and American ambassadors were able to negotiate Aristide's exile. Within days of his departure, President George H. W. Bush issued an executive order freezing Haitian government assets in the United States. A few weeks later, he imposed a trade embargo excepting food and humanitarian supplies.

But the coup led thousands of Haitian refugees to flee their country, taking to boats that were barely seaworthy to reach the Florida coasts. Keeping with procedures established under the Reagan administration, the US Coast Guard intercepted the boats and took the Haitians to the Guantanamo Naval facility located in Cuba. Initially, the Bush administration did not consider the increase in Haitian refugees to be a problem because it anticipated that the de facto regime would soon collapse.

But that was a miscalculation. The regime did not collapse. Haitian migration continued to increase. A Supreme Court ruling allowed the involuntary return of Haitians to the island. In the House a bill called the Haitian Refugee Protection Act of 1992 was introduced, barring the involuntary return of any Haitians. The bill passed in the House but was never approved by the Senate. With the increased influx of Haitian refugees, President Bush signed another executive order providing for the direct repatriation of any Haitian refugees. This policy remained in place through the remainder of the Bush administration, leaving it for the Clinton administration to handle.

Throughout Bush's mishandling of the Haiti crisis, members of the CBC had been critical, arguing that the United States should have been able to find other countries willing to accept the refugees. New York congressman Major Owens, whose district included the largest number of Haitian residents in the United States outside of Miami, demanded that our government restore Aristide to his presidency. Congressman Owens regularly appeared on the floor of the House to advocate for Haitian democracy and to push President Clinton for tougher action to restore President Aristide to power.

The caucus developed eleven steps that should be taken, including a trade embargo except for food and medicine, stopping all air travel to Haiti, freezing military leaders' assets, and sending a multinational force to the Dominican Republic. How could we promote freedom around the world when a vicious military coup had derailed a democratically elected government in our own backyard? We brought this argument to members of the Clinton administration.

Not every member of the CBC backed President Aristide's government, but Representatives John Conyers, Charlie Rangel, Corinne Brown, Major Owens, Maxine Waters, Carrie Meek, Donald Payne, and I were unrelenting in pressuring the Clinton administration to do the right thing. Eventually, the State Department arranged talks in New York between President Aristide and leaders of the coup. Several of us attended a meeting with members of the military government. It was clear to me that they were interested in lining their pockets with the country's wealth. They seemed to have little interest in improving the lives of the average Haitian citizen.

In July 1993 a weeklong meeting produced the Governors Island Accord, which specified the terms for Aristide's return to the presidency. But by October 1993, the return had not materialized. New sanctions were imposed. Ultimately, the United Nations adopted a resolution authorizing a multinational force under United States leadership to return Aristide to the presidency. With that resolution in September 1994, President Clinton authorized the use of military forces. Simultaneously, he sent former president Jimmy Carter, former chairman of the Joint Chiefs of Staff General Colin Powell, and Senator Sam Nunn to negotiate an agreement. President Clinton also appointed former congressman William Gray as a special envoy to Haiti and accepted former president Jimmy Carter's offer of involvement as a special negotiator. The possible deployment of a force of twenty thousand US soldiers and the participation of these negotiators caused the military junta to relinquish power, and a government aligned with President Aristide was installed.

After serving one year of his remaining term, President Aristide was succeeded by one of his associates, President Preval. Later, after being elected to a second term, President Aristide was forced to leave the country after being abandoned by the George W. Bush administration and opposed by elements of Haiti's military elite. The CBC met with President Bush, who said that he could not protect Aristide's life. President Aristide fled Haiti aboard an American plane and eventually relocated to South Africa.

African Growth and Opportunity Act, Title 1 of the Trade and Development Act of 2000

For decades the United States' policy to African nations had focused on development assistance based on a donor-recipient relationship. The African Growth and Opportunity Act (AGOA) developed a trade relationship that was a more genuine partnership and stimulated African economic development. The act provides duty-free access to thousands of products. To get these trade benefits, a country had to be making progress toward a market-based economy, a functioning and fair judicial system, the protection of workers' rights, the elimination of government corruption, and the observance of the rule of law. The bill passed on a bipartisan basis. Establishing this trading relationship has produced jobs for the United States and the African nations. Because the statute included a time limit, it had to be extended to continue. The last extension will expire in 2025.

US relations with African nations has always been a concern of mine. Since the passage of the AGOA, I have been involved with strengthening trade and other economic ties with African nations. In 2007 I traveled as a member of a CBC delegation to Ghana. When President Obama traveled to Kenya to visit his ancestral homeland, I was privileged to accompany him. In addition to the personal reason for the trip, we also had meetings with government representatives to address opportunities for economic relationships between the countries. There is such opportunity and mutual benefit in strengthening ties and trade with those countries.

Serving on the Committee on Science

When I arrived in Congress, I was assigned to the Committee on Science. At the time I was not familiar with the multitude of topics and concerns that would come before this committee. Perhaps more than any other House committee, Science, Space, and Technology encounters the rapidly changing landscape impacted by research, invention, and discovery. The chair of the committee often sets the priorities and the committee's focus.

That first session we held meetings focusing on the federal role in civilian research and development while emphasizing the importance of science as a national issue. Our nation's economic advances are rooted in the transfer of technology from the laboratory to the private sector for commercialization. Collaboration between the federal laboratories and private industry is needed for our economic growth.

After the 1994 election and the Republican majority in the House, the number of subcommittees was reduced to four—Basic Research, Energy and Environment, Space and Aeronautics, and Technology—ostensibly to increase efficiency and reduce expenses.[33] Even though my focus was always my district and North Texas, our committee addressed concerns affecting the entire nation, and indeed, the world. During my first years of service, we were involved in legislation relating to safe drinking water, federal aviation operations and technologies, hydrogen research as a potential energy source, metric conversion, and aquatic nuisance research. One of the bills that I cosponsored was the Antarctic Science, Tourism, and Conservation Act of 1996. This bill, signed by President Clinton in October 1995, addressed protocols for federal scientific investigation and tourism in Antarctica.[34] It reaffirmed the government's commitment to conservation of Antarctica.

The Science Committee addressed the development of methodologies for risk assessment of health, safety, and environmental concerns to be used to assist agencies and governmental decision-makers to make cost/benefit analyses. We also reviewed the National Sea Grant College Program Act and funding for the International Space Station. Programs managed by the Office of Research and Development for the Environmental Protection Agency were also reviewed, as funding had not been provided for years. We studied the absence of comprehensive authorizations for NOAA projects and Department of Energy civilian research. We looked at funding for the United States Fire Administration for work with state and local fire departments; the NSF's strategic plan for upgrading major research facilities and equipment, such as telescopes; and NASA's operations. We reviewed requests relating to the National Institute of Standards and Technology to promote technological innovation. We had eighty-three bills referred to us for consideration covering a broad range of activities.[35]

The Committee on Science regularly makes proposals about funding the NSF. As the only federal agency with the sole mission to support basic science and engineering research and education, the NSF is the largest source of federal funding for research and education in all science, mathematics, engineering, and technology disciplines. It helps to prepare future generations of scientists, mathematicians, and engineers.

The National Science Foundation Authorization Act of 1998[36] provided a focus on NSF research projects, including tornado forecasting, atomic lasers, and nanotechnology. There were important research facility construction projects, including facility needs for the US Antarctic Program, replacement of the South Pole Station, the new Polar Cap Observatory, and detectors for the Large Hadron Collider. It included educational initiatives promoting partnerships with educational institutions to provide opportunities for development of math and science teachers. The bipartisan support acknowledged that NSF helps to discover the new knowledge that fuels our technological innovation, which in turn fuels our economic strength.

Also in 1998 I proposed the Information Technology Partnership Act,[37] which I viewed to be a complement to the National Science Foundation Authorization Act of 1998. This bill called for the NSF to award grants to five eligible local educational agencies under the Urban Systemic Initiative to develop a technology program to build or expand mathematics, science, and information technology curriculum. The grants would also fund the purchase of equipment and provide teacher training to implement the curriculum. The educational institutions would be required to obtain private sector services and funds to purchase equipment.

Unless someone works in the science or engineering fields, the breadth and importance of the work done by the NSF may not be known. We frequently see and use the benefits of research that it funds and oversees without realizing it. Internet advances are an example. NSF supported researchers who developed the first web browser. That development linked millions of computers and users but those increases made the connections move slower. NSF supported research that expanded understanding of networking and new platform development.

Serving on the Science Committee, you have to develop an awareness and understanding of these research projects so that you can work to ensure the necessary support and funding for the projects to continue. Obviously, we don't become experts or research scientists, but we must develop a working knowledge and determine what questions to ask, what information to get, and trust the opinions that we are being given. We are always mindful of the interrelationship between scientific advances and technology with our economic strength.

One example was the Commercial Space Act of 1998,[38] dubbed a "revolutionary piece of legislation opening up space for commercial use."[39] This act targeted improving legal and regulatory framework for commercial space. Among other things it authorized a market study of the progress in commercialization of the International Space Station. Another example is the Next Generation Internet Research Act of 1998, created to support research and development to expand capacity and capabilities of internet.[40] The nation needed cutting-edge research on networking hardware and software technologies. This statute, in a very real way, helped to shape our future.

The committee also introduced legislation to create a Commission on the Advancement of Women and Minorities in Science, Engineering, and Technology Act.[41] The commission was to determine why women are underrepresented in the high-tech workforce, examine successful practices, and provide Congress with a list of recommendations for encouraging women to pursue careers in science and engineering. Although the term of this commission has now expired, its 2000 landmark report *Land of Plenty: Diversity as America's Competitive Edge in Science, Engineer, and Technology*[42] concluded what I had been advocating: unless the science, engineering, and technology (SET) fields became more representative of the general US workforce, the nation would suffer severe shortages, impacting our economy. The report called for a major shift in education, addressing the barriers limiting women, underrepresented minorities, and persons with disabilities from SET fields. The report warned that while lack of diversity was an old problem, there was a new urgency.

Shortly after this report came out in April of 2001, I sponsored the National Science Foundation Authorization Act. By this time I was ranking member of the Subcommittee on Basic Research. The legislation authorized increased funding for the NSF, which had been significantly underfunded. Disciplines such as nanotechnology were emerging. It was critical that our scientific community lead the way on such new areas. In addition to increasing the budget of the NSF, the legislation also provided grants to strengthen scientific research at HBCUs. Disproportionately low funding had been a persistent problem. This provision was very important to the CBC, as many of our members had attended HBCUs.

Shortly after I introduced that bill, I spoke on the floor in support of a resolution that I had cosponsored, Honoring the National Science Foundation for 50 Years of Service.[43] I used that opportunity to talk about the importance of providing adequate funding for the NSF. If we wanted to celebrate the foundation's achievements, we needed to provide the resources to continue that good work. I pointed out that NSF programs were critical to science education at a time when we were experiencing manpower shortage in many high technology fields. Honoring past accomplishments was fine, but it was of much greater importance that we ensure that the foundation receive the resources to carry out its essential role in in support of scientific engineering research and education.[44]

The Science Committee continued to identify legislative areas to assist underserved populations. For example, the Small Business Technology Transfer Program Reauthorization Act of 2001 required Small Business Administration officials to consider programs to address services being provided to women- and minority-owned businesses.[45]

In December 2002 Congress passed the National Science Foundation Authorization Act of 2002, which authorized almost $38 billion in appropriations for fiscal years 2003 through 2007.[46] This law recognized that our country's economic strength, national security, and quality of life are grounded in our scientific and technological capabilities. At the time I was the ranking member of the House Science Research Subcommittee and had been deeply involved in the drafting of this act, which included provisions directly incorporating a bill that I had earlier introduced, the Mathematics and Science Proficiency Partnership Act of 2001.[47] That bill sought a demonstration program to build or expand mathematics, science, and information technology curricula. With the support of private entities such as Texas Instruments, a focus was to be placed on achieving proficiency in mathematics and technology to assure American competitiveness.

The 2002 National Science Foundation Authorization Act also included the text of another bill I had worked on, the Regional Plant Genome and Gene Research Expression Act, which supported merit-based grants for crop research.[48] That legislation established research grants on crops that can be grown in the developing world to address hunger, malnutrition, and disease. An important feature of that authorization required US scientists to partner with scientists in developing nations to stimulate ideas and develop the scientific capacities of those nations.

The 2002 Authorization Act also contained provisions that authorized appropriations to substantially increase the budget for the NSF and provisions to help secondary schools leverage private-sector funds for math, science, and engineering scholarships. The act also instructed the NSF director to encourage inclusion of HBCUs, Hispanic serving institutions, tribally controlled colleges and universities, Alaska Native–serving institutions, and Native Hawaiian–serving institutions in funded research partnerships.

There is a certain amount of expectation and faith when supporting scientific initiatives. We can't always predict the exact impact of research. But it is elementary that we must provide resources for research if we want to enjoy the benefits and successes of that research, even though we may not be able to define the benefits at the time of the research. For example, two research projects funded in 2002 laid the foundation for the COVID-19 vaccines. It would not have been possible to predict the importance of that research in addressing a pandemic almost twenty years later. But how fortunate we are that the funding had been provided.

Approaching the End of My First Ten Years in Office

As I approached the end of my first ten years in office, there were three major events that will stay with me the rest of my life: the end of Bill Clinton's presidential term, my election as chair of the CBC, and the terrorist attacks of September 11, 2001.

President Bill Clinton, My Friend

On a very cold winter night in 2000, there were approximately thirty of us at Camp David, the presidential retreat on a hillside in Maryland. The president began the evening by telling us how much he appreciated our support and that he would never forget how we stood with him and his family. Then, to my great surprise, he turned to me and began to talk about the many years that we had known one another, the closeness that we had developed, and how much he respected me as a legislator and as a friend. I could not allow his comments to go without response. I told him that I deeply appreciated his friendship. I expressed that his leadership was exemplary and that the American people were grateful for all that he had done for the nation. This was a very special moment for me because I was the only person whom he recognized for such acknowledgement and tribute. It was a moment that I will never forget and will carry with me until my very last breath.

While listening to the president talk that evening about his family's plans after leaving Washington, I thought of seeing him on a street in Little Rock in 1979 when I told him that I was proud that he had been elected attorney general of Arkansas. I predicted that he could one day become a great president. He would have my support, I said, because I knew that he would be a good leader for our country. On that day my words were not simply pleasantries for a friend. They were exactly what I believed.

After working closely with him for eight years while he served as president, I realized that my prediction had come true. Bill Clinton, despite being targeted by partisan attacks, had served this country well.

From the beginning of Clinton's candidacy, there were those who seemed to make it their duty to bring the president down. His detractors alleged that as governor of Arkansas he gave political favors to banking interests in return for financial gain. Those allegations were repeated and fueled until there was a call by Congressman Newt Gingrich for the appointment of a special prosecutor to investigate Whitewater, a failed real estate investment dating back to 1979.

The independent prosecutor, Ken Starr, unable to find evidence of any wrongdoing related to the Whitewater real estate deal, expanded his investigation into allegations of sexual harassment made by Paula Jones. Sometime after, Monica Lewinsky, a White House intern, alleged that she had an inappropriate personal relationship with the president. At the time of Lewinsky's allegations, many individuals associated with the Clintons had been dragged into court or targeted by the Whitewater investigation. Starr's insistent expansion of the scope of his investigation had an appearance of being politically motivated. With Lewinsky's allegations shocking the Washington political establishment, there were questions of whether she had been planted in the White House by the president's enemies to create a situation that would lead to the destruction of his administration, marriage, and legacy. There had been such viciousness in the partisan attacks against President Clinton that even I had to question whether this situation had been orchestrated.

After four years of his investigation, Starr had not been able to put together a case against President Clinton on Whitewater or any of the other areas he had investigated. But he convened a grand jury to examine President Clinton's answers in a deposition that he had given in the Jones case—an answer that revolved around his relationship with Lewinsky.

The president's ultimate admission that he had an inappropriate relationship with Lewinsky shocked and upset his wife and their daughter, Chelsea. To me the alleged conduct did not rise to the level of a "high crime" to warrant impeachment and should not have been the subject of the independent investigator. Most Democrats in the House voted against the articles of impeachment. I viewed the proceedings as a targeted personal assault against President Clinton and an attack on our nation's democratic principles.

It was difficult for friends and admirers of the Clintons to watch the profound toll that the Lewinsky affair and the impeachment proceedings had on their marriage. At one point First Lady Clinton visited with me and other members of the CBC. It was obvious that she was personally exhausted and wounded. She shared that she still believed in her husband as her spouse and as president of our country. She thanked us for standing with President Clinton during a very bleak period in the life of their family. She knew us. She had worked with many of us. Our support and continued friendship was crucial support in their survival of this ordeal. She ended the meeting asking that we continue to keep the Clinton family in our prayers.

And I did keep the Clintons in my prayers. I knew that they would find the strength and courage to move on. I believed that throughout the entire ordeal President Clinton knew that my support of him and his administration was unwavering. He knew that he could count on me as a friend and as an advisor.

On that evening at Camp David, I remembered all of these things, grateful for the relationship that I had with Bill and Hillary. But most of all, I was proud because I knew that our country and the world were better because William Jefferson Clinton had served as president of the United States.

Chair of the Congressional Black Caucus

Appreciating the importance and value of the CBC, I had eagerly served the caucus in nearly every position except chair. Within my first term, I was serving as the whip. I had volunteered for the position, anticipating that it would allow me to meet all the members and for them to get to know me. It would also allow me to join in the leadership meetings, gaining an introduction to the CBC operations. I prepared weekly summaries of upcoming legislation, bill sponsors, and other such information. Preparing those summaries kept me very aware of what legislative initiatives were being considered. Tracking the votes of the CBC members on pending legislation solidified my understanding of the importance of identifying vote counts.

I also served two one-year terms heading the Annual Legislative Conference. This conference was the primary fundraising activity for the CBC Foundation. This weekend of activities and workshops drew people and businesses from across the country to Washington. Reaching out to North Texas companies that had never participated, I was able to raise more money than in the past and bring in new participants.

The contested 2000 presidential election reminded the nation of the importance of voting and fair elections. Now more than ever the voice of the CBC had to be heard. I had served as secretary and vice-chair. I had been integrally involved in the CBC for years. Serving as chair was a natural progression of the work that I had been doing. My experience and appreciation of the role of the CBC would allow me to serve the organization and the country well as chair.

Having made that decision, I started visiting with members to see if they would support my candidacy. I explained to my colleagues that there were five principal concerns that I intended to address if they elected me. The first was technology. I wanted to increase the number of minorities who had computers in their homes and students who had access to computers in their classrooms. Second was health care. As a nurse concerned with the physical and mental health of all citizens, I believed that our country should provide affordable health care coverage for all. Third was voting rights. The 2020 presidential election and the persistent efforts to deny the right to vote to minority citizens had to be addressed. Fourth was the District of Columbia. I wanted to pursue full citizenship for people who resided in the District of Columbia and work toward their right to have expanded representation in Congress, including two senators. Fifth was expansion of capital. I firmly believed that wealth generation was achieved through entrepreneurship. Minority and women business owners and entrepreneurs were severely hindered by the lack of access to capital. This platform received the endorsements of Charles Rangel of New York, Bobby Rush of Chicago, and Chakah Fattah of Pennsylvania, three of the more influential members of the caucus.

I counted the votes prior to the election and was comfortable that I would be elected. Because I'd been very active, I was getting commitments from colleagues. But then I was told that Congresswoman Maxine Waters was recruiting Congressman Bennie Thompson to seek the chairmanship. This was surprising to me as I regularly had breakfast with Thompson and Congressman Clyburn, then the chair of the CBC. Thompson had never shared any thoughts about seeking the position.

I asked Bennie if he was going to run. He told me that he had not decided yet, but later he did enter the race, apparently influenced by Waters's assurances that he could win. His agenda was the pursuit of economic development for cities and rural areas throughout the country, ending the Cuban embargo, and continuing to build bridges between the CBC and other progressive groups.

The race was competitive. California congressman Julian Dixon, hospitalized during the vote, sent his ballot by express mail from his hospital bed in Los Angeles. The vote was held on a Wednesday. Congressman Dixon died the following Friday. When the ballots were counted, I had won, although the actual vote count was not announced. Congressman Hilliard of Alabama then made a motion to have me elected by unanimous acclamation. It passed without dissent. I had been elected the seventeenth chair of the CBC.

My leadership team consisted of Congressman Elijah Cummings from Maryland as first vice-chair, Congresswoman Sheila Jackson Lee from Texas as second vice-chair, Congressman Bobby Rush from Illinois as secretary, and Congressman Gregory Meeks from New York as whip. I included my leadership team in every important activity or meeting. For instance, if a member of the administration wanted to meet with me, I included officers of the caucus in the meeting.

My vision as chair was that all Black members of the House should participate in the CBC, even if their political views were drastically divergent from those of the majority of the members. Because inclusion had always been important to me, I reached out to the only Republican African American in the House of Representatives, J. C. Watts. I invited him to a caucus meeting and he attended. Speaking to the members, he was passionate and emotional in his remarks. To my great surprise, two days later he issued a press release denouncing the caucus. I later learned that he had been instructed by House Republican leaders to keep his distance from us. We remained friendly and I shared with him my plans to protect programs that gave preference to minority businesses, something that he did assist me in doing.

The first major issue that I had to confront was the election of President George W. Bush. The overwhelming majority of our members were adults during the Civil Rights struggle and personally knew the struggle for equal voting rights. One of our members, Congressman John Lewis, had nearly been beaten to death on March 7, 1965, while leading a protest march for equal voting rights in Selma, Alabama. There were others in the caucus who had experienced voter inequality, paid poll taxes to vote, and had their right to vote challenged. Given our collective experiences, we had to comment on the Bush election results.

Hearings held in Florida by the NAACP after the election had documented numerous blatant violations of the Voting Rights Act. Minority voters had been removed from the voting rolls without their knowledge. Police intimidated voters in minority districts. Voting machines in several minority precincts were inoperable, denying those voters the ability to cast their ballots. Tens of thousands of lawfully registered voters had been turned away from the polls by Republican officials. Kathleen Harris, a senior Florida state official, had not added their names to the list of registered voters. Harris was also a member of Bush's Florida campaign committee. Governor Jeb Bush, the president's brother, had ordered state troopers to patrol polling places in minority districts. The cars of some voters were searched. People were intimidated. Ballot boxes from numerous African American precincts were not counted.

Over the years the caucus had become the "conscience" of Congress. We could not, and would not, be silent. We had to speak on the results of the election. On behalf of several African American representatives, we sent a letter to Vice President Gore clearly setting forth our opinion that the twenty-five Florida electoral votes should not be counted for Bush.[49]

When Vice President Gore called for objection to the certificate from Florida, I and other members of the caucus rose in opposition. Caucus members spoke for more than thirty minutes in protest to the Florida electoral votes. Speaking on behalf of the CBC, I objected to the twenty-five electoral votes. Because there were not any senators joining in this objection, the Florida electoral votes were accepted without further review. Members of the caucus walked out of the chamber in protest. As a body we wanted the world to know that we were outraged with the injustices and the denial of voting equality.

As chair of the CBC, I immediately led a press conference. Beginning by saying that I had marched for justice in the Civil Rights movement fully believing that I was protecting future generation's right to vote, I said that we could simply not ignore all of the complaints and issues of the 2000 presidential election. I pointed out that there was overwhelming evidence that Bush did not win the election either by national popular vote or the Florida popular vote. Supporters had engaged in official misconduct, deliberate fraud, and voter suppression to undermine minority voters. "We will ensure that there is no peace in the Congress until [Bush] reaches across party lines," I promised. "Millions of Americans have already expressed their public outrage at the injustices which occurred in the making of George W. Bush's mistaken victory," I stated. "The laws of this country provide for the objection which we herein make on behalf of freedom, justice, and democracy. We, members of the Congressional Black Caucus, therefore wholeheartedly object to the acceptance of the presidential electors from Florida."[50] The electors from Florida should have been rejected. Vice President Al Gore should have succeeded President Clinton.

We knew that there were some in Congress who believed our position to be radical. It didn't matter. The Supreme Court ruling blocking the continued vote recount had incensed the caucus members from Florida who had worked diligently to register minority voters, sponsored unprecedented voter rallies, and worked closely with faith-based institutions to register new voters. That denial of a recount awarded Florida's twenty-five electoral votes to

Bush, giving him 271 electoral votes, only one vote more than the required 270 electoral votes.

Even as we walked out in protest of his election, we understood we would have to work with the new president. But we wanted President Bush to know that the tactics used to secure his election had been uncovered. During a press conference outside of the chamber, I said, "Bush did not win this election by the national popular vote or the Florida popular vote. He should be on notice that without justice there will be no peace."[51]

To achieve our goals, I knew that the CBC had to reach out to the new administration, no matter how we felt about its legitimacy. We had to work closely with other members of the House and Senate; partner with our allies in the religious communities, labor unions, business communities, and civil rights organizations; and reach out to the newly inaugurated president, whose election we had contested. At our request we met with President Bush on January 31, just days after he had taken the oath of office. We wanted him to know the issues that the CBC was focusing on: election reform, education, civil rights enforcement, racial profiling, tax policies, Africa, and our heated opposition to former US senator John Ashcroft, the president's nominee for attorney general.

Prior to the meeting, President Bush phoned me personally to inquire about the issues that we would be raising. I had met him when he was one of the owners of the Texas Rangers baseball team. He had sought my support when he ran for governor, but I was solidly behind Ann Richards, the Democratic incumbent. In response to this inquiry, I told him that caucus members had a variety of issues and that he should listen carefully to them.

That day, most of the members of the CBC and I traveled to the White House to meet with President Bush. After we entered and got seated, the president welcomed us and thanked us for meeting with him. He acknowledged that he and I had worked together on several important projects while he was governor of Texas and I was a member of the state Senate. He was cordial, projecting himself as a fair and decent human being.

We began by telling the president that the American people expected Congress and the White House to work together. He had only received 9 percent of the African American vote. He would have to do more than hold press conferences and distribute funds to conservative Black churches to win support in the nation's Black community, we said. There were specific issues that were of extreme importance to minorities that he needed to address. He acknowledged our role and said that we were his "partners in government."

Voting rights was top on that list. Floridian caucus members had refused to attend the meeting due to discontent and mistrust of the Florida election results. The hard-fought campaign for voting rights had been undermined by the ballot issues in Florida. But President Bush couldn't see the connection between his election and the bitter, ongoing struggle for equal voting rights in the South.

We also shared our objections to his nominee for attorney general, John Ashcroft, a former senator who had lost reelection. We pointed out that the attorney general is to be the protector of civil rights and enforcer of laws protecting equal rights. But Ashcroft's record showed that he would not fairly enforce civil rights laws. As a senator he had been a fervent opponent of court-ordered busing to achieve racially balanced schools. He had opposed a Black Missouri Supreme Court justice's nomination for a federal judgeship, opposition that was significant because there was a distinct need for the president to name more people of color to the federal judiciary. Our insistent opposition to Ashcroft's nomination and call for more minority federal judges was politely heard, but that was all.

As the meeting progressed, we raised other issues, such as public education and the negative impact of budget recommendations upon the children on this nation. On every issue that we raised, President Bush politely acknowledged our concerns and assured us that he would consider our points.

As our meeting went past the allotted time, Vice President Dick Cheney had risen from his seat and started pacing. I attempted to bring the session to a close. But the president pointed out that we had not discussed one of our agenda items, Africa. We addressed the HIV/AIDS epidemic in Africa, and he said that he would place it on the list of issues that his administration would address. With that commitment our meeting ended.

Leaving the White House, I could see the looks of disgust on the faces of many of my colleagues. They knew that we had to work with a president whose agenda was vastly different from our own, a man who had surrounded himself with conservatives whose political positions were in direct contravention to those that we held. President Bush may have run as a "compassionate conservative," but he surrounded himself with men and women who were deeply conservative and hardly compassionate.

We knew that large numbers of minorities would be hurt by the spending cuts resulting from the tax cuts for wealthy Americans that he was proposing. The federal government under the Bush proposal would be hard-pressed to provide any significant assistance to the people who lived in inner cities or to those who existed on the margins of our society. Our meeting had only sharpened our awareness of what we had to do. We had to be prepared to confront the draconian policies that we were certain would come from the White House. We were somewhat certain that one of our principal policy objectives, universal health care for all Americans, would not find a sympathetic ear on Pennsylvania Avenue. But we realized that we had to push and fight if we wanted to see any of our objectives considered.

We composed a legislative agenda of eighteen topics that included health care, budget and taxation, redistricting, voting rights and election reform, science and technology, small business and capital access, criminal justice, trade policy, national defense, veterans affairs, and African policy. Each caucus member was assigned an area where he or she had special expertise or personal experience. Congressman Rangel was assigned to the policy group on budget and taxation. Congressman Conyers, a brilliant lawyer and a senior member on the House Judiciary Committee, was assigned to criminal justice. Congress- woman Christensen, a physician, was assigned to health care, and I was assigned to science and technology and redistricting. With the experiences of voter fraud in Florida, Congressmen Hastings and Meek, both from Florida, as well as Congressman Clyburn, were assigned to voting procedures and irregu- larities with an eye toward preventing the problems that had plagued the 2000 election. We established a working group of caucus members, also headed by Congressman Conyers, whose major function was to research and study issues related to the reauthorization of the Voting Rights Act.

As part of our strategy to advance our issues, we knew that it was critical to interact directly with members of the president's cabinet, so we arranged meetings with Secretary of State Colin Powell, Secretary of Labor Elaine Chao, Secretary of Health and Human Services Tommy Thompson, Secretary of Transportation Norman Mineta, Secretary of Education Roderick Paige, and other key members of the administration and White House staff. We wanted direct communication so that there could be no claim that they were not aware of our policy concerns and legislative objectives.

Within days of that meeting, in early February, we convened a budget and tax briefing with experts from the Center for Budget and Policy Priorities, a Washington-based financial think tank that researched and analyzed the impact of proposed federal and state budgets on low-income families. The session focused on the impact that the administration's proposed $1.6 trillion tax plan would have on the nation's domestic programs. Progressive economists who opposed the tax plan predicted that the nation's unemployment rate would increase, that the poverty rate would rise, and that more Americans would be pushed into poverty if the plan was approved.

Making every single vote count was one of the most significant legislative priorities of our caucus. A month after the inauguration, we held the first congressional election-reform hearing. We took a very close look at the Florida presidential election results, the mistreatment of registered voters, and the efforts by Florida officials to sway the election. Witnesses included leaders from organizations that represented racial minorities and members of Congress who represented the state of Florida. Members of Congress from the House and the Senate testified. Recommendations were developed for the prevention of the voter fraud and intimidation that had taken place during the Florida election. A second hearing was held sixty days later. Panelists included former members of the executive branch, members of Congress, state government officials, and election-reform experts. The hearings received significant press attention. We wanted to catch the attention of the occupants of 1600 Pennsylvania Avenue—for them to know that we were watching and that any attempt to deny fair elections in the future would be challenged in courtrooms and on the streets of our country. Making every vote count was an essential component of the tenets of an all-inclusive American agenda that the caucus introduced in the 107th Congress.

Health care reform continued to be a focus. We recognized it as a human rights issue. Disparities existed because our current system favored the affluent and neglected the vulnerable. Our country was the only one in the free world that did not have a health care system for its citizens, and we remained determined to change that. There were those who argued that universal health care was socialism. But we asked, What was socialist about a system in which babies were given a chance to survive infancy and American people with preventable diseases were given a chance to extend the length of their lives?

. Knowing that we had to keep the issue of health care reform on the nation's agenda, with Congresswoman Christensen using her medical training and expertise, we convened a Health Brain Summit in April of 2001. Using the theme Health Care Justice Now!, the summit began with a massive rally at the Capitol. It ended with a luncheon featuring US Surgeon General David Satcher, former president of Meharry Medical College, speaking about the health disparities in our system.[52]

Government support and engagement with minority-owned businesses was another targeted topic. We knew that small businesses were the backbone of our economy. Entrepreneurship was also the way to build wealth. Access to capital, small business loans, and opportunities for government contracts were all activities that could encourage the creation and development of minority-owned businesses. As a country we had experienced the longest economic expansion in the nation's history. The wealthy among us had prospered significantly. It was the job of the CBC to ensure that every citizen shared in this growth.

To identify potential government contract opportunities, we closely monitored the activities of various agencies. We met with agency representatives responsible for procurement. After the terrorist attacks in September of 2001, we held meetings with officials from the Defense Department, pressing for minority business owners to be included in their programs. These meetings proved successful as a number of minority-owned businesses were awarded contracts to repair infrastructure.

Part of our strategy to advance our issues was to collaborate with others. I had always believed that it was important to get to know the people with whom you worked. I thought that it was important that we connect with senators. We had weekly Tuesday morning meetings with the Senate leadership. During our meetings with members of the Senate, the first such gatherings in the history of the Congress, we discussed how the caucus and the Senate could work together. The discussions of issues were comprehensive. Topics included education, judicial nominations, election reform, taxation and budget policies, and campaign finance reform. These gatherings allowed caucus members to discover that some senators shared the same political beliefs that were important to them. The meetings allowed me to grow close to senators such as Tom Daschle, Chris Dodd, Ted Kennedy, and John Kerry. The relationships that developed through such formal and informal interaction made it easier to pick up the phone and call a Senate colleague for advice or to share information that helped with a policy issue.

I also believed that it was important to form alliances with members of Congress who represented other minority groups. Blacks and Hispanics had worked well together in the Texas Legislature, and this convinced me that we could accomplish more for the communities that we represented on the national level if we worked together.

The Congressional Hispanic Caucus was formed in 1976 by five Hispanic members, including two from Texas, Congressmen Kiki de La Garza and Henry B. Gonzalez. It was an advocacy group for the interests of Hispanic Americans. By 2001 the Hispanic Caucus had experienced significant growth. Their constituents also faced voting discrimination, and they were concerned about election reform. Another important issue to our Hispanic colleagues was immigration reform, something that we promised we would assist them in addressing. Programs that helped the nation's Hispanic communities would also be ravaged by the proposed Bush tax cuts. Hispanics were aligned with us to protect social programs that benefited minorities and poor people in rural and urban areas.

I also reached out to Asian Pacific American Caucus chair David Wu. The three caucuses had been working on various policies and initiatives relating to health issues, campaign finance and election reform, and immigration. It was time to come together formally and increase the impact of our combined members; the Congressional Tri-Caucus was born. With our collective membership of fifty-four, we constituted a potent congressional voting bloc.

The extension of the Voting Rights Act was important to the caucuses. Our efforts led to bipartisan legislation that authorized $3.9 billion dollars to reform the nation's outdated election system. It provided funds to eliminate antiquated voting machines, for the training of poll workers, for a centralized voter registration system, and for greater access to voting machines for disabled voters.

Whenever the issue of immigration reform came up, members of the Hispanic Caucus knew that they could count on the support of the CBC. When the Dream Act was voted on in the House, every single member of the CBC joined our Hispanic allies in supporting the legislation.

Even with strategic alliances, as progressive forces we had our work cut out for us in the 107th Congress. In the House of Representatives, the Republicans had a nine-vote majority. Congressman Dennis Hastert, a former schoolteacher from Illinois, was Speaker of the House. He was chosen as a compromise candidate, beating Congressmen Dick Armey and Tom Delay from Texas, both considered too divisive to lead such a closely divided House. Hastert, a moderate, generally well-liked by his colleagues, was a pleasant change from former House Speaker Newt Gingrich.

At the beginning of the session, the Senate was evenly divided between Democrats and Republicans. With the newly elected Vice President Dick Cheney casting the tiebreaking vote, Republican senators selected Trent Lott as their leader. But within four months, Vermont senator Jim Jeffords left the Republican Party to caucus with Democrats, giving us the majority in the Senate. Tom Daschle, a liberal from South Dakota, was then elevated to the post of Senate majority leader. This shift in Senate majority impacted our weekly meetings because it allowed a joint focus on mutual priorities.

In addition to promoting our own agenda, the caucus also had to address the administration's legislative proposals. One such example was the ill-conceived No Child Left Behind legislation. It required school districts to increase student test scores and issue annual report cards on student performance. One of the stated goals of the legislation was to encourage urban schools to raise standards by hiring "better teachers." The legislation was supposedly designed to improve student achievement, and it mandated punishment for schools that did not meet certain minimum testing standards. It relied upon artificial measurements without candidly addressing the impact of years of discrimination and underfunding.

Being the leader and spokesperson for experienced elected officials was sometimes challenging. But one of my most difficult and personally embarrassing moments resulted from the unfortunate CBC Foundation award of scholarships to my grandsons and great-nephews. The CBC Foundation had for years awarded scholarships to students. When the impropriety of that award was brought to my attention, the funds were immediately repaid by my trustee who handled all of my personal finances. All matters related to this situation were reviewed by the House Ethics Committee and fully resolved.

Going a step further, I expanded the CBC Foundation Scholarship Committee to make any subsequent awards related to my district. I was honored that Ms. Mavis Knight, member of the Texas State Board of Education; Randy Skinner, director of Greater Dallas Area Justice Revival; Dr. Roscoe Smith, Dallas Independent School District teacher and administrator; Raul Magdaleno, director of Diversity and Outreach for Southern Methodist University's Meadows School of the Arts; and Dr. Al Roberts, educator and professor emeritus of Paul Quinn College, agreed to serve on this inaugural committee.

I was passionate about my work with the CBC and all that we accomplished through this body. My approach reflected my basic belief that everyone should be given an opportunity to participate and to contribute their talents and skills to our work. My attitude earned me the support and cooperation from nearly every member of the caucus. My strongest supporters were Representatives Clyburn, Corrine Brown, Eleanor Holmes Norton, Charles Rangel, and the late Stephanie Tubbs Jones.

The caucus's strength comes from our view of ourselves as a cohesive body representing a larger family of American citizens. We know that we could not allow egos and personal difficulties to get in the way of accomplishing the people's business. That is why we are in Washington. That is why we pursue public service. That is why we work together.

September 11, 2001, Terrorist Attack

The other event that I will always remember as I approached the end of my first decade in Congress is the al-Qaeda terrorist attacks of September 11, 2001. Those attacks changed America forever.

I was at the Capitol in a breakfast meeting about small business. As I got up to leave, people were running down the hallway. Surprised, I asked what was going on. They yelled for me to go to the basement. I joined the people going to the basement. But once we got there, we were told to leave the building and go outside.

Once outside, I could see the fire at the Pentagon. The flames were reaching into the sky. As I stood there, looking, wondering what was going on, my cell phone rang. Roscoe Smith, my district director, was calling me from Dallas to see if I was safe. I didn't understand his question because I didn't know what was going on. He told me that two buildings had been hit in New York and the Pentagon. It was just unbelievable, but the flames that I was watching were so real.

Capitol police came up and told me to get off the premises. They advised me not to take my car and to just walk away. I walked to the congressional building because I needed to check on my staff. But Capitol police would not let me enter. They told me to just keep on walking.

And so I walked, eventually stopping at the Democratic National Committee building. Security was called, picked me up, and took me to the underground shelter. There were many members of Congress assembling. It was supposed to be a secret shelter, but when we turned the corner to drive into the building, I noticed that news media lined the sidewalk. We received a briefing on what was known at that time about the attacks. We were then encouraged to find a way home. I went back to the Capitol, got my car, and drove home without any problems.

Shortly after arriving home, I received a beeper message instructing me to return to the Capitol at 7:00 p.m. We met on the Capitol steps, Democrats and Republicans, to show the world that our nation and Congress was still strong. Standing in the front row, I joined in the singing of "God Bless America." Some of the captions on the photos of us from that evening would comment that for one day at least, Democrats and Republicans had come together.

September 11, 2001, obviously changed this nation. But just two days earlier, on a Sunday, I had returned to the United States from Durban, South Africa, where I served as coleader of the United States delegation to the World Conference against Racism in South Africa. This UN-sponsored conference was building upon the end of apartheid in South Africa to produce an international declaration recognizing and addressing the consequences of the trans-Atlantic slave trade, colonialism, and race.

At the conference there seemed to be an anger directed at our country. Confronting the consequences of centuries of racism and imperialism released suppressed resentment and bitterness. It wasn't spoken out loud, but it was something that you sensed in formal meetings and casual conversations. The United States was held responsible for the uncertainty, poverty, and misery in various parts of the world. The feelings were so intense that sometimes it seemed that some delegates even wished us harm.

Upon my return arrival in Dallas, I gave an address to a group of clergy members. I shared with them my experience in South Africa, telling them that I was highly concerned about the reputation and safety of our nation. I was troubled by the attitudes toward the United States that I had witnessed. Having returned to Washington, I was reminded of these thoughts and feelings when the attacks occurred on Tuesday.

I quickly learned that four passenger jets, two from United Airlines and two from Dallas-based American Airlines, had been hijacked by terrorists. Two planes were deliberately flown into the World Trade towers, symbols of American capitalism and economic power. The plane flown into the Pentagon was an attack on our military strength. But to me it was a complex that I had visited many times, coming to know many people who worked there. My thoughts and prayers immediately went to the victims and to our nation.

We later learned that the last plane, United Airlines Flight 93, crashed in a field in rural Pennsylvania. We were told that this plane was headed toward Washington, possibly the Capitol building. The passengers on that jet who decided to confront the terrorists very likely saved the lives of many legislators and staff that day, including me. The degree of disruption that would have been caused to our government was unimaginable.

President Bush had been in Florida speaking to a class of elementary schoolchildren at the time of the attack. House Speaker Dennis Hastert, along with other senior House and Senate leaders, was rushed from the Capitol to a secure bunker located in Virginia, where he remained until late afternoon. First Lady Laura Bush, who had been scheduled to appear before a congressional panel in the Senate, was rushed away, protected by Secret Service agents with machine guns yelling at people to move aside.

This was the first attack in centuries by enemies of our country on our nation's mainland. It was unsettling. It was unimaginable. There was an immediate impact. Wall Street closed, all airline flights in the United States were halted, and international flights headed to the United States were diverted to other airports.

Like many Americans, I listened as President Bush spoke to the nation. He clearly declared that "the United States would hunt down and punish those responsible for these cowardly acts."[53] The rest of that day and the following days were filled with decisions and actions to protect the country. Like many of my colleagues, I spoke in support of the Joint Resolution Expressing the Sense of the Senate and House of Representatives Regarding the Terrorist Acts Launched against the United States on September 11, 2001. Acknowledging the victims who had been killed, their families, those who had given their lives trying to save others, and the American Airlines and United Airlines family that had been so impacted, I spoke the vow that was in many Americans' hearts: the United States would never, ever cower to terrorists.

There was an astounding chorus of world leaders denouncing the attacks and offering to assist the United States. Bank accounts of those suspected of association with the terrorists were frozen. The United Nations Security Council adopted a resolution condemning the attacks. Law enforcement agencies across the globe worked together to arrest those suspected of terrorism.

I spoke out against the senseless, horrendous tragedies of September 11th. I gave special tribute to the American Airlines family because of their unique to contributions to the Dallas–Fort Worth area. I recognized that our flags were at half-mast, but I asserted that our heads were high because we were Americans whose freedom would ring loudly forever.[54]

On September 14 the administration asked Congress to authorize the use of military force against those who "planned, committed or aided the attacks." Authority was also requested to use force against anyone that aided the terrorists. Days later at a joint session of Congress, President Bush specifically thanked Congress for its leadership, commenting that "all of America was touched at seeing Republicans and Democrats joined together singing 'God Bless America.'" He thanked the American citizens, foreign leaders, and the world for the outpouring of support for our nation. And then he spoke directly to the Taliban, stating that they needed to hand over the terrorists or share in their fate. We were at war against al-Qaeda, terrorists, and nations that harbor or support terrorism. He famously declared that "either you are with us, or you are with the terrorists." His message was clear: the future depended on what America decided to do in the face of global terrorism.[55]

Congress had to quickly address the aftermath of the attacks. Within ten days the Air Transportation Safety and System Stabilization Act was introduced and referred to House committees, including the House Transportation and Infrastructure Committee on which I served. The Senate and House both passed bills providing for airport and airline security. The bill was presented in the full House later that night.[56] As I spoke in support of this bill, I noted that the airline industry had already lost over $1 billion and that its future was bleak due to reduced consumer demand because people were afraid to fly. The airline industry is an indispensable part of the American economy. If the airlines were not supported, other economic areas would be negatively impacted. Employees of American Airlines and citizens of DFW had flooded my district office with phone calls asking for legislation to help the airlines ride out the storm. The bill had to pass.[57] After other comments and debate, a voice vote was called, and at 11:06 p.m. the bill to help the airline industry was passed.

Some weeks later we again addressed the safety of flight through the Aviation and Transportation Security Act. Through a conference agreement, additional security was achieved by requiring that all passengers and baggage be screened, cockpit doors be reinforced, flight crews be trained to respond to hijacking situations, and funding be provided for additional air marshals. The agreement also called for criminal background checks for all persons with access to sensitive areas within airports and for foreign nationals seeking instruction of larger-sized aircrafts.

As I said on the floor, passengers had still not returned to flying, and private baggage checkers had missed a loaded gun that was in a passenger's briefcase. Congress needed to do something. These two provisions relating to background checks had been identified to me by representatives of the DFW airport as critical to assuring security, and so I was proud that they had been included. This legislation, added to the measures that we had already enacted, helped to maintain the airline industry.[58]

But we also addressed the impact on airline workers. I was a cosponsor for the Displaced Workers Relief Bill of 2001, a bill to provide extended unemployment benefits, training opportunities, and continued health care coverage for airline workers.[59] I wholeheartedly supported this bill. I also drew attention to a bill that I had introduced earlier that year, before the September 11 attacks, that would help the displaced workers: H.R. 886 to eliminate federal income taxation of unemployment benefits. It made little sense to me that we would tax unemployment benefits.[60]

On October 7 American forces, assisted by troops from many other nations, launched Operation Enduring Freedom in Afghanistan. The effort was to dislodge the Taliban-backed government that was suspected of backing al-Qaeda. Suspicion had immediately fallen on the terrorist group al-Qaeda and its leader, Osama bin Laden. While I always continued to encourage diplomatic efforts, talking and listening, communicating with our neighbors, and developing alliances, I also supported our right to defend ourselves, our right to take whatever action was necessary to protect our people and our nation. I publicly supported proactive steps to address the threat of terrorism.[61]

In the wake of the attacks on the United States and the military actions abroad, President Bush's popularity rating approached 90 percent. The president began to talk about the need for new laws that he said would ensure the country's safety. On October 23, 2001, the Uniting and Strengthening America by Providing Appropriate Tools Required to Intercept and Obstruct Terrorism (USA PATRIOT) Act was introduced.[62] This bill incorporated language from legislation introduced earlier in the session. Those bills had gone through the committee process, were amended, and received bipartisan support. This particular version, consisting of more than 130 pages, was put to a vote in the House the very next day. The House vote was 357 to 66.

I was one of the sixty-six who voted against the bill. I did so because I believed that some of its provisions were excessive. For instance, it expanded the authority of the FBI to review email, phone, and bank records without a court order. It also gave law enforcement the authority to search a personal residence without consent and it authorized the indefinite detention of immigrants. The potential for abuse was alarming. Following passage in the House, the Senate considered and passed the bill, again the very next day. In the Senate only one member, Wisconsin senator Russ Feingold, voted against it.

The decades since September 11 have seen a marked change in this country. We have become accustomed to airport screening procedures, investigations under the PATRIOT Act, and the military actions that were born out of the terroristic attacks.

As we came together, rallying behind the nation and its leaders, uniting in a spirit of patriotism and recommitment to the ideals of this nation, there was a sense of mutuality that is unimaginable in this current era of vicious partisan divide. We shared a common bond born out of the shock, fear, and sadness of the attack. We faced the uncertainties and used our collective judgments. We did not always agree, but never did we question anyone's love for this nation. We were all Americans forever bound by the tragedy of September 11.

Chapter 14

My Second Decade as a Congresswoman (2002–2012)

My second decade was spent under the presidential administrations of George W. Bush and Barack Obama, two very different presidents, two very different approaches to addressing issues and problems, two very different relationships.

The Iraq War

As I was campaigning for the November 2002 election, the possibility of a war in Iraq had become a reality. Starting a war against Iraq had been an objective of President Bush's for some time. It had been confided to me by someone close to President Bush that he held a personal antipathy toward Iraqi president Saddam Hussein. I was told that the need to confront and neutralize Hussein was discussed at one of the administration's first cabinet meetings.

Following the Persian Gulf War, President Bush's father, former president George Herbert Walker Bush, was the target of an assassination attempt in Kuwait. In April 1993 he was in Kuwait for a celebration of the allies' 1991 victory and the forced retreat of Iraqi troops from Kuwait. His son, Neil, and his three daughters-in-law were with him. There was a plot to kill President Bush by using explosives hidden in a car parked near the motorcade route.

Investigation determined that there was a strong case that Saddam Hussein had been behind this attempted plot to kill the president. Saddam had publicly promised on Iraqi television that he would hunt down and punish Bush, even if he was no longer in office. Based upon the gathered evidence, President Clinton had ordered a retaliatory missile strike against the Iraqi Intelligence Service building in Baghdad. But I doubt that the Bushes ever forgot about the assassination plot.

Importantly, there were individuals in President George W. Bush's administration who were on record as supporting regime change and the removal of Saddam Hussein. Vice President Dick Cheney had served from 1995 to 2000 as CEO and board chairman of Halliburton, a Texas-based multinational contractor with strong ties to the military-industrial complex. Cheney had also served as secretary of defense under President George H. W. Bush and had pushed to continue the Persian Gulf War until Saddam was captured. Members of President George W. Bush's administration— Elliott Abrams, national security advisor; Donald Rumsfeld, secretary of defense; John Bolton, undersecretary of state for disarmament; Richard Armitage, deputy secretary of state; and Paul Wolfowitz, deputy secretary of defense, had all signed an open letter to President Clinton in 1998 urging him to take steps to protect American interests in the Gulf, including removing Saddam.[1] Undoubtedly these individuals, especially Cheney, advised President George W. Bush to proceed to war against Iraq.

While the buildings targeted on September 11 were still smoldering, Secretary Rumsfeld urged that Iraq be included in the first round of attacks against terrorism. The proponents of preemption, urged on by the attacks of September 11, seemed to smell blood. They wanted to go back into Iraq to complete a job that they had reluctantly ceased ten years earlier.

They were advocating the Bush Doctrine, which said that the United States possessed an absolute right to engage in preventive wars, using its military might to bring down foreign governments that threatened our security. The Bush Doctrine declared that military force by the United States was acceptable when American interests and safety were at stake. It was used by ideologues who believed that America had a duty to spread democracy throughout the Middle East as a means of fighting terrorism.

Wolfowitz argued for an immediate attack against Iraq at a meeting of the president's national security team. But Secretary of State Colin Powell, a combat veteran, persuaded the president to direct his attention on Afghanistan rather than attack Iraq. And fortunately Congress's focus was also on finding the terrorists and those responsible for the attack on American soil. The joint resolution signed on September 18, 2001, expressly stated that Congress supported the determination of the president to bring to justice and punish the perpetrators of the attacks and their sponsors.[2] Iraq had not been connected to those attacks. Yet during his State of the Union address on January 29, 2002, the president turned his attention to Iraq, saying that it continued to flaunt its hostility to the United States and to support terror.[3] He claimed that Iraq had developed anthrax, nerve gas, and nuclear weapons for over a decade. He included Iraq as part of an "Axis of Evil" and pledged that he would not wait for dangerous regimes to threaten the world with the most destructive weapons. He wanted us to conclude that the Iraqi government was in possession of "weapons of mass destruction" that posed a grave danger to the interests of the United States.

The president spoke to a global audience with a degree of certainty as if he had seen the weapons with his own eyes. The speech created a bewildering moment for me and for many of my colleagues. In the months following the address, the administration produced CIA data claiming that it confirmed Iraq was involved in rebuilding its nuclear weapons program and that the country's military had misled United Nations officials about its possession of chemical and biological weapons.

During a graduation address at West Point in June of 2002, the president said that America should be ready to take preemptive action against other nations when our freedom was in question. He recognized that the military would be transformed, able to strike at a moment's notice at any dark corner of the world. He vowed that America's safety would not be left in the hands of "a few mad terrorists and tyrants."[4]

A central part of the administration's continuing argument was that there was a relationship between the Iraqi government and the terrorists that attacked the United States on 9/11. The suggestion was that if Iraq were not confronted, weapons of mass destructions would one day fall into the hands of al-Qaeda and other extremist elements. But serious questions arose as to whether Iraq possessed weapons of mass destruction, as President Bush and his operatives, such as Vice President Cheney, argued. The administration pressed its case even when faced with numerous doubters.

On July 26, 2002, Representative Peter DeFazio sponsored a resolution for the House to consider and vote on for the use of force by the United States Armed Forces against Iraq before such force was deployed.[5] The resolution recited that Iraq had developed weapons of mass destruction, including chemical and biological capabilities, and had made progress toward developing nuclear weapons capabilities. It noted that the president and vice president had made statements expressing an intention to use force against Iraq, to have regime change, and use military resources if necessary. On that date the bill was referred to the House Committee on International Relations.

While the resolutions were pending, on September 12, 2002, President Bush gave an address to the United Nations General Assembly. Invoking the memory of the September 11 terrorist attacks, President Bush presented his case for military action against Iraq. He said that Iraq presented an aggressive threat. He declared that Saddam continued to develop weapons of mass destruction. He closed with a challenge to the nations of the UN to stand up for global security.[6]

Less than a week later, President Bush met with the vice president and the congressional leadership. Speaking from the Rose Garden on October 2, 2002, flanked by Republican and Democratic leaders, President Bush in press remarks following that meeting said that Saddam "deceives, delays, and denies." He added that he had talked with the leadership about the need for a strong bipartisan resolution, which his administration would send over in a couple of days. He said that confronting Iraq as a threat was central to the war on terror because Saddam had longstanding and ongoing ties to international terrorists. He claimed that Iraq had stockpiled enough biological and chemical agents to kill millions of people. And he told the nation that Saddam had killed his own people and was developing weapons of mass destruction.[7]

House Joint Resolution 114 was introduced by Speaker J. Dennis Hastert.[8] The resolution expressly stated that Iraq had weapons of mass destruction that posed a continuing threat to the United States. Comments by Speaker Hastert from the Rose Garden made it clear that the memories of September 11 were also pressing. Representative Gephardt, speaking as the minority leader, said Iraq's use and continuing development of the weapons of mass destruction and terrorists' efforts to get those weapons mandated the authorization to use force to meet that threat.[9]

Debate on the resolution was held on October 8, 2002. As I rose to speak, I remembered my husband, father, grandfather, uncles, and many others in my family who had proudly served in our armed services. They had been willing to take up arms to defend our nation when combat was necessary and justified. Over the years I had consoled many families who had lost a loved one on a battlefield. As a psychiatric nurse at the VA hospital in Dallas I had daily witnessed the physical and mental costs of war. I had cared for veterans who had lost limbs and others who had lost their minds.

I was mindful that there were American forces already fighting in Afghanistan. We had launched Operation Enduring Freedom a year earlier in an effort to dislodge the Taliban control. We were searching for Osama bin Laden, and that had to be our top priority. And so I told the members that I felt the moral weight of deciding whether to send our men and women into battle. I acknowledged that no one liked being on the opposite side of the president on this issue but that I could not support the resolution. I first read specific principles that the CBC believed had to be addressed before there was military action: (1) no unilateral, first-strike action without a clearly demonstrated and imminent threat of attack on the United States; (2) only Congress had the authority to declare war; (3) every conceivable diplomatic option had to be exhausted; (4) a unilateral first strike would undermine the moral authority of the United States, destabilize the Middle East region, and undermine the ability of our nation to address unmet domestic priorities; and (5) any poststrike plan for maintaining stability in the region would be costly and require a long-term commitment.

I acknowledged that Saddam's regime posed a threat and that military action might be necessary in the future. But, in my view, a better approach was to solidify the support of the international community and act under the auspices of the United Nations rather than proceeding unilaterally. Significant progress had been made in weapons inspections by working through the United Nations. If the United States acted alone, without exhausting all peaceful options, we could damage the global support that we had received from other countries after the 9/11 attacks.

To me the administration had not provided sufficient credible evidence of an imminent threat to invoke a doctrine of self-defense. I did not believe that giving the president the authority to launch a unilateral, first-strike attack was appropriate given the attendant risks and possible consequences. An assault on Iraq, I believed, would create additional enemies for us and unleash anti-Western sentiment from allied groups that would one day attempt to harm us and destroy our way of life.

I was also concerned that there had not been any consideration of the long-term commitment for nation building that would be necessary after the Saddam regime fell. Would we have to bear the financial burden of the economic reconstruction and democratization that would be required? We were still struggling from the financial and economic impact of September 11. How would we manage that recovery if we were focused on military action in Iraq? I ended my remarks by posing three specific questions: Does a war with Iraq improve our national security? Does it allow the United States to make peace through the power of our example? Does it allow us to focus on the economic suffering of our own people? Answering each question with a resounding "no," I announced that I would be voting against the resolution.[10]

Every member of the CBC voted against the resolution, including Representative Charles Rangel, who had served in the Korean War with distinction and often spoke of his comrades and pride in having served his country. He insisted that there were questions that needed to be answered before Congress gave up its authorization to declare war and turn it over to the president. He posed questions as to why neighboring countries had not raised alarms to threats posed by Saddam. But the House Resolution passed by a vote of 296 to 133.[11] The Senate Resolution also passed, 77 to 23. The war resolution was signed by the president on October 16, 2002. It would prove to be a dark day in our nation's history.

A few weeks later, President Bush signed legislation that created the Department of Homeland Security Agency.[12] The stated objective of the new department was to keep Americans safe from terrorist acts, enhance the country's response to terrorism, and prevent such acts from occurring in the future. I spoke and voted against this bill, believing that it was rushed. Bringing disparate elements from over federal government needed to be thoughtful. But this agency created a sprawling bureaucracy while leaving many important security questions unanswered.

I also opposed the arming of our nation's pilots rather than a deployment of air marshals to improve airline security. Furthermore, the bill authorized an unproven approach to classified research, rejecting the existing policies of the Departments of Defense and Energy. I had great misgiving in opposing this bill because it would have been ideal for members to stand together in a united front against terrorism. But the provisions that diminished aviation security forced me to vote against it.[13]

The bill passed in the House on November 19 by a vote of 295 to 132, and in the Senate by a vote of 90 to 9. The director of the new department became a member of the president's cabinet.[14]

In the January 2003 State of the Union address, President Bush told the American people that Saddam Hussein had continued to pursue chemical, biological, and nuclear weapons despite his agreement to disarm. He said that Saddam had shown utter contempt for the UN and the world. He said that intelligence sources had established that Iraq was hiding its weapons programs from inspectors. He directly invoked the memories of September 11, urging listeners to imagine the hijackers possessing a vial of chemical agents or lethal viruses provided by Saddam. He left no doubt: he was ready to confront Saddam and go to war.[15]

A little more than a week later, Secretary of State Colin Powell, one of the few senior officials in the cabinet that world leaders respected, was dispatched to the United Nations to press the case that Iraq possessed weapons of mass destruction. Armed with data given to him by the White House and the intelligence community, Secretary Powell argued that Iraq was a dangerous state and that it had not cooperated with United Nations weapons inspectors. He claimed that the United States had firsthand descriptions of sophisticated mobile biological weapons.[16] I did not believe a word of what Secretary Powell presented to the United Nations. I knew he had been misled. The administration invited me to private briefings at the White House in an attempt to convince me that its position was correct and that war was necessary. But those briefings were not persuasive.

President Bush continued the press for a war on Iraq in a speech in late February. He claimed that the safety of the American people depended on ending the Saddam threat. And he again said that Saddam was a wealthy patron who paid for terrorist training and offered rewards to families of suicide bombers.[17] There was a part of me that felt sorry for President Bush. He was a likable person, but he was severely in over his head. He was surrounded by warmongers who simply wanted to promote their personal agendas no matter how egregious the human and personal suffering that resulted from an armed conflict. But his plans were putting our military personnel at grave risk.

On March 19, 2003, President Bush announced to the nation that military operations to disarm Iraq had begun. In his declaration he justified the military action, saying that the people of the United States and its allies would not live at the mercy of a regime that threatens peace with weapons of mass murder. The administration had pulled together a group of nations called the "coalition of the willing."[18]

Baghdad fell in a matter of weeks. Two of Saddam Hussein's sons and his grandson were killed by American forces. Saddam escaped capture and went into hiding. He was later captured near his hometown of Tikrit. But as the United States entered this war with Iraq, antiwar forces protested vehemently, both in this country and abroad. American young men and women were being severely injured and killed in Afghanistan. Now the administration was risking additional lives in Iraq. It made no sense.

It was ultimately discovered that some of the claims that had been made to justify the war simply were not true. The claim that Iraq had tried to purchase uranium from sellers in Niger was false. In 2002 Joseph Wilson, a former US ambassador to Gabon, had traveled to Niger at the request of the Central Intelligence Agency to investigate whether Iraq had attempted to purchase raw materials to manufacture chemical weapons. The US ambassador to Niger told him that she had determined that those allegations were false, something that she had already communicated to Washington. Wilson spent more than a week talking with government officials and people associated with the uranium business. Based upon his investigation, he also determined that those allegations were baseless. His conclusions were provided to the CIA and the State Department of African Affairs Bureau.

In July 2003 Wilson wrote an editorial for the *New York Times* setting forth this information. Shortly after his editorial appeared, Wilson's wife, Valerie Plame, was identified in the press as a CIA operative. "Scooter" Libby, an aide to Vice President Cheney, was charged with having leaked the confidential, life-threatening information to the media.

Despite Wilson's report, the administration insisted that there were weapons of mass destruction. We know now that those claims were false. Secretary Powell would later say that his appearance before the United Nations was a "momentous failure" and there was no evidence to connect Saddam and Iraq to the September 11 terrorist attacks. There were investigations and inquiries throughout 2003 and 2004, efforts to determine whether such weapons existed. But the administration still insisted upon American military presence in Iraq.

Approaching the first Iraqi election, the struggle to get the Bush administration to establish a plan for withdrawal of US troops became a disgraceful political battle. President Bush and Vice President Cheney had continued to deny allegations that the prewar intelligence was falsified or outrageous. They insisted that troops needed to remain in Iraq.

A well-respected veteran and ardent supporter of our military, Democratic representative John Murtha, called for the creation of a plan that staged withdrawals of forces. The presence of the US military, he was convinced, was actually fueling the insurgency rather than pacifying the country. Recent polling asserted that over 80 percent of Iraqi people wanted the US forces out of their country, that 45 percent believed that the attacks against US soldiers was justified. Continued US military presence was not in the interests of the United States, Iraqi people, or Persian Gulf region. Representative Murtha proposed language that because US military action in Iraq was not in the best interests of the American people, "the deployment of United States forces in Iraq, by direction of Congress, is hereby terminated and the forces involved are to be redeployed at the earliest practicable date." He also proposed deployment of a quick reaction force and an over-the-horizon presence of US Marines to be deployed in the region.[19]

The very next day Republican Duncan Hunter filed a one-sentence resolution that "it was the sense of the House of Representatives that the deployment of United States forces in Iraq be terminated immediately." The Hunter resolution was called for vote that very same day.[20]

Republicans had argued that any mention of withdrawal lowered the morale of our soldiers and emboldened the terrorists. They offered this resolution to put Democrats on the spot and force a vote against the resolution, making it appear as if we were against removing troops from Iraq. Such a vote, Republicans argued, would send a needed message of support to our troops.

This legislative maneuvering was unfortunate. As I said in opposition to that resolution, Murtha's resolution was designed to stimulate a thoughtful and profound debate on Iraqi policy. It was a necessary debate. I pointed out that a Texan had just become the two thousandth soldier to die in Iraq.[21] Such sad milestones compelled looking back to see what lessons had been learned. Standing by while damage was being done was not patriotic. It was not being strong on national security. It was not being tough on terrorism.

What we opposed was an irresponsible withdrawal. We wanted a plan for ending this engagement of US military rather than the administration's limitless stay the course. We argued that we had to limit our commitment to Iraq. We had to work to make our country secure, but we also had to keep my commitment to our men and women in uniform by saying publicly that we needed to "change our course."

The war became an issue in subsequent elections. Through 2012 nearly five thousand United States servicemen and women were killed in Iraq. More than sixteen thousand were seriously injured. It is estimated that more than one hundred thousand Iraqi civilians were killed. But one entity that benefited quite handsomely from the Iraq War was Halliburton, the company once headed by Vice President Cheney. It or its subsidiaries received billions of dollars in contracts from the federal government. Some of them were single-source agreements that a former assistant to Cheney awarded to hand-picked contractors.

Our relationships with allies in the Middle East became extremely frayed. Many in the world viewed us as thirsty for war and aggression. Once again the CBC had been on the right side of the issue. We had protested vehemently against the war, but the leadership of the nation went against our concerns and our position, creating a decimated economic and political climate that would take years to recover.

After the war I went on a congressional trip to Iraq. I encountered young soldiers who had to endure 120-degree heat. Their living conditions were horrible. There were no places for them to sleep. No restrooms. I discovered that when, having to use the bathroom, an officer made one out of cardboard so that I could answer nature's call.

My congressional colleagues and I did not have to remain in Iraq as did the brave young women and men in the military. Many of them came home with injuries, mental and physical, that essentially ruined their lives. Those who had sent our soldiers seemingly there had little concern or thought for the consequences of that decision. Sadly and regrettably, it was simply politics for them.

Ryan White HIV/AIDS Treatment Modernization Act of 2006

Ryan White was 13 years old when he was expelled from school because he had been diagnosed with AIDS. Due to his hemophilia, he needed regular transfusions, and he contracted the disease through one of those transfusions. He was expelled from school despite reassurances from doctors that he did not pose a health risk to the student body. That decision was appealed, bringing national attention to how he was being ostracized and treated due to this disease.

Ryan became a poster child for the AIDS crisis. He made numerous public appearances, participating in fundraising and educational events, appearing on TV. He worked tirelessly to destigmatize the disease. He spoke before the President's Commission on the HIV Epidemic, sharing the impact that information about the disease had on his reception when he transferred to a different high school. Although originally given just six months to live, Ryan surpassed that prediction, living almost five more years, just months short of his high school graduation. His activism helped change the nation's attitude toward AIDS patients. Four months after his death in 1990, Congress passed the Ryan White Comprehensive AIDS Resources Emergency (CARE) Act. This act funds programs to improve access to care for low-income, uninsured, and underinsured AIDS patients and their families.

I was aware of Ryan's story. I had seen the impact of HIV/AIDS diagnoses on individuals and within communities through my work as vice chairperson to the City of Dallas's Health and Human Services Commission. And I had seen the benefits of the Ryan White Act, prompting me to be a cosponsor of the Ryan White CARE Reauthorization Act of 1994.

The act has been reauthorized multiple times, each occasion giving me the platform to address the disproportionate impact that AIDS had on the African American community. When I spoke in 2006, I was speaking on behalf of the CBC and myself, a former nurse. At that time more than eighteen thousand Texans were living with the disease. Sixty percent of women with HIV were African American. We had to support programs making progress against this disease. Governments, corporations, foundations, religious groups, and private citizens had to unite to win the war on AIDS. There simply was no other moral or practical choice.[22]

Historically Black Colleges and Universities Week

While I did not attend a historically Black college or university, growing up in Waco, Texas, I was very familiar with Paul Quinn College, one such institution. HBCUs have educated millions of African Americans at times when other institutions of higher learning were not opening their doors. These colleges and universities served not just as beacons for individuals wanting to advance their education but also as powerful symbols of pride and community.

HBCUs of America have been and continue to be the equal opportunity colleges and universities of the higher education institutions in America.

The progress made socially, economically, politically, and educationally by African Americans has been made because of these institutions.

Appreciation for HBCUs was not theoretical. My district included Paul Quinn College, which had moved from Waco to Dallas. A part of my childhood, it was now a resource in my district, allowing me to witness the impact of its education on young people. This appreciation moved me to introduce a resolution recognizing HBCU week.[23] I also worked with Representatives James Clyburn and John Duncan to establish the first bipartisan HBCU Congressional Caucus. But my greatest contribution was my consistent advocacy on behalf of HBCU inclusion in research and educational funding, an insistence rooted in my firm belief that they are untapped resources for our nation.

Science, Space, and Technology Committee, Cybersecurity, and NASA

After the September 11 attacks, the Science Committee turned its attention, like most of the nation, to terrorism. Recognizing that the war on terrorism would be won in the laboratory as much as on the battlefield, we focused on scientific and research investments to fight terrorism. We tackled cyberterrorism, leading to the passage of the Cyber Security Research and Development Act. We conducted hearings and introduced legislation to enable the government to more quickly investigate building failures by giving the National Institute of Standards and Technology jurisdiction and authority over such investigations. We were also actively involved in the establishment of the Department of Homeland Security, making certain that a focus on science and technology existed through the creation of an undersecretary with that role.

The tragic disintegration of the space shuttle *Columbia* in February 2003 put a spotlight on the committee, especially the Space and Aeronautics Subcommittee. We held hearings on the cause of the accident, monitored the investigation by the independent Columbia Accident Investigation Board, worked with NASA to effectuate a return to activities, and sought to give meaning to the lives that were lost and compassion for the families who were grieving.[24] As legislators we passed two bills: the NASA Flexibility Act of 2004 and the Commercial Space Launch Amendments Act of 2004. These acts addressed the need for an exceptional technical workforce and a regulatory approach to assessing risk in space tourism.[25]

I spoke in support of the NASA Authorization Act of 2005, pointing out the technologies that were rooted in NASA research that had become part of our everyday lives: cell phones, cordless appliances, Velcro, Teflon, GPS, CAT scans, and MRIs. NASA went beyond space exploration. It contributed to our lives, helped our military, and improved medical services.[26]

Just a few weeks later, I again had the opportunity to applaud the work and successes of NASA. A resolution had been introduced in the House to recognize Space Shuttle Commander Eileen Collins, Mission Specialist Wendy Lawrence, and the Contributions of All Other Women Who Have Worked with NASA. Speaking in support of that resolution, I applauded the work of all women in preparation of the *Discovery* shuttle launch. I specifically recognized my friends, Drs. Mae Jemison and Mary Ann Webber and Commander Eileen Collins.[27]

I didn't always initially speak in support of a bill. The Energy Policy Act of 2005 was such a bill. It ultimately went through a conference report yielding a bill that I could support and that would be ultimately signed by President George W. Bush. Even though I was mindful that I was from an energy-producing state, I could not in good conscience remain silent. The initial bill delayed anti–air pollution measures, allowing smog pollution to continue unabated while giving billions in tax breaks to politically favored energy industries. It was our responsibility, as representatives of the people, to demand clear air policies. Air pollution means more asthma attacks, hospital visits, and premature deaths for residents of ozone odor nonattainment areas. The preceding year Children's Hospital in Dallas had four thousand emergency department visits for children, with an average age of 5. Prolonging dirty air was not an answer. Clear air was needed for us and our children. The conference version added critical clean air provisions and removed drilling in the Arctic National Wildlife Refuge. With these and other changes, I was able to support the bill.[28]

With the 2010 Republican victory in the House, I became the ranking member of the House Science, Space, and Technology Committee. I was the first African American and woman to be elected to this position.

Chair of the House Transportation and Infrastructure Committee Subcommittee on Water Resources and Environment

The Army Corps of Engineers traces its origins back to the Revolutionary War. Through various statutory amendments, the corps is now responsible for the navigation, flood damage reduction, environmental restoration and protection, coastal storm damage prevention, emergency response, hydroelectric power, water supply, and recreation for American's waterways. Significantly for North Texas, the corps is responsible for flood damage reduction, navigation, and environmental protection and restoration.

Members of Congress identify needed water projects in their districts and present them to the staff assigned to the Water Resources and Environment Subcommittee of the Committee on Transportation and Infrastructure. These proposals stretch the breadth of water concerns, coastlines, wetlands, harbors, rivers, flooding, drinking water, dams, bridges, levees, pumping stations, wastewater, and pollution; all are covered under Water Resource Subcommittee bills.

These projects are referred to the Corps of Engineers to evaluate and report on. The Water Resources Subcommittee then reviews the Corps of Engineers assessment. Hearings may be conducted. The subcommittee determines which projects should be included in a bill and recommends those projects to the full Transportation Committee. When approved by the full committee, the projects are included in a Water Resources Development bill. For each water project, Congress must first pass legislation authorizing the corps to do an in-depth study of that project. Pursuant to that legislation, the corps conducts a study and prepares a recommendation. A recommendation to proceed with a project needs subcommittee acceptance to be included in a subsequent bill. Then Congress considers the bill and if passed, the projects are authorized. Actual funding comes through a separate appropriations bill.

These steps anticipate that water resource legislation will be introduced every two years to act on each of these decision points.

The Water Resources Development Act of 1994 was my first opportunity to address flooding in Dallas. This act authorized water resources development and conservation projects of the Army Corps of Engineers. It oversaw water infrastructure. Designed to be renewed every two years to authorize new projects, it is how Congress provides federal funding for water-related projects.

The WRDA of 1994 identified twenty projects from across the country and Puerto Rico that had been approved by the committee.[29] I had been able to get the Dallas Floodway Extension to construct flood protection works for Rochester Park and the north section of the Central Wastewater Treatment Plant included in the bill. For each project the estimated total cost, federal cost, nonfederal cost, and those monies to be contributed by other entities were specified. The bill provided that any authorized projects are to be carried out as described in the plans that had been presented to the committee.

As a member of the subcommittee on Water Resources for the next thirteen years, I reviewed hundreds, if not thousands, of projects. The ones deemed meritorious were included in a Water Resources Development Act that was introduced every Congress. Even if the bill passed our committee, there was no guarantee that it would be passed by the House and Senate. The Water Resources Development Act of 1996 included a project to address flooding in Rochester Park of Dallas and the Central Wastewater Treatment Plant. It was not until 2000 that a Water Resources Development Act was again passed. Each term that Congress did not pass a water development act, projects involving our waterways, harbors, levees, and flood protection systems would languish.

Years would pass before Congress considered another water bill. The chairman of the Transportation Committee, the late congressman James L. Oberstar, appointed me to chair the Subcommittee on Water Resources and Environment. I eagerly accepted this position, becoming the first female and first African American to head this subcommittee. Focusing on water and addressing our related infrastructure needs was a priority.

Chair Oberstar and I were the principal sponsors of the Water Resources Development Act (WRDA) of 2007. The bill that we drafted, with the assistance of Representative John Mica, a Republican and ranking member on the committee, provided funding for water resources projects throughout the nation. There was funding for bridge construction and repair, improvements to harbors and navigable channels, expansion of the Mississippi River locks, and improvement of systems to reduce flooding and storm damage. The devastating experiences of Hurricanes Katrina and Rita had underscored the need for flood prevention measures. Ultimately, it was about the economic livelihood of our nation and our ability to be competitive.

The bill included Dallas projects for bridge construction, flood control, ecosystem development, and improvements to the Trinity River. I had included a picture of a flooded home in Cadillac Heights, a section of south Dallas, in my campaign materials as my continuing promise to work toward a solution to the flooding. Dallas had prepared a comprehensive plan for the Trinity that emphasized flood protection while being environmentally responsible and creating recreational and open space. If the project was determined to be sound, almost $300 million of federal funds would be provided under this bill.

The bill, which was hundreds of pages and included projects for every state, had to go through conference. I was a member of the Conference Committee. We finally reached agreement, authorizing $29 billion for projects supervised by the Corps of Engineers. Of that sum almost $300 million was allocated for the Dallas Floodway Project addressing the Trinity River and its tributaries. The bill was sent to President Bush for signature.

President Bush knew the conditions that confronted Texas. He lived in Dallas and was aware of the flooding and the decaying bridges. I spoke with him and his chief aide, Karl Rove, about the importance of the legislation. Rove and I had worked together in Austin. I suggested to him that if the president could not bring himself to sign the bill, he should allow it to become law without his signature. The president waited until the very last day before vetoing the legislation.

I immediately began to work with other members in the House, Democrats and Republicans, to override President Bush's veto. My strategy was clear. I visited with as many members as I could. I emphasized the needs in their districts that the legislation addressed, pointed out the infrastructure insecurity, and walked them through the projects in the bill. This was important legislation. We could not abandon it simply because the president had vetoed it.

At the House debate to override President Bush's veto, I pointed out that it had been almost two years since Hurricanes Katrina and Rita had torn through the Gulf Coast leaving tragedy and despair. I reminded the members of the heartbreak they had caused. How would those who had lost homes, families, and livelihoods be able to restore their lives? I quoted President Bush, his promise that we would do what it takes, we would stay as long as it took, to help citizens rebuild their communities and their lives. Then I asked, How was his veto of the Water Resources Development Act consistent with this pledge?

We couldn't always respond to tragedy after the fact. We needed to act to prevent the tragedies in the first place. Gulf Coast wetlands that help stunt water surges had disappeared. An underused shipping channel that contributed to the New Orleans flooding needed to be closed, and we needed to build stronger, higher levees around the city. I argued that we could not keep postponing our infrastructure projects. Every time we put something off, it was just going to get more expensive. Our failure to have the regular, every-two-year approval of infrastructure projects merely postponed the inevitable and cost us more money.

This act reached across the country. With population growth outpacing land management, the Florida Everglades were disappearing. Funds were needed to launch three of fifteen projects directed to restore them. Locks and dams were needed in the Upper Mississippi River to improve shipping. Ecosystem restoration in the Midwest was addressed. There were small water projects as well, focusing on improving quality of drinking water.

I pointed to the needs of my district. The Dallas Floodway received 1,600 square miles of Trinity River runoff and moved that water through Dallas by virtue of levees forming both sides of a 2,000-foot-wide floodway. The waters had been predicted to flood downtown Dallas, causing a projected $8 billion damage to property and infrastructure. This catastrophe was not theoretical. Exploding population growth had increased the water runoff, overwhelmed the antiquated interior drainage pumps, and greatly reduced the effect of the levee system. Dallas and the nation needed this water bill. I just couldn't accept that President Bush, who lived in the Dallas area, was denying the country these resources. And fortunately, Congress could not accept President Bush's position either. His veto was overridden.[30]

The next time that we saw one another he greeted me by saying, "Hello Miss Trinity." I asked him if he was going to return to Dallas once his presidency ended. He said that he and Mrs. Bush intended to reside in Dallas. "Well, all I will need is your address," I said in a cordial manner. "Because I intend to construct a trench from the Trinity River to your front door so that when it does flood you will be the very first to know."

We were also concerned about water quality. Approximately 40 percent of the nation's rivers, lakes, and coastal waters did not meet state quality standards. Without substantial investment the water quality would be worse than before the Clean Water Act had been enacted. It had been more than twenty years since Congress had authorized appropriations for the Clean Water State Revolving Fund. We needed to act. The Water Quality Investment Act of 2009 was introduced by Chair Oberstar and me.[31] My work as subcommittee chair to get this legislation to the floor was acknowledged by Chair Oberstar and others. While the bill passed the House, it did not proceed any further.

I had to decline a leadership position on a subcommittee of the House Science Committee to serve as chair of the Water Resources Subcommittee. But I didn't hesitate in making that decision. I knew how critical water is to the nation when there isn't enough or when there is too much. Devoting my talents and focusing on bipartisanship for such critical issues was natural for me.

John, Hillary, and Barack

Shortly after President Bush's second inauguration, Senator John Edwards, a young lawyer from North Carolina, reached out to me. I had always liked Edwards, who was elected to his first term in 1998. We had mutual friends in Dallas and he phoned me whenever he visited the city. He had regularly attended the weekly meetings with members of the CBC. He had also traveled to Texas to address the Dallas County Democratic Party, favorably impressing the attendees as a potential future presidential candidate.

As Senator John Kerry was considering running mates for his 2004 presidential race, I encouraged him to consider Edwards as his vice president. I believed that he would bring an energy and youthfulness to the ticket. In many ways he reminded me of former president Carter, another southerner whose social policies were progressive and visionary.

During one of our personal meetings shortly after the 2004 election, Senator Edwards informed me that he had decided to run for president in 2008 and asked if I would support him. He had spoken at a prayer breakfast that I sponsored, so I had been able to witness his interaction with a southern African American gathering. I also knew that Senator Edwards had written a plan outlining universal health care coverage for millions of uninsured Americans. And when he asked for my support, he was the only person who had expressed an interest in running. Universal health care was a priority issue of mine, so I told him that I would support his candidacy.

Months after agreeing to support Senator Edwards, another young senator came knocking on my door, seeking my support for his presidential run. This time it was Senator Barack Obama, a first-term African American legislator from Illinois who had electrified the entire nation as the keynote speaker at the 2004 Democratic National Convention. I was conflicted by this request. He had become a personal friend and active member of the CBC, where he was well-liked. I appreciated his hard work and diligence. He had winning ways with people and a broad smile that could light up a room. Any reservations that he did not have enough experience to be president because he had only been in the Senate less than four years no longer existed.

But I told Obama that there was a problem, that I had already committed to Edwards and that as much as I would like to support him, I could not go against my word. Obama understood, replying that he respected my position. He shook my hand, thanked me for being honest with him, and left for another appointment. When he left, I felt a sense of sadness. He was like a son to me. It was very difficult. Here was a young African American who was seeking the highest office in our country. I'd had to say no to him when he asked for my support. Years earlier, I had written an editorial that appeared in a Dallas newspaper endorsing Reverend Jesse Jackson's 1988 campaign for president. I wrote that even if Reverend Jackson's presidential bid was not successful, he was opening the door for other young African Americans. Thinking about that editorial after meeting with Senator Obama, I wondered if I was helping to close that door.

Trying to sleep that night was very difficult for me. I had been the first African American nurse at the VA hospital in Dallas, the first African American to chair a major committee in the Texas House, and the first African American woman elected to Congress from North Texas. And hours earlier I informed a very intelligent, industrious, studious, and honest young African American that I was unable to support him. I felt as though I had betrayed all the things that I stood for, that I had worked for. But I knew that I had to keep my word because in politics, and in life, your word is your bond.

Things did not get any easier for me when my very good friend and ally Hillary Clinton told me that she was running for president and needed my support. I had known Hillary since Bill's run for governor. Over the decades we had worked together and supported each other's political efforts. I had become even closer to them while they were in the White House. I had been a regular guest at 1600 Pennsylvania Avenue, had frequently flown on Air Force One, and had supported them during the impeachment struggle. I had grown to love the Clintons as much as I loved members of my own family.

Hillary had served admirably in the Senate, representing the people of New York. She knew her way around Washington. Her learning curve would not be steep. She was accustomed to hardball politics. I felt that it was time for the nation to have a female commander in chief. Hillary was the woman with the most experience and would be a great president. But still my word was my bond. I had to tell her that I had already committed to Edwards. That night was another night of sleeplessness. During my entire political career, I had been an African American and a feminist. I was proud of being both. And yet I had to decline to support a Black man and a woman in historic bids to lead the most powerful nation on the face of the earth.

Senator Edwards announced his run for the nomination in December of 2006 in New Orleans. He was running on an agenda of bringing our troops home from Iraq, passing national health insurance, creating jobs, and fighting global warming. In the early national polls, he was behind both Senators Clinton and Obama, who were polling first and second, respectively. He also lagged behind them in fundraising.

I was one of the few Edwards supporters in the CBC. I was joined by Mel Watt and G. K. Butterfield, both from North Carolina. The rest of the caucus was fairly evenly split between Senators Clinton and Obama. Senator Clinton had the support of John Lewis and David Scott from Georgia; Emanuel Cleaver of Missouri; Sheila Jackson-Lee from Texas; Stephanie Tubbs Jones from Ohio; Dianne Watson and Laura Richardson from California; Donna Christensen from the Virgin Islands; Corrine Brown, Kendrick Meek, and Alcee Hastings from Florida; and Gregory Meeks, Edolphus Towns, and Charlie Rangel, all from New York.

Senator Obama's supporters included Elijah Cummings from Maryland; Artur Davis from Alabama; Barbara Lee from California; Hank Johnson and Sanford Bishop from Georgia; Keith Ellison from Minnesota; Al Green from Texas; Chaka Fattah from Pennsylvania; Gwen Moore from Wisconsin; Lacy Clay from Missouri; John Conyers from Michigan; Bobby Scott from Virginia; and Bobby Rush, Jesse Jackson Jr., and Danny Davis, all from Illinois.

Eight members of the caucus had not publicly announced their positions. Caucus members were torn between whether they should support a woman or an African American for the presidency. If elected, either would make history and be groundbreaking for our country. In the first major contest between the three major candidates, the Iowa caucuses, Edwards finished second behind Obama, who won nearly 40 percent of the vote in a state where African Americans numbered less than five percent. Edwards and Clinton were nearly ten points behind.

Five days later in New Hampshire, Edwards finished third. He finished third in Nevada. Two days after the Nevada vote and five days before the South Carolina primary, I attended the debates in South Carolina. After the debates ended, Obama walked over to me. He said that he thought that Edwards would be withdrawing from the race. If that happened, he asked, would I support his candidacy? "I need you to come over to me."

The primary results were disappointing for Edwards. He finished third in both South Carolina and Florida. The South Carolina showing was particularly disappointing for him because he had been born there and it bordered the state that he represented in Congress. He phoned me and told me that in about an hour he was having a press conference to announce his withdrawal. Two years and one month after his announcement, he dropped out of the race.

The moment that Senator Edwards removed himself from the presidential stage, phone calls came from both the Obama and Clinton camps. I was in Ghana when Hillary called me. I told her that I had informally decided to go with Obama. But she asked if we could talk further when I got back home. I received phone calls from people I had worked closely with over the years who were Hillary supporters. Some had been contributors to my campaigns.

But then one weekend when I returned to Dallas, I discovered that the enthusiasm for the Obama candidacy among young people had reached a boiling point. I had never witnessed that level of excitement about a political race. My son and his family were fervent Obama supporters. If I supported Hillary, he made it clear that we would be voting for different candidates. He was solidly behind Obama.

I still did not believe that Obama would win the nomination. In my heart I just did not believe that the nation would elect an African American president. I felt that race prejudice was so intense that I would not see a Black president during my lifetime. But I knew that I could not dampen the high intensity level in young people, Black, white, and brown, by publicly endorsing Hillary. I thought that I should support the young people's efforts, help them to organize.

Hillary called me later asking for my support. I told her that I had to go with Obama and explained my reasoning. She said that she understood, but I could tell that she was disappointed with my answer. Bill then called and I told him that I was supporting Obama, but that I believed that Hillary would win the nomination. When she was the nominee, I would put all of my support behind her candidacy. He said that he understood but asked if I would remain silent about my support of Obama until after the California primary debate. I told him that I would. I felt that I owed him that much.

I made it clear to everyone that I was supporting Obama but was not opposed to Hillary. The Clinton people, who continued to see me as an ally, made daily visits and phone calls to my office, suggesting to some that I was really a closet Hillary supporter. Never in my wildest dreams did I think that I would be on the opposite side of an issue from the Clintons.

My endorsement of Obama was included within their campaign materials. Before agreeing to go to churches to speak on behalf of Obama, I went into deep prayer and meditation. One night the Lord spoke to my heart saying, "This could be the moment that you have been waiting on for a lifetime."

I spoke to congregations throughout the south on his behalf. The crowds that Obama drew were enormous. There was a level of commitment that I had not witnessed before, and it was not long before I began to believe that he could beat Hillary. Obama would become the first African American presidential nominee for the Democratic Party.

He had massive voter appeal. People were drawn to his charismatic pull. While an Illinois state senator, he developed a reputation for being able to work with members of both political parties. That was a rare trait for most politicians, but a necessary one to get things accomplished. He helped pass legislation that created a $100 million Earned Income Tax Credit for Illinois families, increased childcare funds for poor families, and supported legislation that benefited workers faced with layoffs.

His concern for families was reflected in his personal life. He was happily married to Michelle, also a graduate of Harvard Law School, who he had met in a Chicago law firm. They had two precious daughters, Malia and Sasha. Obama would absolutely beam when he would look at them. He was seen as a rising star in the Democratic Party. Then Senator Biden characterized him as "articulate, and bright and clean and a nice-looing guy."[32] I began to think that he was acceptable to many white voters, and especially to those who had suffered economically during the Bush presidency.

On February 5, 2008, Super Tuesday of the primaries, Obama beat Clinton by winning thirteen of the twenty-two contested states. His showing, winning states in several regions of the country, demonstrated that he was a serious contender for the White House. He defeated Clinton in the Texas primary caucuses, something that few expected him to do.

Texas Congresswoman Sheila Jackson-Lee from Houston, who supported Hillary during the Texas primary, was asked not to come to the Texas State Convention. That was how serious the support for Barack Obama was among Democrats in Texas.

Obama's candidacy excited voters, especially young people, in a way that I could have never imagined. That excitement was contagious. I had not believed that I would see a Black man become the presidential nominee of a major party. But I was seeing it, and realizing the possibility that he might actually win the election. That hope, that possibility, filled my heart. But I knew that my decision to support Barack had hurt my friend Hillary. And that is something that I have always regretted.

The Obama Election

When Senator Obama received the nomination, it was as if a breath of fresh air had been blown into the life of the nation. The very fact that a person of color was the nominee of a major American political party was a victory in and of itself. I knew that something special was taking place, something that I had not seen since the time that John Kennedy ran for president.

Still, even with the excitement and enthusiasm, I was optimistic but not certain that he could defeat Senator John McCain of Arizona, the Republican Party nominee. A Vietnam war hero and former prisoner of war, he had spent two decades in the navy, retiring on a disability pension. He had been elected to the House of Representatives in 1983. Four years later he was elected to the United States Senate. He served on the Armed Services Committee, the Commerce Committee, and the Indian Affairs Committee.

I knew McCain as we were neighbors, living in the same condominium in northern Virginia. We had worked together in Congress. A very nice man, he could sometimes be a very difficult politician. In the Senate he had a reputation for being a maverick. He broke from his party on a number of occasions, including when he voted to confirm Ruth Bader Ginsburg, a Clinton nominee to the US Supreme Court. His efforts to bring about campaign finance reform did not earn him many friends among conservatives.

McCain had first run for the Republican Party presidential nomination in 2000 but lost to President George Bush. He had named his campaign bus the Straight Talk Express, a motto that he would use again on his 2008 campaign bus that took him from airports to campaign events.

For this presidential run, McCain chose Sarah Palin, who was two years into her first term as governor of Alaska as his running mate. She was an extreme conservative. McCain and his advisors believed that she would bring balance to the ticket, offsetting his moderation. There was also the belief that as the first woman on a Republican national ticket, her selection would generate excitement and enthusiasm for the campaign. Immediately after the Republican Convention, the McCain/Palin ticket had an impressive lead over the Obama/Biden ticket.

When I first saw the polls, I thought that perhaps I would not see a Black president. But selecting Palin for vice president turned out to be a problem for the campaign. Her interviews with prominent reporters showed the nation that she was wholly inexperienced, uninformed about foreign affairs, and unqualified to be the vice president of the United States. Far from bringing a sense of normalcy to the ticket, Palin brought chaos. Independent and progressive women were frightened by her because of her stance on women's issues. Her statements were unpredictable. Joe Biden, who had been selected as Obama's running mate, destroyed her in the first vice presidential debate. Voters became concerned that if anything happened to McCain, she would become president.

Obama clearly won the first two presidential debates. By the time the third and final debate occurred in October of 2008, McCain was so desperate that he suggested to millions of viewers that Senator Obama had socialist leanings. The final weeks of the campaign were brutal. Yet McCain refused to attack Obama's character or suggest that he was not a Christian. In fact, when a woman referred to Senator Obama as an Arab during a town hall, McCain said, "No, he is a decent family man. We just disagree on fundamental issues."

I worked as hard for Obama as I had for myself in any of my own elections. During the campaign I had volunteers in my campaign office calling voters in other states, urging them to vote for Obama. Given McCain's less than solid support among moderates and independents, and Palin's erratic behavior, I sensed that Obama stood a chance of being elected, but I was not certain given the outcomes and shenanigans during the presidential races in 2000 and 2004. The Republicans could once again steal the election, I feared.

On election night I went to the Dallas Obama headquarters to watch the results. Hundreds of young people of all colors were there, waiting with anxious anticipation to become witnesses to history. They had given their hearts and legs to his campaign. I was so very proud of them. I had never seen that type of energy before. I was overcome with emotion and began to cry. Most of them were students, unpaid volunteers who worked in the Obama/Biden campaign because they believed in the dream, reminiscent of Dr. Martin Luther King Jr.'s vision. These young people were the new marchers, the new freedom riders. They were the reincarnation of Medgar Evers, Viola Liuzzo, and Reverend James Reeb, who were killed because they fought for racial equality. To these visionary and courageous young people, the campaign was not simply a race to see who would become president, it was a continuation of a movement that had commenced long before any of them were born.

I was so proud. I knew that something new had taken place in America. It was something that I could not fully describe but that I felt deeply. As the television monitors displayed the results of the early vote in various sections of the country, I did not think that the Obama/Biden ticket would carry Texas, but if the energy that was present in this room existed across the nation, there was a good chance that Obama would be declaring victory that evening. History would be made.

At 10:00 p.m. Central Standard Time, the networks and cable channels called the election for Senator Barack Obama. He had been elected president with 53 percent of the popular vote and had 365 electoral votes. He had even won Florida and Ohio, the two states that I had worried about the Republicans stealing. He had accomplished a feat that many had believed impossible.

When the results were announced, the room erupted, strangers embraced one another, and tears began to flow from the eyes of men and women of all colors. Shouts of "Glory, hallelujah" could be heard. People were screaming at the top of their voices, jumping, dancing, and shouting. Even outside the streets erupted in joy. Car horns were blasting, whistles were blown, people were walking and shouting.

Having been a single mother who raised a young son, on election night I thought of Senator Obama's mother, Ann Dunham. She had died of cancer in 1995. She had not lived to see what her son had accomplished. But that night I had the feelings of a mother, and I was so very proud of him.

But I was also feeling honored and gratified for the opportunity that I had had to help to make history. It was one of the most marvelous moments in my life. I only wished that my father, who had told me that I could achieve anything that I set my mind to, was alive to share in this awesome experience and see how his little girl had played a role in making it a reality. Because this time, when I returned to Washington to take the oath of office, this time a Black man would be in the White House, not as a driver, a cook, a butler, or an aide, but as president of the United States of America.

Black Man in the White House

It was a bitterly cold day when president-elect Obama took the oath of office on January 20, 2009, becoming the forty-fourth president of the United States. I had chartered a plane from Dallas to Washington so that friends and members of my family could witness the inauguration. I had been to several inaugurations but had never seen the streets of Washington as crowded as they were on that day. Almost two million people from all over the world came to witness this world-changing event. People from across the country and around the world watched it on television. It was, as Senator Dianne Feinstein described it, "a day when a dream that once echoed across history from the steps of the Lincoln Memorial finally reached the walls of the White House."[33]

The temperature hovered around ten degrees. I shivered in my seat at the Capitol as the ceremony began. Aretha Franklin sang, Yo-Yo Ma played the cello, and Reverend Joseph Lowery from the Southern Christian Leadership Conference gave the benediction. As the ceremony proceeded, I watched the faces of my colleagues very closely. Some beamed with joy, unable to control their delight. There were others, however, whose faces were as cold as the temperature we were enduring. They were still in shock and dismay that Senator Obama had been elected to the highest office in the land.

The Chief Justice of the Supreme Court, John Roberts, administered the oath of office. He was so nervous that he misspoke and Obama had to assist him. In fact, the oath was administered again the next day because a word had been spoken out of order.

President Obama's inaugural address was compelling. With his opening acknowledgment of the sacrifices borne by our ancestors, he heralded a new day in America. He acknowledged the problems confronting us as a nation: the war against terrorism, the economy, the conflict and discord. He spoke of shared sacrifices, the need to assume a new sense of responsibility for one another and for the country. He talked of reforming the nation's health care system, dealing with global warming, improving the economy, developing alternative uses of energy, creating jobs, and bringing American troops home from Iraq and achieving peace in Afghanistan. His oratory and choice of words were compelling. He spoke words of inspiration, calling us to be keepers of the American legacy.

That evening my family and I attended the Texas Black Tie and Boots Ball. It was packed with celebrants who had come from Texas to participate in a history-making event. Not everyone in the large banquet room had supported Obama's nomination, but that did not matter because he had energized a new core of Democratic voters and had delivered one of the most compelling inaugural addresses in our country's history.

There were so many events and activities. I received invitations from so many organizations, well-known and lesser known. Organizations specifically targeting African American concerns and issues, inspired by the election of the first Black president, especially celebrated the occasion: the CBC Foundation; National Congress of Black Women, Inc.; National Council of Women's Organizations; National Association of Minority Government Contractors; Meharry Medical College; the Council for Leadership Equality and Diversity; the Historically Black Colleges and Universities; National Bar Association; National Black Chamber of Commerce; National Newspaper Publishers Association; and so many more. And, of course, there were Texas-connected events: the Black Tie and Boots ball, the University of North Texas reception, the Craig Washington's reception, and Texas Style Chili. A binder of invitations and activities and sheets of daily itineraries were evidence of the excitement and optimism born out of this election. It was a new birth of freedom.

Obama was targeted by some conservatives and other divisive forces from the moment he was declared the winner. The administration of the oath only seemed to intensify their opposition. They seemed to be still in shock that an African American was now considered the most powerful individual on the face of the planet. They certainly could not stomach the fact that he was their commander in chief. They made plans to derail his programs and his policies.

Members of the CBC sensed the atmosphere among some of our colleagues in the House. We were told that a similar attitude was present among some in the Senate. Many of us pledged to help the administration succeed. We knew that the president had a lot to learn, and that many of the people that surrounded him were new to Washington. We opened our office doors. We encouraged them. We gave advice, telling them that they could call on us at any time.

Of all of my years in Congress, I have only served under two Democratic presidents, Bill Clinton and Barack Obama. Both addressed the nation's problems, advancing robust legislative agendas. The country was in dire straits when President Obama was elected. We were in a recession and in a seemingly endless war in Iraq. President Obama, working with a Democratic Congress for the first two years of his administration, took an aggressive, broad approach to tackle the nation's challenges.

Lilly Ledbetter Fair Pay Act of 2009

One of the first bills signed by President Obama was the Lilly Ledbetter Fair Pay Act. It was introduced on January 6, 2009, and I joined as a cosponsor of this bill, which was made necessary because a Supreme Court ruling had unduly restricted the time period for wage discrimination claims. Lilly Ledbetter had filed a lawsuit against Goodyear Tire & Rubber Company alleging that she had been given poor evaluations because of her sex and that because pay raises were based on the evaluations, she was denied equal pay. The Supreme Court ruled that she could only sue on the last pay decision, not for the lower pay that she had suffered over the years. This statute was written to make it clear that Congress intended for a victim of wage discrimination to be able to claim back pay for up to two years preceding the filing of their claim.

Speaking in support of this bill, I pointed out that there was undeniable gender disparity because of loopholes in the Equal Pay Act of 1963. Women were earning seventy-eight cents on the dollar to their male counterparts, amounting to $400,000 to $2 million in lost income. When women are underpaid, their children and families are harmed. It did not make sense that a woman would not be allowed to recover damages when a company treated her unfairly and paid her less. This type of discrimination needed to stop. This statute was an important step to ending pay discrimination.[34]

Hate Crimes Prevention

Frustratingly, it sometimes takes multiple introductions of bills for them to be adopted by Congress. This is the case with the passage of a statute criminalizing acts of violence against a person because of their race, gender, religion, or national origin. The Hate Crimes Prevention Act of 1997, which I cosponsored, was first introduced on November 13, 1997. The bill did not advance.

It was introduced again on March 3, 1999. I was again a cosponsor. And again, although Bill Clinton was president, Republicans controlled both the House and Senate. On June 7, 2000, as the bill had not moved through the House, I rose to speak. I asked how we could sit in Congress and profess how far America has come. Why did we always seem to need to stress how we had grown economically and socially? Wasn't this the time for America to grow morally? For those who were afraid to answer that question, I answered it for them: now was the time.

I reminded them that the bipartisan Hate Crimes Prevention Act had been introduced over a year earlier. This legislation would make it easier for federal authorities to assist in the prosecution of racial, religious, and ethnic violence. This legislation had been referred to the Subcommittee on Crime, where it sat.

I spoke of the brutal death of James Byrd Jr. in Texas, who had been beaten shamelessly by two white supremacists, then chained to a pickup truck and dragged to his death. I implored my colleagues to act. We could not allow another minute to pass before enacting the Hate Crimes Prevention Act. Now was the time. But my words did not move the opposition.[35]

Over the years variations of hate crime prevention bills were proposed. Congressman John Conyers introduced Local Law Enforcement Hate Crimes Prevention Act in the House on April 3, 2001.[36] I joined as a cosponsor. There was a similar bill introduced in the Senate. Congressman Conyers reintroduced the act each subsequent session, and each time I joined as a cosponsor. Under the Bush administration and the Republican-controlled Congress, there simply wasn't any interest in moving hate crime prevention bills forward.

After all those efforts, and multiple votes over the years, finally in October 2009 President Obama signed the Matthew Shepard and James Byrd Jr. Hate Crimes Prevention Act expanding federal crimes to include assaults targeting persons because of race, color, religion, national origin, sexual orientation, gender identity, or disability. It had been added to the 2010 National Defense Authorization Act to secure passage. Signing the bill, President Obama paid tribute to Senator Ted Kennedy, who had worked diligently in support of this legislation up to his death just a couple of months earlier. The persistence required to secure passage of this bill and the working relationships needed to coordinate between both chambers speak to benefits of having legislators who are not artificially restricted by term limits and can be tenacious in pursuing legislation.

Repeal of Don't Ask, Don't Tell

It had been a long time coming, the formal legislative action to repeal the Department of Defense's policy of "Don't Ask, Don't Tell" banning openly gay persons from serving in the military. When in 1994 the Defense Appropriations Act was passed, it led to the implementation of a policy of "don't ask, don't tell, don't pursue, and don't harass." It was a compromise attempt to remove an absolute ban on military service by gays and lesbians, actively supported by military leaders and leading senators to fulfill a campaign promise to remove the ban.

However, any ban or restriction on persons qualified to serve in the military didn't make sense, especially during the Iraq War when the military needed personnel. Don't Ask, Don't Tell had unintended consequences. It put a burden on servicemembers, as they were still subject to involuntary discharge.

President Obama had campaigned on the repeal of that compromise. I stood in support of the bill to repeal those restrictions, noting that almost thirteen thousand servicemembers had been discharged since the 1994 passage of Don't Ask, Don't Tell. I expressed my disbelief that we were allowing incredibly qualified and trained individuals to be excluded from the military for being themselves. It was important, I said, that Americans embrace openly gay individuals as equal and essential to our nation's armed services. We had to work together toward ending discrimination against every minority and create more opportunities for all Americans. The contributions of every person serving in our military should be highly valued.[37]

Getting Out of the Recession

When Barack Obama was elected president in 2008, America was in a recession. Low interest rates had spurred a boom in real estate and housing construction. Various types of mortgages—including subprime, adjustable rates—had been created, which allowed unqualified borrowers to purchase homes. Housing prices started to fall because too many houses had been built. Homeowners were becoming upside down in their mortgage, causing defaults. This created a housing bubble that collapsed in 2007. Financial businesses that had purchased the mortgages as investments suffered losses. Unemployment rose. Banks and financial institutions were failing.

During the time between Obama's election and inauguration, Democratic congressional members worked to develop legislation to address the economic problems. President-elect Obama had set a goal that the legislation should save or create at least three million jobs. Obama aides held meetings with the group drafting legislation.

American Recovery and Reinvestment Act

On January 26, 2009, the House version of the American Recovery and Reinvestment Act of 2009 was introduced.[38] The Recovery Act was designed to jumpstart our economy, create or save millions of jobs, and begin addressing long-neglected concerns. The very next day I spoke in support of this bill, especially its focus on infrastructure needs. Our roads, bridges, transit systems, airports, and water-related systems needed attention. The Water Resources Subcommittee had identified $50–60 billion of vital Army Corps of Engineer projects that needed to be funded. Investment in infrastructure supported tens of thousands of jobs and billions of dollars in economic activity. The $3 billion in infrastructure investment funding allocated for Texas under the proposed bill would provide a tangible benefit not only to the state but also to the nation by the increased efficiency in the movement of goods and services. If we kept on doing the same things that we had been doing, we would get the same results.[39]

I continued my remarks the next day. This time I focused on the science and educational stimulus activities. We needed a high-tech workforce, so we had to have the educational resources for developing that talent. There were provisions for funding the National Institute of Standards and Technology to provide grants for research science buildings at colleges and universities. There was funding for modernization of K–12, additional support for Head Start, grants for college students, and financial incentives for effective teachers. But my concern about HBCUs compelled me to address the digital divide between those campuses and others. HBCUs are a unique resource and remain extremely effective in educating and graduating African American students. I urged federal funding for support of HBCUs.[40]

My firm belief that passing the bill was an important first step to helping our nation's economy was shared by a majority of the House. Despite amendments and modifications urged by Republican members, not a single Republican member voted for the bill. I was the only North Texas member to vote for it. In the Senate the debate was intensified by the participation of Senator Ted Kennedy, who was suffering through a fight with a brain tumor in the early rounds of voting. With three moderate Republicans joining the Democratic senators, the bill narrowly passed but drew Senator John McCain's scathing rejection of any claim that it was a bipartisan bill.[41] It was difficult to believe that it was possible, but the divisions between Democrats and Republicans had become even more deeply hardened and sharpened. But the bill passed and was signed into law. The foundation for pulling our nation out of the recession had been laid.

Some months later I spoke on the floor. I wanted to go on the record to report that I had held two economic recovery workshops in Dallas with almost a thousand people attending. This attendance was due to the American Recovery and Reinvestment Act, an unprecedented effort to dig ourselves out of the recession and move toward economic recovery and long-term sustained prosperity. Communities in my district had already received recovery money. The Los Barrios Unidos Community Clinic was able to open a satellite clinic. DFW Airport was going to immediately start a $2 million runway rehabilitation project. The Dallas Independent School District had already received more than $78 million to support low-income students. Four other schools district that I represented collectively received about $3.6 million. Overall, the state of Texas was awarded almost $338 million in School Improvement Grants to help with low achieving schools.

As I said at that time, we had inherited quite a mess with the last administration, but the Democrats were restoring the country's economic well-being. There was plenty of work to be done, but the American Recovery and Reinvestment Act had been a strong beginning. I was proud, then and now, to have voted for the Recovery Act.[42]

Saving the Automobile Industry

At the same time that the Recovery Act was being considered, President Obama also had to address the declining auto industry. While some wanted the major automobile companies to go into bankruptcy, President Obama believed that they should be given government assistance. He developed a plan that provided for billions of federal dollars to be invested in the struggling automobile industry for General Motors, Chrysler, and Ford to be retooled and restructured. The GM CEO had to resign. It was an investment in an important segment of the economy. With this lifeline millions of jobs were saved. This decision has led a retired Chrysler executive to write a column saying that he hoped that there would be a statue of Barack Obama in Detroit with the inscription: "He saved the domestic auto industry, 2009."[43] I agree.

Dodd-Frank Wall Street Reform and Consumer Protection Act

The crisis that rocked financial institutions during 2007–2009 was rooted in lax lending standards that promoted easy mortgages, creating a housing bubble. When the bubble burst, millions of homeowners were upside down on their mortgages, owing more than their homes were worth. Financial institutions were holding trillions of dollars in worthless investment. Lehman Brothers, one of the largest financial banks, had to declare bankruptcy. The stock market plummeted. Unemployment climbed.

These events caused an examination of the financial regulatory system. It was outdated and provided little to no oversight. To address these problems and to provide some stability, the Dodd-Frank Wall Street Reform and Consumer Protection Act was passed.[44] It reorganized the financial sector and created the Consumer Financial Protection Bureau. Regulation was necessary because companies in the financial industry had nearly caused a total economic collapse of the American economic system.

While Dodd-Frank was under consideration, I addressed the House to encourage the American public to stand with Democrats to stop Wall Street from "gambling with our economic security." I pointed out that for far too long the executives on Wall Street had reaped rewards by bending the rules and dodging financial regulation. Wall Street executives had taken big bonuses while gambling with our homes, our jobs, and our economy. And when their financial world collapsed, they had turned to the American taxpayer to bail them out. The Dodd-Frank bill put an end to the taxpayer-funded bailouts. Never again would average Americans be on the hook for Wall Street's greed. Big banks were accountable for their own failures. Regulators would now have the tools to stop the unregulated greed that had almost destroyed our financial world.[45]

The Generations Invigorating Volunteerism and Education (GIVE) Act was a bill to encourage volunteerism as one component to address our economic problems.[46] The bill helped connect Americans to high-quality, meaningful service and service-learning opportunities. It was especially designed to provide opportunities and incentives to middle and high school students to participate. I had proposed language to engage public safety officers to volunteer with disadvantaged youth and provide opportunities for community-based crime prevention efforts. I recognized that too often there was a disconnect between law enforcement and the citizens of high crime areas. It was important that these two groups recognized that they were partners in crime prevention, not adversaries. I was pleased that my language was incorporated into the bill.[47]

After the House had passed the GIVE bill, the Senate considered the bill, renaming it the Edward M. Kennedy Serve America Act. The bill proposed $5.7 billion dollars over five years to encourage volunteerism by expanding the AmeriCorps programs, creating a new service corps addressing energy efficiency, student engagement, health care, and veterans.

As he signed the bill, President Obama said that it was fitting that it was named after Senator Edward Kennedy, for he was a person who had never stopped asking what he could do for his country.[48] The legislation was not just a tribute to Senator Kennedy; it was a call for action to all of us, to do our part to lift our fellow Americans. We all had a role to serve our communities and to shape our history.

Taking Care of Our Veterans: Veterans Health Care Budget Reform and Transparency Act of 2009

While attention was being focused on health care reform for the general population, I was also giving my attention to the health care provided to our veterans. In early February 2009, I introduced the Veterans' Medical Personnel Recruitment and Retention Act of 2009.[49] The salaries being paid to VA health professionals—our nurses, physicians, dentists, and pharmacist executives—were not competitive. My bill called for waiver of pay restrictions and increases in pay to enable the VA to recruit and retain professionals who were on the front lines of health care. It provided for limits on overtime duty, weekend duty, and alternative work schedules for nurses. It created an educational loan repayment program.

Months later, the Caregivers and Veterans Omnibus Health Services Act was introduced in the Senate.[50] This comprehensive bill, among other things, provided support for veterans' caregivers, focused on women veterans' health care matters, and addressed mental health issues. Along with these measures, the bill incorporated the provisions set out in my Veterans' Medical Personnel Recruitment and Retention Act of 2009.

The day the House considered this bill, following a public acknowledgement of the importance of my provision for retention and recruitment of the professionals needed in the VA, I rose to urge members to vote for the bill. I said that it was our duty to assure that our veterans who had so courageously served our country receive the medical support they deserve.[51] Being a part of strengthening the health care given to our veterans allowed me to once again serve our veterans.

Patient Protection and Affordable Care Act

Early in his administration, President Obama appeared before a joint session of Congress, talking not just to elected officials but, as he said, also speaking frankly to the American people. President Obama assured the nation that we would recover from our economic crisis. He specifically mentioned the cost of health care, the rising costs that impair savings. Recalling that health care reform had been an issue as far back as President Teddy Roosevelt, he urged that health care reform could not wait, that it had to be addressed.[52]

On May 18, 2009, Congresswoman Barbara Lee, chair of the CBC, took to the floor to present the caucus's position on health care issues. The comprehensive set of principles that the caucus had developed were presented. The elimination of health disparities had to be a central goal of any health care reform process. Mental and dental health care had to be addressed. There had to be increased focus on preventive measures. Health information technology had to be integral to any reform. Collection of data by race, ethnicity, language, geography, and socioeconomic factors must be mandated. Community-based research examining causes of health disparity and including minorities needed to be conducted.

As the chairwoman of the CBC announced these principles, she expressly recognized me, noting that as a former nurse, I brought a wealth of knowledge and expertise to the health care debate and had been involved in health care reform for many, many years.[53] I had been fighting for health care reform for a long time. It had been fifteen years since President Clinton had tackled health care, a point that I would make in my remarks on the floor. During that time insurance companies had held the public hostage, controlling them, rationing medicine, and telling the physicians what to do. I had repeatedly called for quality health care for all Americans, noting that over 20 percent of the African American community and 35 percent of the Hispanic community did not have health insurance. Just a few weeks earlier, during a telephone town hall with over 3,500 constituent participants, I heard firsthand the concerns about rising health care costs.

The fight for affordable health care continued through the summer. Speaker Pelosi and other Democrats introduced H.R. 3962, the Affordable Health Care for America Act. On July 15, 2009, the next day, I joined other nurses at the Rose Garden as President Obama emphasized the importance of nurses in health care.[54] Joined by other nurses from the American Nurses Association, this was yet another opportunity to spotlight the need for health reform.

On September 17, 2009, Representative Charles Rangel introduced the Patient Protection and Affordable Care Act, H.R 3590.[55] I repeatedly urged the House to approve health reform bills. When I spoke, as I told my colleagues, I was speaking from my experience as a state and federal legislator and as a nurse. Having worked with psychiatric patients, I knew firsthand that health care for persons with mental health issues was especially weak. But the entire health care system had faltered, and we were now in a crisis. Americans were spending more on health care than housing or food; some were choosing between health premiums, rent, or prescription medicines. We needed to have an alternate system to compete with insurance companies. We could not let the millions of dollars that were being paid to insurance lobbyists determine what health care reform we would provide. We call ourselves the richest country and leading nation, but we did less to make sure that our people were healthy. We needed affordable health care.

On another occasion I focused on the impact that health premiums had on small businesses. The increase just for small businesses to cover their employees had gone up 129 percent since the year 2000. Small-business workers pay an average of 18 percent more in premiums. How far does this have to go before we have the common sense to change it?, I asked my colleagues.

But the debate continued. As I had said on the floor, insurance companies were spending millions of dollars to oppose any health care reform, promoting mistruths and falsehoods. At a time when the American people deserved to have all of us working together to get decent health care reform, misinformation was being spread around. If the insurance companies had wanted to cover the millions of uninsured people, they would have already done so. Scare tactics were used. Republicans were deliberately mischaracterizing the bill's provisions. There were false claims that we were canceling Medicare. It was long past time that health care reform be passed.[56]

The bill that had been introduced by Representative Charles Rangel in November 2009 was the basis for the reconciliation bill that came up for vote in March 2010.[57] On that day I spoke one more time in support of affordable health care for all Americans. I declared that the time had come, that indeed it was long past time, that the House should choose consumers over insurance companies. They had held the public hostage, controlling health care, telling physicians and hospitals what to do. It was time to let the people have their right to pick their health care. Voting in favor of this bill was something we simply had to do.

On March 23, 2010, I joined others in the east room of the White House to witness the signing of the health care reform bill. I had been invited by President Obama to attend the ceremony in recognition of the work that I had done to support the health and well-being of all Americans.

During the first four years of the law, Republicans in the House of Representatives challenged it more than fifty times. And I would rise in opposition or issue statements denouncing those efforts. Yet despite such opposition, by spring 2015, nearly twelve million people had signed up for health care under the Affordable Care Act. Some states such as Texas refused to establish an exchange that allowed people to purchase insurance. To fill that void, the federal government established an exchange in Texas, as well as the other states that had refused to establish their own.

Despite the opposition and efforts to undermine the Affordable Care Act, also known as Obamacare, it has helped millions of Americans access health care. The years that I and other members of Congress had spent keeping a focus on health care issues had finally brought help to Americans. It was a win for our country.

Other Accomplishments from Obama's First Term

During Obama's first administration, there were a number of statutes for which I successfully offered amendments. It is always important to gauge the viability of proposed legislation and the possibility of including provisions advancing related but unaddressed interests and projects. One such amendment to the Commerce, Justice, Science, and Related Agencies Appropriations Act secured $32 million in funding for HBCUs.[58] My continued concern about mental health care for military families with members stationed outside of the United States was reflected in the successful amendment to the Defense Authorization Act requiring the Department of Defense to report on the need for and availability of such mental health care services.

Added on as a rider to the Patient Protection and Affordable Care Act were important provisions drawn from the Student Aid and Fiscal Responsibility Act of 2009 (SAFRA.) This legislation changed how students could access federal funds for education. Instead of the government subsidizing private loans, which promised banks profits even in the case of default, students would borrow directly from the government, eliminating millions of dollars by removing the private banks from the process. The bill also provided critical funding for community colleges and HBCUs. With rising tuition costs at private and public institutions, it was important that financing vehicles were in place to help students attend college or get career training. As I had said in support of SAFRA, because we are only as rich as our poorest citizens, fiscal education is important to the nation.[59]

There were other spending bills that provided significant benefit to North Texas. We received approximately $34 million dollars in grants from the Department of Housing and Urban Development from the Community Development Block Grants to expand economic and housing opportunities in urban communities. There were grants to the city of Dallas and Dallas County totaling almost $860,000 for homeless relief and another $8.3 million to expand affordable housing for low and very low-income families. The city of Dallas also received $3.6 million for Housing Opportunities for Persons with AIDS. Securing this federal funding is important because it enables the local governments to provide programs for the benefit of their residents that they probably would not otherwise have.

These selected bills were just part of the accomplishments of the first Obama term. In the years immediately preceding his election, the Iraq War was dividing the nation. Candidate Obama had campaigned on a platform favoring withdrawal of the US military from Iraq. Prior to the election, he visited Iraq, meeting with the Iraqi prime minister, insurgent leaders, and US military commanders. He developed and kept a timeline for the withdrawal of troops from Iraq.

The 9/11 attacks had been orchestrated by Osama bin Laden, the leader of al Qaeda. For ten years, as we strengthened our defense and disrupted terrorist attacks, we had hunted him, determined to get justice for the brazen terrorist attack that killed thousands and injured even more. On May 2, 2011, Navy Seals conducted an operation that killed bin Laden, marking the most significant achievement in our efforts to defeat al Qaeda. It was an achievement that we were able to do because, as President Obama said, we are one nation, under God, indivisible, with liberty and justice for all.

As I watched President Obama confront the breadth of issues before him, I was proud that I was among those who had nurtured him when he first came to Congress. Both he and Michelle are impressive professionals who had both attended exemplary schools and achieved success and committed themselves to public service. As a couple they represented the United States well, driven by a belief that they were fighting for the world as it should be. They were pushing us to become that more perfect union.

It was that message and compassion that was reflected in the Deferred Action for Childhood Arrivals, which provided a process for children brought into the country unlawfully to be eligible for work permits. It was with the belief that Supreme Court justices should bring perspective and empathy in consideration of the cases before them that he sought the appointment of two progressive women, Elena Kagan and Sonia Sotomayor, as associate justices. It was with the understanding that diversity is important that his administration appointed significant numbers of persons of color to positions within his administration. He also appointed minority judges to federal district and appellate courts, a total of sixty-six over both terms.

President and Mrs. Obama represented this nation well. Watching them as I attended events at the White House and other public appearances, not only was I filled with pride, but I also had confidence that this nation was moving in the right direction.

Preparing for the 2012 Election

The candidacy and ultimate election of a Black man to the presidency of the United States had unleashed a racist backlash. At the University of Kentucky, someone hung a life-size likeness of Obama from a tree, symbolizing a lynching. Newspapers reported racially charged incidents across the country: a burning of a Black church in Springfield, Massachusetts; the Maine "Osama Obama Shotgun Pool," soliciting bets on when he would be assassinated; the US flag being flown upside down, to signal distress because a Black man had been elected; a radio show host blogging that his dream was for a drone to attack the inauguration crowd; the beating of an Obama supporter dressed in a campaign T-shirt; cross burnings; schoolchildren chanting "assassinate Obama."

The Republican strategy, openly discussed at a dinner on the night of Obama's inauguration, was to oppose every legislative proposal or initiative. And they did. It didn't matter that we were in an economic crisis; Republican leadership demanded that its members challenge any Obama legislation. Even the American Recovery and Reinvestment Act, addressing the economic problems that were affecting all Americans, did not receive a single Republican vote.

When the Republicans won a majority of the House during the 2010 elections, they were even better positioned to thwart Obama's initiatives. The partisanship really showed itself in the consideration of the Budget Control Act of 2011.[60] As I said on the floor in July 2011, the Republican bill was yet another attempt to balance the budget on the backs of seniors and the middle class. They were going to slash Medicare, Medicaid, and Social Security but not put any burden on the nation's most wealthy corporations and individuals.[61]

I urged bipartisan efforts to work on fiscal issues and maintain investments in our communities that would create jobs and grow the economy. It was terribly disappointing that ending Medicare for seniors is so important to Republicans that they continue to pursue this agenda at all costs and willingly put our national economy in peril. The House of Representatives had been under the control of the Republicans for nearly two hundred days, and they had yet to bring a single job-creating bill to the floor.[62] The economy should always be above partisan politics. It seemed that they would rather see the United States default on its existing debt for the first time in history, watch our economy lose hundreds of thousands of jobs, and cause interest rates and consumer goods to skyrocket in the process.

I had spoken to people all over Dallas, Tarrant, and Collin Counties, and unanimously they were seriously concerned about the lack of a true job plan from the Republican majority. We knew that spending needed to be cut. We knew that long-term fiscal health had to be ensured. But gridlock over spending cuts did not create jobs. We needed a bipartisan compromise that focused on fiscal responsibility while maintaining investments in our community that continue to create jobs and grow the economy. To get Americans back to work, we had to invest in science, education, research, and innovation to create the jobs of the future. We had to focus on America's ability to build, construct, and grow manufacturing across the country to remain globally competitive. I urged that something had to be done, that we had to do something about it. But there had to be a genuine desire to reach a compromise, not just an agenda to undermine a president.

But the greatest challenge to the future of this nation were the efforts to suppress voter participation in upcoming elections. The 2008 election turnout had not only shattered previous records at the time, but it was also the most racially and ethnically diverse, with unprecedented turnouts of Blacks, Hispanics, and Asians. Such demographics alarmed Republicans and caused a crusade to disenfranchise eligible voters.

A year before the 2012 election, I spoke out against these voter suppression efforts. Voting is a fundamental pillar of our democracy. Laws requiring a government ID even if the voter had a voter registration card and was listed on the registration roll burdened students, elderly, and the poor in exercising their right to vote. Restrictions on voter registration drives were designed to frustrate the registration of minorities. Not surprisingly, the voting laws being enacted did not address the purging of entire voter rolls or intentionally long wait times during early voting that had impacted recent elections. I thought that it was important to spotlight these efforts and raise the alarm about what was happening across our nation.

Chapter 15

My Final Decade
(2012–2022)

My last decade as a congresswoman began with the 2012 election. For this election my district lines were changed once again, this time due to the data from the 2010 census. Because the district lines are drawn in the state legislature, once the Republicans controlled the Texas legislature, I was not consulted about any boundaries or the composition of my district. This meant that when I was confronted with a new configuration, I would have to develop outreach strategies for the new areas added to the district. I had to educate new voters about my record. I had to share with them my legislative priorities. And I had to let them know that I was sincerely interested in hearing their concerns and issues.

My campaign strategy has generally remained the same: make contact with the voters. I used town halls, church meetings, personal robocalls so it would be my voice asking for their support. I had to abandon the door-to-door walks because the size of the district made that impracticable. But there was one thing that I never did: I never took for granted that I would be reelected. I always respected the voters' right of choice.

Obama's Second Term

The 2012 election was exciting because it returned Barack Obama to the presidency for a second term. And while the Republicans had control of the House, the Democrats were in the majority in the Senate.

President Obama's second inauguration was still invigorating and exciting. The celebration had a slightly different feel. The reelection proved that his first victory was not a fluke, not an aberration, but the democratic process at work. It was a recognition of his policy and legislative successes, the respect and dignity that he and his family brought to the White House, and his undeniable commitment to upholding the ideals of our nation. Again there were a multitude of events to attend, a binder of itineraries and invitations. This time the celebration was less idealized; we knew how the Obamas could be mocked, insulted, and denigrated, sometimes with Republican encouragement. But we were celebrating nonetheless because there were even more people who appreciated and valued his leadership.

Ranking Minority Member, Committee on Science, Space, and Technology

The real challenge in the Science Committee came in late 2012 with the appointment of Lamar Smith as chairman. Although he was from Texas, which is commonly a basis for collegiality, he was the most difficult member I have ever encountered. Abandoning tradition, he did not meet with me as the ranking member to discuss his agenda and programs for the committee. He did not invite me to work with him to set a general direction for the committee. Instead, he led the majority to blatantly weaponize the committee to attack science. He was relentless. He was harmful.

We did not share funding priorities. The majority heavily supported basic research rather than developing a balanced portfolio of investments that reached across the full range of fields. We urged the majority to find funding for wide-ranging research and development activities and STEM education programs. We were especially concerned when the NOAA, Department of Energy, Environmental Protection Agency, and NASA were hit with 20 percent higher cuts, with those monies shifted to the Department of Education. Past issues caused us to be concerned with STEM education not being housed in science mission agencies.

Under House rules each committee is to submit a report each quarter as to its activities. Under the Republican majority, one of my duties as the ranking member would be to author the statement of views by the minority party. As the committee considered cuts to the FY 2012 budget, I was compelled to point out that the investments in research and education programs had yielded very significant economic payoffs for the American people. The choice before the nation was clear: we could focus on the need to stay competitive in an international marketplace or we could engage in shortsighted reduction of our capability for innovation and education to meet arbitrary budget cuts. I pointed out that the proposed cuts would undermine years of bipartisan effort to increase student interest in science, engineering, and math, tantamount to posting "Help not Needed" signs on laboratories and universities across the nation. Failing to provide funding to invest in education, new ideas, and new processes would deny our children the capacity to deal with the crises that their generation would face.

Programmatically, we had to point out that the cuts to the NASA budget did not reflect the priorities that had been established in the NASA Authorization Act of 2010. The budget recommendations relating to the Department of Energy relied on an unrealistic assumption that private industry would spearhead a long-term solution to the depletion of fossil fuels or reduction of pollution.

And we had to strongly condemn the characterization that the Environmental Protection Agency was engaging in a pattern of regulation based on insufficient or faulty scientific evidence. The problem at the EPA, as we saw it, was not that the agency did not use science well or abused it. It was that science was used by those who feared regulation to postpone risk assessments with consistent requests for yet additional review, frequently causing matters to be considered for over a decade. We also noted our support for the Department of Transportation continuing research into development of energy efficient and environmentally friendly infrastructure. We had to address deterioration and safety concerns in our existing infrastructure.

As I wrote in the minority view, the majority had abused the committee's legitimate oversight powers by its efforts to tarnish the reputations of federal scientists, science-based nongovernmental organizations, and federal science agencies that did not go along with the majority's politically biased views.[1] Subpoenas were issued for the New York and Massachusetts state attorneys general for records used in their investigations of ExxonMobil for fraud for failing to disclose scientific data establishing that climate change was real and that fossil fuel was contributing to global warming. Never before had Congress sent a subpoena to a state law enforcement agency.

Chair Smith led the majority to involve the Science Committee in yet another investigation of Hillary Clinton's private email server. It didn't matter that the FBI and five other congressional committees were conducting reviews. This political use of the Science Committee was extremely alarming. It sidelined legitimate oversight activities that were needed; caused widespread criticism by mainstream media, including seven major newspapers; and created a risk that the negative impact would be long-lasting and put at risk the committee's ability to conduct necessary and appropriate oversight.

Normalizing Relations with Cuba

Midway through his second term, President Obama began the process of normalizing relations with Cuba. For more than fifty years, the official United States policy had reflected the Cold War policies opposing Communism. Trade and travel to the island were limited.

For years I had participated with a CBC program that had been born out of a meeting with the caucus and Fidel Castro. In 1999 a group of us had traveled to Cuba. During one of our meetings, we were discussing the lack of doctors for African American communities. President Castro offered to provide medical education and training for low-income students who committed to return to their communities and work for at least six years. Since 2000 this program had offered medical scholarships to students who would not have otherwise been able to achieve their medical training. Over the years there have been several students from my district, some who were graduates of Dallas Independent School District schools, who studied in Cuba under this program. I traveled to Cuba, bringing supplies and personal items to support our students. We went to a number of provinces, as Cuba's health care and medical education systems were set up on a localized, regional approach.

During my two earlier trips, I had been in meetings with Castro. He was very charismatic and engaging. It was easy to see that he was very much in charge, adored by his people. On one of those trips, there was a hurricane that ripped across the island. He was on television regularly, giving updates and encouragement to the residents. His messages were very soothing and calming.

I was pleased when President Obama, simultaneously with President Castro, announced a new period in the relationship between the United States and Cuba. President Obama met with Cuban president Raul Castro, brother of Fidel Castro, in Panama in the spring of 2015. After various steps, including the reopening of the US embassy in Havana; meetings on law enforcement issues such as counterterrorism, counternarcotics, and cybercrime; and joint statements on marine protections, environmental issues, and migration, President Obama traveled to Havana.

I and several members of the caucus accompanied President Obama on this history-making visit. A number of US companies were seeking to do business with Cuba and advocated the lifting of the trade embargo. We participated in meetings with Cuban officials and representatives of those companies. We were working to promote trade between our countries and renew our connection.

Iran Nuclear Treaty

The Joint Comprehensive Plan of Action (JCPOA), known as the Iran nuclear treaty, was a landmark treaty. In this treaty between Iran, the United States, China, France, Russia, the United Kingdom, and Germany, Iran agreed to dismantle its nuclear program, which was leading to the development of nuclear weapons. Iran provided increased access by international nuclear inspectors to their facilities to assess Iran's compliance with the treaty.

In exchange, the signatory nations would relieve some of the sanctions against Iran.

Although the House does not have a formal role in the ratification of a treaty, there is always a possibility that some ancillary legislation or budget support may be needed. The CBC was briefed on this treaty at the direction of President Obama. His national security advisor, Susan Rice, would frequently meet with the caucus to keep us informed and up to date on important foreign policy matters, such as the treaty.

I fully supported the Iran nuclear treaty. Limiting Iran's efforts to create nuclear weapons was in the interest of every nation. The treaty was a shining example of diplomacy and multi-national cooperation that yielded measurable results.

21st Century Cures Act

After Trump's election but before his inauguration in a remarkable showing of bipartisan support in the House and the Senate, we passed the 21st Century Cures Act.[2] This act, as I said on the floor, reflected congressional commitment to investment in health research and innovation in development of new treatments. It also ensured that there would be strategies to increase minority representation in clinical trials. The bill's focus on innovative cancer treatment and mandatory funding for the Food and Drug Administration and the National Institutes of Health would keep America in the forefront of medical research.[3]

This legislation incorporated much of the framework of the Helping Families in Mental Health Crisis, a bill that I had cosponsored earlier in the year. That bill had passed in the House by a vote of 422–2.[4] It was especially satisfying that Congress had recognized the need for mental health and substance abuse programming and had advanced innovation in mental health care.

Being at the White House to watch President Obama sign this bill was especially poignant because it was one of the strongest examples of bipartisanship that had come out of Congress in recent years. It also came toward the close of the Obama presidency, one that had been marked by Republican attacks and divisiveness.

Game Changer: 2016 Election

When Hillary Clinton announced her candidacy for the presidency in 2016, I was a strong supporter. I had always been troubled by having to decline supporting her in 2008 because of my endorsement of Barack Obama. This time I could, and did, actively campaign for her. I traveled to other states, visiting African American churches, focusing on get-out-the-vote initiatives. I knew that Hillary was well qualified. And now she had added secretary of state to her already impressive resume and job qualifications. The broad Democratic field of candidates quickly became Hillary Clinton and Bernie Sanders. It felt as if this was her time.

There can be no denying the fact that the 2016 election was both shocking and disturbing. I had already chartered a plane for travel to the inauguration. I watched the election results come in at my campaign office with volunteers who had participated in the get-out-the-vote activities. I was stunned as the results from Michigan, Pennsylvania, Ohio, and Indiana showed Trump receiving the higher vote. These were states with strong labor unions, and Trump did not have a track record of supporting labor. It didn't make sense to me. I had agreed to go to the Dallas Democratic headquarters, but I stayed at my campaign office until 3:00 a.m., overcome with disbelief. Finally I turned to the volunteers, saying, "I guess we need to go home." At that point there was nothing to be done.

In terms of objective qualifications, Hillary Clinton undeniably had more experience with legislative operations, governance, and foreign relations. For some reason she could never overcome the intense negative feelings that grew out of her leadership of the health care task force, the Whitewater and Vince Foster allegations, and her support of Bill Clinton through the impeachment proceedings. In my opinion those attitudes and feelings, which had been fanned by Republican partisans over the decades, blinded voters to her fitness to be elected as the first woman president.

In sharp contrast, Donald Trump didn't have any experience in government. His popularity seemed to be rooted in a television show noted for his dogmatic pronouncement, "You're fired." Even his record as a businessman was tarnished with bankruptcies and lawsuits. But he had an uncanny ability to tap into the segment of our population that was feeling detached and disconnected from the two-term presidency of Barack Obama. The repeated Republican histrionics opposing the Affordable Care Act, suggesting that President Obama was a Muslim and supported terrorism and vowing that his initiatives should be blocked, had broadened and hardened the divisions between Republicans and Democrats that had started with Speaker Newt Gingrich. His repeated denouncement of trade policies influenced labor unions.

He appealed to an audience who enjoyed his abrasive, cocky, "in your face" style. They were entertained by his insulting labels, name calling, and offensive comments about women, persons with disabilities, and Democrats. They relished his braggadocios manner, even when he boasted that he could shoot someone and not lose any voters.[5] His behavior revealed issues about his character and narcissism that were alarming to those of us concerned about this country.

But it was his flaunting of norms and standards of civility that raised even more alarms. The castigation of the press, the baseless slogans of "fake news," and the encouragement of chants of "lock her up" concerned me. Our government depends upon mutual respect and institutional norms. Legislators handle differences of opinion and work through disagreement. But an attitude that encourages and promotes bullyism, that praises and applauds obstructionism, does not serve our nation.

The role of each branch of government—legislative, judicial, and executive—needs to be understood and valued. Our democracy demands that the members of Congress and the executive branch commit to sincerely working together in the best interests of the nation. We may disagree about priorities and the pathways to achieve objectives, but we do so in a spirit of respect, believing that each person truly holds the interest of the country at heart. Above all, we approach the issues that we confront with an attitude of civility that we can discuss and debate those differences and reach a compromise.

Donald Trump Is President

President Trump's election shattered many hopes for working together. He demanded an allegiance that smothered any open cooperation between Democrats and Republicans. Members of Congress with whom I had worked for years were now afraid to have our collaboration publicly acknowledged. Our work would, and did, suffer.

I didn't have any relationship with President Trump before his election. At the luncheon following the oath for the leadership of the House and Senate, I approached him and said, "Congratulations, Mr. President." President Trump responded, "I know you didn't expect me to be here, I didn't either."

As I stood there, hearing his words—such a bizarre comment—my concerns for the country deepened. I was aware of his position on subjects that I had a lot of knowledge about: trade, climate control, relations with Cuba, DACA, and the Affordable Care Act—concerns that were well-founded, fears that proved to be justified.

Candidate Trump loudly attacked trade agreements and vowed to end NAFTA. I had been in Congress when NAFTA was adopted, so I knew the rationale and had seen the benefits in my district. Any agreement may need modification with the passage of time, but NAFTA was fundamentally sound. But the claim that he would make Mexico and Canada yield to his demands appealed to his supporters. In the end President Trump's trade policies were not successful. Deficits with China and the world were significantly higher than under President Obama. American consumers ended up paying higher prices for goods because of the tariffs he unilaterally imposed. And the US-Mexico-Canada Agreement was an update of NAFTA. In the end President Trump's trade policies hurt American interests, companies, and consumers.

But it was candidate Trump's calling climate change and global warming "a hoax" that most distressed me. Having served on the Science, Space, and Technology Committee, I knew the real challenges facing our country and the world with climate change. While he was campaigning, I again took the floor, spurred by the flooding that had taken the lives of sixteen Texans during the wettest spring season on record. We simply had to keep moving forward in addressing fossil fuel emissions and atmospheric changes and protecting wetlands. Our literal existence was being threatened.

Again, my concerns were well-founded. My fears proved to be justified. Within months of his presidency, he pulled the United States out of the Paris Climate Agreement, action that I criticized at the time as being the height of shortsightedness when we were facing the most serious environmental challenge in human history. The EPA oversaw the reversal or revocation of environmental rules that protected natural resources, addressed pollution, and targeted the climate. Standards for fuel efficiency, carbon emissions, and methane gas emissions were all lowered, causing more carbon dioxide to be added to the atmosphere.

Even the EPA had to recognize that the Obama policy had reduced harmful air pollutants by 73 percent. But it reversed those standards and instituted a policy that allowed higher greenhouse gas emissions while acknowledging that there could be thousands of deaths because of increased air pollution. This action was appalling. I immediately released a statement pointing out that President Trump was ignoring the science and putting Americans' health at risk. We were sacrificing our nation's health to appease the coal industry.

Almost halfway through his term, President Trump even disputed whether there was climate change in a *60 Minutes* interview. That was too outlandish; that was too far. I issued a statement that "feelings are not facts," warning that the president was pedaling misinformation. I said that as president he should have been advancing measures to attack the causes of climate change, but to the harm of the country and the world, he abdicated that responsibility.

We continually opposed Trump's efforts to deny climate change. As the ranking member of the House Science, Space, and Technology Committee, I issued a minority report, "'Much Ado about Nothing': A Minority Review of the Majority's Climate Science Investigation," that directly confronted the administration's unsubstantiated allegations that scientific data had been manipulated by NOAA scientists for political reasons. Like so many positions advanced by this administration, there was no evidence to support those claims and many had been proven to be false.

After the first one hundred days of the Trump presidency, I joined other members of the CBC to spotlight the dangers posed by his position on the environment and global climate change. In January 2018 I went to the floor to speak out in support of climate research. I pointed out that in 2017 alone, there had been sixteen extreme weather events. Houston had three five-hundred-year floods in three years. We were breaking the wrong weather records. We had to accept that climate change was real.[6] But President Trump never admitted that there was climate change. As a result we lost four years in the fight against climate change. Our way forward to protect the country, the world, and the planet has been made more difficult and become more critical because of him.

Candidate Trump also vowed to terminate the relationship with Cuba that had been established by former president Obama. I understood the Obama strategy of opening the door and letting the relationship build and grow. It was in stark contrast to Trump's anticipated approach to insist on concessions and conditions. It was an approach that would undo that which had only recently been achieved. Again, my concerns were well-founded. My fears proved to be justified.

Within months of taking office, President Trump instituted a new policy imposing tougher restrictions on American travel and business with Cuba. He renewed the statutory embargo. He ended joint medical research on infectious diseases. I criticized these actions, saying that he was dragging American-Cuban relationships back fifty-five years to a time of extreme tension. He was hurting American and Texas farmers, businesses, and airlines by limiting opportunities.

Another initiative that President Obama had instituted was the Deferred Action for Childhood Arrivals (DACA). During the campaign candidate Trump denounced that program as one of the most unconstitutional actions ever undertaken by a president. President Trump announced an end to DACA, with Dreamers becoming subject to deportation within six months. It was, he said, a system that victimized millions of Americans by taking away jobs. His threats to end DACA had created anxiety and apprehension for the young people who had been protected under this program. His announcement of ending DACA increased the alarm and fear. I called his announcement the beginning of a dark era that would tear families apart. Speaking on the floor, I shared the stories of Texan Dreamers, graduates of Yale and Southern Methodist University, who were working hard every day to live the American dream. I urged my colleagues to pass a DREAM act that let those young people know that they could consider American to be their true home.[7]

Fortunately, about three years later, the Supreme Court ruled that President Trump had not addressed the fact that thousands had relied on the program to enroll in school, begin careers, buy homes, start families, and pay $60 billion in taxes. Failure to address those issues made President Trump's decision arbitrary and capricious. This ruling saved Republicans in Congress from having to address the issue of the Dreamers.[8]

President-elect Trump nominated former senator Jeff Sessions to serve as his attorney general. This appointment was opposed by the CBC. Senator Chuck Grassley presided over the Judiciary Committee confirmation hearings. Breaking the tradition of professional courtesy, he did not schedule Senator Cory Booker, Congressman John Lewis, and CBC chair Cedric Richmond—all representatives of the CBC—to appear at the beginning of the hearings. Instead, he scheduled them for the end. Rather than the Republican committee members attending this final witness session to hear their testimony, only Senator Grassley was present. In an obvious effort to counter the testimony of these representatives of the CBC, collectively representing millions of citizens, Senator Grassley arranged for three African American former staffers out of Senator Sessions's thirty years in office to testify about their experiences working in his office. The disrespect was blatant. The insult was intended and obvious. The arrogance and tone were reflective of the president-elect. And it was hypocritical because members of the CBC had just weeks earlier been admonished by the Speaker pro tempore to refrain from "engaging in personalities against Member of the Senate and the President-elect."[9]

Infrastructure was one focus of President Trump's attention during his inauguration speech. He characterized our infrastructure as being in disrepair and decay. He declared that he would "build new roads and highways, and bridges and airports, and tunnels and railways all across our nation."[10] I knew about infrastructure. For years I had worked addressing our highways, railways, and airways. I knew that we could not rely solely upon the public/private partnerships he touted.

I addressed his remarks a few days later from the floor. A healthy mix of direct spending, tax incentives, public/private partners, and sensible public policies was needed. I pointed out that Texas was projected to account for nearly 15 percent of the national population growth through 2030. Dwindling federal funding for highway projects severely impacted our ability to build up the state's infrastructure. I urged President Trump to be serious about bringing real solutions to the table, something that was not merely handouts to corporations.[11]

As President Trump's term progressed, there were other issues that were of concern: packing the courts with ultraconservative judges, manipulating the 2020 census procedures, and condoning racist and inflammatory statements and conduct and police brutality. I spoke out individually against many of his statements and actions. The CBC and the Tri-Caucus, which had grown since it was formed under my CBC chairmanship to be the Tri-Caucus plus two, diligently worked together to oppose his actions that threatened our communities. We stood in solidarity against his harmful initiatives and troubling rhetoric.

Bipartisan Efforts under President Trump

Despite the acrimonious election and the rank appeal to partisanship, there were occasions when we were able to reach across the aisle. It is always important to identify those issues that can be advanced through Congress.

Inspiring the Next Space Pioneers, Innovators, Researchers, and Explorers (INSPIRE) Women Act

Passed by the House in 2016, we reintroduced this bill in early 2017 because it had not made it out of the Senate.[12] To encourage young girls and women to be interested in aerospace, this act provided support for existing programs, such as NASA Girls, a virtual mentoring program; Aspire to Inspire; and a summer institute for middle-school girls. The act also required NASA to submit a plan for its current and retired workforce to mentor female K–12 students. As I said in supporting the bill, mentorship is one of the best ways to show young girls that STEM careers are possible.[13]

Women in Aerospace Education Act

As a nation, assuring that we have the needed number of aerospace engineers and related technologies is critical to our space program. Faced with the need to expand and diversify the aerospace workforce, the Women in Aerospace Education Act was passed.[14] We had to improve our efforts and strategy to recruit women and individuals historically underrepresented in the science, technology, engineering, and mathematics to the aerospace industry. Signed by President Trump on December 11, 2018, this bill directed the NSF to prioritize the recruitment of women and historically underrepresented persons for internships and fellowships at NASA. As I said in support of this legislation, women were still woefully underrepresented in aerospace, constituting only 8 percent of that engineering specialty. By recognizing the space travel by astronaut Peggy Whitson, we acknowledged that we needed more successes like hers.

Innovations in Mentoring, Training, and Apprenticeships Act

The passage of a bill is exponentially increased when a majority member introduces the bill. To signify my support, I would sign on as an original cosponsor. That is what happened with the Innovations in Mentoring, Training, and Apprenticeships Act.[15] While Majority Leader Kevin McCarthy introduced the bill, as noted in the *Congressional Record*, I supported that introduction.

For years I had been focusing attention on the fact that our nation needs a skilled, diverse workforce in order to stay competitive in our world market. This bill recognized that truth and called for the NSF to develop a grant program involving junior or community colleges and industry partners in outreach for recruitment and enrollment of women and underrepresented populations in STEM fields. Grants would also be awarded for the development of curriculum and internships and research relating to STEM education.

As I said in support of the bill, it was high time that we as a society recognized the value of apprenticeships as avenues to high-quality careers. A strong STEM workforce is built on the foundation of blue-collar STEM workers, those who use their extensive STEM knowledge day in and day out without the traditional four-year degree. We need laboratory managers, technicians, mechanics, machinists, and welders to transform the ideas of engineers and scientists into reality. This bill helped to align education and training at community colleges with the knowledge and skills needed by employers.[16]

A Focus on History: Hidden Figures Congressional Gold Medal

The celebration of the fiftieth anniversary of the Apollo moon landing provided me with the opportunity to spotlight the unsung contributions of women to the success of the NASA program.

On February 27, 2019, I introduced the Hidden Figures Congressional Gold Medal Act.[17] As I spoke in support of the bill, I noted that in the early days of the space program, women and their talents were critically important but often overlooked. Women were generally not permitted to serve in any visible position or recognized publicly for their contributions. Women of color faced the additional daily indignity of racial discrimination. But the efforts of these women led to what can easily be called one of our nation's crowning achievements, landing the first humans on the moon. It was important that they be granted the Congressional Medal of Honor to recognize their achievements and to inspire our children. As I rhetorically asked, what better example can we hope to give our sons and daughters than the brilliance, hard work, and perseverance of these women computers, mathematicians, and engineers.[18]

While this act specifically named Katherine Johnson, Dr. Christine Darden, Dorothy Vaughn, and Mary Jackson, a fifth Congressional Gold Medal was awarded to honor all women who contributed to NASA. One such woman was Dr. Gladys West, who was instrumental in the development of global positioning systems (GPS) and the SEASAT remote sensing technology. Her receipt of the Pioneer in Tech Award from the National Center for Women & Information Technology gave me the opportunity to once again honor the brilliance, hard work, and determination of such trailblazers. Her career was inspirational for the next generation, especially the members of the Alpha Kappa Alpha sorority to which we both belong.

Henrietta Lacks Enhancing Cancer Research Act of 2019

Henrietta Lacks was an African American woman who suffered from cervical cancer. While receiving treatment at the Johns Hopkins Hospital in Baltimore, Maryland, in 1951, two tissue samples were taken from her cervix: healthy tissue and cancerous tissue. A researcher at Johns Hopkins took those tissue samples, without Lacks's knowledge or permission, and used them, a practice that was common at that time. Mrs. Lacks's cells were unlike any other cancer cells that had been received in the lab. Her cancerous cells multiplied and survived at an extraordinarily high rate. Where other cells would die, Mrs. Lacks's cells would double every twenty-four hours of so. Her cells were used to create the HeLa line of cells, eventually used by Jonas Salk to create the polio vaccine. HeLa cells, using the first two letters of her first and last name, continue to be widely used in research, including in vitro fertilization, HIV/AIDS, leukemia, Parkinson's disease, and the development of COVID-19 vaccines.

Many companies and researchers have used HeLa cells to develop new, profitable treatments. The Lacks family was never asked to consent to the use of those cells, nor were they compensated for that use. Revenues that were generated were never shared with the family. Equally important, her contribution was never acknowledged.

This act, which I cosponsored, was a way for us to recognize her legacy and its importance to medical research.[19] It also highlighted unacceptable past practices of using African Americans for medical testing without their knowledge or consent. The Henrietta Lacks Act requires the federal government to publish a report on government-funded cancer research trials, including the participation by underrepresented populations and describing any barriers to participation. Years after her cells had been cultivated, this statute honored her by improving access to clinical trials for communities of color.

National Suicide Hotline Designation Act

My days at St. Mary's and my rotation in psychiatric services gave me a strong interest in and commitment to improving resources for individuals encountering mental health issues. Working as the chief nurse for the psychiatric section of the VA hospital reinforced that interest and concern. Throughout my congressional terms, I had introduced legislation targeting mental health issues, especially for veterans. But the opportunity and ability to provide a resource to assist with suicide prevention across the nation was certainly one of my proudest moments.

About 45,000 Americans committed suicide annually, an average of 123 daily suicides. It was estimated that there were an additional 1 million–plus Americans who attempted suicide. Addressing this situation made it ripe for bipartisan action.

The first step was the passage of the National Suicide Hotline Improvement Act of 2018.[20] We had a National Suicide Prevention Lifeline, but it used 1-800-273-TALK as the phone number. It was cumbersome and hard to remember. This 2018 statute required the Federal Communication Commission, working with the assistant secretary for mental health and substance use and the secretary for veterans' affairs, to determine the feasibility of a designated dialing code, similar to 911, for the national suicide prevention hotline. Such a three-digit hotline would also be a tool to consolidate various state entities that were providing suicide-prevention services.

My hard work and leadership, along with that of Congressman Chris Stewart, Republican of Utah, was publicly acknowledged in the congressional debate. In my remarks and those of other members, the bipartisan support was acknowledged.[21] The bill passed the House with 379 in favor, 1 Republican member against, and 48 members not voting. It was a resounding endorsement of the need for a simplified dialing code.

After passage through the Senate by unanimous consent, the act was signed by President Trump on August 14, 2018. But that was just the first step. The FCC and other designees had to conduct the research.

In September 2020 the designated Suicide Prevention Month, the National Suicide Hotline Designation Act of 2020 was introduced. Working with Congressmen Chris Stewart, Seth Mouton, and Greg Gianforte, we garnered support for passage. This act designated 988 as the three-digit code to be used for suicide prevention.

In December 2021 the Substance Abuse and Mental Health Services Administration issued a report relating to the funding required to support the Suicide Prevention Lifeline. That report applauded 988 as a "once in a lifetime opportunity to strengthen and expand the Lifeline and transform America's behavioral crisis care system to one that saves lives by serving anyone, at any time, from anywhere across the nation."[22] It recognized that there was still work to be done to integrate state mental health resources, but the simplified 988 digital code provided the doorway to that much-needed network of resources.

On July 16, 2022, the universal 988 phone went live on all United States devices. Through federal funding, the 988 system provides states with resources to support people in crisis and prevent suicides. The rollout has been as successful as I could have hoped.

Our efforts to prevent suicide did not stop with the hotline. On October 16, 2019, I was a cosponsor of the bill Advancing Research to Prevent Suicide Act. The bill came out of the Committee on Science, Space, and Technology, which I chaired. Expressly recognizing that suicide is a major public health concern, this bill directed the NSF to support multidisciplinary research on suicide to advance knowledge and understanding of aspects of suicide. The bill passed and was signed into law by President Trump on January 13, 2021, just days before he left office.

Honoring American Veterans in Extreme Need Act of 2019 (HAVEN Act)

Fortunately, our veterans are highly regarded by most members of Congress. The Honoring American Veterans in Extreme Need Act of 2019 (HAVEN Act) enjoyed broad support.[23] Veterans who were experiencing severe financial difficulties might file for bankruptcy relief. The amount of income they had would determine whether they could file Chapter 7 and have their debts discharged or had to file a Chapter 13 debt-repayment plan. Disability or service-related compensation was included in determining the veteran's income. This bill, which I cosponsored, recognized that it simply wasn't fair to include veterans' disability monies as income in a bankruptcy proceeding. Those veterans who were experiencing hard times and had to file bankruptcy needed to have their disability to support themselves.

National Defense Authorization Act

Fulfilling our duties and responsibilities to our servicemen and women and their families is always a tremendous responsibility. We have to provide adequate funds for our military branches. We have to be ever mindful of our soldiers.

The National Defense Authorization Act of 2020 contained two amendments that I sponsored that focused directly on those serving our nation.[24] Because it was fundamental that all military family housing units should be safe, Amendment 210 that I offered required installation of maintenance of carbon monoxide detectors in military housing.[25] Amendment 209 directed the development of a strategy to better recruit and retain mental health providers in a manner that addresses the need for cultural competence and diversity among those providers. It is not just the amount of funds that we approve that matters; it is also important that that funding is providing for items and services that address our military personnel's needs.

Impeachment: The First Time

One of the most solemn responsibilities of the House is investigation of presidential conduct that could lead to the presentation of articles of impeachment. When President Trump conditioned support of Ukrainian military training on the provision of information on Hunter Biden, he abused the office of the president. His attitude conveyed that what he wanted he expected to get, and he didn't care if it was legal. I was troubled that he would request damaging information on a fellow American for personal political gain and threaten to withhold congressionally approved military aid. Such conduct was an abuse of power that justified the impeachment proceedings.

I had earlier been vocal in my support of an independent investigation into allegations of collusion between the Trump campaign and the Russian government. That investigation caused President Trump to fire the director of the Federal Bureau of Investigation, James Comey. I joined the calls for the appointment of Robert Mueller as a special prosecutor.

When the articles of impeachment were presented to the House for a vote, I voted in support of those articles.[26] Announcing that vote, I said that the truth was that President Trump had abused the power of his office by both obstructing the impeachment inquiry and soliciting interference by the Ukrainian government in the 2020 US presidential election. The evidence of corruption was overwhelming. I was compelled to vote in favor of the resolution of impeachment. But the solemnity of that day and that vote shall always be with me.

The Senate vote was to be expected. There were fifty-seven votes for guilty and forty-seven votes for not guilty, but a two-thirds majority vote was required.[27] But that vote only encouraged President Trump. To my mind it emboldened him, fueling an attitude that he was above the law. It made him even more dangerous, a greater threat to our democratic institutions.

Chair, Committee on Science, Space, and Technology
The Committee for the Future

Serving as the chair of the Committee on Science, Space, and Technology has been one of the greatest honors of my career. While a chairmanship reflects seniority on the committee, it also requires the support of the majority leader and the proven respect of committee members. The party's Policy and Steering Committee makes the chair nominations to the party, which then elects the chair. In 2019 I was honored to be elected to this position.

There is such a breadth of areas and programs that are touched by this committee. It has jurisdiction over: (1) all energy research, development, demonstration, and related projects and all federally owned or operated nonmilitary energy laboratories; (2) astronautical research and development, including resources, personnel, equipment, and facilities; (3) civil aviation research and development; (4) environmental research and development; (5) marine research; (6) commercial application of energy technology; (7) the National Institute of Standards and Technology, standardization of weights and measures, and the metric system; (8) NASA; (9) the National Space Council; (10) the NSF; (11) the National Weather Service; (12) outer space, including exploration and control thereof; (13) science scholarships; (14) and scientific research, development, and demonstration.

For our committees we work closely with and depend upon our staff. We must have people who have studied and worked in the fields under our jurisdiction. We use their expertise and knowledge of agencies and departments to gather the research, identify witnesses to come before the committee, and help us to develop the most effective legislation. Oftentimes, their historical knowledge of the committee allows them to be the resident experts on the earlier legislative initiatives.

There are probably over twenty-five distinct areas of research relating to matters that come before the Science Committee. Because the majority has more staff members than the minority, when I became chair I had to find staff members willing to return to work for the committee. Fortunately, we were able to assemble a good team to support the committee's work.

I had served as ranking member under Chairs Ralph Hall and Lamar Smith. With Chair Hall we met at the beginning of the session. We talked about the direction of the committee for that session and identified and set the goals and focus for that term. It was an invaluable planning session. But it also served as a foundation for bipartisanship, a recognition that we would need to work together to achieve our goals. I decided that I would use that approach as I began my chairmanship. I met with Frank Lucas, ranking member, to talk about all that we could accomplish during the session. We had worked together for years on the committee; now we would work together to lead the committee.

Through my continued membership on this committee, I have been involved in decades of work and legislation touching on all of these areas. It is not possible to detail all the initiatives, proposals, and legislation that I touched during those years. Each bill proposal reflected my best judgment that it benefited the nation. But there are some events and activities that I must simply talk about.

Climate Change and Energy

The first full committee hearing for the 116th congressional session was *The State of Climate Science and Why It Matters*.[28] I convened this hearing because President Trump had campaigned as a climate change denier. In June 2017 he announced his intent to withdraw the United States from the Paris Agreement, the commitment of over 185 nations to a global pact to address climate change. But under the terms of the Paris Agreement, the United States could not begin the actual withdrawal process until

November 2019. Our hearing, held on February 13, 2019, was designed to provide a big-picture assessment of the current state of climate science. It was my hope that rigorous scientific discourse would enable the creation of sound public policy.

As I said in my opening remarks, we are responsible for the alarming rate of global warming. Increases in sea-level rise and ocean acidification, severe weather incidents, and poor air quality are caused by greenhouse gas emissions. The evidence is clear. The Trump administration had regrettably chosen to ignore its scientists' findings. But we, the lawmakers, had a responsibility to protect the interest. On this committee we were going to be informed by the most relevant and up-to-date science as we worked to fulfill our oversight responsibilities. Our role was critical in preparing the nation to deal with climate change. I committed that we would continue this focus on the need to act on climate change throughout this congressional session.[29]

Demonstrating a bipartisan approach to climate control, Ranking Member Frank Lucas candidly stated that we knew the climate was changing and that global industrial activities have played a role in that change. He shared his belief that the federal government has a responsibility to prioritize research to better understand causes of climate change and to develop the next-generation technologies to address climate change.

Our very first witnesses were quite direct: "First, climate change is real, it is happening now, and humans are responsible for it. The planet is running a fever."[30] Climate change is not just an environmental challenge, it's an economic challenge, an infrastructure challenge, a public-health challenge, and a national-security challenge. Net global carbon dioxide emissions must be brought to zero. Climate change needs to be an integrated part of decision making at all levels, public and private.[31] These points were repeated and reiterated by the other witnesses. A consensus letter from thirty-one nonpartisan scientific societies confirmed the severity of climate change and the human contributions to that change.[32]

A few months later, we held another full committee hearing, this time focusing on *Earth's Thermometers: Glacial and Ice Sheet Melt in a Changing Climate*.[33] There were almost daily news reports about the world's ice melting. Studies showed that the rate of change in the Artic and Antarctic has increased quickly. Sea levels are rising. Coastal cities are at risk of being flooded if the Antarctic ice sheet melts, something that scientists are predicting. Melting glaciers in the Himalayan mountains put freshwater sources at risk.

In September we held another hearing on *Understanding, Forecasting, and Communicating Extreme Weather in a Changing Climate.*[34] The nation had been experiencing climate-change-fueled weather and disasters causing over $1 billion in losses. There is consensus among scientists that humans have caused an undeniable role in the extreme weather conditions. We needed to understand the physical science that supported observations and forecasting. We also needed to understand how our biases impact the forecasting process. And we had to recognize that our past experiences can influence how the public responds to notices from emergency managers.

Our subcommittees also convened hearings. There were hearings exploring wind, solar, and clean energy sources, the impact of climate change on our oceans and coasts, and the impact of rising sea levels on American property owners. We also held hearings focusing on the environmental consequences of climate change, such as the pollution of the Great Lakes— an important source of drinking water and recreation—that is killing fish and wildlife habitats. By the end of the first session, we had considered and moved a number of climate related bills.

At the end of 2019, I and a number of the members of the committee traveled to Madrid for the twenty-fifth UN Conference of Parties. We went to demonstrate the United States' continuing commitment to the ideals of the Paris Accord. The conference was disappointing. Instead of a bold signal that coordinated, concerted action was going to be taken to address climate change, the participants were unable to reach consensus. Critical decisions were carried over to the next conference.

As a committee we were determined that we would follow the science. Climate change is a serious challenge to this planet. We must understand the urgency; we are running out of time. But there's still hope, if only we take actions.

Combating Sexual Harassment, H.R. 36

The National Academies of Sciences, Engineering, and Medicine issued a report in 2018 entitled *Sexual Harassment of Women: Climate, Culture, and Consequences in Academic Sciences, Engineering and Medicine.*[35] While applauding the gains women had made in the science, engineering, and biomedical disciplines, the report noted that persistent sexual harassment jeopardizes that progress. Academic institutions were second only to the military for incidents of sexual harassment. Based on that research, the subcommittees held three hearings. That testimony helped to inform the bill that Ranking Member Lucas and I introduced, Combating Sexual Harassment in Science Act of 2019.[36] This bill called for the establishment of a grant program to promote research to better understand the factors contributing to and consequences of sexual harassment and gender harassment and develop policies and interventions to address and prevent such harassment. The bill passed the House but regrettably did not advance through the Senate.

NASA

Throughout my years on the Science Committee, I have been a consistent supporter of our initiatives in space. When I first joined the committee, the development of the International Space Station was a focus of the committee's work. President Clinton had praised it as a national space priority.

Funding for various space projects were included within civilian space authorizations. In 1997 I unequivocally announced my full support for the space station. I recognized the benefits of space-related research, including the commercialization of products and manufacturing that yield good jobs. But being penny-wise and pound foolish did not make sense to me.[37]

I always appreciated that the men and women who pursue our dreams of space exploration bravely accept the risks of space travel. Some have tragically lost their lives. We had honored those astronauts who perished in the space shuttle *Challenger* and *Columbia* disasters by a memorial shrine at Arlington National Cemetery. We had not so honored the first three casualties of our space program, Command Pilot Virgil "Gus" Grissom, Senior Pilot Edward H. White II, and Pilot Roger B. Chaffee, who had died on January 27, 1967, in a fire inside their Apollo command module while it sat atop the launch pad at Cape Canaveral. On the fiftieth anniversary of that tragic accident, I introduced the Apollo 1 Memorial Act.[38] While it did not pass that session, it was included within the 2018 National Defense Authorization Act, finally correcting this oversight and giving the acknowledgement due the crew of Apollo 1.[39]

Early in my chairmanship, March 2019, I convened a hearing titled *America in Space: Future, Visions, Current Issues.*[40] The purpose of the hearing was to provide big-picture perspectives on the future of the nation's civil space activities. What would our future in space look like in ten, twenty, fifty years?

This meeting was particularly poignant because that year would be the fiftieth anniversary of the Apollo moon landing. As a committee we would be building upon past reports, studies, and workshops that defined the goals for the national space efforts. We would also have to address the constraints and distractions that were impeding NASA's operations. There was a lack of consensus on the next steps of human space flight, increasing financial pressures, an aging infrastructure, and the emergence of additional space-capable nations, some friendly, some potentially unfriendly.

As we began the hearing, I noted that the administration had just released its budget proposal that called for cuts to NASA's budget, which caused me to remark that there isn't much room for vision in continually shrinking budgets. The Trump NASA budget was especially troubling because of a directive he had issued on December 11, 2018, calling for a return to the moon as a foundation for eventual exploration of Mars. Vice President Pence, supporting that directive, declared that we were in a "space race" and told NASA to undertake a crash program to put astronauts on the moon within five years by any means necessary.

At our hearing on the proposed NASA budget, I pressed NASA administrator Bridenstine to provide specifics: How much money was needed each year, what increases was the President going to make to the proposed budget to provide that funding, and would international partners be included or frozen out?[41] I wanted the specifics, not hot air.

Our Space and Aeronautics Subcommittee held a hearing to gain a better understanding of what would be needed for human space exploration. But as

I said in my remarks, setting arbitrary deadlines uninformed by technical or programmatical realities and failing to present a credible plan with identified needed resources would, in effect, be setting NASA up for failure. Such an approach would be a disservice to the men and women of NASA and its contractors. It would end up weakening US leadership in space. I felt the committee's responsibility and burden to present the objective, unbiased, and impartial assessments so central to scientific analysis. Like many of my colleagues on both sides of the aisle, I wanted a bold and visionary human exploration program, one worthy of our great nation.

Infrastructure, some mundane items such as upgraded utilities, some specialized needs such as wind tunnels, gigantic clean rooms, vacuum chambers supercomputers, and buoyancy tools had to be addressed. Some of NASA's critical facilities are located in coastal, low-lying regions vulnerable to sea-level rise and extreme weather events caused by climate change. The Wallops Flight Facility Causeway bridge, the only access to the launch complex for the International Space Station, was degrading and needed repairs. The deteriorating condition of NASA's infrastructure was said to be its single greatest threat to mission success, one that needed to be addressed.

While the public routinely associates NASA with space exploration, it is the research relating to aviation and aeronautics that has most touched Americans' lives. NASA was born out of the 1915 National Advisory Committee for Aeronautics, which had been created with a mandate to promote civilian and military aviation. NASA has been instrumental in the development of modern-day commercial and military aircraft and systems for efficient air traffic management. Today it is in the forefront of aviation advances and emerging markets such as urban air mobility, using automated aircraft to move passengers or cargo at lower altitudes within urban and suburban areas.

In addition to NASA's proven impact on our economy, the world has also benefited from the technological advances that are rooted in its research: cell phones, GPS systems, air purifiers, water filters, Mylar insulation, cordless tools, memory foam, scratch-resistant glasses, Super Soakers, workout machines, weather-forecasting capabilities—an almost endless list of everyday items. There is no telling what new contributions will be rooted in today's research.

There are significant issues facing NASA as I retire. What will happen when the International Space Station is no longer usable? If a privately owned space station is created, will the government just be another customer alongside tourists, film crews, or other groups interested in microgravity experiments? What would be the impact of reducing the government's management of such a space station? How can the needed security concerns be reliably maintained under a commercial rental arrangement? These questions must be intentionally and deliberately considered by Congress because the transition will be challenging and as a nation, we need to get it right.

The End of the Trump Administration

During the last year of the Trump administration, three major situations dominated: the pandemic, the killing of George Floyd, and the presidential campaign.

George Floyd Killing

As the presidential campaign proceeded, on May 25, 2020, the nation was transfixed by a nine minute, twenty-nine second cell phone recording of a Minneapolis police officer pressing his knee against George Floyd's throat. The sheer horror of that video, the tragedy of a needless death, galvanized people. Communities across the nation and world took to the streets in anger born of despair: marches, protests, demands for criminal prosecution, calls for police reform.

For many the pain was nothing new. I remembered a conversation with my parents about how to act during a police encounter. I had been forced to have that same conversation with my son, and my son had to repeat that morbid discussion with my grandsons. African Americans have long suffered the consequences of racism. In the aftermath of George Floyd's murder, in the wake of so much pain and grief, Congress had a moral responsibility to meet the calls for bold and transformative change.

The public response to the video was outrage. The protest marches were impressive. With voices raised crying out for justice, most of the nation could not escape the anger and rage born out of watching a police officer continue to kneel on Floyd's neck despite his pleas that he couldn't breathe and his cries for his mother. This time there wasn't any question about what had happened. It was recorded. The denials would be exposed as lies.

Just in the first half of 2020 we had seen the deaths of Ahmaud Arbery, Breonna Taylor, and now George Floyd. It was too much. The senseless murders of African Americans had to stop.

But President Trump didn't make any public comments about Floyd's death. He tweeted about the protest in Minneapolis, calling the marchers "thugs" and saying, "When the looting starts, the shooting starts." Over the next days he would issue tweets challenging the protestors, threatening to call out the unlimited power of the military, urging that the most vicious dogs and ominous weapons be used to protect the White House.[42]

In Dallas we held a George Perry Floyd Remembrance Day on June 4, 2020. I told the assembled people that I was the mother of a son who is the father of three sons. As my son was growing up, as my grandsons grew up, I never rested until I knew they were home, not because they were bad kids but because they were Black. I pointed out that racism is part of the fabric of this country and that we wouldn't truly live in peace until we came to grips with racism.[43]

I was proud to be an original cosponsor of the George Floyd Justice in Policing Act when it was introduced on February 24, 2021.[44] The act would ban the use of no-knock warrants and deadly chokeholds, limit the transfer of military-grade equipment to police departments, and put in place reforms to more easily hold police officers accountable for misconduct. This bill wouldn't solve all of the problems or redress all past wrongs. But we had to empower our communities to reimagine public safety in an equitable manner. As I spoke in support of the bill, I stated that we needed to empower our communities to reimagine public safety in an equitable manner. That means reinvesting—not defunding—police department resources to prioritize community policing. I closed by saying that Black lives matter, and that it was past time that the laws of our nation reflected that reality.

While the House passed the bill, unfortunately, the Senate did not. The votes were pretty much along party lines. Once again, Congress had failed African Americans.

2020 Election

Sensing an opportunity to elect a new president after President Trump's tumultuous term, a number of Democrats announced for the 2020 presidential campaign. I had known Joe Biden for years and had supported his candidacy for the 1988 Democratic nomination. I had worked with him during his time as vice president in the Obama administration, and I knew that he was experienced as both a legislator and a member of an administration.

Once again I had to face emotional conflict in making my endorsement. I had to explain to Senators Kamala Harris and Corey Booker, both African Americans, that I could not support their candidacies because I was supporting Biden.

President Biden's candidacy received a tremendous boost with his victory in the South Carolina primary. I had gone to South Carolina to join my colleague and friend Congressman Jim Clyburn in support of Biden's campaign. With that primary victory, there was greater attention given to the impact of minority voters, particularly African American women, on a candidate's success. In the first Democratic debate, candidate Joe Biden pledged to select a woman as vice president and to appoint an African American woman to the Supreme Court.

Managing an election amid COVID restrictions prompted the use of voting mechanisms beyond the casting of votes on election day. Ballot drop boxes, drive-through voting, expanded early voting, and mail out of ballots to all registered voters were used in various measures across the nation. Voter turnout was high: 154.6 million voters cast ballots, or almost 67 percent of citizens over 18 years old.

Having refused to say that he would accept the results of the election and condemning mail-in voting, President Trump rejected the results of the election. Watching his attempts to manipulate the American public with his repeated false statements was sickening. Seeing attorneys appear at news conferences advancing wild, unsubstantiated claims of fraud was maddening.

Elections are the lifeblood of a democracy. We need to revere the process, not exploit it.

Trump's claim that the 2020 election was fraught with fraud was absurd on so many levels. There was no factual support for his claims. He could never muster any evidence to establish the allegations. Audits conducted at the Republicans' insistence did not reveal any widespread issues. More than sixty lawsuits brought by Trump or his allies were dismissed. The very voting procedures Trump targeted with his falsehoods had been the subject of legislation proposed by Democratic members of the House—legislation he did not back, bills that were not supported by Republican members, except for an occasional lone vote.

The For the People Act of 2019, H.R. 1, addressed voter access and election integrity by increasing election security for federal elections, reforming campaign finance laws, ethics laws, and other procedures passed the House.[45] The Securing America's Federal Elections (SAFE) Act authorized funding for voting system security improvement grants and states' election infrastructure; required states to conduct post-election, risk-limiting audits; set strict cybersecurity standards for technology vendors and voting systems; and required voting machines to be manufactured in the United States.[46] The Voting Rights Advancement Act of 2019 established the criteria to be used for determining which states had to submit to preclearance requirements for any changes to voting practices.[47] All of these bills passed the House on strict party lines.

Notably, Republicans opposed the voter registration and same-day voter registration changes, saying that the states were already adopting those practices in ways that best suited the state's geographic concerns, resources, and laws. For another bill they said the proposed requirements of paper ballots and manual hand counts were backward steps that would erase all of the hard work of state and local officials. The Republicans had rejected our efforts, saying the states were managing the election systems. Yet these would be the very practices that Trump and other Republicans would point to as they denounced the 2020 election.

Yet other bills relating to elections had been introduced in 2017. The Voter Empowerment Act of 2017,[48] introduced by John Lewis, which I and 185 other Democratic representatives had cosponsored, sought to modernize voter registration, promote access to voting for individuals with disabilities, and protect the ability of individuals to vote in an election. The Federal Election Integrity Act of 2017,[49] Same Day Registration Act of 2017,[50] Help Our Service Members and Citizens Abroad Vote Act,[51] Servicemember Voting Protection Act,[52] and Protecting the Right to Independent and Democratic Elections (PRIDE) Act[53] were before the Congress. But there was no support for any of these bills in the Republican-controlled Congress.

After the 2020 election, it was clear that President Trump would not accept the results of the election. But I never thought that he would pursue such an active campaign to undermine the credibility of the electoral process. I could not have predicted the eagerness with which his supporters and indebted Republican officials embraced the ludicrous and outlandish claims, epitomized by the rhetoric of Rudy Giuliani, Sidney Powell, and others. And I certainly did not foresee the violent attack on the Capitol building that occurred on January 6.

I had been a part of the certification of the vote on multiple occasions. The CBC had objected to the receipt of the delegates from Florida during the Bush-Gore election. But we followed the procedure, accepted the outcome, and moved on. Vice President Gore, who presided over that certification of elections results, repeatedly disallowed our objections for lack of a senator's signature. That is what the rules required, and that is what he did. That is what happens in a democracy: you voice your objections as allowed under the procedures and then accept the results. There was no rioting, forced entry, or assault on police officers. So we, at least the Democrats, could not foresee the violence that would surround us that day.

I had cast my vote and was returning to my office. I encountered a man walking by himself in the Rayburn Building and asked if I could help him. He replied that he was just looking around because it was his first trip to Washington. I don't know if he was part of the crowd that had come to interfere with the election certification, but I have often wondered.

When I got to my office, I couldn't get in. My staff had gathered and locked the doors. Once they let me in, looking through my window at the Capitol, I was horrified watching the mob scaling the walls, smashing windows, and attacking the police. The Capitol—the building that represented the heart of our government, where I had worked for so many years, where I and my legislative colleagues had dedicated ourselves to service of our constituents—was under siege by Americans. Like many Americans I could not pull myself away from the news broadcasts. The cries of "Hang Mike Pence" or "Where's Nancy?" were terrifying. I believed then, and now, that if either of them had been found by that mob, they would have been seriously injured.

While the violence outside of the Capitol demanded our attention, I was also dismayed by the number of legislators who objected to the count of votes from millions of Americans. Legislators especially should be committed to the sanctity of the vote. There was no evidence to back the claim that there had been widespread fraud in the election. Allegation after allegation was roundly exposed as unfounded. We had painfully watched the shenanigans of Rudy Giuliani and Sidney Powell. We had watched the pressure applied to state election officials who bravely demonstrated the integrity to stand behind their ballot counts. But the truth didn't matter to certain legislators because it did not advance their agenda: retain power in any way possible.

I'm not sure which troubled me the most: the external acts of sedition by the mob or the betrayal of legislators who had sworn an oath to preserve the Constitution. But I knew that there had to be accountability. There needed to be immediate prosecution of those who stormed the Capitol and impeachment proceedings against President Trump.

I had earlier expressed my appreciation for the Capitol Police in a concurrent resolution that I had introduced in June 2017, recognizing that they made innumerable contributions and sacrifices to secure the Capitol complex and protect members of Congress, staff, and the public.[54] That year we passed a bill, the Wounded Officers Recovery Act of 2017,[55] that authorized payments to families of employees were killed or suffered serious injuries in the line of duty. But never did I think that our Capitol Police would be called on to stand in front of American citizens, be yelled at, sprayed with bear spray, hit with flagpoles, or crushed in door frames.

The second impeachment hearings, this time investigating President Trump's connections to the attempted insurrection, once again showed the importance of the three branches of government. Presidents cannot act with impunity and contempt toward our governmental structure. If our elected officials refuse to fulfill their constitutional responsibilities, then we as a nation are truly doomed. It was regrettable that members of Congress would not look past party affiliations and base their votes on the evidence. The correctness of the impeachment vote was affirmed by the report of the January 6th Committee. Despite the repeated obstruction, the efforts to block testimony, and the refusals to cooperate, it is clear that the mob that attacked the Capitol on January 6 was inspired and summoned by President Trump and people acting on his behalf.

In addition to these articles of impeachment, the House established a bipartisan commission to investigate the events of January 6. As I said on the floor in support of this bill, January 6 was one of the darkest days in the history of our nation and of democracies everywhere. We had to understand the events that led up to that horrible day, the security failures and any possible corrective measures. We needed to understand the hatred that drove the insurrectionists, a hatred that I feared was even present within the House. This hatred, left unaddressed, would only remain prevalent. We had to have the commission.[56] The trust that is placed in us as elected officials requires that we objectively evaluate evidence and fairly consider allegations of abuse of power. Our oath to defend and uphold the Constitution demands nothing less.

The Biden Administration

Between COVID restrictions and the January 6 attack, the inauguration of President Joe Biden was a somber, serious affair. I attended the ceremony, sitting in the cold, wearing my mask. Due to Covid, I didn't attend the traditional inaugural parties and balls. I was intentionally avoiding crowds.

The baseless Republican allegations of a stolen election continued as an incessant undercurrent. Even so, there was a feeling of relief because Biden had won.

Emmett Till Antilynching Act

Even while Congress was wrestling with the continued impact of COVID-19 and the January 6 attack, there was still time to address one of the darkest incidents in American history—the 1955 brutal lynching of Emmett Till, a 14-year-old African American boy in Mississippi. Till was abducted and tortured, his eye gouged out, and tied to a cotton gin fan with barbed wire, supposedly for flirting with a white woman. His disfigured body was then thrown into the Tallahatchie River, where it was recovered three days later, so distorted that he could only be identified by a ring.

For decades before and after Till's lynching, bills had been introduced to include lynching as a federal crime. Those bills had always failed. One of the first bills introduced in 2021 was the Emmett Till Antilynching Act.[57] An early cosponsor, I knew that this nation still owed a tribute to that 14-year-old Black boy. It was never too late to pay that debt.

American Rescue Plan Act of 2021

In early 2021 the nation was still reeling from the effects of COVID-19. There was an economic crisis and continuing public health emergency. There was recession, joblessness, poverty, homelessness, and hunger. We needed to be efficient and effective.

Early in his administration President Biden laid out a multipronged approach to address our nation's needs. By using the budget resolution and reconciliation process, Congress moved quickly to enact legislation to prove $1.9 trillion in funding for necessary programming. The bill, the American Rescue Plan Act of 2021,[58] passed along party lines in both the House and Senate. On March 11, 2021, the first anniversary of the World Health Organization declaration that COVID-19 was a pandemic, President Biden signed the American Rescue Plan.

I strongly supported the American Rescue Plan Act of 2021. The legislation was needed to provide much-needed relief to both individuals and communities. Our nation's scientists and engineers, biologists, physicists, computer scientists, and social scientists jumped into action, contributing to the efforts to deal with the pandemic. The vaccines would not have been possible without expertise from many fields and many researchers. The act included $750 million in funding through the NSF and the National Institute of Standards and Technology for additional research related to COVID-19. Because important scientific work remained to be done, I urge adoption of the rescue package.[59]

Infrastructure Investment and Jobs Act

Having served on the Transportation and Infrastructure Committee, I was well aware of the nation's need for funding to achieve much-needed infrastructure repairs. As a nation we enjoy the advantages and ease of highway travel across our country through our system of highways, bridges, and tunnels. But our usage requires that we maintain them. There must be regular, sustained maintenance and repair.

When we look at our nation today, infrastructure extends beyond concrete and asphalt. It reaches to broadband and internet access. It includes accessibility to safe drinking water. It develops electric vehicles to help us transition as a nation to more environmentally responsible transportation. It focuses on continued development of public transit systems. It targets the electric grid. The very breadth and scope of resources that are used daily by Americans requires substantial ongoing financial commitment.

On June 4, 2021, the Infrastructure Investment and Jobs Act was introduced in the House.[60] It was called the Bipartisan Infrastructure Law because it had the support of Republican and Democratic legislators. I was in favor of the bill because it included many critical measures relating to extreme weather resiliency, public transit, and funding for highway construction and clean energy.[61] The act is comprehensive, covering roads, bridges, rail, public transit, broadband, water infrastructure, airports, power and grid, electric vehicles, and research. The authorization of $1.2 trillion reflected the years of neglect and disregard for the fundamental expenditures needed to maintain our infrastructure. It was the largest investment in roads and bridges in seventy years and in passenger rail in fifty years.

After the passage of the act, our Transportation Committee held a meeting on the implementation of the act. With allocation of $1.2 trillion in new spending over five years, it was important to me that pathways of access existed for disadvantaged businesses. As recognized by the title, the act will spur the creation of strong, good-paying jobs, essential to the continued strength and growth of our nation. I was concerned, once again, about the ability of minority-owned companies to participate in business activities and share in the benefits created by the act. At the Transportation Committee hearing, I asked Secretary Buttigieg directly what steps the Department of Transportation was taking to assure the participation of minority and women-owned businesses.[62]

Creating Helpful Incentives to Produce Semiconductors (CHIPS) and Science Act

The pandemic painfully showed us the consequences of the United States' decline in the manufacturing of microchips. The integrated circuit, the microchip, invented by Jack Kilby, an employee of Dallas-based Texas Instruments, is used in items from coffeepots to cars, computers to game consoles, medical equipment to military weapons systems. Chips have become essential to our way of life. During COVID the interruption of the supply chain collided with increased demand. Consumer goods saw longer delays and increased costs.

National security concerns are also implicated by microchip manufacturing because fighter jets, ships, and weapons use chips, many of which are produced in Taiwan. China had become a leading exporter of microchips. Anytime that the United States is primarily dependent upon another country to manufacture critical components for our military equipment, we must be concerned about the vulnerability of our military and that supply chain.

We were once the leading nation of microchips. By the time of the bill, we were down to producing only about 10 percent of the world's chips and none of the most advanced chips frequently used in military equipment. The CHIPS and Science Act, passed in July 2022, was designed to bring semiconductor manufacturing back to the United States, reduce costs, address supply chain interruptions, and boost national security.

Legislatively, the act was born out of a bill that I introduced, along with Ranking Member Frank Lucas, in July 2021, the Bioeconomy Research and Development Act.[63] This bill, although amended and retitled, provided for a coordinated federal research initiation to ensure continued US leadership in engineering biology. This bill was used as the vehicle for the America COMPETES Act of 2022. It passed the House on February 4, 2022.

The Senate, in its consideration of this bill, had passed it with an amendment. That amendment was the inclusion of a bill that had been proposed in the Senate, the United States Innovation and Competition Act of 2021. Senator Charles Schumer had introduced this bill in the Senate on April 20, 2021.[64] Over six hundred amendments were proposed. As passed, it was thousands of pages long and covered a broad span of subjects. It included sections relating to "Countering Chinese Communist Party Malign Influence"; "Investing in Alliances and Partnerships," which addressed diplomatic concerns for multiple nations across the continents; "Investing in Our Values," which addressed human rights concerns; and the "Trade Act of 2021," which listed almost 1,500 items. It was simply too much. It covered too many unrelated, independent topics. We needed to find another approach.

The commitment to semiconductor manufacturing was strong and solid. We had to strengthen our competitiveness against China. Companies were poised to make investments in semiconductor manufacturing. Intel had delayed a groundbreaking ceremony in Ohio. Micron Technology's plans for expansion in Idaho had been stalled. We needed to move.

At the same time, the House had passed a number of bills relating to science, research, and STEM that the Senate did not even consider. Those initiatives had been set out in these bills: Supporting Early-Career Researchers Act,[65] STEM Opportunities Act,[66] Rural STEM Education Research Act,[67] COAST Research Act of 2021,[68] MSI STEM Achievement Act,[69] National Science Foundation for the Future Act,[70] Combating Sexual Harassment in Science Act,[71] Department of Energy Science for the Future Act,[72] National Science and Technology Strategy Act of 2021,[73] Bioeconomy

Research and Development Act of 2021,[74] Regional Innovation Act of 2021,[75] Steel Upgrading Partnerships and Emissions Reduction Act of the SUPER Act of 2021,[76] Energizing Technology Transfer Act,[77] National Institute of Standards and Technology for the Future Act of 2021,[78] and the Micro Act.[79] I had sponsored or cosponsored a number of the bills, which had either passed or been introduced in the House and became provisions within this section of the act.

As these bills were individually considered by the House, I would emphasize the importance of the bill, especially pointing out the bipartisan support for science initiatives. For example, speaking on the Department of Energy Science for the Future Act, I pointed out that it was a substantial effort in the fight against climate change, authorizing research for the next generation of clean energy sources so that we might have clean, sustainable, reliable, and affordable energy.[80]

Rising in support of the National Science Foundation for the Future Act, I emphasized the need for funding research, leveraging of our STEM talent, and providing access to science and technology.[81] It seemed logical and reasonable to me to incorporate the provisions of those bills into the legislation for semiconductor manufacturing. They would be the "Science" component of the act, supporting important initiatives for NASA, STEM, and research and development. I proposed that approach to Speaker Pelosi and representatives from the White House.

A conference committee met in May 2022. Passage of the bill took weeks of bipartisan negotiations and long hours put in by staff. The act takes a holistic approach, targeting construction of manufacturing facilities, support for research and development initiatives, and workforce development. Finally, by August 2022, it had passed both houses of Congress and been signed by President Biden.

About two months after the signing of the act, President Biden traveled to New Albany, Ohio, for the groundbreaking of a new Intel manufacturing facility. I was honored to travel to Ohio and join other members of Congress as the president stood on the edge of the vacant acreage that will be the new home of semiconductors factories. After recognizing members of the Ohio delegation who were there, President Biden said, "We're also joined by congressional leaders from around the country who fought so hard for this bill. Eddie Bernice Johnson, Chair of the House Science Committee. Eddie, this whole bill . . . wouldn't have gotten done without you. It really wouldn't have."[82]

This support of the semiconductor industry was also important to Texas. Samsung is building semiconductor facilities near Austin. Texas Instruments, working with GlobalWafers America, an international company led by CEO Doris Hsu, is building a silicon wafer plant in Sherman, Texas. These plants will provide thousands of solid, good-paying jobs for Texans while strengthening our supply chain. This is a clear benefit for the American people.

But the CHIPS Act was truly a bipartisan effort, not only in the House. Senator Roger Wicker, a Republican from Mississippi, was the ranking member of the Senate Committee on Commerce, Science, and Transportation. He pushed for the expansion of the Established Program to Stimulate Competitive Research (EPSCoR), which ensured 20 percent of funding would be set aside for states and areas that had traditionally received a small share of research funds. Other Republican senators supported the bill and voted in favor of it. I was pleased that we were able to get this bipartisan support for the CHIPS Act. I have always maintained that science is for everyone.

Chapter 16

Some Things Took Decades

Not all the work that I did could be accomplished in single two-year legislative terms. Sometimes there were pressing national situations, such as 9/11 or the Iraqi War, that so demanded our attention that we had to, understandably, shelve other concerns. For much of my tenure, I was in the minority party fighting against a conservative agenda.

There were some issues that I fought for throughout my three decades in Congress, bringing them up year after year, session after session: getting funding for public works projects, redressing decades of discrimination and inequality, pushing new technology and scientific developments, spotlighting inequities resulting from historic discrimination, advocating for STEM education. These issues, now seen as crowning achievements of my career, were only realized because I was consistent, insistent, and persistent over the decades. I had to stay on message. I had to reach not just across the aisle but across the years. I had to seize moments and create opportunities. I had to be creative and strategic. But most of all, I could not allow myself to feel defeated because there was no instant success; I had to be patient.

Building Public Transportation Projects and Infrastructure

Many of the infrastructure projects that are the work of elected officials can take years to be achieved. The interests of citizens in each of our fifty states are represented. There are projects and funding needs for each state. Every elected official is competing for funding and support for the programs and projects needed in their districts. Continuity is needed to initiate and shepherd projects and legislation that must be adaptable to ever-changing and growing concerns, technology, and population dynamics.

From my earliest days in Congress, I was involved in transportation, water resources, and brownfield abatement. These activities directly addressed Dallas–Fort Worth and the North Texas area. But legislation in these areas impacted communities across the country. Over my thirty years in Congress, I have been involved in infrastructure projects aggregating in literally hundreds of billions of dollars to build and maintain the infrastructure, bridges, highways, public transit systems, and waterways of this nation.

Transportation was not an issue that had commanded much of my attention during my days in the Texas Legislature. There had been legislation addressing highway speed limits in relation to pollution and lead levels in gasoline. But I realized that without proper highways, reliable public transportation systems, and appropriate infrastructure, people have great difficulty getting from their homes to their places of employment. Without efficient, multifaceted transportation systems, including intermodal, multimodal, bicycle, and pedestrian systems, the North Texas region could not maintain its desired quality of life or its economic vitality.

When I went to Congress, the Dallas–Fort Worth area was the largest and most dynamic regional economy in Texas. Population growth for the region was projected to attract three million new residents. Two million new jobs were anticipated. I knew that a large part of my job as a member of Congress was to secure the appropriate funding to sustain the infrastructure required for the region's growth. In 1993 Dallas had adopted a Thoroughfare Plan that identified extensive reconstruction and expansion of the freeways and implementation of the Dallas Area Rapid Transit (DART) systems as two critical components. Achieving those objectives would require significant federal support and intergovernmental cooperation. This is why I believed that it was important that I serve on this committee.

Transportation is the largest House committee. Every form of transportation—cars, buses, trains, subways, planes—are within the committee's jurisdiction. It has to be a forward-looking committee, considering new technologies, new fuels, and environmental concerns. Research must precede every project approval. We have to consider estimates of population growth, geographic expansion, and development demands. We look at the resilience and projected life span of proposed construction materials to assess their ability to withstand weather conditions.

I served on the Transportation Committee with its various names during my entire time in Congress. Much of my work was done through the Aviation, Highways, and Transit and Water Resources and Environment Subcommittees. At various times I served either as the ranking member or chair of the Subcommittee on Water Resources. But I didn't need a leadership role to be active in assessing and addressing the issues brought before the committee.

Surface Transportation

When we talk about surface transportation, our interstate highway system comes immediately to mind. As residents we regularly drive on our roads and highways, cross bridges, and go through tunnels. We have seen the deterioration of our infrastructure—crumbling bridges and outdated highways and tunnels. Our ability to travel safely, both on land and in the air, contributes to our way of life.

Surface transportation is central to our economy because roads and trains are essential to the efficient and effective movement of freight and goods. There must be a network that moves products from ships and planes to destinations across the country.

Highways

In assessing highway needs, we had to have a sense of the state's priorities. Early in my tenure, there was an issue in Texas. Should funds be allocated for maintenance of five hundred miles of the north-south I-35 interstate because of increased trade from Mexico? Or should we fund an alternate route preferred by some Texas lawmakers, upgrading US 39 from Laredo to Texarkana to an interstate? In making such decisions, the voice of state leadership is important.

One of the earlier bills that I worked on through the Surface Subcommittee was the National Highway Designation Act of 1995. It provided $455 million in funding to Texas and designated as high priority corridors I-35 from Laredo, Texas, to Duluth, Minnesota, and the Camino Real corridor in El Paso to various international ports of entry and the New Mexico border. I was concerned, however, about the safety impact of repealing the mandatory 55 mph speed limit and removing federal mandates requiring motorcycle helmets for persons under 18. Road fatalities had declined under the 55 mph speed limit.

We also passed amendments to the Intermodal Safe Container Transportation Act. Intermodal shipping refers to transporting freight by two transportation modes, such as ships, trains, and trucks. With the passage of NAFTA, the Dallas–Fort Worth highways had become major trade routes. Interstate highways and railways converge in southern Dallas, prompting steps to create an inland port there. This involved a coalition of neighboring cities, including Cedar Hill, DeSoto, Balch Springs, Duncanville, Lancaster, Mesquite, and Seagoville. Some of these cities were in my district.

In 1998 we passed the Transportation Equity Act for the 21st Century (TEA 21).[1] I was an early cosponsor of this comprehensive statute. It guaranteed a record $198 billion in surface transportation investment; provided grants and incentives to increase seat belt and child seat usage, develop air bag technology, and encourage adoption of .08 alcohol limits; provided for bicycle and pedestrian pathways and bicycle trails; and designated $3 billion for projects to improve communities' cultural, aesthetic, and environmental qualities to begin to remedy past damage to communities of color by highway placement and construction.

A key component significantly changed how highway, highway safety, and transit programs were funded. States were guaranteed funding from the Highway Transportation Fund. One feature of that statute for which I had strenuously fought was our intent that all monies devoted to high-priority projects would have to be spent on those projects or otherwise forfeited by the state. States could not divert those monies. I had insisted on that provision. Funding allocations for desperately needed road and infrastructure improvements in southern Dallas had been largely ignored by the Texas Department of Transportation in favor of projects in more affluent areas of the state. I felt strongly that federal money allocated to specific projects should be spent on those projects.

Yet the Department of Transportation and Related Agencies Appropriations Act passed in 1999, which appropriated the monies authorized in the TEA 21, included a provision that gave states the very veto ability that we had addressed in passing the TEA 21. Despite the needed transportation funding, I rose in opposition because it allowed states to veto those projects and reallocate the funds to other projects. I pointed out that the House Transportation Committee had rejected that position and that it was clearly the committee's intent that states should forfeit the funding if it was not used for the designated project. I specifically shared our experience in Dallas. Calling it an irresponsible contradiction of the intent and spirit of the House bill, I urged Republicans to remove that provision.[2] I had to put my concerns on the record. I had to again fight for South Dallas.

Because projects were now funded through the Highway Trust Fund, determining the recommendations for expenditures became one of the major responsibilities of the Surface Transportation Subcommittee. Every state pays into the fund through its collection of gasoline taxes. Certain states, such as Texas, that are highly dependent on automobiles, are donor states, contributing more funds to the federal government than received in state appropriations for federal programs. Part of this imbalance can be caused by a state's rejection of funds for specific programs, such as Texas's decisions relative to Medicaid funding.

Working with others such as Jim Clyburn, we focused on funding state projects that would raise the appropriations to be more proportionate to the states' contribution. A number of programs are supported by such funding: Interstate Maintenance Program, National Highway System, Bridge Program, Surface Transportation Program, Congestion Mitigation and Air

Quality Improvement Program, Appalachian Development Highway System Program, Recreational Trails Program, Federal Lands Highways Program, National Corridor Planning and Development and Coordinated Border Infrastructure Programs, Construction of Ferry Boats and Ferry Terminal Facilities, National Scenic Byways Program, Value Pricing Pilot Program, High Priority Projects Program, and Commonwealth of Puerto Rico Highway Program. To serve effectively I had to become familiar with the parameters of each program to evaluate the requests for funding that were being received. We had to review transportation proposals submitted by cities, counties, states, and federal agencies.

We relied upon the Department of Transportation with its various components—Federal Railroad Administration, Federal Highway Administration, Federal Aviation Administration, the Federal Transit Administration, and the Environmental Protection Agency—to provide us with information and evaluations. When considering community needs and funding priorities, we needed material and data from these agencies to help us make informed decisions. And in drafting legislation we had to consider and identify the appropriate federal agency to manage the expenditure and assure compliance with the approved projects. TEA 21 authorized funding only through 2003.[3]

Two years later I was an original cosponsor for the Safe, Accountable, Flexible, Efficient Transportation Equity Act: A Legacy for Users (SAFETEA-LU), a transportation reauthorization bill.[4] States and municipalities had been awaiting federal funding contributions. Their highway and road projects were effectively on hold, needing Congress to act. As I said in support of the bill, traffic gridlock caused a waste of time as well as a waste of fuel. Infrastructure was continuing to deteriorate. "Below average" was the most recent assessment of Texas's infrastructure by a civil engineers association. This bill, although not authorizing all of the funding needed, was a good step in the direction of meeting the nation's transportation needs. The bill authorized $244.1 billion, at that time the largest surface transportation investment, although far short of the $375 billion estimated as needed by the Department of Transportation. But it brought funding certainty that had not existed since TEA 21 had expired.[5]

Securing funding for highway and infrastructure projects is often laborious and frustrating. State and local governments submit proposals. Those proposals are reviewed by the appropriate federal agency. There are usually meetings with agency representatives and the project sponsors, and there may be subcommittee hearings to gather more information about a project. Once the subcommittee has assessed and prioritized the projects, the draft legislation itemizing each project and associated funding is prepared. These bills can be well over a hundred pages in length. That draft bill is then reviewed by the full Transportation Committee, voted upon, and introduced in the House. If passed, the funding for the projects still has to be included with the funding bill created by the Appropriations Committee. This process results in the actual appropriation of funds being made the year after the surface transportation projects were approved.

Even when these steps have been taken, there is always the possibility that in the next budget cycle, the funds will be reallocated. This is what happened when President Bush took monies allocated for surface transportation and used them to help pay for the Iraq War. I was deeply saddened by this action. The Iraq War was misguided, while our infrastructure was in dire need of repairs and improvement. Taking money from our streets to continue an ill-advised war was simply wrong.

It would be almost ten years before another federal spending law to provide long-term funding for surface transportation infrastructure, the Fixing America's Surface Transportation Act (FAST Act).[6] That Act called for $305 billion in funding for 2016–2020. I was the senior Texan on the House Committee and a conferee to the transportation bill. I was pleased that the bill supported research and development and expanded university transportation center outreach to women and underrepresented populations. While I had wanted an even higher level of funding, this bill was a strong first step to building and maintaining our critical transportation infrastructure. President Obama signed the bill on December 4, 2015.

The last major transportation bill that I was involved with was the Infrastructure Investment and Jobs Act that was passed in 2021.[7] This act provided $550 billion in new federal investment in roads, bridges, water infrastructure, internet, railways, public transportation, and more.

This act also recognized that communities of color had been divided by the construction of highways and provided funds to support the reconnection of those communities.

Over the years I have likely reviewed hundreds, if not thousands, of highway, bridge, and railway projects crossing this country. It was frequently difficult to decide which projects should be given priority because there were competing needs and concerns. Our colleagues would frequently urge approval of projects proposed within their districts and states. Using the information from the appropriate agencies, the analysis of the proposals, and the insight from our colleagues, we would have to determine which projects would receive funding.

But there was one highway project that was always close to my heart and central to my district. Known as the Mixmaster, it is the convergence of interstate highways I-35 and I-30 in downtown Dallas. For years there were no ramps allowing access from one highway to the other. Drivers had to exit the highway and drive city streets to reach access ramps. Left-hand exits caused accidents, as drivers would dart across the highway to access the exits. There were bottlenecks, lengthy traffic delays, and safety concerns. With an estimated 450,000 to 500,000 motorists a day, it was one of the most congested roadways in Texas. But with $500 million in federal funding to assist with the $798 million project, bridges were replaced and the interchange reconstructed. It took decades, but finally in 2017 the new exchange was complete.

Railways and Mass Transit: DART

In the 1940s streetcars were the dominant transportation system in Dallas, moving people from the southern sector of the city to North Dallas. With Dallas's rapid growth, it was clear to those of us in public life and in the business community that if we were to become one of the country's elite economic, academic, commercial, and social arenas, our system of highways, airports and public transportation would have to expand and maintain pace with our rapidly growing population.

Our public transportation agency, the Dallas Area Rapid Transit authority (DART), was founded as a regional entity in 1983 by voters from fourteen cities and Dallas County. DART replaced the Dallas Transit Authority, which had been responsible for public transportation in the city of Dallas since the early 1960s. In its early years, DART focused on bus service improvements, expanding bus routes and extending service to suburbs while developing plans for rail transit, high occupancy vehicle (HOV) lanes, carpooling, and mobility-impaired transit planning. It transported hundreds of thousands of passengers daily and was poised to develop the first light-rail system in the southwestern United States.

When I joined the House Transportation Committee in January of 1993, I was positioned to contribute to DART's development. Having once worked in Dallas without a car, I knew the importance of a public transportation system that was affordable, reliable, and safe. I was, perhaps, the only member of Congress from North Texas who had depended on public transportation. Knowing how important DART was to people and their livelihoods, I was determined to do all that I could to assist those who were responsible for the operation and expansion of the system.

The light-rail system received significant federal funding, beginning with $82.6 million in September 1993 for the development of the South Oak Cliff rail, which served the VA hospital where I used to work. Providing support for DART also meant adapting to its revisions and reassessments of how to best serve its constituent populations. In 1995 DART revised its Transit System Plan to expand the light-rail system, increase HOV lanes, include commuter rail transit linking Dallas and Fort Worth, and include extensions to DFW International Airport.

Over the years I was able to secure hundreds of millions in grants and awards for DART. I also worked with DART and Dallas officials to provide input on the development of rail lines. For example, I encouraged the development of a DART rail to the American Airlines arena area. It was my belief that having public transportation accessible to those attending events at the arena would contribute to the arena's use. I secured the funding to create the Rosa Parks Plaza in downtown Dallas so that we would remember that her refusal to give up her seat on the bus helped spark the Civil Rights Movement.

DART rail is now well established. There is a connection between Denton and Dallas, enabling students from Dallas to travel to Denton to attend either

University of North Texas or Texas Woman's University. Passengers can travel to DFW Airport using the orange line. In the years that I have served in Congress, DART has literally created a network of rail, buses, and vans to provide transportation throughout Dallas and contiguous cities—network that was developed with the input of federal funds that I was able to secure.

Trinity Railway Express

Dallas and Fort Worth are thriving cities approximately thirty miles apart. The population increase that fueled the growth of Arlington and Grand Prairie, cities between Dallas and Fort Worth, created a need for a rail option to travel between the cities. The Trinity Railway Express (TRE) had its first run on December 30, 1996, drawing more than four thousand riders during its first day of operation. The TRE operates between Fort Worth T&P Station by downtown Fort Worth to what is now the Eddie Bernice Johnson Union Station in Dallas.

Inland Port

The intersection of Interstate Highways 20, 35, and 45 made a natural location for the site of an inland port. This area of southern Dallas that was long undeveloped now sees thousands of trucks in and out of manufacturing and distribution centers. The highways and rail lines link to ports in Houston and California. The Union Pacific terminal houses containers that are then transferred to trucks. With almost 7,500 acres located in five municipalities—Dallas, Lancaster, Ferris, Wilmer, and Hutchins—the inland port is a bustling arena for goods, warehouses, and shipments. Although challenged by economic recessions, the port has grown, yielding over thirty-thousand good-paying jobs. The population influx also contributes to a housing and construction boom for these cities.

From Brownfield to Sports Home: Victory Park

They're called brownfields. Real estate that has been contaminated by the potential presence of a hazardous substance or pollutant drives down property values, provides little to no tax revenue, and contributes to community blight. The contamination makes the reuse or development of the property problematic. Making this land usable for development reduces blight and spurs economic development.

In the early 1990s, much of the population growth that we had experienced in Dallas took place away from the downtown area. To counter that population shift, Dallas created the Brownfields Redevelopment Program as part of its approach to downtown revitalization. Working with the EPA, I was able to secure a $200,000 assessment pilot grant to determine the extent of the contamination. That initial grant spurred development and additional EPA funding of over $1 million dollars. With those funds Dallas was able to leverage more than $3.4 billion in private/public investment.

The brownfield cleanup and development of Victory Park was overwhelmingly successful. In 2001 the EPA awarded Dallas the Phoenix Award, declaring that Victory Park was one of the nation's largest and most successful brownfields projects.[8] Approximately seventy-two acres that formerly had been home to an outdated power plant, car repair shops, soil contaminated with heavy metals, and groundwater polluted by hydrocarbons were transformed. A well-known sports arena, the American Airlines Center, home to the Dallas Mavericks basketball team and Dallas Stars hockey team; restaurants; office space; residential units; and hotels were built on this acreage. Previously unusable acreage was now populated with income-generating businesses reportedly valued at billions of dollars. This transformation from eyesore to economic engine confirmed the program's vision.

In 2008 I presided over a subcommittee hearing to discuss reauthorization of the EPA's brownfield program. As I said in my introductory remarks, I had seen firsthand the positive effects of brownfield redevelopment. I talked about Victory Park and the dramatic turnaround, the result of collaboration between the state of Texas, the EPA, the city of Dallas, and private developers.[9]

Dallas councilwoman Vonceil Jones Hill also spoke of another successful brownfield project: the construction of the Dallas Jack Evans Police Headquarters facility.[10] Also awarded the Phoenix Award, the police headquarters was part of a neighborhood revitalization project that transformed an old Sears regional complex into residential housing and commercial and retail space. Another abandoned, neglected area of Dallas had become a thriving community with assistance from the EPA brownfield program.

But as I pointed out, in order to achieve such successes, funding was necessary. In the decades-long program, the $660 million in seed money had yielded assessments of 11,500 properties, helped to create more than 47,000 jobs, and led to the leveraging of over $10.3 billion in cleanup and development activity. But the brownfields program was consistently and significantly underfunded despite congressional authorizations. I firmly believe that the economic impact and potential for job creation more than justified the increased funding for the brownfields project.

Aviation Subcommittee

At various times I have served on the Aviation Subcommittee, which has jurisdiction over civil aviation. This covers infrastructure, safety, labor, commerce, and international issues. We work closely with the Federal Aviation Administration and the National Transportation Safety Board. We oversee, among other things, air traffic management, airport construction and capacity, and air passenger protection.

The Wright Amendment and Dallas Airports and Airlines

One of the major issues confronting me during my early years in Congress was the Wright Amendment. Decades earlier the federal government had ordered the cities of Dallas and Fort Worth to create a regional airport or potentially lose continued federal funding. As a result, the cities came together to create such a regional airport. The 1968 bond ordinance funding for DFW Airport required the airlines flying from Dallas's Love Field and Fort Worth's Meachum Field to transfer all operations to DFW. The airlines agreed to this requirement, effectively closing Love and Meachum Fields.

However, Southwest Airlines did not exist at the time of this ordinance. When Southwest was created, it was allowed to fly out of Love Field. It refused to leave that airport. A federal judge upheld Southwest's claim, allowing it to continue to operate flights within Texas.[11]

In 1979, using the momentum of the Airline Deregulation Act of 1978, Southwest announced plans to expand its service outside of Texas, beginning with flights to New Orleans. Local officials were concerned that increased use of Love Field would weaken DFW. They reached out to Rep. Jim Wright, then the Speaker of the House. An example of legislative negotiation, Wright sponsored and passed an Amendment to the Air Transportation Competition Act of 1979 that prohibited interstate commercial aviation out of Love Field and allowed only commuter airlines. But Southwest flights from Love Field would be allowed to fly to a Texas destination or one of four neighboring states: Arkansas, Oklahoma, Louisiana, and New Mexico. The amendment, which became known as the Wright Amendment, recognized that DFW was the primary airport in North Texas.

The Wright Amendment had been a repeated issue of controversy between Dallas and Fort Worth before I arrived at Congress. Dallas officials believed that removal of restrictions at Love Field would promote more economic opportunity for the city. More flights meant lower fares, which meant more travelers and more economic benefits for Dallas. They were joined in this position by some nearby states such as Kansas and Missouri, which wanted their cities to have opportunities for direct flights to Love Field. But Dallas residents living near Love Field were opposed to any expansion of flights.

Fort Worth generally opposed removal of the restrictions because it did not want to impede the growth of Alliance Airport, an airport located in northern Fort Worth that was the southwest hub for Federal Express. Just a year earlier, Fort Worth had filed a lawsuit against Dallas to block a city council vote to reconsider the Wright Amendment.

DFW Airport officials were concerned about its operations and the impact of more flights out of Love Field. Would airlines split operations between DFW and Love Field? What would be the economic impact? Questions and concerns swirled around the question of what should be done about Love Field.

Once I was elected and appointed to the Transportation Committee, it was only natural that overtures would be made to me about changing the restrictions. There were competing interests and concerns revolving around the continuation or modification of the Wright Amendment. Southwest had grown over the years, developing a far-reaching network of destinations of long-distance flights, originating at any airport except Love Field. But that flight restriction still hampered its operations. These limitations also hindered competition, which contributed to higher airfares for direct flights to and from North Texas. While DFW had certainly become more established and was a key national airport, there was still concern that an unrestricted Love Field could undermine that stability. And residents of the Love Field neighborhood remained concerned about the noise and pollution that would accompany any expansion of flights.

While I believed that the arrangement was balanced and had served the best interests of the stakeholders in the Dallas–Fort Worth area, I also thought that it was important that the interested parties, Dallas, Fort Worth, and other area cities talk to each other to attempt a resolution. To me the cities that had come together in 1968 to create an arrangement that would build DFW Airport should now, in that same spirit, continue to work together. I suggested that stakeholders convene a conference and hammer out a resolution to the common problem.

A transportation summit was convened in 1995 in Irving, Texas, a city centrally located between Dallas and Fort Worth. Rodney Slater, the secretary of transportation, attended. I made it clear to all of the participants that I was not going to take a position on the Wright Amendment until I listened to and weighed the arguments of all who were involved.

Two years later, in 1997, Congress enacted the Shelby Amendment, which expanded Southwest's market to include three additional states and further defined the aircraft that could use Love Field. This amendment was instituted by the Appropriations Committee, not the Committee on Commerce, Science, and Transportation. It was not widely debated, but the basic premise of the Wright Amendment as envisioned by Congressman Wright remained.

The early years of 2000 saw the airline industry face significant challenges. The terrorist attacks of 9/11, high oil prices, technological advancements, design of new aircraft, and other factors combined to cause an upheaval in the industry. Consumers had more fare choices. Airline employees were concerned about labor contracts. All of these issues were implicated in continued efforts to revise the Wright Amendment.

In May 2005 Representatives Jeb Hensarling and Sam Johnson, both from North Texas, introduced the American Right to Fly Act.[12] The bill proposed the immediate end of the Wright Amendment by allowing direct flights from Love Field to any US state. The bill was referred to the Subcommittee on Aviation. As the only member from North Texas to sit on the House Aviation Subcommittee, my position carried considerable weight. I consulted with North Texas colleagues who had smaller airports in their districts. I spoke with stakeholders from DFW Airport, Love Field neighborhood groups, airline representatives, and labor union leaders. I reviewed data and studies related to economic considerations. By 2003 nearly twenty-five million passengers used DFW while nearly three million people used Love Field. American Airlines, with DFW as its home airport, served 18 percent of the nation's passenger air travel; Southwest held nearly 8 percent of the market share. Gross revenues for 2004 for Southwest were $6.5 billion; American had gross revenues of $18 billion. DFW, Love Field, American Airlines, and Southwest Airlines were undeniably significant contributors to the DFW economy.

Reports were also generated attempting to predict the economic impact of the repeal of the Wright Amendment. One study projected that DFW would lose 204 flights a day, 21 million passengers annually, and would slash airport passenger traffic such that DFW would not recover for an estimated twenty years.

Based on those conversations, such data and research, and my knowledge of North Texas, I was convinced that a stable DFW was crucial to the financial health and continued development of North Texas. An immediate repeal of the Wright Amendment would jeopardize that continued growth and potentially negatively impact the Love Field community. I was also mindful of the agreements that had been made when DFW was created and the subsequent modifications that resulted in the Wright Amendment. A deal had been reached and that deal should be respected, not legislated out of existence by Congress. I firmly believed the issue should be resolved locally, not by congressional mandate. In response to advocates of expanding service at Love Field, I announced that I was prepared to introduce legislation that would end commercial flights to Love Field if there was unfettered opening of the airport. In a statement released after my announcement I said, "The Wright Amendment was agreed to by both cities, area constituent groups and Southwest Airlines. The balance between our two airports has served North Texas well and should not be disturbed."[13] It was my hope that Congress would not preempt the local cities of Dallas and Fort Worth.

With the bill not progressing in the House, on July 19, 2005, Senators John Ensign of Nevada and John McCain of Arizona introduced the American Right to Fly Act, which would immediately expand direct air service from Love Field to all of the United States.[14] They said they introduced the bill because air travelers across the country were paying higher fares and had fewer flight options because the Wright Amendment restricted market competition. Southwest passengers desiring to travel outside the designated destinations had to purchase two tickets, actually deplane, secure their luggage, and then check in through security again and recheck their luggage to board the second flight.

That same date Senators James Inhofe and Tom Harkin of Iowa introduced the True Competition Act, which, after reciting congressional findings about the creation and construction of DFW Airport, provided for the termination of all scheduled passenger service from Love Field within three years. Two days later Representative Hensarling introduced the What's Love Got to Do With It Bill, which called for the closing of the airports in Tulsa, Oklahoma, and Des Moines, Iowa.

It was against this backdrop that the Senate Subcommittee on Aviation held its hearing on November 10, 2005. I provided testimony at that hearing explaining the concerns underlying my opposition to a preemptive repeal of the Wright Amendment instead of a negotiated resolution. To me the 1968 restrictions and subsequent modifications were born out of cooperation between the cities. Any further modifications or repeal should come again from such a cooperative spirit rather than an imposition from Congress. There were legitimate concerns surrounding what course of action should be pursued. Love Field was located in a residential area, and expanded use negatively impacted the environment, safety, and quality of life of those residents and the approximately thirty thousand students being educated in schools located near the airport. Noise pollution and traffic control were especially concerning. Polls that suggested over 80 percent of DFW people favored the repeal did not capture the fears of the residents; the persons polled would not have to suffer the consequences of increased air traffic at Love Field.

Secondly, a weakened DFW Airport would have a potential negative impact on the North Texas economy. The airport generated $14.3 billion in economic output, 268,000 jobs, and $6 billion in payroll. There had to be caution in taking steps that could weaken this impact.

I recognized there were countering arguments that repeal was needed to lower airfares and to encourage competition. Those arguments had legitimacy. The question was always one of how you balance these concerns and who should make the ultimate decision. I believed that the cities of Dallas and Fort Worth, just as they had reached agreement when DFW was first built, should exercise the authority to reach a resolution that best addressed their respective interests and concerns.

Senator Kay Bailey Hutchinson expressed these same sentiments in her testimony. She believed that local community leaders in Dallas and Fort Worth should be the ones to come up with the right plan. Otherwise, everyone would be put in a very bad situation of dictating from Washington what is right for the citizens of North Texas, especially the people who live near Love Field, and trying to project the economic impact that would reach to smaller cities in Texas such as Abilene and Amarillo.

Congresswoman Kay Granger echoed similar views in her testimony. She bluntly stated that she thought a change in the Wright Amendment would be a blow to DFW Airport. She also pointed out that Southwest had the ability to offer direct flights by using gates at DFW, noting that it had been offered millions in incentives to use DFW.

Other states could be negatively impacted by a repeal. Senator James Inhofe testified that airline service to Oklahoma cities would be reduced. Senator Mark Pryor expressed the same concerns about airline service to Arkansas. Representatives from smaller airports presented their perspectives.

The hearing confirmed that there was no quick and simple resolution. But this examination of the issues and repeated encouragement for local officials to negotiate spotlighted the need for discussions between Dallas mayor Laura Miller, Fort Worth mayor Mike Moncrief, and executives at American and Southwest Airlines. In early March 2006, Dallas and Fort Worth passed resolutions formally requesting that members of Congress refrain from taking any action on the Wright Amendment to give North Texas officials time to develop a local solution. Those resolutions were honored and no further congressional action was taken until the announcement of an agreement.

Once the cities announced that they had reached an agreement, I contacted Jim Wright. I believed he deserved an opportunity to share his opinion on proposed legislation impacting the amendment. We talked about the reasons for the initial restrictions, the rationale for the Wright Amendment, and the need to change the current arrangement. He told me that he fully supported the resolution reached by the cities. His comments reflected the assessment that I had made, both on the merits of the resolution and the importance of the process by which the resolution had been reached.

On July 18, 2006, I and twelve other representatives introduced the Wright Amendment Reform Act.[15] Representative Don Young, as chairman of the House Transportation Committee, introduced the bill. This proposal reflected the approach that had been consistently urged during the Senate hearing: collaboration and negotiation between stakeholders crafting a resolution that was acceptable to all. This successful ending was not always predicted. Indeed, the *Fort Worth Star-Telegram* had opined that there was "no middle ground, no make-it-feel-all-better compromise."[16] But I had always believed that the best resolution had to come from the local elected officials.

The Senate version of the bill was sent to the House on September 28, 2006. There had been delays in Senate approval. Senator Patrick Leahy, a close personal friend of Representative Wright, was a holdout. I made arrangements to have Wright call Senator Leahy and address his concerns. With Wright's assurances that this bill would best serve North Texas and the country and that it had his approval, Senator Leahy withdrew his opposition.

Once again I had the honor of joining other representatives in sponsoring a slightly revised Wright Amendment Reform Act, now called House Bill 6228. The key aspects of the Wright Reform Act were: (1) direct and through flights were expanded throughout the United States, (2) no international travel from

Love Field (3) the number of gates at Love Field would be reduced, and (4) the FAA would notify Congress that the modifications could meet safety standards. The Wright Amendment Reform Act was signed into law on October 13, 2006.

The fight over aviation in North Texas had been going on for decades. There had been repeated lawsuits and threats of yet more lawsuits. There had been congressional action trying to direct and manage the airports and air travel. Hundreds of hours had been spent meeting with city officials, airline representatives, DFW Airport representatives, Love Field residents, and other interested parties to help facilitate a resolution. But the position that I took in 1995 that local government officials needed to craft the solution never changed. And in the end that was the approach that succeeded, that was the best way to serve the people of North Texas.

While the Wright Amendment was being resolved, other airport needs still demanded attention. At DFW runways needed to be repaired and extended, service roads repaired, and an aircraft rescue and fire training facility constructed. A new baggage handling system was needed at Love Field. More than $54 million in grants helped to fund these projects. Because of my position on the Transportation Committee, over the years I was able to press for funding for DFW and Love Field, even though DFW was no longer in my jurisdiction.

Flooding

Dallas had historically experienced flooding due to the Trinity River. However, by the time that I arrived in Congress, it was clear that two areas of the city, Rochester Park and Cadillac Heights, two predominantly African American communities, had been intentionally overlooked and neglected in flood-prevention measures. During my first congressional campaign, I featured a picture of a house in Cadillac Heights that had been flooded. That picture became the symbol of my commitment to address the causes of flooding along the Trinity River Basin.

Due in large part to its segregated housing laws and patterns, Dallas had allowed developers to construct homes for African Americans in areas that would not have been otherwise approved for development. Construction of developments, such as the 350-plus homes of Rochester Park on a known flood plain, was approved by city officials.

In November 1992 a disastrous flood in Rochester Park occurred, the result of decades of flood control measures targeting white neighborhoods and industrial areas, knowingly neglecting African American communities. Federal plans to address the problem were rejected in 1983 by the then Dallas mayor. And when a levee was finally constructed to protect Rochester Park, outdated engineering information was used, leaving the area still vulnerable to flooding.

When I got to Congress, with my appointment to the Transportation Committee, I was able to focus on measures to address the Trinity waterway and flooding. In 1996 we directed that Rochester Park and Central Wastewater Treatment Plants be added to the federally authorized floodway system. The floodway project had to be coordinated with the city of Dallas because it was responsible for securing the nonfederal portion of the necessary funds.

Additionally, there were several development initiatives proposed for the Trinity River, each idea demanding time or a referendum to determine which proposal the city would pursue. Dallas mayor Ron Kirk, members of his staff, and I had regular meetings with planning experts in Dallas and in Washington. In 1998 Mayor Kirk teamed with Dallas-area elected officials, community leaders, and members of the business community to pass a $246 million bond proposal to raise public funds for the Trinity River Project.

While the development of a comprehensive flooding plan was complicated and moved laboriously slowly, the city was able to move forward more quickly with the construction of two bridges to cross the Trinity River. The bridges were intended to improve transportation in the city, connecting West Dallas with downtown. They were to be signature structures. Named after two leading women philanthropists, Margaret Hill Hunt and Margaret McDermott, both bridges have been built. In 2007 the American Institute of Architects awarded the Trinity River Project its highest award for regional and urban planning.

Around the same time, although not in my district, reducing the flooding of Johnson Creek in Arlington, a neighboring city, and restoring it for recreational use had gained importance. The project had been previously proposed, but now the Dallas Cowboys were looking for a site for a new football stadium and were considering building in Arlington. The Johnson Creek flooding had to be resolved for the stadium to be built on the Arlington site. Working with Representative Joe Barton, a Republican, I was able to secure $12 million of federal funding to contribute to the anticipated cost of over $20 million through the Water Resources Act of 1999. The Cowboys broke ground on the new stadium in Arlington in 2005. If we had not resolved that flooding problem, the Cowboys stadium would not have been built.

We had struggled to get biennial Water Resources Development legislation passed. In 2007 President Bush had vetoed WRDA, a veto that I worked hard to override. That statute authorized almost $300 million for the Trinity River Floodway. But the Corps of Engineers had to conduct a feasibility study before construction could begin. After two years of study, the Corps determined that the plans were inadequate, and a new strategy had to be developed. It took several years for the city and the Corps to conduct the necessary testing and assessments to develop a new floodway plan, which called for wetlands, grasslands and woodlands, recreational trails, pumping stations, and levee improvements.

Another major flooding problem presented itself when in 2015 Lewisville Lake Dam was determined by the Corps of Engineers to be unstable and almost certain to fail. If the dam had been breached, residents in cities in Lewisville, Coppell, Carrollton, Dallas, Farmers Branch, and Irving would have flooded. Downtown Dallas could have flooded to a depth of fifty feet, jeopardizing all the hospitals and medical facilities because of their ground-level generators. It would have been a major catastrophe. Funding was needed to secure and strengthen the dam. In 2018 I was able to secure $92 million to be used for the Lewisville dam, averting such a catastrophe. Making the dam safe and secure again was a top priority for me. I was extremely pleased and relieved when were able to secure the funding; the alternative was simply unthinkable to me.

In that same bill, Dallas received almost $300 million for the continued work on the Dallas Floodway. Pumping stations are used to pump storm water, sometimes hundreds of thousands of gallons of water a minute, away from residential and business districts. Part of this money is being used to update a pump station to almost triple its capacity to pump water.

Finally, on June 7, 2022, I was able to stand at the groundbreaking ceremony for the construction of this project to improve levees and renovate and build pumping stations. It had taken over two decades to get to this point, but I had not forgotten what had motivated me all of these years to stay focused on addressing the flooding. Remembering the photo that I had used on my first campaign, I said to the assembled group, "Imagine waking up and finding water up to your window line, your beds and couches soaked with water." Removing that fear, knowing that we had to provide the infrastructure to prevent such anxiety, is what drove me to stay focused and determined that we could get it done.

Fighting for STEM Education and Opportunities

The participation of women in science, technology, and engineering has always been an area of focus for me. Perhaps that interest was rooted in being a nurse, a science-based profession. My work in strengthening and improving science, technology, engineering, and math (STEM) education began when I was a member of the Texas House. My colleague Carlos Truan and I worked on science and math legislation to ensure that minorities and women were included in programs created by the state.

But I was also influenced by seeing the identifiable impact of Dallas-based Texas Instruments and its founders, Cecil Green, Patrick Haggerty, Erik Jonsson, and Eugene McDermott. Watching Texas talent leave the state to pursue education, they established the Graduate Research Center of the Southwest, which became the foundation for the University of Texas at Dallas. While in the Texas Senate, I was a cosponsor of a bill to expand that institution to a four-year college by allowing the admission of freshmen and sophomores. That bill included an explicit expression of legislative intent that minority students be full participants in the school's educational opportunities, especially natural sciences, mathematics, and engineering. It further provided that enrollments be set aside for minority students until minority enrollment was fully representative of the state's minority population.[17]

So it was natural for me to look at ways the federal government could advance STEM education, especially for women and minorities when I was elected to Congress. Little did I know that it would become one of my longest and hardest battles, requiring persistence, insistence, and unwavering determination. But what I did know was that I would need to use a variety of avenues to mount my campaign to strengthen our nation's focus on science and technology and to expand educational STEM opportunities to minorities and women. It was critical to our nation's continued global and economic leadership. Naturally, I would sponsor legislation, but I would also organize, host conferences, support research and studies, liaise with professional organizations, and travel the country advocating for STEM opportunities.

The CBC gave me an immediate platform to talk about STEM. In 1993 I designed the CBC Science and Technology Brain Trust. I envisioned a program that would support and inspire young Black students across the country to pursue opportunities in STEM. The brain trust would be a tool to connect those students with prominent leaders and professionals who by example could help students realize that they could excel in such careers.

For almost thirty years, during the CBC Foundation's Annual Legislative Conferences, I convened annual brain trust conferences, bringing together leading scientists, engineers, computer technologists, pilots, astronauts, and physicians to speak with African American students.[18] While students came from as far away as Houston, most students were from DC, Maryland, Virginia, and East Coast cities. With busloads of youth, we would often have between four and five hundred students present. During COVID we gathered virtually, emphasizing that a STEM education to workforce pipeline was essential to the continuing progress of this nation.

I also kept a focus on STEM as the cofounder of the Technology, Infrastructure, Development Task Force of the CBC. There is a significant digital divide in this country, one that has existed for decades. Technology should be a part of rebuilding and modernizing the Black community. To help accomplish this, there must be greater access to STEM education and resources. This lack of access to broadband for communities of color was vividly exposed during COVID. The resulting inequities in digital learning can no longer be ignored.

I knew when I went to Congress that we could achieve these objectives by building on existing legislation. The Science and Engineering Opportunities Act of 1980 requires the NSF to regularly publish data relating to the participation of women, minorities, and persons with disabilities in the science and engineering fields. Its1994 report noted that underrepresentation continued, despite some improvement. But the past decade had created greater alarms because of a national decline in educational quality. There was now a problem of equity and quality, a problem that threatened our ability to achieve equity or sustain international competitiveness.

In 1998 the Committee on Science published a report titled Unlocking Our Future: Toward a New National Science Policy.[19] While I commended the effort to create a comprehensive science policy report, I joined my colleagues Barbara Lee, Sheila Jackson Lee, and Darlene Hooley in submitting a dissenting view. We identified four areas that the report failed to address: (1) the role of underrepresented populations in the fields of science and technology, (2) social and behavioral sciences, (3) K–12 science and math education, and (4) the challenges of environmental quality.[20]

Representative Sensenbrenner, the chair of the committee, introduced a resolution that the publication should be the framework for deliberations on congressional science policy and funding. The next day I spoke against that resolution, noting our criticism of the report. While I commended the chair and other committee leaders for the effort to create a comprehensive science policy report, I had to speak against the resolution. I listed the four areas that the report failed to address. I pointed out that any policy needed to include underrepresented populations or otherwise a technological divide would be created. I used statistics relating to access to computers to illustrate the disparity between white, African American, and Hispanic students.

We needed programs such as the NSF's urban systemic and rural systemic initiative programs focusing on specialized high school math and science curriculum. I pointed to scientific community partnerships with HBCUs and Hispanic Service Institutions (HSIs). From 1993 to 1994, $10 billion had been allocated to research institutions, with John Hopkins alone receiving $701 million. In contrast, eighty-one HBCUs and HSIs divided $140 million in funding. These inequities must be addressed.[21]

That same year the Congressional Commission on the Advancement of Women and Minorities in Science, Engineering, and Technology Development was established. Its mandate was to identify opportunities and barriers for participation of women, minorities, and persons with disabilities in science, engineering, and technology fields. Two years later the commission released its report *Land of Plenty: Diversity as America's Competitive Edge in Science, Engineering and Technology*.[22] Again there was recognition that there were barriers that limit participation in science and technology fields. And once more there was acknowledgment that to compete effectively in the global marketplace required full and equitable participation of all Americans in the science, engineering, and technology fields.

There continued to be studies and reports warning of the decline in STEM education and the attendant consequences for our economy and security. We couldn't simply ignore that reality. So I repeatedly sponsored or cosponsored legislation to advance technology and science, especially targeting expanded outreach to underrepresented communities, even when prior bills had not advanced. The Information Technology Partnership Act[23] would have required the NSF to create demonstration grant projects for educational agencies in urban areas to develop math, science, and information curricula. Building on hearings that the committee had held, programs were again proposed in the Mathematics and Science Proficiency Partnership Acts of 1999 and 2001.[24]

Educational improvements to increase the number of college graduates was the focus of the Undergraduate Science, Mathematics, Engineering, and Technology Education Improvement Act introduced in 2002.[25] Despite twenty years of education reform, there still was little understanding of the factors that influenced study in sciences or technology. Once again, data demonstrating the link between technological advances and economic growth and national security was included within the congressional findings. The need was clearly identified. The bill, which I cosponsored, presented reforms to address those needs. Direct grant programs for higher education institutions to increase the number of underrepresented students, enable students at community colleges to matriculate directly into baccalaureate programs, and introduce career opportunities and other activities were specified. Minority-serving institutions were eligible for grant funding to strengthen and improve the curriculum, support faculty, and encourage research activities. When I spoke in support of this bill, H.R. 3130, I said that it would "put in place a range of programs and activities that will strengthen undergraduate education in science and technology and will help provide the human resources that this Nation will need for economic strength and security in the postindustrial world."[26]

Finally, in December 2002, Congress passed the National Science Foundation Authorization Act of 2002, which authorized almost $38 billion in appropriations for fiscal years 2003 through 2007.[27] The NSF is the largest source of federal funding for research in all science and engineering disciplines and in science, mathematics, engineering, and technology education at all levels. It helps to prepare future generations of scientists, mathematicians, and engineers. This law recognized that our country's economic strength, national security, and quality of life are grounded in our scientific and technological capabilities.

At the time I was the ranking member of the House Science Research Subcommittee and had been an original cosponsor, deeply involved in drafting this act. A year earlier I had proposed a bill to increase NSF authorization. This bill accomplished those goals.

During the House hearings, Congressman Ralph Hall acknowledged that I was responsible for a lot of the bill, but especially the section on the Partnership for Math and Science for Economically Disadvantaged Students. Senator Ted Kennedy had assisted with including sections of the Mathematics and Science Proficiency Partnership Act into this authorization. We included programs to build or expand mathematics, science, and information technology curriculum. We created the Robert Noyce Scholarship Program to support the training of science and mathematics teachers.

The act also contained provisions that authorized appropriations that substantially increased the budget for the NSF and provisions to help secondary schools leverage private sector funds for math, science, and engineering scholarships. By getting the support of private entities such as Texas Instruments, a focus was to be placed on achieving proficiency in mathematics and technology.

The act also instructed the NSF director to encourage inclusion of HBCUs, HSIs, tribally controlled colleges and universities, Alaska Native–serving institutions, and Native Hawaiian–serving institutions in funded research partnerships. It was always important to me that HBCUs be provided access to these funded programs. Historically, our HBCUs had graduated more minority scientists, engineers, and computer scientists than other educational institutions. It was logical to me to tap into that resource for expanding our pool of minority STEM professionals by providing funding to strengthen and expand that programming.

But in addition to those aspects, the statute included the text of the Regional Plant Genome and Gene Research Expression Act that I had sponsored earlier in the year. That legislation established research grants on crops that can be grown in the developing world to address hunger, malnutrition, and disease. An important feature of that authorization required US scientists to partner with scientists in developing nations to stimulate ideas and develop the scientific capacities of those nations.

There is a certain amount of expectation and faith when supporting scientific initiatives. We can't always predict the exact impact of research. But two research projects funded in 2002 laid the foundation for the COVID-19 vaccines.

The focus on science, technology, engineering and mathematics education became sharpened with the October 2005 release of the initial report of the National Academy of Sciences' *Rising above the Gathering Storm*.[28] Ten weeks earlier Senators Lamar Alexander and Jeff Bingaman had asked the National Academies to consider "the top 10 actions, in priority order, that policymakers could take to enhance the science and technology enterprise so that the United States can successfully compete, prosper, and be secure in the global community of the 21st century."[29]

To respond to this request, a commission was created to gather information, consult with leading experts, and develop recommendations with action steps. This report helped crystallize a focus on technology preparedness. It disclosed that then current trends indicated that the United States economy might not be as strong in the future without government intervention. It declared that "this nation must prepare with great urgency to preserve its strategic and economic security. . . . The United States must compete by optimizing its knowledge-based resources, particularly in science and technology." It went on to say that "without a renewed effort to bolster the foundations of our competitiveness, we can expect to lose our privileged position" and that the issues explored showed "a recurring pattern of abundant short-term thinking and insufficient long-term investment." Holding on to a mentality that isolation and "circl[ing] the wagons" will preserve American quality of life simply "won't work."[30]

The alarms raised by the report were not surprising to those of us who had been following trends in education and technology. We were validated. We had been correct in pushing for increased education and training. But there were some members of the committee who were shocked. They seemed to want to believe that our economy would just always be strong, that we would somehow remain competitive even without investing the necessary resources.

I knew that we had to act. I served as a congressional spokesperson for the report, staying focused on the report's identified objectives. The highest priority had to be given to increasing the nation's talent pool by vastly improving K–12 science and mathematics education. We had to make a robust effort to increase the number and proportion of US citizens earning degrees in science, engineering, and mathematics.

There were specific recommendations to achieve these objectives, included the annual hiring of ten thousand kindergarten through twelfth-grade teachers trained in STEM fields. Students were to receive four-year academic scholarships if they studied science, engineering, or mathematics. Participating students were required to spend five years teaching in public schools. Those teaching in urban and rural schools would receive a $10,000 annual bonus. Federal funding was also recommended for colleges and universities that created undergraduate programs in science, mathematics, and engineering.

The report also recommended that the skills of existing teachers be improved through participation in educational programs during the summer months and pursuit of advanced degrees in math, science, and engineering.

The pool of students taking advanced science and math courses in junior and senior high schools also needed to be expanded.

Key barriers such as implicit bias and the expectation that scientists had to look like men had to be tackled. The lack of accessible childcare had to be addressed because it was a barrier to recruitment and training of female scientists.

I had introduced House Democratic Leader Nancy Pelosi to Norman Augustine, the chair of the committee that had done the research and authored *Rising above the Gathering Storm*. To me this research was so significant and important that I wanted it to be widely known.

As we approached the 2006 midterm election, Leader Pelosi unveiled the Democrats' Innovation Agenda: A Commitment to Competitiveness to Keep America #1. Underscoring the importance of America being the leader in science and industry, she noted American investment in research had been flat or failing for almost twenty years. Drawing from the *Rising above the Gathering Storm* report, she called for a renewed commitment for discovery, invention, and growth. The agenda called for qualified science and math teachers for K–12 classrooms; an addition of one hundred thousand new scientists, mathematicians, and engineers to the American workforce; increased federal funding for basic research; affordable access for every American to broadband; and development of clean, sustainable energy alternatives.[31]

Building on the momentum of the *Rising above the Gathering Storm* report and the Democratic agenda, the America Creating Opportunities to Meaningfully Promote Excellence in Technology, Education, and Science Act of 2007 (America COMPETES Act) was introduced in May 2007.[32] This bill was a comprehensive effort to address the nation's technology and science needs by focusing resources for the NSF, the Department of Energy's Office of Science (DOE/OS), and the National Institute of Standards and Technology (NIST).

It was very important to me that members of the Science Committee understand how crucial this legislation was to minority Americans who were still not fully participating in the country's technological revolution. I arranged a meeting for committee chair Congressman Bart Gordon with members of the CBC so that he could hear firsthand the concerns and ideas of other minority representatives.

During Science Committee deliberations, I encouraged my colleagues to include provisions that would increase the number of women and racial minorities that pursued STEM training and careers. I successfully offered two amendments. One created a program to enhance the participation of women in academic communities by a directive that science agencies establish clear policies for researchers who were on leave of absence because they were caregivers. Another required the secretary of energy, when utilizing COMPETES funding, to give special consideration to HBCUs and land grant universities. At the urging of the caucus, the collection of data was addressed by directing the National Academy of Sciences to prepare a report detailing barriers confronting minorities who wanted to study STEM courses.

I pushed for additional funding for the NSF to support educational programming for minority students. The Louis A. Stokes Alliances for Minority Participation and the NSF Minority Postdoctoral Research Fellowships, HBCU-UP program, and Noyce Scholarships were all programs to encourage increased education and training of African Americans in the STEM fields. These funding levels simply were necessary to diversifying our science and technology workforce.

Because of differences between the House and Senate versions, a conference was required. After the conference report, I again spoke on behalf of this bill. We had held numerous hearings. We had participated in markups. It was time for the bill to pass. Quoting my father, "Nothing is free; you get what you pay for."[33] We hadn't been investing in STEM education, and we had allowed ourselves to get behind. Now was the time to make the investment in our future.

The bill authorized $33 billion over fiscal years 2008–2020. Pointing out that we had been spending a lot of money on the Iraq War, we declared it was time to spend money to take care of our nation. With bipartisan support, the COMPETES Act passed. It was a proud moment.

President Bush signed the bill, but he had already determined that he would not seek full funding to meet the authorization levels. Nonetheless, its passage created a sense of optimism and encouragement that the nation would finally be giving needed attention to our science, technology, and engineering needs.

This legislative focus on STEM issues spurred me to join with my Texas colleague Silvestre Reyes to create the House Diversity and Innovation Caucus. Its purpose was to generate policy ideas that would target the underrepresentation of women and minorities in the STEM fields. This caucus has received the support and collaboration of significant organizations, including the National Center for Women and Information Technology, the Society for Women Engineers, United Negro College Fund, the National Science Teachers Association, the Society of Mexican American Engineers and Scientists, and the Society of Hispanic Professional Engineers.

In June 2008 to highlight the failure to appropriate the needed level of funding for the COMPETES Act, I introduced a concurrent resolution expressing the Sense of Congress Regarding Science Education. The COMPETES Act had to be properly funded. The most recent assessment of educational progress revealed that a majority of those 17 years of age were poorly equipped for informed citizenship and productive performance in the workplace. It was also reported that women and minorities continued to be underserved by and underrepresented in science and mathematics. We had to focus on training our youth. Youth are the key to our future prosperity. They are our responsibility. Passing a statute has little value if Congress doesn't appropriate the funds for the authorized programs.

I spoke of two of Dallas Independent School District's Townview Magnet schools, the School of Talented and Gifted and the Science and Engineering Magnet. Those schools were nationally ranked as top schools. Their programs had benefited from support by Texas Instruments. I described the UTeach Program initiated by the University of Texas in Austin that offers pathways for STEM college students to obtain teaching certification and place engaged, highly trained teachers in the classroom. I continued to emphasize that we needed a skilled workforce. Our companies had to be able to find the scientists, engineers, and mathematicians they needed.[34]

This congressional resolution recognized that this nation should dedicate its resources to developing a broad pool of citizens literate in science, mathematics, and technology. Representative Holt, as he thanked me for introducing this resolution, warned that "without taking a bold, different approach in this year's appropriation cycle, Congress will be delivering a blow to our future economic security and competitiveness."[35] The resolution was agreed to in the House on a voice vote. It was received in the Senate where it was referred to the Committee on Health, Education, Labor, and Pensions. It died in committee.

Just a few weeks earlier, on May 8, 2008, the Committee on Science and Technology had held a hearing on my proposed legislation Fulfilling the Potential of Women in Academic Science and Engineering Act of 2008.[36] My bill noted that while there had been progress in women obtaining undergraduate degrees in engineering, less than 20 percent of bachelor's degrees in engineering and physics were awarded to women. It further pointed out that women held a small portion of leadership positions in institutions of higher education, scientific societies, and honorary organizations. The bill called upon federal science agencies to develop policies for a program of workshops to educate program officers, grant review panels, and higher education department chairs on how to minimize the effects of gender bias. I believed that such an educational program was necessary to start to address the barriers to women in engineering and science.

Dr. Lynda Carlson, NSF; Dr. Linda Blevins, Office of Science, Department of Energy; and Dr. Donna K. Ginther, University of Kansas, appeared as witnesses. The hearing was to identify approaches to change the culture and structure of their institutions to implement changes to recruiting, hiring, promotion, and tenure practices. Before their testimony, I gave an opening statement. I candidly expressed my frustration about the uphill battle that I was encountering in getting equality for women. I had attempted to incentivize the formation of an interinstitutional monitoring organization through a competitive grant. That grant was accepted into the Higher Education Act but was stripped out during conference proceedings.

I told the witnesses and committee members that I did not feel that enough was being done to educate persons of influence on the subtle gender bias that exists and that was holding women back from achieving at the same levels as men. I posed questions highlighting the absence of federal action. And then I pointed out that the most recent study published by the NSF on doctorate recipients from United States universities had intentionally omitted numbers relating to women and minority candidates, saying such suppression was necessary to protect the confidentiality of the individuals. Even if the numbers are embarrassingly low, I said, they need to be disclosed so that taxpayers and legislators have the truth about the sad state of women and minority achievement in the sciences. I acknowledged the support of the American Association of University Women, National Coalition for Women and Girls in Education, the Society of Women Engineers, the National Science Teachers Association, the American Chemical Society, and other organizations. Their interest in this information demonstrated the breadth of concern.

The bill did not progress through the House, but I was determined to keep the spotlight on STEM opportunities for women and minorities. I reintroduced this bill again in 2009 and 2011. The National Academies' 2007 study, *Beyond Bias and Barriers: Fulfilling the Potential of Women in Academic Science and Engineering*, had succinctly stated the challenge: for the United States to remain a leader in economic and educational globalization, we had to aggressively pursue the innovative capacity of all of our people, women and men.[37] It was not a lack of talent but rather institutional biases and outmoded institutional structures that were the barriers. My bills addressed those barriers, and I was determined that they should be removed.

With the election of Barack Obama to the presidency, we had an administration that actively promoted STEM initiatives. His Educate to Innovate campaign identified three specific STEM education goals: increasing STEM literacy, improving math and science instruction, and expanding STEM education and jobs for underrepresented groups.[38] The American Recovery and Reinvestment Act included a major funding increase for the National Institutes of Health.

But once again, a publication by the National Academies Press sounded the alarm. *Rising above the Gathering Storm, Revisited: Rapidly Approaching Category 5* was published in 2010,[39] the same year that the COMPETES Act was up for reauthorization. The book concluded that despite the positive response to the initial report, the nation now faced even greater challenges. Other nations had taken the recommendations of the initial *Rising above the Gathering Storm* report and implemented them in their countries. Our competition was rapidly moving forward while we were only inching along. We needed consistent funding for the science initiatives, but it was not provided. Despite some bright spots in the public school system, overall, we had not improved in math and science. The highest priority remained strengthening the public school system and investing in basic scientific research.

On April 22, 2010, the America Creating Opportunities to Meaningfully Promote Excellence in Technology, Education, and Science (America COMPETES) Reauthorization Act of 2010 was introduced as H.R. 5116.[40] The House Science, Space and Technology Committee conducted a number of hearings. Our committee report addressed virtually every provision of the bill. There was an admonition that there was an expectation that any partnership between a major research university and a minority-serving institution was to be a true partnership engaging all players in the development and shaping of the proposal. We pointed to the astronomy bridge program between Fisk and Vanderbilt Universities as an example of a mutually beneficial partnership.[41]

Because the bill passed the House and the Senate had approved its version, it was necessary for the differences to be resolved. The conference version removed the language relating to my Fulfilling the Potential of Women in Academic Science and Engineering Act. But I vowed that I would continue to propose that legislation. I reintroduced it on March 2, 2011. It was just too important to simply abandon it.

The COMPETES Act of 2010 created the Committee on STEM education. This was an important step because it was charged with reviewing STEM education programs and activities in each federal agency and developing a STEM education strategic plan. The first strategic plan published under this mandate was in 2018. It recognized three principles that I had been advocating for years: we needed to have a STEM-literate public; we had to have diversity, equity, and inclusion, especially of historically underserved and underrepresented communities for this nation to realize the full benefits of STEM; and we had to educate a STEM-literate workforce for our economy.

In the December 2010 Science Committee report to the 111th Congress, I was compelled to submit a written additional view. I pressed for funding allocations that would reflect the urgency described in the report and create and strengthen STEM educational opportunities. I wrote that it was time to act boldly to produce a more diverse, well-educated workforce in STEM. We must invest in segments of our population that are not pursuing STEM training. We also had to target gaps in the STEM workforce because we were losing precious human capital.[42]

As always with funding decisions, priorities needed to be assessed. I identified allocated funding that should be diverted to provide robust funding for NSF. Certain NSF and Department of Energy programs had not been specified in the appropriations or the president's budget. I included them for funding, with specific funding requests. The Office of Science and Technology Policy had not been fully staffed and it needed to be restored to coordinate science activities. NASA education account funding should be increased. And the Department of Commerce–National Institute of Standards and Technology needed funding to allocate technological assistance to small businesses.

As I said in closing, these were programs with demonstrated success. They were needed to create a diverse educated workforce ready to face the "gathering storm" of international competition that had grown even more intense. We needed to make a shift in our priorities.

After the success of the original Competes 2007 and COMPETES Reauthorization of 2010, I introduced America Competes Reauthorization Act of 2014.[43] But that bill did not progress.

I was extremely disheartened when the act was again up for reauthorization in 2015. This time, Chair Lamar Smith authored the legislation.[44] He steered its perfunctory passage in the House Science Committee, keeping it behind closed doors without any legislative hearings or subcommittee markups. Neither the agencies that were the subject of the authorizations nor the stakeholders were given the opportunity to review the bill or to provide comment. The only bipartisan negotiations were limited to a few pages in the STEM title. Rather than reinforcing a commitment to science, it was preoccupied with questioning the motives of the NSF and the integrity of the scientists being funded. It created roadblocks to clean energy research and development. Even the sitting secretary of energy wrote a letter to the committee critical of the bill, disagreeing with the budget cuts to his agency.[45] The bill failed to do anything substantive or meaningful in regard to STEM. Efforts to ensure that minority-serving institutions were equal partners in NSF-funded research were rejected.

Slightly more than a month after its introduction the bill came up for debate. For three and a half hours, members spoke, the remarks and positions predictable along party lines. Republicans supported the restrictive funding, characterizing it as fiscally responsible. I spoke in opposition. I had to begin by pointing out that I had been a strong supporter of the original COMPETES Act and the 2010 reauthorization. So it was very unfortunate that I had to oppose this reauthorization. I pointed out that since 2010, spending in research and development had, at best, stagnated and, at worst, declined. In contrast, China had averaged an annual increase of 28 percent and had overtaken the United States as the world's largest economic power. H.R. 1806 did not provide adequate funding for research and development. It continued Chair Smith's politicization of the grant-making process. As I stood on the House floor, I was armed with letters and statements of concern and opposition from more than seventy different groups.[46]

The bill passed the House. It was received in the Senate and referred to the Committee on Commerce, Science, and Transportation. There it died. But my work on STEM and expanding opportunities could not die. Through the rest of Chair Smith's tenure, I was as determined as ever. I introduced the STEM Opportunities Act of 2015. Later that session, Chair Smith and Congresswoman Elizabeth Esty introduced the STEM Education Act of 2015.[47] This bill reflected a bipartisan effort to provide programming that supported teacher training, scholarships, and competitive grants for out-of-school STEM activities. In announcing her support for the bill, Congresswoman Esty graciously acknowledged me as leading the Science Committee to truly recognize the importance of a robust and multidisciplinary STEM education and inspiring the committee to do more across the board to support STEM.[48]

While I supported this bill, I did have my reservations. My concern rested with the new definition of STEM. Under this bill, STEM was "science, technology, engineering, and mathematics, including computer science."

Yet just a year earlier, the House had agreed to define STEM as "science, technology, engineering, and mathematics, including other academic subjects that build on these disciplines such as computer science."[49] That definition had been developed in collaboration with the STEM Education Coalition. The more expansive definition was needed to allow other critical subjects to be included that did not fit cleanly within the letters—such subjects as statistics and geology; statistics, an essential tool in research; and geology, fundamental in energy development. The narrower definition meant that resources could not be specifically targeted for these fields. That did not make sense to me.

While I was working diligently on legislation, I thought that it was important to acknowledge schools with successful STEM programs. I entered remarks in the *Congressional Record* congratulating the students, parents, and faculty of Cedar Hill Collegiate, Drew Freeman Middle School, Eastern Senior High School, Howard University Middle School, Ron Brown High School, Lasalle-Backus, and others for their programs in the STEM arena.[50]

In November 2017 Congresswoman Barbara Comstock and I sponsored the STEM Research and Education Effectiveness and Transparency Act.[51] This bill would require all federal sciences agencies to collect data to identify best practices to expand and sustain effective practices. Although it was not acted on by the Senate, Congresswoman Comstock had publicly thanked me for joining as a sponsor and for my longtime commitment to ensuring STEM reaches into all communities and provides opportunities for all.[52]

Once I was elected chair of the House Science Committee, we were able to continue focusing on STEM. Ranking Member Lucas and I introduced the STEM Opportunities Act of 2019.[53] It was designed to promote research and grant opportunities for women and historically underrepresented groups. A truly bipartisan bill, it passed the House and was referred to the Senate Committee on Health, Education, Labor, and Pensions. It did not advance in the Republican-controlled Senate. There were other bills related to research and STEM that passed the House but could not make it through the Senate, bills that had received strong, bipartisan support, such as the National Science Foundation for the Future Act[54] and the Department of Energy Science for the Future Act.[55]

But the best opportunity to advance STEM initiatives arose in 2021, during the first year of the Biden administration—the Creating Helpful Incentives to Produce Semiconductors (CHIPS) and Science Act. The bill had gone nowhere under the Trump administration. But this time the focused attention to chip manufacturing presented an opportunity to secure passage of other much-needed legislation. The concern about China becoming a major chip exporter created an urgency that had not previously existed.

This determination to bring chip manufacturing back to the United States allowed me a platform to advance other scientific and STEM provisions. The lack of access to childcare had been identified as a barrier to women's participation in research and engineering, so childcare was required. By attaching the STEM bills to the semiconductor legislation, we were able to incorporate other strategies for expanding opportunities in STEM areas.

One section of the act was named after me: NSF Eddie Bernice Johnson Inclusion across the Nation of Communities of Learners of Underrepresented Discoverers in Engineering and Science (INCLUDES) Initiative. I did not ask that this section be named after me. That idea came from Senator Maria Cantwell. We were elected to the House of Representatives the same year. In talking about this honor, she said that they thought it was very appropriate to name a key NSF program for increasing diversity in STEM the "Eddie Bernice Johnson INCLUDES" program. In her words, she said that this program would continue to bear my name, to tell my story, to attract the next generation of STEM women. It would be a reminder to our colleagues of all the STEM legislation that I had helped pass, including the bipartisan Minority Serving Institutions STEM Achievement Act and the bipartisan STEM Opportunity Act.[56]

I am so grateful that we were able to pass this landmark legislation and cement STEM initiatives for the benefit and prosperity of this nation. Our nation must have a trained workforce to manage the technology if we are to remain globally competitive. I couldn't give up. I wouldn't let up. It was too necessary. It was too important.

Protecting the Right to Vote

Having grown up in the segregated south, paid poll taxes, and applauded the passage of the Voting Rights Act of 1965, I have a deep-rooted commitment to the protection of everyone's right to vote. To me it is fundamental. The right to vote is to be recognized and respected. Access to the polls is to be provided. The votes are to be legitimately counted. That is the bedrock of our republican democracy.

Unfortunately, too often there have been threats and attacks on the right of people of color to vote. Sometimes it seems that every time that the impact of minority voting has been demonstrated, there is an effort to restrict and constrain the exercise of the right to vote.

Throughout my adulthood, I have fought to protect the right to vote. I have participated in voter registration drives. I've worked with get out the vote campaigns. I have helped to draw redistricting plans.

In 1987 the confirmation of a Texas judge to be a chief appellate judge gave me the opportunity to spotlight voter intimidation. During the 1982 campaign, as part of a Republican ballot security program, signs were posted throughout Black polling places in Dallas. The judge had been identified as having distributed some of the signs. I had obtained one of the signs and during the hearing, I held it up for the judge, audience, and cameras. I wanted the sign to be seen, just as it would have been seen by Black voters on election day. There was a heading that it was unlawful to remove the sign by order of the Sheriff of Dallas County. Large red lettering warned: YOU CAN BE IMPRISONED, and then in small type was set out a list of six prohibited activities. At the bottom, again in bold letters, it said DON'T RISK IT, OBEY THE LAW. To me it was important that the sign be displayed. It was intimidating. It was threatening. It was made to cause Black voters to be frightened.

The Senate committee questioned the judge about his participation in the ballot security program. He admitted that he had joined in posting the sign at a Black polling place. But it was his understanding that the Texas Secretary of State, the Dallas County Election officials, and the sheriff's department had authorized the sign. He recognized that it was a mistake and improper for him to participate in that program. With that apology his confirmation was secured.

I have remained concerned about voting rights. When I got to Congress, I joined the efforts of the CBC and other caucuses to be vigilant, introducing legislation pushing Congress to be the guardian of the right to vote.

Help America Vote Act

The 2000 election had revealed problems with voting practices and equipment. Millions of votes had not been counted. While the debacle in Florida with hanging chads received the greatest attention, hearings and reports discovered that there were problems with other voting systems, such as lever voting machines that would jam. Military and overseas personnel encountered obstacles to registration and voting. Eligible voters had been inexplicably removed from the voting rolls and turned away at the polls. As chair of the CBC, I had worked to keep a spotlight on this outrage and on the need to assure voting integrity. My work was recognized by my colleagues in their public comments, being called heroic. We had to assure that Congress met its duty to address this historic failure.

I was an original cosponsor of H.R. Bill 775 introduced in the House on February 28, 2001. Titled the Voting Improvement Act,[57] it was designed to establish a program to provide funds to state and local governments to replace the punch-card voting system and to establish the Election Administration Commission. This bill was referred to various House committees for consideration.

Several months later, on November 14, 2001, H.R. 3295, the Help America Vote Act, was introduced in the House.[58] This bill contained many of the same provisions as H.R. 775. The bill was referred to the House Science Committee to consider a provision creating a Technical Standards Development Committee. The committee would ensure the usability, accuracy, security, and integrity of voting systems and equipment. The National Institute for Standards and Technology would assist the committee and provide grants for voting technology research and pilot programs.

This bill passed the House and the companion bill passed the Senate. Ultimately, it was referred to conference for resolution of any differences between the bills. The final Help America Vote Act (HAVA), a result of a bipartisan conference report, was, as I said on the floor, the civil rights bill of the new millennium. It had taken twenty-one months of floor speeches and field hearings. The act created mandatory minimum standards for states to follow in federal elections. It provided funding to improve and upgrade voting equipment, train poll workers, upgrade voter lists, and make polling places accessible for disabled individuals.

More importantly, HAVA established the Election Assistance Commission, an independent, bipartisan commission tasked with providing guidelines for election equipment, gathering information on the administration of elections, and providing guidance to the states on elections procedures. This bipartisan commission, since becoming operational in January 2004, has developed best practices reports designed to assist state and local election officials to enhance their voting processes and provided guidelines for provisional voting and voter identification requirements. It responded to foreign interference in the 2016 elections and COVID-related issues in the 2020 election cycle. Significantly, the commission was integral to the certification of voting equipment that was used in the 2020 election and the rejection of claims of widespread voter fraud.

As I had said years earlier in support of this bill, we had to make sure all Americans could register to vote, remain on the rolls once registered, vote free from harassment, and have those votes counted. The least that could be expected is that when people vote, those votes are correctly counted.[59] We simply had to create mechanisms that would improve our electoral system. We had to encourage, support, and respect the rights of all citizens to participate in our government, not restrict or impede their participation. This act was a good beginning, but it was only a beginning.

My efforts to assure voting rights continued through my time in Congress. In 2003 a constitutional amendment that I supported was proposed.[60] This amendment guaranteed that all citizens 18 or older would have the right to vote, assured that elections would be administered in accordance with standards set by Congress, established same-day registration and voting, and required that electors vote for the candidate receiving the majority votes of their states. While the proposed amendment did not pass the House, our concerns have been proven to be justified. President Trump's efforts in 2020 to have certain substitute electors cast votes for him in contravention of their state's majority vote would have been unconstitutional had the amendment been adopted and ratified.

In September 2004 I joined over fifty other representatives in support of House Resolution 793, which condemned all efforts to suppress and intimidate voters in the United States and reaffirmed the fundamental right to vote of all eligible United States citizens.[61] Going back to the passage of the Fifteenth Amendment, the resolution listed repeated efforts to suppress and intimidate African American voters. We believed that the House needed to make a definitive condemnation of any efforts to suppress and intimidate voters and reaffirm that voting is a fundamental right. Disappointingly, but not surprisingly, the resolution was not adopted.

Just a few months later, President George W. Bush was reelected for a second term. His first term had proven to be a disaster for the nation. We had record surpluses when President Clinton left office, but Bush's economic policies had quickly taken the country down a slippery slope. His foreign policies could best be described as reckless, leading us into a war in Iraq based on claims of weapons of mass destruction that were later proven to be false. He was unable to articulate an appropriate vision for our nation, and in some parts of the world we became a laughingstock during his administration.

John Kerry, a respected US Senator from Massachusetts and a Vietnam War veteran, was our party's nominee in the 2004 presidential election. I thought for sure that President Bush would soon return to his ranch in Crawford, Texas, where he could pursue two of his passions, raising cattle and hunting deer. Polls had Kerry leading Bush by as many as five percentage points. Even on Election Day, credible exit polls had Kerry beating the sitting president by as many as eight points.

But then came vote results from Ohio, a battleground state where our party had worked tirelessly to register minority voters. And once again the shadows appeared. In some counties with large numbers of minority voters, the polling places did not open. In another voters were unable to vote for

Kerry because his name had been removed from the ballot. And in others the voting machines were locked in offices with Republican election officials claiming that they could not find keys to open the doors of the offices where they were stored.

At the end of the night, Ohio was called for President Bush. He was reelected. Those of us who had worked in Ohio and who understood the desperation of the Republican Party knew that we had been robbed once again.

Fannie Lou Hamer, Rosa Parks, and Coretta Scott King Voting Rights Act Reauthorization and Amendments Act

Just two years later, voting rights were again a focus of Congressional activity. The 1965 Voting Rights Act was one of the most significant pieces of legislation ever passed. It reinforced every American's right to vote by outlawing discriminatory voting practices that had existed in many southern states. It required preclearance of voting procedures. Over the years the act had been amended four times, either because sections were expiring or to respond to Supreme Court rulings.

In 2006, more than forty years after the original bill, there were still discriminatory practices denying minorities the right to vote. Without a continuation of the Voting Rights Act, minority citizens would continue to have their voting rights denied or diluted. We had to address that problem. We had to continue the protections so that the right to vote was protected. Our democracy rests upon the ability of citizens to participate in free and fair elections to choose their representatives.

As I said in support of the Fannie Lou Hamer, Rosa Parks, and Coretta Scott King Voting Rights Act Reauthorization and Amendments Act, our values, our freedom, and our democracy are based on the idea that every eligible American citizen has the right to vote. Every citizen has the right to expect that their vote will be counted. At that time it had been only forty years earlier that minorities lived under the oppression of Jim Crow. As a result, millions of Americans were unable to fairly participate in our democracy. In this battle for the most basic of rights, many heroic Americans were imprisoned, beaten, or even killed in the name of freedom and justice.

The Voting Rights Act changed the face of this nation. We had made amazing progress, but having made progress did not mean that we could stop working to address voting inequality. We should not and could not give up until every American citizen had the access and opportunity to vote—regardless of their skin color, ethnicity, or language ability. Despite the progress there were still thousands of cases of voter intimidation and discrimination reported at every election. Minorities continued to face the uphill battle of misinformation over polling locations, the purging of voter rolls, scare tactics, and inaccessible voting locations. The reality was that there were still some people who didn't want minorities to vote.[62]

As an example, I pointed to the treatment of students attending Prairie View A&M University, a historically Black university in Waller County near Houston. When two students decided to run for county office, the district attorney attempted to prevent Prairie View students registering to vote in fear that the students might support the student candidates. The Supreme Court had ruled years earlier that students had a right to register and vote in Waller County. This attempt to deprive them of their right to vote was blocked. The county had not sought DOJ approval. At the same time, the NAACP and five students brought a lawsuit against the district attorney. He had to back down. The students had the right to vote.

The Voting Rights Act was not and never will be about special rights; it is about equal rights and ensuring the rights of every American voter. It was time to reauthorize this historic cornerstone of civil rights. It was imperative to our values, our rights, our freedom, and our democracy that the act be passed.

The bill did pass the House with a vote of 390–22 and in the Senate 98–0. On July 27, 2006, the approval of the Voting Rights Act not only extended the protections, but it also recognized that racial discrimination was still denying people of color their fundamental right to vote. The fight for equality could not relax; the fight was not over.

For the People Act of 2019 and 2021

The For the People Act was introduced in two successive sessions of Congress, 2019[63] and 2021.[64] It was an integrated approach that addressed voter access, election integrity, election security, political spending, and ethics for the three branches of government. For individual votes it expanded registration and restricted removal of voters from voter lists. For states it provided support for election security, sharing of election-related intelligence information, development of a national strategy, and the creation of a National Commission to Protect United States Democratic Institutions. It addressed campaign financing. It required presidential and vice presidential candidates to produce ten years of tax returns. And it required codes of ethics for all federal judges and justices, legislators, and federal employees.

As I urged my colleagues to vote for this bill, I reminded them that the right to vote free from intimidation or obstacle is the most precious right of any American. It was the pillar of our democratic system. And, as I prophetically told them, if that pillar is threatened for anyone, it is a threat to us all, to our democracy and to our very way of life.[65]

I urged the Senate to pass the For the People Act because this was a fight for the future of the nation. It was received in the Senate less than two weeks after its passage in the House. No action was taken.

John Lewis Voting Rights Enhancement Bill

An effort to amend the Voting Rights Act was presented with the introduction of the Voting Rights Advancement Act of 2019[66] and the John R. Lewis Voting Rights Advancement Act of 2021.[67] These bills, which I proudly cosponsored, were the legislative response to the Supreme Court's ruling in *Shelby County v. Holder*, which had removed the preclearance requirement for enumerated states and jurisdictions. The elimination of the preclearance requirements had enabled the adoption of restrictive voting laws.

Naming this bill after the late congressman John Lewis on its second introduction was deliberate and intentional. He had written the first three hundred pages of the bill. As a young man, Congressman Lewis had been active in the Civil Rights Movement, marching with Dr. Martin Luther King Jr. across the Edmund Pettus Bridge in Selma, Alabama, to fight for the rights of African Americans to vote. He had been severely injured in that march. A Civil Rights icon, he had fought vigorously to protect voting rights through his decades of service in Congress. Attaching his name to the bill symbolized that legacy and devotion to ensuring free, fair, and equitable access to the polls.

As I said in support of the bill, it was time for Congress to meet the moment. The recent efforts in Texas to unfairly and unduly restrict access to the vote that had caused Democratic members of the state house to risk arrest in protest was a vivid reminder of the decades and decades of unfair voting procedures. Passage of this bill would prohibit restrictive voter requirements and restore the original provisions and intent of the Voting Rights Act. More importantly, it was the fundamentally right thing to do for democracy.[68]

The John Lewis Voting Rights Enhancement Act passed the House. Not a single Republican voted for the bill. It was received in the Senate about thirty days later. Nothing happened after that.

The voting rights bills have not been able to advance in the Senate, even with the 2020 Democratic majority. Senate rules require that sixty senators vote to end debate on a bill and move it forward for a vote. There have not been enough Republican senators to join in a vote to move the bills forward. The basis of our democracy, the right to vote and to have your vote counted, has been kidnapped because of Republican fear of losing power.

Pandemic: COVID Changes a World

We will always remember spring 2020, not for its flowers or budding leaves but for the introduction of the COVID-19 virus and the resulting pandemic. We received confirmation of the first United States case of coronavirus in January. We were immediately assured by President Trump that everything was under control, that everything was going to be fine. He praised China, its efforts to contain the virus and its transparency in sharing information.[69] We were repeatedly told that everything would be fine, despite the rapid spread of cases in the United States. Travelers from China were banned. Eventually, a public health emergency was declared.

As we passed into February, we were told that the virus would naturally die during the warmth of spring and summer months. The COVID impact was compared with the flu and we were told that it would disappear one day like a miracle. And, expectedly, Democrats were criticized, charged with politicizing the coronavirus as we tried to focus attention on this rapidly growing crisis. Rather than a call for unity, for the nation to rise together to combat this virus that did not care about party affiliation, gender, race, or other differences, President Trump provided false assurances that everything was under control.

As a health care professional, I knew and respected the work of the Centers for Disease Control (CDC). More than ever our situation was defined by the science. When states closed offices, businesses transitioned to working at home, teaching moved from classrooms to homes, and the CDC recommended wearing masks, there should have been a presidential call for everyone to put on a mask. Dr. Fauci knew as a health professional and scientist that you had to deal in the real world, not the world of false assurances. Everyone had to work together. Wear a mask, avoid crowds, maintain physical distance, wash your hands. These were relatively easy but important steps for all of us to take.

I was very concerned about the COVID-19 virus. The Committee on Science, Space, and Technology held a hearing on March 5, 2020, entitled *Coronaviruses: Understanding the Spread of Infectious Diseases and Mobilizing Innovative Solutions.*[70] With Vice-Chairman Ami Bera presiding, doctors from Boston Children's Hospital, the National School of Tropical Medicine, Baylor College of Medicine, Johns Hopkins School of Public Health, and Smithsonian Global Health Program appeared before the committee.[71] As I recognized in my written submission for the hearing, the COVID-19 outbreak had created a public health crisis with significant international dimensions. I noted that the spread of misinformation during this current outbreak had been accelerated by social media. I urged a holistic research and development response, one that focused on the science for understanding the virus and treatment and on social science to fight disease outbreaks and combat misinformation. I closed by declaring that we must do everything in our power to ensure that science guided our response to this outbreak and prepared us for the future.

At another hearing we took testimony to explore scientific foundations for repurposing existing drugs for treatment of COVID-19. As I said,

"Repurposing existing therapeutics for COVID-19 treatment would be an important tool in the world's pandemic toolkit." While there was urgency in exploring this repurposing, we had to always remember that "paramount importance of upholding scientific integrity at all times."[72] Any federal policies had to be based on the best available science and free from political interference. Referencing the FDA debacle over hydroxychloroquine, I warned against damage that can occur when political considerations inappropriately influence the scientific process. Our decisions needed to be guided by scientific evidence, not political pressure.

There were other hearings involving COVID-19. We explored the impact of COVID-19 on the fire service community and explored the need for additional grants for personal protective equipment. Our concern about extreme heat and COVID-19 on vulnerable, low-income communities and communities of color was addressed in other hearings.[73] A hearing was held to examine the research being conducted at the Department of Energy Office of Science's Biological and Environmental Research and how that research could be leveraged to respond to COVID-19. Another hearing focused on the twin stressors of climate change and COVID-19. The extent of the impact of COVID-19 on university research and pipeline for STEM was the focus of another hearing. One subcommittee hearing that was especially important explored data management at the local, state, and federal level.[74] We wanted to determine how hospitals and researchers could best be served by the federal government and what investment was needed in data infrastructure.

As I said in my prepared statement, our ability to fight the pandemic depended greatly on accurate, objective, and accessible data. But career scientists were being attacked. Political officials at Health and Human Services challenged the science behind the CDC's Morbidity and Mortality Weekly Reports. There were attempts to silence agency officials to paint the administration's response in a better light. It was important to state our position that the members of the committee did not stand for such blatant disregard of scientific integrity in the federal government.

Navigating through a pandemic would be challenging under the best of circumstances. But the Trump administration was not the best of circumstances. The denials and misinformation that came from the

White House added confusion and turmoil. Dr. Fauci, well recognized and respected, tried to provide the nation with well-reasoned information and guidance. Our scientists worked diligently and professionally. It was disheartening to watch the unfounded attacks. But it was rewarding to see their dedication and determination, knowing that ultimately following the science would give us the pathway through the pandemic.

Serving as the chair of the House Science Committee was a great honor. I did not set out to make history. But I was the first African American and female to serve as chair of the Committee on Science, Space, and Technology. As a consequence, when my portrait is hung in the committee room, it will be the only portrait of a woman and African American on those walls. My hope is that it will serve as an inspiration to young girls and people of color throughout this country. But my greater hope is that America will keep a commitment to scientific advancement and exploration. Our nation's status and strength are dependent upon that.

Fighting for Women's Issues

When I won my 1972 primary, news accounts invariably noted that I was the first African American woman to represent North Texas. Many articles pointed out that I had defeated three male opponents. While I knew that my election was historic because of my gender and race, I believed that it was my competency and ability to represent the people in my district that led to my election. But throughout my career, I was always keenly aware that I was a Black woman. That identification has motivated me to always fight for the political, social, and personal equality of women.

Throughout my life I have belonged to organizations that actively embraced and focused on issues that impact women, especially African American women. I proudly joined Alpha Kappa Alpha Sorority, the oldest Greek letter organization for African American women, while I was campaigning for the Texas House. The sorority has grown since I joined, with chapters now throughout the United States, Virgin Islands, Liberia, South Africa, Germany, Canada, and Japan. But it is still known for its focus on women's issues and service. Having a network of college-educated African

American women to turn to for support and encouragement has been critical to my career.

On January 15, 2008, on the one hundredth anniversary of the founding of AKA, I proudly rose on the floor of the House to speak. As I proudly shared, AKA had grown into a worldwide organization with 200,000 members in 975 chapters across the globe and on every continent.[75] Eight years earlier I had paid special tribute to the sorority, so it was only fitting that I recognize the centennial anniversary.[76] I gave tribute to the spirit of the women who, living in a society that imposed inferiority and second-class citizenship, banded together to create this sorority. The founders were determined to provide support for each other and to work together to promote solutions for African Americans. I named recognizable members of the sorority, such as Coretta Scott King, Rosa Parks, Maya Angelou, Toni Morrison, Ella Fitzgerald, and Dr. Mae Jemison, to exemplify the leadership that the sorority had nurtured. The impact of the AKA sorority was truly immeasurable and had helped America to become what it was.

In June of that year, I was pleased to join in a House Concurrent Resolution that allowed Alpha Kappa Alpha Sorority to celebrate its centennial anniversary on the Capitol grounds.[77] Speaking in support of that resolution, I was proud to give the names of the founders, one generation removed from slavery, who helped to jump-start a movement of education African American women. It was expected that more than twenty thousand members would travel to Washington to celebrate the one hundredth anniversary. It was fitting that they be allowed to host an event at the Capitol.

Women's History Month in 2013 gave me another opportunity to honor the women of the Alpha Kappa Alpha Sorority from the floor of the House.[78] As a proud member, I wanted to highlight the many accomplishments of the organization, reflecting our mission of Service to All Mankind. Our human rights outreach raises awareness of human trafficking and domestic violence. We promote social justice through voter empowerment, civic engagement, and expanding access to education in minority communities. Global poverty initiatives allow us to focus efforts to end hunger throughout the world and to promote sustainability and independence through women-owned businesses and sustainable agricultural practices. AKA's outreach expands as it promotes high academic standards, mentorship, global health services, and the advancement of human and civil rights.

But it was truly personal when in 2014 I paid tribute to my chapter, Alpha Xi Omega, in Dallas.[79] Having been founded on June 6, 1929, its members had provided outstanding community service to Dallas, from tutoring children, raising money to fight cancer, and increasing awareness to combat AIDS, to supporting research for sickle cell anemia and feeding the hungry. Our sorority understands that the price of liberty is the duty of each of us to freely give back. I was proud when I said that the city of Dallas was a better place because of the eighty-five years of dedicated and selfless service by the distinguished women of the Alpha Zi Omega Chapter.

I have long believed that it was important, especially for African American women, to join organizations that would be not only supportive but also reflective of our values. Early in my tenure in Congress, I spoke in recognition of Cardiss Collins's retirement, then the longest-serving African American woman in Congress. It had been my privilege to have been one of her sponsors for membership in both Alpha Kappa Alpha Sorority and The Links, Inc. These two organizations have been, and are, near and dear to my heart.

The Links, Inc., established in 1946, is an international organization bringing together more than seventeen thousand professional women of African descent. Sharing core values of friendship, integrity, honesty, service, commitment, courage and respect for self and others, The Links are heavily involved in community service. I had been invited to join Dolly Adams, the First Lady of Paul Quinn College, in the early 1970s to establish a chapter of The Links in Waco. I had just won the Democratic primary, which brought a certain degree of notoriety. We hoped that my participation would help to give the chapter exposure and publicity to strengthen its launch. Unexpectedly, Fannie Smith, A. Maceo's wife, approached me asking why I had not joined the Dallas chapter. For me the answer was straightforward: I had not been invited to join. However, several years later, I did join the Dallas chapter and have maintained my membership since then.

The Links, Inc., was extremely involved in promoting interest in STEM careers for young African American girls. At my suggestion the national organization adopted a STEM program, encouraging its chapters to develop activities and programming that would introduce girls to careers in these fields. Chapters of The Links have developed yearlong activities, taking girls to manufacturing plants, hospitals, and even NASA. I cannot think of a better organization with which I could have partnered to spread the importance of teaching young Black girls about STEM and involving them in programming to give them the confidence to pursue such careers. I applaud The Links, Inc., for its vision and willingness to be in the forefront of this initiative. I am forever grateful for their partnership in promoting STEM to our young women.

For these and many other reasons, I introduced a resolution to recognize the seventy-fifth anniversary of The Links, Inc. As I said in that resolution, between 2018 and 2020, more than 2,600 scholarships had been awarded to Black youth to support their pursuit of academic interests. Its programming targeted closing the achievement gap from pre-K through college. It provided support for mentoring programs, STEM activities, and HBCUs. My membership in such organizations complements my natural activism with respect to women's issues. Even before I became a candidate, I had been active in issues that supported the participation of women in political activities.

In August 1970 I joined over 1,400 other women to attend the first Texas Governor's Conference on the Status of Women.[80] With United States District Court Judge Sarah T. Hughes and Barbara Jordan as key organizers, developing strategies to increase the number of women appointed to state boards and commissions and elected to the legislature was a primary objective. At that time Barbara Jordan and Frances "Sissy" Farenthold were the only women in the legislature.

Joining other women, I was a part of the effort to create a permanent commission on the status of Texas women. We believed that such an entity, funded by the state with an office, staff, and resources, could target research on women's issues and spur action by legislators and state government officials. Predictably, there was opposition. Opponents argued that a women's commission would cause women to neglect their roles as homemakers and threaten traditional family values. Because of those senseless fears, the women's commission was rejected by state officials.

The 1972 election saw the candidacy of several women for legislative positions, including myself. Sissy Farenthold was the Democratic gubernatorial candidate. Additionally, with the support of Farenthold and Barbara Jordan, the Texas Equal Rights Amendment was put before the electorate. I actively supported the amendment, encouraging voter turnout and support. With a rallying call of "Oh thank heaven for Amendment Seven," the amendment was approved.

The adoption of the Equal Rights Amendment put a focus on Texas's family and penal codes. The Women's Caucus took the lead in identifying which statutory provisions would need to be addressed. Within weeks of being sworn into office, I hosted a meeting in my office attended by Representatives Sarah Weddington and Chris Miller and Senator Betty Andujar. While some wording edits were straightforward, such as changing "husband" to "spouse," there were others that were more substantive, such as deleting a provision that allowed a husband to plead justifiable homicide for killing his wife's lover.

There were other legislative issues that we tackled as women. Working with Representatives Kay Bailey and Weddington, I supported the introduction of legislation to encourage the reporting and prosecution of sexual assaults. We took on child abuse and childcare center licensing by introducing legislative amendments to the Family Code and Penal Code to better define child abuse to include psychological and emotional damage and failure to thrive.

In 1973 the Institute on Women's Wrongs was founded by Eleanor McGovern and Dr. Judianne Densen-Gerber to sponsor research into the lives of women who did not have a voice. Again, Sarah Weddington, Chris Miller, and I became very involved, establishing a Texas chapter. To underscore the first project, Women in Prison and Their Minor Children, we held the first meeting at the FCI Fort Worth, a federal prison that housed both men and women. The subject was particularly poignant because Texas also had the largest women's state prison. Until this research Texas female offenders had not been asked any questions about whether they had children, what arrangements had been made for the children, or the impact of their incarceration on the children. It was an effort to put a spotlight on the cycle of crime and poverty through generations.

Despite progress on women's issues, I found the environment in state
government laden with bigotry and sexism. Grown men, responsible for
governing, perceived women as lesser beings. The term *girlie* was in frequent
use. Whenever I reflected on the daily slights and tensions, it reaffirmed that
I carried two major burdens that were also responsibilities: I would always be
identified as an African American and as a woman. And I would always be
fighting for equal rights for African Americans and women.

I frequently participated in conferences and speeches focusing on the
role of women, especially in politics and government. Texas Woman's
University invited Sarah Weddington and me to participate in a program
titled Setting Legislative Priorities: A Woman's Point of View.[81] East Texas
State University, now Texas A&M–Commerce, invited me to participate
in the Contemporary Woman and American Justice conference.[82] Whether
speaking to college students or women's missionary societies, my message
was always the same: our country will benefit when women are recognized
and afforded opportunity and equality.

The November 1975 three-day Conference on Women in Public Life,
sponsored by the Lyndon B. Johnson Library in Austin, brought over one
thousand women to Austin to discuss women in local politics as leaders. Joining
speakers such as Judge Sarah T. Hughes, Frances Farenthold, Representative
Barbara Jordan, Liz Carpenter, and Ann Richards, I shared my story with the
group. I told them of my personal hesitation about managing the demands of
the legislature and my responsibilities as a mother. It was a grave decision,
one that I had made only thirty seconds before the filing deadline. "I was
Black, divorced, and the mother of a 14-year-old son. The only thing that
I had going for me in Dallas County was that I was Baptist." But I added that
the "policy at my house was not to allow anyone to cripple me." My message
was simple: women needed to have the courage and confidence to be leaders
in their communities.[83]

I had to always be mindful of stereotyping and how situations would
appear. When the other representatives from Dallas asked me to serve as the
delegation's secretary, I refused. Accepting that position would have been
a perpetuation of gender roles, something my male colleagues did not, and
could not, understand.

During my first term it was common for people to come into my office, ask for coffee, and ask when the representative was coming in. I quickly learned that as a woman I could fight to be respected, but I would never be one of the in-crowd. Traditional lobbying revolved around "booze, beefsteak, and broads" and had grown to lavish hunting and golfing trips, with women remaining on the outside looking in. Oftentimes, I'd only hear about such trips through stories in the newspapers. The troubling thing wasn't that I wanted to attend or participate in these activities, it was the reality that this doorway to influence and power would never be open to me.

I was fortunate that I had my prior professional experiences to rely upon, because during my first years as an elected official, I didn't have many mentors in the political arena. The female public figures who were already established, Judge Sarah T. Hughes, Barbara Jordan, and Sissy Farenthold, were remarkable role models. They were respected leaders, eloquent speakers, and dedicated public servants who taught by example. They were strong advocates for affordable childcare, parental leave, programs for children, mental and physical health, and focusing on issues that impacted women. And they willingly embraced, encouraged, and counseled the first African American woman elected to the Texas House from Dallas.

As I moved into other positions, especially with the Department of Health and Human Services, I continued to advance issues impacting women and children. Teen pregnancy was a central focus of mine.

When I returned to the Texas legislature, I chaired a Special Senate Advisory Committee on the Creation and Expansion of Minority and Women Owned Business Ownership Opportunities. The Supreme Court had ruled that there needed to be evidence of discriminatory practices, systemic barriers, or customs to justify governmental action to remedy discrimination. The committee was charged to obtain that evidence, to examine the barriers, practices, and policies that had deterred and/or denied opportunities for small socially and economically disadvantaged businesses. We held public hearings that confirmed what we knew: a good-old-boys system limited business opportunities for women and minorities.

We made recommendations. Procurement goals for women- and minority-owned businesses, an end to redlining in accessing capital, and resources for technical and procurement assistance were needed. Recognizing the importance of certification of disadvantaged businesses for access to state contracts, we urged the official adoption of the term *historically underutilized business*.[84] This work was especially important because entrepreneurship is a valuable tool in the creation of wealth.

With my election to Congress, I had an even broader platform to address issues particularly relevant to women. Even though bills may not be passed into law, their introduction spotlights concerns and problems, generating discussion and attention. Finances and economic security were addressed with the introduction of the Comprehensive Women's Pension Protection Act of 1996[85] and the Economic Equity Act of 1996.[86] Working with Representative Constance Morella, our bill for a Commission on the Advancement of Women in the Science and Engineering Work Forces advanced a focus on the recruitment, retention, and advancement of women in science and engineering.[87] With the Sexual Harassment Prevention Act of 1996, we sought to allow civil litigation in claims of sexual harassment against anyone working in interstate or foreign commerce. The Breast and Cervical Cancer Information Act of 1993,[88] Women and HIV Outreach and Prevention Act,[89] and Women's Health Equity Act[90] focused on woman's medical needs. The Gender Equity in Education Act[91] sought the creation of an Office of Women's Equity within the Department of Education. Protecting children by preventing the construction of public schools and childcare centers on property with unhealthy electromagnetic fields was the objective of the Children's Electromagnetic Field Risk Reduction Act.[92] My legislative proposals spanned quality childcare, women's participation in sports and exercise activities, medical needs and services, and economic and educational equality. I would remain focused on these issues throughout my time in Congress.

I also understood the importance of honoring and recognizing women's achievements. Sacrifice and contribution were acknowledged by Congressional Gold Medals for Addie Mae Collins, Denise McNair, Carole Robertson, and Cynthia Wesley, the four young girls killed in the

1963 Birmingham church bombing;[93] Congressional Gold Medals for the Hidden Figures, Katherine Johnson, Dr. Christine Darden, Dorothy Vaughan, Mary Jackson, and all women who served as "computers, mathematicians and engineers in the space program";[94] a joint congressional resolution that women suffragists should be revered and celebrated[95] and a proposal that March 1993 and 1994 be designated as Women's History Month.[96]

Over the years I sponsored or cosponsored a number of bills seeking Congressional Gold Medal recognition for other noteworthy women: Sally Ride, the first woman in space;[97] Judge Constance Baker Motley, the first African American federal judge and civil rights lawyer;[98] Honorable Shirley Chisholm, first African American woman elected to Congress and to run for the presidency;[99] and Aretha Franklin, first woman inducted into the Rock and Roll Hall of Fame, recipient of Presidential Medal of Freedom.[100]

Another vehicle for congressional acknowledgment of individual contributions and milestones is through a formal resolution. I sponsored or cosponsored resolutions recognizing Zora Neale Hurston,[101] Betty Shabazz,[102] Rosa Parks,[103] Coretta Scott King,[104] and others. I joined a 2005 resolution adopted by the House commending Kuwait for extending the vote and eligibility for public office to women.[105] Another House resolution adopted in 2006 recognized the Iraqi women's radio station for providing women an opportunity for free speech and inclusion in the country's reconstruction.[106]

I also entered statements in the *Congressional Record* acknowledging women who had made an impact. I spoke about Louise Raggio, known as the Lone Star State's First Lady of women's legal rights;[107] DeMetris Sampson, the Thirtieth Congressional District Woman of the Year for 1996;[108] Juanita Craft, a Dallas civil rights leader who successfully fought segregation at North Texas State University, now University of North Texas, and the State Fair of Texas;[109] Dolores Huerta for her commitment to the improvement of working conditions for children, women, and farm workers;[110] Malala Yousafzai, Pakistani victim of a Taliban assassination attempt for supporting the right of girls to attend school;[111] Ambassador Lindy Boggs, who had worked on the Head Start Program and an amendment to the Equal Credit Opportunity Act to protect women from lending discrimination;[112] the Honorable Ellen Johnson

Sirleaf, the first female president of Liberia;[113] the Honorable Carolyn Wright, the first African American to serve as chief justice of a Texas appellate court;[114] and many others. It was important to me that women of achievement be publicly acknowledged.

In 2005 I rose in honor of the Women's International League for Peace and Freedom in the celebration of their ninetieth anniversary. Located in thirty-six nations, it was formed during World War I. Born out of a meeting that was scheduled to focus on suffrage for women but turned to activism to promote the ending of the war, it had worked to promote peaceful and nonviolent solutions to conflicts around the world.[115]

In addition to these activities, I knew that my position allowed me to bring attention to the role that women across the globe could bring to peacekeeping. As a member of Congress, I traveled the world. I worked with women from Bosnia, Bahrain, Afghanistan, the Sudan, South Africa, Israel, Palestine, Singapore, Iraq, Germany, and many other parts of the world. Having been disappointed by the failure of the Equal Rights Amendment to be ratified, when I assisted in drafting constitutions for Iraq, Bahrain, and Afghanistan, I made certain that the recognition of women's rights was included in the constitution from its beginnings.

Much of my travel has been to countries impacted by war. I have seen the suffering of women and children, the physical scars from shrapnel and bullets and the emotional effects reflected in the listless eyes. Over and over again I met women and children displaced by war, robbed of family, deprived of civil and human rights. They shared their experiences, the terror of bombings and shooting, the fear of starvation and homelessness, the physical and emotional pain of sexual assault. The pain and anguish was the same. It didn't matter what country or what language was spoken. War was destructive. I have learned that war cannot be an acceptable or logical alternative if we are serious about the survival of the human race.

I have always believed that women, if provided a platform, could be instrumental in addressing differences and conflict. Conflict resolution will never be achieved without the meaningful participation of women. On December 18, 2001, still reeling from the September 11 terrorist attacks, I introduced a concurrent resolution encouraging worldwide efforts to involve more women in peace building and peacekeeping efforts. That resolution recognized that women had been involved at grassroots level to create stability and build nations. It sought to bring women together for workshops and forums, assuring that women were positioned to influence global political conflict resolution. Even though the United Nations had already issued a resolution touching upon these issues, the House did not adopt my resolution.[116]

That resolution also reflected my sharpened interest in building a women's movement for world peace. In October 2001 I had read a magazine article about civil war in Liberia. On the cover was a picture of two teenage boys holding automatic weapons. The picture saddened me tremendously. That night I could not sleep, thinking of Kirk and my grandsons, Kirk Jr., David, and James. I couldn't imagine them being confronted with the horrors those young men faced. I did not want any children to grow up in a world where conflict was only resolved by weapons rather than diplomacy and peaceful measures.

I decided to do something that would focus on a culture of world peace. The words "A World of Women for World Peace" became embedded in my mind. I didn't know how to start. I just knew that I had to do something. I called Vivian Castleberry, a journalist for the former *Dallas Times Herald* newspaper in Dallas who I trusted and respected. She was a cofounder of the Dallas Peace Center and would understand what I was trying to accomplish. She offered her support.

Another woman I phoned was Jan Sanders, the wife of Judge Barefoot Sanders Jr. She suggested that I phone Swanee Hunt, the youngest daughter of a Texas oil magnate, H. L. Hunt. A former ambassador to Australia under President Clinton, she was the director of Women in Public Policy Program at Harvard's Kennedy School. I called Swanee and told her of my idea. She listened encouragingly and said that I should come to Harvard that Friday because she was having an international women's conference, including a reception for Leymah Gbowee of Liberia, who would ultimately be awarded the Nobel Peace Prize in 2011. It was an exciting suggestion. I dropped everything and traveled to Cambridge.

Out of that visit grew annual conferences designed to bring greater visibility to women who are victims of war and who promote peace-making, peacekeeping, and peace-building activities in their communities. These conferences include panel discussions and keynote speakers, bringing women from across the world to Washington, DC, or Dallas. Guests have come from Bosnia, Afghanistan, Pakistan, Uganda, Kenya, England, and other countries. Panelists and guest speakers have included Bisera Turković, the former Bosnian ambassador to the United States; Mary Njoroge, the former director of basic education in Kenya; Dr. Qudsia Mirza, a law professor and Islamic scholar; Gillian Combs, chair of the Women's Foundation; Munira Beba Hadzic, executive director of BosFam; Sister Rosemary Nyirumbe, founder of the Ugandan Sewing Hope Foundation and supervisor of St. Monica's Girls Tailoring Center; Gulalai Ismail, founder of the Pakistan organization AWARE Girls; Dr. Otunba Basirat Nahib, founder of Women Advancement for Economics and Leadership Empowerment in Africa; and many others.

As a legislator I have been able to take tangible steps to affect the status of women. I have sponsored house resolutions calling for ending all forms of discrimination against women, recognizing the historic election of women to the parliament of Kuwait, designating May as the month during which the global peace-building activities of women are recognized, and supporting the goals of International Women's Day. I introduced a bill to provide assistance to women and children in Iraq to enhance their political participation and personal safety. Keeping a focus on the impact of global conflict on women and the need for women participation in peace strategies lobal conflict has been a priority for me.

I have traveled to war-torn countries. In 2003 I met with Iraqi women leaders in Washington, DC, including the female minister of reconstruction and development of northern Iraq and president of the Assyrian Women's Union in Iraq. Shortly after that meeting, I went on the first congressional delegation to Iraq. That trip compelled me to introduce a concurrent resolution for US agencies to assist women and women's organizations' participation in the work to strengthen and stabilize Iraqi democracy.

My 2008 trip to Bosnia inspired me to start a Women's Peace Initiative to spotlight both the horrific impact of war on women and the efforts of women working to achieve peace in their countries. I had a similar focus in 2009 in relation to Afghani women when the House considered the Foreign Relations Authorization Act, Fiscal Years 2010 and 2011; I successfully offered two amendments important to women. The first amendment provided financial assistance for the creation of a State Department program to support mentorship and leadership exchange opportunities for Afghan women. This program encouraged more women to actively participate in politics and support democratic values. The other amendment called for Congress to express its condemnation of child soldiers. There were international estimates that over 250,000 children had been forced to fight in conflicts, suffering cruel conditions and physical assault. Forcing children to become soldiers was unacceptable and a violation of human rights.

For more than fifteen years, this message that women needed to be a part of any peace process would be a central tenet of several legislative proposals. In 2013 I joined with Representatives Janice Schakowsky, Mike Honda, and Niki Tsongas to introduce the Women, Peace, and Security Act. This bill built upon President Obama's executive order establishing a National Action Plan on Women, Peace, and Security.[117] We reintroduced this bill each session until it was finally enacted in 2017. This act, the Women, Peace, and Security Act of 2017, required US agencies to provide training that ensured women's meaningful inclusion and participation in peace processes.[118]

Over the years I have hosted many conferences and roundtables in addition to my annual World of Women for World Peace events. Such events allow for productive and creative exchange of ideas, reinforced commitment to inclusion of women in global peace efforts, and increased public awareness. The importance of women's leadership to ending conflicts through peaceful negotiations and creating access to humanitarian assistance during disasters and wars cannot be overstated. Women can make the difference in our nation and world.

Chapter 17

Looking Back

Candidly, working on this book has been difficult for me. Through my years as an elected official, I did not seek attention. I was not motivated by self-aggrandizement, I didn't need to have my name on the bill, and it wasn't necessary that I conduct the press conferences. What was important to me was to help people. I wanted to solve problems that were making people's lives hard. I wanted to make a difference in people's lives. I simply wanted to serve my constituents, my state, my country, and my world. I believe that I have done that.

My Waco connections and roots are strong. The foundation that my parents, Edward and Lillie, gave my siblings and me has been with me always. My father passed in 1981, my mother in 2007. But even with the passage of years, the love that they gave and the teachings that they taught are with me always. The three pillars on which my life has rested were learned from them: faith, family, and purpose.

Throughout my life faith and church have sustained me. The religious faith taught to me by my parents only grew and became stronger as I entered adulthood. Being a member of different denominations, each with unique worship experiences, I have never wavered in my beliefs. Prayer remained a foundation of my life as I moved to South Bend, into nursing, through the Texas Legislature, through governmental appointments, and to Congress. Beginning in 1993 I hosted annual prayer breakfasts that featured guest speakers who were open about the role of faith in their accomplishments. There have been times of trials and challenges and there have been trying times in Washington, but those times have only reinforced my faith. Prayer has sustained me.

Family has always surrounded me. My sister Sallye has to this day been a source of encouragement, advice, and counsel. My sister Helen and my brother, Carl, have passed. But despite the significant age differences, we were close. Our lives have reflected the values and principles taught to us by our parents. Sallye and Carl were educators while Helen followed me into nursing. We embraced the importance of making a difference and a contribution.

My grandparents, uncles, aunts, cousins, and extended relatives were active parts of my childhood. The close-knit Waco community, neighbors, and friends were like family in their encouragement and support. The importance of family was such that Kirk, when asked what he would want people to know about me that they may not know, answered, without pause or hesitation, "She never stopped being a mother." Whether serving in Austin or Washington, I made it home to Dallas almost every weekend. When Kirk was young, I was determined to provide him with activities with other young Black children, especially through the Jack and Jill organization. As my family grew with grandchildren, my trips home included attending their events and activities, even if it meant just flying in for the day. It was important that we have family gatherings and make life as normal as it could be.

I am so very grateful for the friends and relationships that have blessed my life and become family. It is the emotional investment, the closeness and tightness of sharing common beliefs and goals, that drew us together. Kirk calls it the "enterprise"—those people who surround you, becoming your circle of support, who allow you to be the outward face of all the work that is done. They make sacrifices, bear burdens, and accept the responsibility to play their parts so that the work might succeed. They became my and Kirk's world, folks from my life experiences, South Bend, Austin, Dallas, Washington, the world, friends, supporters, staff. With all of the

organizations—Jack and Jill, Inc., The Links, Inc., Alpha Kappa Alpha Sorority, the Girl Friends, Inc., Circle-Lets, CBC, the myriad other House caucuses,
and my church homes—I have always tried to show my gratitude, to let them
know that I appreciated their contributions and that I know that I could not
have lived the life that I have, done the work that I've done, without them.

But my life has been built on what I believed to be my purpose: to serve.
Service across the spectrum of needs, families struggling with economic
hardship, a country facing division and factionalism, nations ravaged by war,
and a planet challenged by pandemics and climate change. From caring for
individual patients to urging policies to help preserve our world, I have tried
to lift my voice to make an impact.

This purpose of service was a foundational message to my staff.
We were there to serve our constituents, the people of our district, state, and
nation. I was moved when Damarcus Offord, one of my Dallas staffers, in
accepting a community service award, credited that teaching for his personal
understanding of the importance of service. No matter how much I do,
how much service I can personally give, I know that I am only one person.
My impact is multiplied when I can inspire others to accept service as their
purpose. That is one of the reasons that mentorship is so important to me.
Just like A. Maceo Smith, Reverend S. M. Wright, Reverend H. Rhett James,
Reverend Caesar Clark, and Reverend Zan Wesley Holmes guided me, I have
strived to reach back and do those things for those coming behind me.

A large area of my work has revolved around science and STEM
initiatives. Perhaps that came to me naturally because nursing is a
science-based profession. But my understanding of the importance of science
was also fueled by seeing the identifiable impact of Dallas-based Texas
Instruments and its founders, Cecil Green, Patrick Haggerty, Erik Jonsson,
and Eugene McDermott.

But I have never forgotten my early career as a psychiatric nurse.
From that experience I understood the importance of easily accessible
outreach, the proverbial lifeline for someone contemplating suicide. The 988
hotline seemed to be a simple solution, but it took several years to establish.
The same awareness of mental health issues spurred me to work with the
Substance Abuse and Mental Health Services Administration to have a

national center created to focus on African American behavioral health and health equity. Housed at the National Center for Primary Care at Morehouse School of Medicine, the center has established a strategic network of partners to expand research and service across the nation.

Collegiality, working across the aisle, has always been important to me. I knew that to accomplish anything, I had to be able to talk with everyone. I firmly believe that this approach, valuing bipartisanship, is important to the success that I had as a legislator. Congressman Ralph Hall in remarks on the 2002 NSF funding complimented me on my bipartisan approach. Similar acknowledgments were made during the debate on the Water Resources Development Act of 2007 and other legislation that I introduced. On the announcement of my retirement, my long-time colleague Frank Lucas wrote that I was an "old-school legislator who cares more about results than headlines."[1] Those words mean a lot to me.

I have flown on Air Force One, visited Camp David, attended many state dinners, witnessed history with the inauguration of Nelson Mandela, assisted with the drafting of constitutions for nations that had fought through internal wars, and seen the impact of poverty and armed conflict. I have had the benefit of travel across the globe, visiting many nations, both developed and developing. With those experiences I sincerely believe that the United States is the best place to live. But knowing and believing that does not absolve us of our responsibility to push forward.

We are not perfect. We are still burdened with racism and discrimination. We have never come to terms with our history, the horrific institution of slavery and the wicked system of Jim Crow. For every forward step achieved by African Americans in this nation, there is a concerted effort to not only halt that progress but to reverse it.

Simply look at the outrage directed to the 1619 Project and Critical Race Theory, the movement to end diversity, equity, and inclusion initiatives. We're told that the harm of centuries of discrimination is to be ignored because such material might cause young white children discomfort, guilt, or anguish. Where was the concern for enslaved Black children torn away from their families? Or Black families robbed of a father because of lynching? Or the schoolchildren forced to walk miles to go to a dilapidated school building to use worn out textbooks? The African Americans told to sit in the back of the bus or being daily confronted with "whites only" signs? Where is the concern for Black youth forced into underresourced schools, living in substandard housing, or targeted by police? Where is the concern about the decades of oppression, discrimination, and inequity for my ancestors and my descendants? What is the fear in facing the truth?

Much of my work has been focused on expanding opportunities for underrepresented communities. Why does the attitude persist that opening doors for some inevitably means that doors are being closed for others? Why is there such refusal to appreciate that when the best and brightest minds are cultivated, encouraged, and supported, that we all win? That when we bring together people with different perspectives, skills, life experiences, backgrounds, and ideas, we create centers for achievement and growth?

We are also still fighting the vestiges of gender bias, denying women the full opportunities accorded men. There have been advances, but there is still a long way to go.

I have been blessed to have my work recognized in so many ways. The Amtrak station in Dallas is the Eddie Bernice Johnson Union Station. The Dallas Independent School District has named a pre-K through fifth grade STEM academy the Eddie Bernice Johnson STEM Academy. A garden at Parkland Hospital surrounding the Women and Infants Specialty Health Center bears my name. My portrait reflecting my service as chair of the House Science Committee hangs in the Science Hearing room, the only woman, the only African American. I hope that portrait, as described by Senator Maria Cantwell, reflects the heart and spirit of a champion, providing inspiration and encouragement, a reminder that we can have an impact through our service.

Ironically, one of my earliest recorded comments in the *Congressional Record* consisted of tributes to women who were retiring from Congress. I remarked then, "I hear that there is life after office."[2] I am on my search to find that life.

Epilogue

On December 31, 2023, while this manuscript was being peer reviewed, Congresswoman Johnson passed without ever settling into the life of retirement she had hoped to explore. She had developed an infection while recuperating from spinal surgery in a rehabilitation facility. Medical negligence, according to her family, had led to a painful, untimely, and unnecessary death.

News of her transition drew accolades and tributes from across the country. The *New York Times*,[1] *Washington Post*,[2] and CNN[3] recognized her as a trailblazer. ABC News[4] and *US News and World Report*[5] called her an "influential former Texas US Representative." From Maryland to Honolulu, Hawaii, media across the nation reported the news of her passing, recounting her firsts—first African American to represent North Texas in Congress, first nurse elected to Congress, first African American and woman to chair a congressional committee, and so many more.

President Joe Biden issued a statement recognizing her "immense courage and commitment to the promise of America," calling her "an icon and mentor to generations of public servants through whom her legacy of resilience and purpose will endure."[6] Vice President Kamala Harris called her a "visionary, pioneer, and a fighter."[7] The Texas Democratic Party released a statement acknowledging that while they mourned "the loss of a trailblazer, they celebrate the life of a remarkable woman who shattered glass ceilings and paved the way for future generations."[8] The *Dallas Morning News*, as part of its extensive coverage, wrote in an opinion piece: "Eddie Bernice Johnson's wisdom, optimism for America will be missed: Her steely will and gentle grace defined her rise in Texas politics."[9]

Her homegoing was celebrated in Dallas over two days, with discrete activities, each with their own tone, each with their own significance. From the quiet reflective lying in state through testimonials at services, the riveting performance of "We Shall Behold Him" by her daughter-in-law, Sondra Johnson, at the funeral, the moment of silence at the Dallas Mavericks game, the decorated store window at the original downtown Neiman Marcus store, the hanging of banners bearing her picture at the Eddie Bernice Johnson Union Station, the outlining of the Dallas skyline with yellow lights, the shining of her initials, EBJ, on the front of the Omni hotel, the yellow and gold lights shining from the iconic ball of the Hyatt Regency hotel, Eddie Bernice Johnson's life was celebrated. Each event fed into the next, reaching a crescendo of praise and gratitude worthy of her fifty years of service.

Around 8:00 a.m., on Monday, January 8, 2024, a procession with a glass-enclosed hearse bearing her casket drove up to the Texas Hall of State. Before the doors opened to the public, the casket was placed in the Great Hall, its position on the carpet, arrangement of flowers, all details meticulously managed with great affection and purpose. She was lovingly attended by her personal stylist, checking the congresswoman's signature St. John's suit, the strands of her hair, the placement of her classic pearl ring on her left hand, the red, white, and blue scarf draped around her neck and the congressional pin adorning her right lapel. All of us—funeral home employees, former staffers, friends, and family—were determined that Congresswoman Johnson's body would be displayed with the same style, sophistication, and elegance with which she had carried herself.

Over a six-hour period, despite the driving rain and extreme weather advisory for hail, thunder, and lightning, almost a thousand people viewed her body. Family, longtime friends, staffers, grateful constituents, elected officials, neighbors, classmates, and Dallas businesspeople and leaders all walked the long, red-carpeted aisle to her white casket flanked by large bouquets of yellow roses. Viewers intuitively waited quietly for others to walk from the casket before they approached. Once they were in front of her casket, hats were removed, heads were bowed, tears flowed, and prayers of respect and appreciation were quietly spoken.

The darkness and somberness of the day was broken by the significance of her lying in state at the Texas Hall of State. As a child growing up in segregated Texas, Eddie Bernice could only attend the state fair on "colored" day, the only time she could walk into the Hall of State. As Congresswoman Johnson, her body was down the hall from a statue of former president of the Republic of Texas, Mirabeau Lamar, with whom Senator Yarborough had decades earlier compared her quick ascendancy in the Democratic party.

And, as an honored stateswoman, lying underneath the words "all free-man and lovers of freedom must reverence and adore the American union," a spotlight shone on her love for this nation and its freedoms.

Later that afternoon Congresswoman Johnson's body was taken to Concord Baptist Church, the procession live streamed on local news. Waiting at the church, symbolically dressed in white, were members of The Links, Inc., Alpha Kappa Alpha Sorority Inc., Jack and Jill, Inc., the Girl Friends, Inc., and Circle-Lets. To them she was EBJ, someone who had been by their side working on community projects, promoting STEM activities and youth outreach, encouraging educational and economic achievement, fighting for voting rights and equality, supporting one another, and so much more. The longevity of her membership, sometimes more than fifty years, made her a senior member. But it was her mighty strength, determination, dedi-cation, and devotion reflecting her understanding that leadership is about making everyone else better, that drew these women in tribute.[10] Her grace and bearing, which allowed her to "walk with kings and queens but never los[e] the common touch," which made her "comfortable in any room,"[11] nurtured the sisterhood they shared. A representative from each organization went to the lectern to share remembrances, their members standing in united tribute to their sister.

The transition into the formal wake service continued with memories of personal connections and shared moments. Speaker after speaker rose, often using the affectionate reference "EBJ," talking of the lessons she had taught them, the mentorship that she had provided. "Don't focus on the title, focus on the truth."[12] "Never give up, never give out, and never give in."[13] She was a "mentor to the women in the [Congressional Black] caucus, a mentor's mentor, she was a woman who said what she meant and meant what she said."[14] She showed "that she did not raise her voice, but her voice is loud."[15]

And then there was the striking story that Congresswoman Johnson didn't speak of in this autobiography. While she wrote of the work that she did in assisting the writing of the Iraqi constitution and her visit to the desert, she made no mention of the bravery required for that trip. That message was given by Sanford Bishop, a former congressman who told of her immediate agreement to travel with him to Baghdad on a fact-finding delegation. He smilingly remembered her steady coolness on their way to visit wounded soldiers. Wearing a St. John's knit suit in 120-degree heat, steel protecting head gear, full body armor, and strapped in the back of a C5 cargo plane that was flying aerial evasive maneuvers because they were under artillery fire, the congresswoman showed no signs of concern or apprehension. She was focused on their mission, the work to be done, not their personal safety.

As the tributes drew to a close, the sanctuary became quiet except for the soft organ refrains of "Great Is Thy Faithfulness." A ripple of applause slowly spread as President Joe Biden came into view, entering through a side door. He walked to the family, Kirk and Sondra, grandsons, embracing them, offering words of comfort. He greeted Eddie Bernice's sister, Sallye, who had been seated in her wheelchair but who had stood up for his entrance. They hugged, his words bringing a gentle smile to her face.

As he walked to the casket, there was once again applause. Reaching the casket, he made the sign of the cross and folded his hands in prayer with a bowed head. He gave his final farewell as he kissed the tips of his fingers and touched her casket. Simple, poignant, genuine gestures. President Biden walked to the members of the CBC, shaking hands and hugging, and then back to the family. The sanctuary again applauded as he walked out, followed by the family. No public remarks were needed for his heartfelt tribute to Eddie Bernice.

Tuesday morning, January 9, 2024, hundreds assembled at Concord Baptist Church for the formal funeral service for Congresswoman Johnson. Over twenty-five members and former members of Congress were present. Former United States senator Kay Bailey Hutchinson, former White House counsel Harriet Meiers, numerous state and local elected officials, former staffers, and constituents gathered in the sanctuary to await the entry of the family. Senior Pastor Bryan Carter, reading scriptures, led the family and close friends into the sanctuary as they walked by the open casket for one final farewell. Setting the tone for the ceremony, he recognized that all had gathered to give her the highest honor, "Well done, thy good and faithful servant," and to thank her for her leadership, lifting her voice for those who didn't have a voice, standing strong, working across the aisle, staying for fifty years of public service, and fighting against racism and discrimination.[16]

Tributes followed, echoing Pastor Carter's praise and gratitude. In a recorded message, Vice President Kamala Harris noted that Congresswoman Johnson saw the nation as it could be and devoted her life to make that vision real, to bring healing and hope.[17] Former president William Jefferson Clinton, appearing by video, recalled their more than fifty-year friendship, in storm or sunshine, and praised her as someone who was always fighting and standing up for what she thought was right.[18]

That became a recurring message—gratitude for her friendship, admiration for her tenacity, determination, mentorship, and service. "If Eddie Bernice was on your side, you knew that you could stand straighter, that your voice was stronger, your path was clearer, because you knew that she always had your back."[19] She was "our congressional mother, guiding us to congressional leadership."[20] She "was quiet, gentle, but as strong as steel."[21] "She would begin her phone calls with 'How can I help?"[22] Fighting with "grace and dignity, . . . she was a 'can do person' . . . always willing to do the hard work."[23]

Her three "adopted" sons, former Dallas mayor and former US trade representative Ron Kirk; Harris County Commissioner, former Texas state senator, and former aide to Congressman Mickey Leland, Rodney Ellis; and Texas State Senator Royce West, rose together to speak of their "matriarch." The lesson she taught: "do the work." Do the work to quell the political discord. Do the work to address accessible health care, higher education, and historically underutilized minority businesses, and build coalitions based on interests, not political affiliation. Do the work even if it means going to bed at 1:00 or 2:00 am. Do the work.[24]

Dallas mayor Eric Johnson took on the task of sharing what he believed Congresswoman Johnson would say to us:

> Knock it off, the divisiveness, the excessive partisanship, the ugliness. . . . She believed very strongly that you didn't have to be ugly to be strong and to stand for what you believe in. . . . She would want me to tell you to get over yourself, you're not the feature presentation

of every show that you're in. . . . She'd want me to make sure that you understood that there is too much work to be done for all of us to be show horses all the time . . . she chose to be the work horse just about every time. . . . And finally she would want me to ask you who do you love besides yourself? . . . She'd want me to tell you that . . . all of her accomplishments, all of the things that you read about, . . . that she did these things not for herself but for all of us, because she loved us.[25]

As much as she loved her colleagues, constituents, city and country, her family was always her foundation. Her three grandsons, through tears and smiles, shared stories of Granny, their one-on-one time with her, smilingly remembering her remarkable ability to make them each believe that they were the favorite grandchild. Their stories attested to her work ethic, going to sleep with briefing materials beside her. They knew she was powerful yet dainty, the epitome of class and elegance. They were touched by her humility but most of all by her deep love.

Her great-granddaughters, Kennedy and Lily, who a little more than a year earlier had stood beside their great-grandmother at the unveiling of her congressional portrait, touchingly reminded us of Congresswoman Johnson's love for children. Their words were accentuated by Kennedy's tall stature and Lily's stretch to barely peer over the lectern and to reach the microphone as they shared the lessons she had taught them. "We might be young, but we've learned a lot from our great-grandmother, Eddie Bernice. This is what she taught us: work hard every day and never give up when things get tough." "Be kind to everyone, be strong here [pointing to her heart] and here [pointing to her head]." "Girls can be good at math and science; no, girls can be *great* at math and science." "Always remember family comes first and always do the right thing even if it is not fun." "We'll never forget what you taught us, Granny." "We love you and we'll miss you every day."[26]

Family did come first for Congresswoman Johnson. Her son, Kirk, paying tribute to his mother, began by saying that he "had a wonderful life, a wonderful mother and [he] felt blessed to have shared her with us." She believed that everyone should have respect and love as God's child. Even though her death was "untimely and unnecessary . . . God chose to take her on 1, 2, 3, 1, 2, 3 [12/31/23]; there will never be another 1, 2, 3, 1, 2, 3; she was unique, she was special"[27]—the date of her death forever a symbol that there will never be another Eddie Bernice Johnson.

Before Reverend Michael Wayne Walker—retired administrative minister of Messiah Baptist Church, Brockton, Massachusetts, and close family friend—rose to give the eulogy, Sondra Dilworth Johnson, the congresswoman's daughter-in-law, gave the final family tribute of the afternoon. While the keyboardist played, Sondra walked up the steps to the sanctuary stage, stood purposefully, and arranged the music stand and microphone. Seconds later, singing the words "the sky shall unfold," Sondra began a riveting, powerful rendition of "We Shall Behold Him," the majesty of her voice blending with the keyboard, giving a performance that poignantly reflected Eddie Bernice's love of choral music.

The next day, Wednesday, a procession made the almost three-hour trip to take Congresswoman Johnson to Austin to be laid to rest. A short detour through her hometown, Waco, took the cars past a waiting crowd, holding a banner that declared, "Well done, EBJ, we love you"—a banner that drew tears and appreciation from inside the cars.

At the Texas State Cemetery, down the hill from the graves of Barbara Jordan and Sarah Weddington, her former colleagues, a small crowd gathered around the congresswoman's casket, the vault lid bearing her picture and an image of a United States flag propped in the foreground. At her gravesite, family, friends, and elected officials gathered to share memories, express gratitude for her service, and give honor to a life well lived. With the gentle tossing of yellow roses on top of her lowered casket, the ceremonies celebrating her life drew to a solemn close.

Endnotes

Note for the Editor's Preface

1. Eddie Bernice Johnson and Molly Galvin, "The More Inclusion We Have in Science, the Better Outcomes We'll Get," *Issues in Science and Technology* 39, no. 2 (Winter 2023): 27–30.

Notes for Chapter 7

1. "Ambassador Robert S. Strauss," Strauss Center for International Security and Law, University of Texas at Austin, accessed on March 30, 2024, https://www.strausscenter.org/robert-s-strauss/.
2. "Toppling of Orr Became Apparent Long Before Final Vote at Convention," *Fort Worth Star-Telegram*, June 14, 1972, 1; "Lubbock's Ralph Brock Aids Revolt Against Democ. Leader," *Lubbock Avalanche-Journal*, June 14, 1972, 141.

Notes for Chapter 8

1. Barbara Jordan Governor for a Day, the Barbara Jordan Archives, Texas Southern University, https://www.tsu.edu/academics/library/pdf/governor-for-a-day-virtual-exhibit.pdf.
2. "State Office Accused of Discrimination," *Victoria Advocate*, May 13, 1973, 19.
3. "Double Bias Laid to Office of Comptroller," *Fort Worth Star-Telegram*, May 2, 1973, 32.
4. "Discussion of Charge Due Today," *Corpus Christi Times,* September 20, 1973, 51; "Sex Discrimination Letter Issued against Comptroller," *Corpus Christi Caller*, September 18, 1973, 6.
5. "Calvert Assails Sex Bias Charge," *Austin American-Statesman*, September 19, 1973, 75; "Calvert Says His Office Doesn't Discriminate," *Tyler Morning Telegraph*, September 20, 1973, 21.
6. "Impeachment Action against Comptroller," *Longview News-Journal,* September 20, 1973, 1; "Minimum Pay: Calvert's Ouster Urged Unless Ways Changed," *Austin American-Stateman*, September 20, 1973, 1.
7. "Hispanic Reps Say Comptroller Should Resign," *Fort Worth Star-Telegram*, September 23, 1973, 15; "Resignation of Calvert Demanded," *Austin American-Statesman,* September 21, 1973, 1; "Daniel Demands

Apology after Calvert's Remark," *Tyler Morning Telegraph*, September 22, 1973, 9.

8. "State Prisoners Ired by Rough Treatment," *Odessa American*, November 15, 1973, 3.

9. "Black Lawmakers Seek Prison Beating Probe," *Valley Morning Star*, July 14, 1973; "Texas Prison Chief Disputes 10 Inmates," *Waco News-Tribune*, August 1, 1973, 13; "Punishment of Inmates at Prison 'Justified,'" *Kilgore News Herald*, August 1, 1973, 16; "2 Black Legislators Call for Probe of Beatings of Prisoners," *Fort Worth Star-Telegram*, July 14, 1973, 8.

10. Ruiz v. Estelle, 503 F. Supp. 1265 (S.D. Tex. 1980).

11. Penitentiaries-Study of Reforms, S.C.R. 87, Adopted by the Senate on May 10, 1973; adopted by the House on May 28, 1973, filed with the Secretary of the State, June 11, 1973.

12. Final Report of The Joint Committee on Prison Reform of the Texas Legislature, December 1974.

13. Letter of Ronald Earle to Senator Chet Brooks, January 23, 1975.

14. Ruiz v. Estelle.

15. H.S.R. 97, 63rd R.S., TX Legislature, April 4, 1973.

16. "The Report on the Interim Study on Child-caring in Texas, Committee on Human Resources, House of Representatives, State of Texas, 63rd Legislature, 1973–1974," November 12, 1974.

17. "Rangers To Investigate Two Deaths," *Odessa American*, August 10, 1973, 3.

18. "Action Urged on Study of Retarded," *Corpus Christi Times*, November 1, 1973, 34.

19. "Report on the Interim Study on Child-caring in Texas."

20. H.S.R. 31, 63rd R.S. TX Legislature.

21. H.S.R. 151, 63rd R.S. TX Legislature.

22. "Dallas Rep Selected," *Grand Prairie Daily News*, October 13, 1973, 9.

23. "Report to the Texas Legislature from the House State Affairs Interim Subcommittee on Law Enforcement Education, Training and Standards," December 1974.

24. Commission on Law Enforcement Officer Standards and Education-Reporting Requirements, Chapter 548, H.B. No. 1203, 64th R.S., Texas Legislature, June 19, 1975.

25. H.B. 451, 65th R.S., TX Legislature

26. "2 Republicans, 1 Woman get Texas House Chairmanships," *Fort Worth Star-Telegram*, January 26, 1975, 2; "Barriers Tumble as Blacks Win Chairmanships," *Corpus Christi Caller*, January 26, 1975, 7B

27. "Report of the Committee on Labor, Texas House of Representatives, 64th Legislature," October 1976.

28. "Jury-Reemployment of Jurors," Chapter 94, H.B. 245, Vernon's Ann. Civ. St. art. 5307b.

29. H.B. 2079, 64th R.S., TX Legislature.

30. H.B. 1557, House Study Group Report, 64th R.S., TX Legislature.

31. H.B. 1403, 64th R.S., TX Legislature.

32. H.B. 1403, House Study Group Report, 64th R.S., TX Legislature.

33. H.B. 1018, 64th R.S., TX Legislature.

34. H.B. 1514, House Study Group Report, 64th R.S., TX Legislature.

35. H.B. 127, 64th R.S., TX Legislature.

36. H.B. 127, House Study Group Report, 64th R.S., TX Legislature

37. H.B. 127, Bill Back, 64th R.S., TX Legislature.

38. "Report of the Committee on Labor, Texas House of Representatives," 64th Legislature.

39. Interim Report, 65th TX Legislative Sessions, Committee on Labor, Texas House of Representatives.

40. Interim Report, 65th TX Legislature.

41. H.B. 247, 64th R.S., TX Legislature.

42. H.B. 178, 64th R.S., TX Legislature.

43. H.B. 136, 65th R.S., TX Legislature.

44. S.B. 1073, 65th R.S., TX Legislature.

45. Minutes of the Texas House Committee on Public Education, May 2, 1977.

46. "School Breakfast Debate Flares," *Corpus Christi Caller*, May 29, 1088, 50.

47. H.B. 136, 65th R.S., TX Legislature.

48. "Robbins Criticizes School Bill," *Lubbock Avalanche-Journal*, July 17, 1977, 48.

49. Rogers v. Brockette, 588 F. 2d 1057 (5th. Cir. 1979).

50. Rogers v. Brockette, 588 F. 2d 1057 (5th Cir. 1979, *cert. denied* 444 U.S. 827, 1979).

51. "After a Nearly 50-Year Career, Johnson Says Greatest Feat Came in 2d State House Term," *Spectrum News* 1, November 23, 2021.

Notes for Chapter 9

1. Strauss Center for International Security and Law, University of Texas at Austin, accessed on March 30, 2024, https://www.strausscenter.org/robert-s-strauss/.
2. "Rep. Johnson New HEW Head," *Kilgore News Herald*, August 11, 1977, 4
3. "Fresh Air and Invigorating Thoughts," *Corpus Christi Caller*, July 23, 1978, 56.
4. "HEW Official Named Nurse of Year," *El Paso Times*, April 8, 1978, 19.
5. "Urban Ministry Turns to Neighborhoods Topic," *South Bend Tribune*, October 15, 1978, 39.
6. "Ville Platte Medicaid Pay Recovered," *Kinder Courier News*, April 25, 1979, 11.
7. "Rural Health Clinics Not Cheap for Texans," *Victoria Advocate*, December 3, 1978, 5A.
8. "Social Security News," *Weekly News*, November 9, 1978, 3.
9. "Boggs, Corrine Claiborne (Lindy)," *History, Art & Archives: United States House of Representatives*, accessed on March 30, 2024, https://history.house.gov/People/Detail/9543#biography.

Notes for Chapter 10

1. S.R. 217, 71st R.S., TX Legislature, March 6, 1989.
2. Editorial, *Dallas Morning News*, October 22, 1986, p. 26a.

Notes for Chapter 11

1. Outgoing Address, Honorable Mark White, Governor of Texas, Journal of the House of Representatives of the Regular Session of the Seventieth Legislature of the State of Texas, January 13, 1987, 101.
2. Legislative Reference Library of Texas, 70th Regular Session, January 13, 1987–June 1, 1987, https://lrl.texas.gov/sessions/sessionSnapshot.cfm?legSession=70-0.
3. H.J.R. 5, 70th Legislature, 2nd Called Session, July 21, 1987.
4. H.J.R 5, 70th Legislature, 2nd Called Session, Election Details, https://lrl.texas.gov/legis/billsearch/amendmentDetails.cfm?amendmentID=460&legSession=70-2&billTypedetail=HJR&billNumberDetail=5

5. "Child Protective Services in Texas," Staff Report to the Senate Committee on Health and Human Services, February 1989.

6. Joint Interim Task Force on Affordable Housing, Report to the 71st Legislature, 1989.

7. Joint Interim Task Force, at 12–22.

8. S.B. 75, 71st R.S., TX Legislature, effective on January 1, 1990.

9. S.B. 75, 71st R.S.

10. Minutes: Senate State Affairs Committee, Monday, March 6, 1989, 2; "Lawmakers Urge Fair-Housing Plan," *Galveston Daily News*, March 7, 1989, 10.

11. S.B. 481, 70th R.S., TX Legislature, effective August 31, 1987.

12. S.B. 1607, 71st R.S., TX Legislature, effective June 14, 1989.

13. S.B. 663, 72nd R.S., TX Legislature, effective June 6, 1991.

14. S.B. 482, 70th R.S., TX Legislature, effective June 20, 1987.

15. S.B. 485, 70th R.S., TX Legislature, effective August 31, 1987.

16. Edgewood Independent School District v. Meno, 761 S.W. 2d 859 (Tex. App. 3rd 1988), 917 S.W. 2d 717 (Tex. Sup. Ct. 1995)

17. S.B. 524, 71st R.S., TX Legislature.

18. Findings and Recommendations of the Senate Special Advisory Committee on Bishop College, 71st R.S., TX Legislature, 1989.

19. Findings and Recommendations, 71st R.S., TX Legislature.

20. S.B. 275, 72nd R.S., TX Legislature, effective May 1, 1991.

21. African Famine Relief and Recovery Act of 1985, H.R. 1096, 99th Congress (1985).

22. "Leland Crash Site Found; All 16 Killed: Wreckage of Plane with Congressman Spotted in Ethiopia," *Los Angeles Times*, August 14, 1989.

23. "Representative Mickey Leland, 44, Dies in Crash," *New York Times*, August 14, 1989, Section D, 9.

24. "Representative Mickey Leland," 9.

25. "Mickey Leland Made a Difference," *New York Times*, August 15, 1989, 20.

26. "Leland Regarded as a Champion of Oppressed," *Charlotte Observer*, August 14, 1989.1

27. Bush v. Vera, 517 U.S. 952 (1996).

28. "Lawmakers Map Lines, Angles in Redistricting Plan," *Austin American-Statesman*, July 16, 1990, 5.

29. "Lawmakers Map Lines," 5.

30. Terrazas v. Slagle, 789 F. Supp. 828 (W.D. Tex. 1991).

31. Bush v. Vera, 517 U.S. 952, 116 S. Ct. 1941 (1996).

Notes for Chapter 12

1. "Lawmakers Agree: Redistricting Process Is a Mess," *Dallas Morning News*, September 1, 1991, 50A.
2. "Key Players: Who to Watch in the Budget Battle," *Dallas Morning News*, July 14, 1991, 30A.
3. "Editorials/Opinions: U.S. House: Democrat," *Fort Worth Star-Telegram*, February 22, 1992, p. 24.
4. "U.S. House: Democrat," 24.
5. 103 Cong. Rec. H45 (1993).
6. 103 Cong. Rec. H47 (1993).
7. 103 Cong. Rec. H47–48 (1993).

Notes for Chapter 13

1. National African American Museum Act, H.R. 877, 103rd Cong. (1993).
2. National African American Museum Act, 103 Cong. Rec. H14461 (1993).
3. National Museum of African American History and Culture Act, H.R. 3491, 108th Cong. (2003), signed December 16, 2003, Public Law No. 108-184.
4. King Holiday and Service Act of 1994, H.R. 1933, 103rd Cong. (1994), signed August 23, 1994, Public Law No. 103-304.
5. Authorizing the Alpha Phi Alpha Fraternity to Establish a Memorial to Martin Luther King, Jr. in the District of Columbia or Its Environs, H.J.Res. 177, 103rd Cong. (1993).
6. Omnibus Parks and Public Lands Management Act of 1996, H.R. 4236, 104th Cong. (1996), signed November 12, 1996, Public Law No. 104-333.
7. South African Democratic Transition Support Act of 1993, H.R. 3225, 103rd Cong. (1993), signed November 23, 1993, Public Law No. 103-149.
8. Breast and Cervical Cancer Information Act of 1993, H.R. 2293, 103rd Cong. (1993).
9. Osteoporosis Risk Reduction Act of 1994, H.R. 4284, 103rd Cong. (1994)
10. Mammography Access Tax Credit Act of 1993, H.R. 2210, 103rd Cong. (1993).

11. Equal Access to Annual Mammography Screening Act of 1993, H.R. 427, 103rd Cong. (1993).

12. Medicaid Mammography Coverage Act of 1993, H.R. 425, 103rd Cong. (1993).

13. Freedom of Choice Act of 1993, H.R. 25, 103rd Congress (1993-1994).

14. Federal Prohibition of Female Genital Mutilation Act of 1993, H.R. 3247, 103rd Cong. (1993).

15. Access to Obstetric Care Act of 1993, H.R. 1814, 103rd Cong. (1993).

16. Lupus Research Amendments of 1993, H.R. 2420, 103rd Cong. (1993).

17. Comprehensive HIV Prevention Act of 1993, H.R. 1538, 103rd Cong. (1993).

18. Reproductive Health Equity Act, H.R. 26, 103rd Cong. (1993).

19. Ryan White CARE Reauthorization Act of 1994, H.R. 5141, 103rd Cong. (1994).

20. Family and Medical Leave Act of 1993, H.R. 1, 103rd Cong. (1993).

21. Violence Against Women Act of 1993, H.R. 1133, 103rd Cong. (1993).

22. National Domestic Violence Hotline Act of 1993, H.R. 522, 103rd Cong. (1993).

23. Child Abuse Accountability Act, H.R. 3694, 103rd Cong. (1994).

24. Jobs and Investment Act of 1994, H.R. 5278, 103rd Cong. (1994).

25. City of Dallas Thoroughfare Plan, Ordinance No. 20860, October 10, 1990, updated June 1993, 11.

26. Civil Rights Protection Act of 1993, H.R. 3331, 103rd Cong. (1993).

27. "Perot Eager for NAFTA Fight Tonight," *Fort Worth Star-Telegram*, November 9, 1993, 1, 6.

28. North American Free Trade Agreement Implementation Act, H.R. 3450, 103rd Cong. (1993).

29. Ken Goodwin, Scott Ainsworth, and Erik Goodwin, *Lobbying and Policy Making: The Public Pursuit of Private Interests* (Los Angeles: Sage Publications, 2013), 20–21.

30. *Larry King Live*, NAFTA debate, Al Gore and Ross Perot, November 9, 1993.

31. 103 Cong. Rec., H29889 (1993), Providing for Consideration of H.R. 3450, North American Free-Trade Agreement Implementation Act, November 17, 1993.

32. North American Free Trade Agreement Implementation Act, H.R. 3450, 103rd Cong. (1993), signed December 8, 1993, Public Law No. 103-182.

33. Summary of Activities of the Committee on Science, U.S. House of Representatives for the One Hundred Fourth Congress, H.R. Rep. No. 104-887, at 7 (1997).

34. Antarctic Science, Tourism, and Conservation Act of 1996, H.R. 3060, 104th Cong. (1996), signed October 2, 1996, Public Law No. 104-227.

35. Summary of Activities of the Committee on Science, January 2, 1997, supra at 17.

36. National Science Foundation Authorization Act of 1998, H.R. 1273, 105th Cong. (1998), signed July 29, 1998, Public Law No. 105-207.

37. Information Technology Partnership Act, H.R. 3496, 105th Cong. (1998).

38. Commercial Space Act of 1998, H.R. 1702, 105th Cong. (1998), signed October 28, 1998, Public Law No. 105-303.

39. Summary of Activities of the Committee on Science, U.S. House of Representatives for the One Hundred Fifth Congress, H.R. Rep. No. 105-847, 19 (1999).

40. Next Generation Internet Research Act of 1998, H.R. 3332, 105th Cong. (1998), signed October 28, 1998, Public Law No. 105-305.

41. Commission on the Advancement of Women and Minorities in Science, Engineering, and Technology Development Act, H.R. 3007, 105th Cong. (1998), signed October 14, 1998, Public Law No. 105-255.

42. *Land of Plenty: Diversity as America's Competitive Edge in Science, Engineering and Technology*, Report of the Congressional Commission on the Advancement of Women and Minorities in Science, Engineering and Technology Development, September 2000, https://www.nsf.gov/publications/pub_summ.jsp?ods_key=cawmset0409.

43. Honoring the National Science Foundation for 50 Years of service to the Nation, H.Con.Res. 108, 107th Cong., agreed to in the Senate, May 9, 2001.

44. Honoring National Science Foundation for 50 Years of Service, 147 Cong. Rec. H1939 (2001).

45. Small Business Technology Transfer Program Reauthorization Act of 2001, H.R. 1860, 107th Cong. (2001), signed October 15, 2001, Public Law No. 107-50.

46. National Science Foundation Authorization Act of 2002, H.R. 4664, 107th Cong. (2002), signed December 19, 2002, Public Law No. 107-368.

47. Mathematics and Science Proficiency Partnership Act of 2001, H.R. 1660, 107th Cong. (2002), introduced November 19, 2002.

48. Regional Plant Genome and Gene Research Expression Act, H.R. 2051, 107th Cong. (2002), passed House, May 14, 2002.

49. Counting Electoral Votes: Joint Session of the House and Senate Held Pursuant to the Provisions of Senate Concurrent Resolution 1, 147 Cong. Rec. H52 (2001).

50. "Congressional Black Caucus Protests Electoral Vote Count," CNN, aired January 6, 2001, 2:00 p.m., http://www.cnn.com/TRAN-SCRIPTS/0101/06/se.02.html.

51. "Florida Electoral Vote Challenge," CSPAN, January 6, 2001, https://www.c-span.org/video/?161634-1/florida-electoral-vote-challenge.

52. J. Chamberlin, "Congressional Black Caucus Spring Health Braintrust Focuses on Universal Health Care," *American Psychological Association* 32, no. 7 (July/August 2001), https://www.apa.org/monitor/julaug01/blackcaucus.

53. "President Bush Responds," PBS News Hour, September 11, 2001, 1:30 p.m., https://www.pbs.org/newshour/politics/white_house-july-dec01-bush-1pm_09-11.

54. Expressing the Sense of Senate and House of Representatives Regarding Terrorist Attacks Launched Against United States, 147 Cong. Rec., H5542 (2001).

55. "Address to the Joint Session of the 107th Congress," United States Capitol, Washington, D.C., September 20, 2001, https://georgewbush-whitehouse.archives.gov/infocus/bushrecord/documents/Selected_Speeches_George_W_Bush.pdf.

56. Air Transportation and Safety System Stabilization Act, H.R. 2926, 107th Cong. (2001), signed September 22, 2001, Public Law No. 107-42.

57. Air Transportation Safety and System Stabilization Act, 147 Cong. Rec. H5901 (2001).

58. Secure Transportation for America Act, 147 Cong. Rec. H7678 (2001).

59. Displaced Workers Relief Act of 2001, H.R. 2946, 107th Cong. (2001).

60. To Amend the Internal Revenue Code of 1986 to Exclude Unemployment Compensation from Gross Income, H.R. 886, 107th Cong. (2001).

61. Support of American Military and the American People, 147 Cong. Rec. E1835 (2001).

62. H.R. 3162, 107th Cong. (2001), signed October 26, 2001, Public Law No. 107-56.

Notes for Chapter 14

1. Project of the New American Century Letter to Honorable William J. Clinton, January 26, 1998, https://zfacts.com/zfacts.com/metaPage/lib/98-Rumsfeld-Iraq.pdf.
2. A Joint resolution Expressing the Sense of the Senate and House of Representatives Regarding the Terrorist Attacks Launched against the United States on September 11, 2001, S.J. Res. 22, 107th Cong. (2001), signed September 18, 2001, Public Law No. 107-39.
3. State of the Union address to the 107th Congress, United States Capitol, January 29, 2002, 103, https://georgewbush-whitehouse.archives.gov/infocus/bushrecord/documents/Selected_Speeches_George_W_Bush.pdf.
4. West Point Commencement, United States Military Academy, West Point, New York, June 1, 2002, 129, https://georgewbush-whitehouse.archives.gov/infocus/bushrecord/documents/Selected_Speeches_George_W_Bush.pdf.
5. Calling for Congress to Consider and Vote on a Resolution for the Use of Force by the United States Armed Forces against Iraq before Such Force is Deployed, H.J. Res. 109, 107th Cong. (2002).
6. Address to the United Nations General Assembly, United Nations Headquarters, New York, New York September 12, 2002, 139, https://georgewbush-whitehouse.archives.gov/infocus/bushrecord/documents/Selected_Speeches_George_W_Bush.pdf.
7. Remarks Following a Meeting with Congressional Leaders and an Exchange with Reporters, George W. Bush, 43rd President of the United States: 2001–2009, September 18, 2002, https://www.presidency.ucsb.edu/documents/remarks-following-meeting-with-congressional-leaders-and-exchange-with-reporters-6.
8. Authorization for Use of Military Force Against Iraq Resolution of 2002, H.J. Res. 113, 107th Cong. (2002), signed October 16, 2002, Public Law No. 107-243.
9. Iraq Resolution, October 2, 2002, https://www.c-span.org/video/?172981-1/iraq-resolution.
10. Authorization for Use of Military Force Against Iraq Resolution of 2002, 148 Cong. Rec. H7210 (2002).
11. Authorization for Use of Military Force Against Iraq Resolution of 2002, H.J. Res. 113, 107th Cong. (2002), signed October 16, 2002, Public Law No. 107-243.

12. Homeland Security Act of 2002, H.R. 5005, 107th Cong. (2002), signed November 25, 2002, Public Law No. 107-296.
13. Homeland Security Act of 2002, 148 Cong. Rec. H8711 (2002).
14. Homeland Security Act of 2002, H.R. 5005, 107th Cong. (2002), signed November 25, 2002, Public Law No. 107-296.
15. State of the Union address to the 108th Congress, the United States Capitol, Washington, DC, January 28, 2003, https://georgewbush-whitehouse.archives.gov/infocus/bushrecord/documents/Selected_Speeches_George_W_Bush.pdf.
16. Address by Secretary of State Colin Powell to the United Nations Security Council, February 5, 2003, https://www.presidency.ucsb.edu/documents/address-secretary-state-colin-powell-the-united-nations-security-council.
17. Remarks on the Future of Iraq, Washington Hilton Hotel, Washington, D.C. February 26, 2003, https://georgewbush-whitehouse.archives.gov/infocus/bushrecord/documents/Selected_Speeches_George_W_Bush.pdf.
18. Address to the Nation on Military Operations in Iraq, the Oval Office, Washington, DC, March 19, 2003, https://georgewbush-whitehouse.archives.gov/infocus/bushrecord/documents/Selected_Speeches_George_W_Bush.pdf.
19. Expressing Sense of House that Deployment of Forces in Iraq Be Terminated Immediately, 151 Cong. Rec. H11007 (2005).
20. Expressing the sense of the House of Representatives That the Deployment of United States forces in Iraq Be Terminated Immediately, H. Res. 571, 109th Cong. (2005), failed House November 18, 2005.
21. Expressing the Sense of the House of Representatives That the Deployment of United States Forces in Iraq Be Terminated Immediately, 151 Cong. Rec. H11021 (2005).
22. The Ryan White Care Act, 151 Cong. Rec. H8493 (2005).
23. Recognizing National Historically Black Colleges and Universities Week and the Importance and Accomplishments of Historically Black Colleges and Universities, H. Res. 518, 107th Cong. (2002).
24. *The Columbia Accident Investigation Board Report, Hearing before the Committee on Science House of Representatives*, 108th Cong. (2003).
25. NASA Flexibility Act of 2004, S. 610 108th Cong. (2004), signed February 24, 2004, Public Law No. 108-201; Commercial Space Launch Amendments Act of 2004, H.R. 5382, 108th Cong. (2004), signed December 23, 2004, Public Law No. 108-492.

26. 151 Cong. Rec. H12132 (2005).
27. Recognizing Space Shuttle Commander Eileen Collins, Mission Specialist Wendy Lawrence, and the Contributions of All Other Women Who Have Worked with NASA, 151 Cong. Rec. H8120 (2005).
28. Conference Report on H.R. 6, Energy Policy Act of 2005, 151 Cong. Rec. H6949 (2005).
29. Water Resources Development Act of 1994, H.R. 4460, 103rd Cong. (1994).
30. Water Resources Development Act of 2007, Veto Message from the President of the United States, 153 Cong. Rec. H12788 (2007).
31. Water Quality Investment Act of 2009, H.R. 1262, 111th Cong. (2009).
32. "Biden's Description of Obama Draws Scrutiny," *CNN*, February 9, 2007, https://www.cnn.com/2007/POLITICS/01/31/biden.obama/.
33. Opening Welcome Remarks at the 2009 Presidential Inauguration, January 20, 2009, https://www.americanrhetoric.com/speeches/diane-feinsteinpresidentialinauguration.htm.
34. Lilly Ledbetter Fair Pay Act of 2009, 155 Cong. Rec. H123 (2009).
35. Hate Crimes Prevention Act of 1999, H.R. 1082, 155 Cong. Rec. E920 (2009).
36. Local Law Enforcement Hate Crimes Prevention Act of 2001, H.R. 1343, 107th Cong. (2001).
37. Repeal the Don't Ask, Don't Tell Policy, Hate Crimes Prevention Act of 1999, H.R. 1082, 155 Cong. Rec. H10512 (2009).
38. American Recovery and reinvestment Act of 2009, H.R. 1, 111th Cong. (2009), signed February 17, 2009, Public law No. 111-5.
39. American Recovery and Reinvestment Act of 2009, H.R. 1, 155 Cong. Rec. H573 (2009).
40. American Recovery and Reinvestment Act of 2009, H.R. 1, 155 Cong. Rec. H640 (2009).
41. "McCain Blasts Obama," Politico, February 6, 2009, https://www.politico.com/story/2009/02/mccain-blasts-obama-018500.
42. Moving Towards Economic Recovery with the American Recovery and Reinvestment Act, 155 Cong. Rec. H4528 (2009).
43. Fred Hoffman, "Thanks for Saving the Auto Industry, President Obama," *Detroit Free Press*, January 19, 2017, https://www.freep.com/story/opinion/contributors/2017/01/19/thanks-saving-auto-industry-president-obama/96797256/.
44. Dodd-Frank Wall Street Reform and Consumer Protection Act, H.R. 4173, 111th Cong. (2010), signed July 21, 2010, Public Law No. 111-203.

45. Stop Wall Street from Gambling with our Economic Security, 156 Cong. Rec. H2890 (2010).

46. Serve America Act, H.R. 1388, 111th Cong. (2009), signed April 21, 2009, Public Law No. 111-13.

47. Generations Invigorating Volunteerism and Education Act, 155 Cong. Rec. H3553 (2009).

48. "Statement by the President on the Edward M. Kennedy Serve America Act," *AmeriCorps*, March 26, 2009, https://americorps. gov/newsroom/official-statements/2009/statement-president-edward -m-kennedy-serve-america-act.

49. Veterans' Medical Personnel Recruitment and Retention Act of 2009, H.R. 919, 111th Cong. (2009).

50. Caregivers and Veterans Omnibus Health Services Act of 2010, S.1963, 111th Cong. (2010), Signed May 5, 2010, Public Law No. 111-163.

51. Caregivers and Veterans Omnibus Health Services Act, 156 Cong. Rec. H2730 (2010).

52. "Remarks of President Barack Obama: Address to Joint Session of Congress," the White House, Office of the Press Secretary, February 24, 2009, https://obamawhitehouse.archives.gov/the-press-office/ remarks-president-barack-obama-address-joint-session-congress.

53. CBC Focus on Health Care, 155 Cong. Rec. H5695 (2009).

54. "Nurses Join President Obama on Health Care Reform," the White House, Office of the Press Secretary, July 15, 2009, https:// obamawhitehouse.archives.gov/video/Nurses-Join-President-Obama-on-Health-Care-Reform?page=4.

55. Patient Protection and Affordable Care Act, H.R. 3590, 111th Cong. (2010), signed March 23, 2010, Public Law No. 111-148.

56. It's Time for All People to Have Access to Insurance, H12370 (2009).

57. Health Care Reform, 156 Cong. Rec. H1456 (2010).

58. Commerce, Justice, Science, and Related Agencies Appropriations Act, Amendment No. 35 Offered by Ms. Eddie Bernice Johnson of Texas, 155 Cong. Rec. H6932 (2009.

59. Student Aid and Fiscal Responsibility Act of 2009, 155 Cong. Rec. H9683 (2009).

60. Budget Control Act of 2011, S. 365, 112th Cong. (2011), signed August 2, 2011, Public Law No. 112-25.

61. Budget Control Act of 2011, 157 Cong. Rec. H5763 (2011).

62. Republicans' Refusal to Act on American Jobs Act, 157 Cong. Rec. H7022 (2011).

Notes for Chapter 15

1. Report of Activities of the Committee on Science, Space, and Technology, U.S. House of Representatives together with Minority Views for the One Hundred Fourteenth Congress, H.R. 114-884 (2016).
2. 21st Century Cures Act, H.R. 34, 114th Cong. (2016), signed December 13, 2016, Public Law No. 114-255.
3. 21st Century Cures Act, 161 Cong. Rec. H5016 (2015).
4. Passing Mental Health Reform, 162 Cong. Rec. E1458 (2016).
5. "Donald Trump: 'I Could . . . Shoot Somebody, And I Wouldn't Lose Any Voters,'" *NPR*, January 23, 2016, https://www.npr.org/sections/thetwo-way/2016/01/23/464129029/donald-trump-i-could-shoot-somebody-and-i-wouldnt-lose-any-voters.
6. We Must Fight Climate Change, 164 Cong. Rec. H420 (2018).
7. Deferred Action for Childhood Arrivals Program, 163 Cong. Rec. E1325 (2017).
8. Department of Homeland Security et al v. Regents of the University of California, et al, 140 S. Ct. 1891 (2020).
9. Impact of Cabinet Nominations, 163 Cong. Rec. H227 (2017).
10. Remarks of President Donald J. Trump, Inaugural Address, January 20, 2017, https://trumpwhitehouse.archives.gov/briefings-statements/the-inaugural-address/.
11. A Response to President Trump's Inaugural Address and New Deal for African Americans, 163 Cong. Rec. H606 (2017).
12. Inspiring the Next Space Pioneers, Innovators, Researchers, and Explorers (INSPIRE) Women Act, H.R. 321, 115th Cong. (2017), signed February 28, 2017, Public Law No. 115-7.
13. H.R. 4742 Promoting Women in Entrepreneurship Act and H.R. 4755 Inspiring the Next Space Pioneers, Innovators, Researchers, and Explorers Women Act., 162 Cong. Rec. E358 (2016).
14. Women in Aerospace Education Act, H.R. 4254, 115th Cong. (2018), signed December 11, 2018, Public Law No. 115-303.
15. Innovations in Mentoring, Training, and Apprenticeships Act, H.R. 5509, 115th Cong. (2018), signed December 31, 2018, Public Law No. 115-402.
16. Innovations in Mentoring, Training, and Apprenticeships Act, 164 Cong. Rec. H10419 (2018).
17. Hidden Figures Congressional Gold Medal Act, H.R. 1396, 116th Cong. (2019), signed November 8, 2019, Public Law No. 116-68.

18. Introduction of Hidden Figures Congressional Gold Medal Act, 164 Cong. Rec. E1249 (2018).

19. Henrietta Lacks Enhancing Cancer Research Act of 2019, H.R. 1966, 116th Cong. (2021), signed January 5, 2021, Public Law No. 116-291.

20. National Suicide Hotline Improvement Act of 2018, H.R. 2345, 115th Cong. (2018), signed August 14, 2018, Public Law No. 115-233.

21. National Suicide Hotline Improvement Act of 2018, 164 Cong. Rec. H6593-94 (2018).

22. Substance Abuse and Mental Health Services Administration, *988 Appropriations Report*, December 2021, https://www.samhsa.gov/sites/default/files/988-appropriations-report.pdf.

23. Honoring American Veterans in Extreme Need Act of 2019, H.R. 2938, 116th Cong. (2019), signed August 23, 2019, Public Law No. 116-52.

24. National Defense Authorization Act for Fiscal Year 2020, H.R. 2500, 116th Cong. (2019), passed House July 12, 2019; Conference Agreement December 11, 2019, S.R. 1790, 116th Cong. (2019), signed December 20, 2019, Public Law No. 116-92.

25. National Defense Authorization Act for Fiscal Year 2020, Public Law 116-92, sec. 3031, Installation of carbon monoxide detectors in military housing, December 20, 2019.

26. Impeaching Donald John Trump, President of the United States, for high crimes and misdemeanors, H. Res. 755, 116th Cong. (2019), passed House December 18, 2019, Senate adjudged not guilty, February 5, 2020.

27. "Roll Call Vote 117th Congress, 1st Session," United States Senate, February 13, 2021, https://www.senate.gov/legislative/LIS/roll_call_votes/vote1171/vote_117_1_00059.htm.

28. *The State of Climate Science and Why It Matters: Hearing before the Committee on Science, Space, and Technology House of Representatives*, 116th Cong. (2019).

29. *State of Climate Science*, at 8–9.

30. *State of Climate Science*, at 21, testimony of Dr. Robert Kopp, director, Rutgers Institute of Earth, Ocean, and Atmospheric Sciences, and professor, Department of Earth and Planetary Sciences, Rutgers, University.

31. *State of Climate Science*.

32. *State of Climate Science*, at 246–47.

33. *Earth's Thermometers: Glacial and Ice Sheet Melt in a Changing Climate: Hearing Before the Committee on Science, Space, and Technology House of Representatives*, 116th Cong. (2019).

34. *Understanding, Forecasting, and Communicating Extreme Weather in a Changing Climate, Hearing Before the Committee on Science, Space, and Technology House of Representatives*, 116th Cong. (2019).

35. National Academies of Sciences, Engineering, and Medicine, *Sexual Harassment of Women: Climate, Culture, and Consequences in Academic Sciences, Engineering, and Medicine* (Washington, DC: National Academies Press, 2018).

36. Combating Sexual Harassment in Science Act of 2019, H.R. 36, 116th Cong. (2019), passed House July 23, 2019.

37. Civilian Space Authorization Act, Fiscal Years 1998 and 1999, 143 Cong. Rec. H1842 (1997).

38. Apollo 1 Memorial Act, H.R. 703, 115th Cong. (2017).

39. National Defense Authorization Act for Fiscal Year 2018, H.R. 2810, 115th Cong. (2017), signed December 12, 2017, Public Law No. 115-91, Section 1087.

40. *America in Space: Future Visions, Current Issues; Hearing Before the Committee on Science, Space, and Technology, House of Representatives*, 116th Congress (2019).

41. *Hearing Before the Committee on Science, Space, and Technology, House of Representatives*, 116th Congress (2019).

42. "Trump's Response to Police Killing Threatens to Further Deepen Unrest in America, Democrats and Republics Say," CNN Politics, May 31, 2020, https://www.cnn.com/2020/05/31/politics/trump-george-floyd-protests/index.html.

43. "Dallas Declares Friday 'George Perry Floyd Remembrance Day,'" NCBDFWChannel5News,June5,2020,https://www.nbcdfw.com/news/local/dallas-declares-friday-george-floyd-remembrance-day/2383273/.

44. George Floyd Justice in Policing Act of 2021, 1 H.R. 1280, 17th Cong. (2021), introduced in House February 24, 2021, received in Senate March 9, 2021.

45. For the People Act of 2019, H.R. 1, 116th Cong. (2019), passed House March 8, 2019.

46. Voting Rights Advancement Act of 2019, H.R. 4, 116th Cong. (2019), passed House July 27, 2020.

47. Voting Rights Advancement Act of 2019, H.R. 4, 116th Cong. (2019), passed House September 27, 2020.

48. Voter Empowerment Act of 2017, H.R. 12, 115th Cong. (2017).

49. Election Integrity Act of 2017, H.R. 2090, 115th Cong. (2017).

50. Same Day Registration Act, S. 360, 115th Cong. (2017).

51. Help Our Service Members and Citizens Abroad Vote Act, H.R. 3300, 115th Cong. (2017).

52. Servicemember Voting Protection Act, H.R. 3343, 115th Cong. (2017).

53. PRIDE Voting Act, S. 3116, 115th Cong. (2018).

54. Expressing the Sense of Congress Regarding the United States Capitol Police and Their Role in Securing the United States Capitol Complex and Protecting Members of Congress, Their Staff, and the General Public, H. Con. Res. 64, 115th Cong. (2017).

55. Wounded Officers Recovery Act of 2017, H.R. 3298, 115th Cong. (2017), signed August 4, 2017, Public Law No. 115-45.

56. National Commission to Investigate the January 6 Attack on the United States Capitol Complex Act, 167 Cong. Rec. H2574 (2021).

57. Emmett Till Antilynching Act, H.R. 55, 117th Cong. (2022), signed March 3, 28, 2022, Public Law No. 117-107.

58. American Rescue Plan Act of 2021, H.R. 1319, 117th Cong. (2021), signed March 11, 2021, Public Law No. 117-2.

59. Providing for Consideration of H.R. 1319, American Rescue Plan Act of 2021, 167 Cong. Rec. H769 (2021).

60. Infrastructure Investment and Jobs Act, H.R. 3684, 117th Cong. (2021), signed November 15, 2021, Public Law No. 117-58.

61. Infrastructure Investment and Jobs Act, 167 Cong. Rec. H5449 (2021).

62. Implementing the Infrastructure Investment and Jobs Act: Remote Hearing Before the Committee on Transportation and Infrastructure, House of Representatives, 117th Cong. 12 (2022).

63. Report of the Committee on Science, Space, and Technology, House of Representatives, Bioeconomy Research and Development Act of 2021, H. R. Rep. No. 117-2345, pt. 1 (2022).

64. S. 1260, United States Innovation and Competition Act of 2021, 117th Congress, passed Senate June 8, 2021.

65. Supporting Early-Career Researchers Act, H.R. 144, 117th Cong. (2021).

66. STEM Opportunities Act, H.R. 204, 117th Cong. (2021).

67. Rural STEM Education Research Act, H.R. 210, 117th Cong. (2021).

68. COAST Research Act of 2021, H.R. 1447, 117th Cong. (2021).

69. MSI STEM Achievement Act, H.R. 2027, 117th Cong. (2021).

70. National Science Foundation for the Future Act, H.R. 2225, 117th Cong. (2021).

71. Combating Sexual Harassment in Science Act, H.R. 2695, 117th Cong. (2021).

72. Department of Energy Science for the Future Act, H.R. 3593, 117th Cong. (2021).

73. National Science and Technology Strategy Act of 2021, H.R. 3858, 117th Cong. (2021), reported to the House, February 18, 2022.

74. Bioeconomy Research and Development Act of 2021, renamed United States Innovation and Competition Act of 2021, H.R. 4521, 117th Cong, (2021), resolving differences, May 5, 2022.

75. Regional Innovation Act of 2021, H.R. 4588, 117th Cong. (2022).

76. Steel Upgrading Partnerships and Emissions Reduction Act or the SUPER Act of 2021, H.R. 4599, 117th Cong. (2021).

77. Energizing Technology Transfer Act, H.R. 4606, 117th Cong. (2021).

78. National Institute of Standards and Technology for the Future Act of 2021, H.R. 4509, 117th Cong. (2022).

79. Micro Act, H.R. 6291, 117th Cong. (2021).

80. Department of Energy Science for the Future Act, 167 Cong. Rec. H3218 (2021).

81. National Science Foundation for the Future Act, 167 Cong. Rec. H3202 (2021).

82. Remarks by President Biden on Rebuilding American Manufacturing Through the CHIPS and Science Act, New Albany Ohio, September 9, 2022, https://www.whitehouse.gov/briefing-room/speeches-remarks/2022/09/09/remarks-by-president-biden-on-rebuilding-american-manufacturing-through-the-chips-and-science-act/.

Notes for Chapter 16

1. Transportation Equity Act for the 21st Century, H.R. 2400, 105th Cong. (1998), signed June 9, 1998, Public Law No. 105-178.

2. Conference Report on H.R. 4328, Department of Transportation and Related Agencies Appropriations Act, 1999, 144 Cong. Rec. H11652 (1998).

3. Transportation Equity Act for the 21st Century, H.R. 2400, 105th Cong. (1998), signed June 9, 1998, Public Law No. 105-178.

4. SAFETEA-LU, H.R. 3, 109th Cong. (2005), signed September 10, 2005, Public Law No. 109-59.

5. Conference Report of H.R. 3, Safe, Accountable, Flexible, Efficient Transportation Equity Act: A Legacy for Users, 151 Cong. Rec. H7573 (2005).

6. FAST Act, H.R. 22, 114th Cong. (2015), signed December 4, 2015, Public Law No. 114094.

7. Infrastructure Investment and Jobs Act, 167 Cong. Rec. H5449 (2021).

8. Environmental Protection Agency, "From Brownfields to a Green Future," *Newsroom*, April 19, 2007, https://www.epa.gov/archive/epapages/newsroom_archive/newsreleases/fd8bd55df2f-70b48852572c10072e303.html.

9. *The Revitalization of the Environmental Protection Agency's Brownfields Program: Hearing before the Committee on Transportation and Infrastructure House of Representatives*, 110th Cong. 1–3 (2008).

10. Revitalization, at 7–8.

11. The City of Dallas, Texas v. Southwest Airlines Company, 371 F. Supp. 1015 (N.D. Tex. 1973)

12. Fight to Fly Act, H.R. 2646, 109th Cong. (2005).

13. *Remarks before Senate Hearing 109-1098, Hearing before the Subcommittee on Aviation of the Committee on Commerce, Science, and Transportation, United States Senate*, 109th Cong. 24 (2005).

14. American Right to Fly Act, S. 1424, 109th Cong. (2005).

15. Wright Amendment Reform Act, H.R. 5830, 109th Cong. (2005).

16. "Editorial: Wright Amendment: No Middle Ground," *Fort Worth Star-Telegram*, July 31, 2005, p. 68.

17. H.B. 42, 71st TX Legislature, 1st C.S., relating to admissions to and programs at The University of Texas at Dallas, signed July 12, 1989, effective same date.

18. See, e.g. "The Conscience of Congress, A tribute to the Congressional Black Caucus, 25th Annual Legislative Conference," Science and Technology Braintrust: "Technology in a Changing World," 3.

19. Committee on Science, Unlocking Our Future: Toward a New National Science Policy, H.R. 105-847 (1992).

20. Sense of House Regarding National Science Policy, 144 Cong. Rec. H10150 (1998).

21. Sense of House Regarding National Science Policy, at H10150-51.

22. *Land of Plenty: Diversity as America's Competitive Edge in Science, Engineering and Technology*, Report of the Congressional Commission on the Advancement of Women and Minorities in Science, Engineering and Technology Development, September 2000, https://www.nsf.gov/publications/pub_summ.jsp?ods_key=cawmset0409.

23. Information Technology Partnership Act, H.R. 3896, 105th Cong. (1998).

24. Mathematics and Science Proficiency Partnership Act of 1999, H.R. 1265, 106th Cong. (1999); Mathematics and Science Proficiency Partnership Act of 2001, H.R. 1660, 107th Cong. (2002).

25. Undergraduate Science, Mathematics, Engineering, and Technology Education Improvement Act, H.R. 3130, 107th Cong. (2002), passed House, July 9, 2002.

26. Undergraduate Science, Mathematics, Engineering, and Technology Education Improvement Act, 148 Cong. Rec. H4374 (2002).

27. National Science Foundation Authorization Act of 2002, H.R. 4664, 107th Cong. (2002), signed December 19, 2002, Public Law No. 107-368.

28. *Rising above the Gathering Storm: Energizing and Employing America for a Brighter Economic Future*, National Academy of Sciences, National Academy of Engineering, and Institute of Medicine, 2005, https://nap.nationalacademies.org/catalog/11463/rising-above-the-gathering-storm-energizing-and-employing-america-for.

29. *Rising above the Gathering Storm*, xi.

30. *Rising Above the Gathering Storm*, 4, 13, 25.

31. "Pelosi: Unveils Innovation Agenda, Part of Vision for a Stronger America," November 15, 2005, Press Release, https://pelosi.house.gov/news/press-releases/pelosi-unveils-innovation-agenda-part-of-vision-for-a-stronger-america.

32. America Creating Opportunities to Meaningfully Promote Excellence in Technology, Education, and Science Act, H.R. 2272, 110th Cong. (2007), signed August 9, 2007, Public Law No. 110-69.

33. Conference Report on H.R. 2272 America COMPETES Act, 153 Cong. Rec. H9597 (2007).

34. Sense of Congress Regarding Science Education, 154 Cong. Rec. H4912 (2008).

35. Sense of Congress Regarding Science Education, 154 Cong. Rec. H4914 (2008).

36. *Fulfilling the Potential of Women in Academic Science and Engineering Act of 2008: Hearing before the Subcommittee on Research and Science Education, Committee on Science and Technology House of Representatives*, 110th Cong. (2008).

37. *Beyond Bias and Barriers: Fulfilling the Potential of Women in Academic Science and Engineering*, National Academies Science, Engineering, Medicine, 2007, https://nap.nationalacademies.org/catalog/11741/beyond-bias-and-barriers-fulfilling-the-potential-of-women-in.

38. "President Obama Launches 'Educate to Innovate' Campaign for Excellence in Science, Technology, Engineering & Math (Stem) Education," the White House, Office of the Press Secretary, November 23, 2009,

https://obamawhitehouse.archives.gov/the-press-office/president-oba-ma-launches-educate-innovate-campaign-excellence-science-technol-ogy-en.

39. *Rising above the Gathering Storm, Revisited: Rapidly Approaching Category 5*, National Academies Sciences, Engineering, Medicine, 2010, https://nap.nationalacademies.org/catalog/12999/rising-above-the-gathering-storm-revisited-rapidly-approaching-category-5.

40. America COMPETES Reauthorization Act of 2010, H.R. 5116, 111th Cong. (2010), signed January 4, 2011, Public Law No. 111-358.

41. Committee on Science and Technology, House of Representatives for the one Hundred Eleventh Congress, Summary of Activities, H.R. Rep. No. 111-698 (2010).

42. H.R. Rep. No. 111-698, at 294–97.

43. America Competes Reauthorization Act of 2014, H.R. 4159, 113th Cong. (2014).

44. America COMPETES Reauthorization Act of 2015, H.R. 1806, 114th Cong. (2015), passed House, May 20, 2015.

45. Committee on Science, Space and Technology, House of Representatives for the one Hundred Fourteenth Congress, America COMPETES Reauthorization Act of 2015, Report together with Minority and Additional Views, May 8, 2015.

46. America COMPETES Reauthorization Act of 2015, 161 Cong. Rec. H3420 (2015).

47. STEM Education Act of 2015, H.R. 1020, 114th Cong. (2015), signed October 7, 2015, Public Law No. 114-50.

48. STEM Education Act of 2015, 161 Cong. Rec. H1099 (2015).

49. STEM Education Act of 2015, 161 Cong. Rec. H1099 (2015).

50. 50 Recognizing Cedar Hill Collegiate's Commitment to STEM Education, 162 Cong. Rec. E1349 (2106); Recognizing Drew Freeman Middle School's Commitment to STEM Education, 162 Cong. Rec. E1330 (2016); Recognizing Eastern Senior High School's Commitment to STEM Education, 162 Cong Rec. E1327 (2016); Recognizing Howard University Middle School's Commitment to STEM Education, 162 Cong. Rec. E1326 (2016); Recognizing Ron Brown High School's Commitment to STEM Education, 162 Cong. Rec. E1323 (2016); Recognizing LaSalle-Backus Education Campus's Commitment to STEM Education, 162 Cong. Rec. E1321 (2016); Recognizing Central City Public Charter School, Brightwood Campus's Commitment to

STEM Education, 162 Cong. Rec. E1352 (2016); Recognizing McKinley Technology High School's Commitment to STEM Education, 162 Cong. Rec. E1352 (2016); Recognizing Jefferson Academy's Commitment to STEM Education, 162 Cong. Rec. E1351 (2016); Recognizing H. D. Woodson Academy of Engineering High School's Commitment to STEM Education, 162 Cong. Rec. E1351 (2016); Recognizing C-STEM Teacher and Student Support Services, Inc.'s Commitment to STEM Education, 162 Cong. Rec. E1350 (2016).

51. STEM Research and Education Effectiveness and Transparency Act, H.R. 4375, 115th Cong. (2017), passed the House, December 18, 2017.

52. STEM Research and Education Effectiveness and Transparency Act, 163 Cong. Rec. H10159 (2017).

53. STEM Opportunities Act of 2019, H.R. 2528, 116th Cong. (2019), passed House, June 20, 2019.

54. National Science Foundation for the Future Act, H.R. 2225, 117th Cong. (2021), passed the House, June 28, 2021.

55. Department of Energy Science for the Future Act, H.R. 3593, 117th Cong. (2021), passed the House, June 28, 2021.

56. "Cantwell Honors Eddie Bernice Johnson on 40 Years of Service and Shaping the Next Generation of Women in STEM," November 17, 2022, Washington D.C. https://www.commerce.senate.gov/2022/11/cantwell-honors-eddie-bernice-johnson-on-40-years-of-service-and-shaping-the-next-generation-of-women-in-stem.

57. Voting Improvement Act, H.R. 775, 107th Cong. (2001).

58. Help America Vote Act of 2002, H.R. 3295, 107th Cong. (2002), signed October 29, 2002, Public Law No. 107-252.

59. Help America Vote Act of 2001, 158 Cong. Rec. H9295 (2012).

60. Proposing an Amendment to the Constitution of the United States Regarding the Right to Vote, H.J. Res. 28, 108th Cong. (2003).

61. Condemning All Efforts to Suppress and Intimidate Voters in the United States and Reaffirming That the Right to Vote Is a Fundamental Right of All Eligible United States Citizens, H. Res. 793, 108th Cong. (2004).

62. Fannie Lou Hamer, Rosa Parks, and Coretta Scott King Voting Rights Act Reauthorization and Amendments Act of 2006, 152 Cong. Rec. H5161 (2006).

63. For the People Act of 2019, H.R. 1, 116th Cong. (2019), passed the House, March 8, 2019.

64. For the People Act of 2021, H.R. 1, 117th Cong. (2021), passed the House, March 3, 2021.

65. Fighting for the Right to Vote, 167 Cong. Rec. H3899 (2021).

66. Voting Rights Advancement Act of 2019, H.R. 4, 116th Cong. (2019), passed in the House, December 6, 2019.

67. John R. Lewis Voting Rights Advancement Act of 2021, H.R. 4, 117th Cong. (2021), passed in the House, August 24, 2021.

68. John R. Lewis Voting Rights Advancement Act of 2021, 167 Cong. Rec. H4413 (2021).

69. "Trump Says He Trusts China's Xi on Coronavirus and the US Has It 'Totally Under Control,'" CNBC, January 22, 2020, https://www.cnbc.com/2020/01/22/trump-on-coronavirus-from-china-we-have-it-totally-under-control.html.

70. *Coronaviruses: Understanding the Spread of Infectious Diseases and Mobilizing Innovative Solutions: Hearing Before the Committee on Science, Space, and Technology House of Representatives*, 116th Cong. (2020).

71. *Coronaviruses*, at 47.

72. *Repurposing Therapeutic Drugs for COVID 19: Research Challenges and Opportunities, Hearing Before the Committee on Science, Space, and Technology, House of Representatives*, 116th Cong. (2020).

73. *Sweltering in Place: COVID-19, Extreme Heat, and Environmental Justice: Hearing Before the Committee on Science, Space, and Technology, House of Representatives*, 116th Cong. (2020).

74. *Data for Decision-Making: Responsible Management of Data During COVID-19 and Beyond: Hearing Before the Subcommittee on Investigations and Oversight of the Committee on Science, Space, and Technology House of Representatives*, 116th Cong. (2020).

75. Honoring the 100th Anniversary of Alpha Kappa Alpha, 154 Cong. Rec. E16 (2008).

76. Recognizing the Contributions of Alpha Kappa Alpha Sorority, Inc. to African American History, 106th Congress, March 6, 2000, E227.

77. Authorizing the Use of the Capitol Grounds for a Celebration of the 100th Anniversary of Alpha Kappa Alpha Sorority, 154 Cong. Rec. H4886 (2008).

78. Honoring Alpha Kappa Alpha Sorority, Inc. to African American History, 146 Cong. Rec. E237 (2013).

79. Recognizing the 85th Anniversary of Alpha Xi Omega Chapter of Alpha Kappa Alpha Sorority, Inc., Dallas, Texas, 160 Cong. Rec. E874 (2014).

80. "1400 Attended Rights Parley: Prestigious Women Abounded at Conference," *Fort Worth Star-Telegram*, August 31, 1970, 17.

81. "Speakers," *Fort Worth Star-Telegram*, March 1, 1975, 23.

82. "Sumposium [*sic*] Set April 6 at ETSU," *Paris News*, March 3, 1975, 3.

83. "Diversity Marks Conference: Women Experience Gamut of Emotions," *Fort Worth Star-Telegram*, November 14, 1975, 25.

84. Senate Special Advisory Committee on the Creation and Expansion of Minority and Women Owned Business Ownership Opportunities: Interim Report to the 72nd Texas Legislature, January 8, 1991.

85. Comprehensive Women's Pension Protection Act of 1996, H.R. 4204, 104th Cong. (1996).

86. Economic Equity Act of 1996, H.R. 3857, 104th Cong. (1996).

87. Commission on the Advancement of Women in the Science and Engineering Work Forces Act, H.R. 3726, 104th Cong. (1996).

88. Breast and Cervical Cancer Information Act of 1993, H.R. 2293, 103rd Cong. (1993).

89. Women and HIV Outreach and Prevention Act, H.R. 2395, 103rd Cong. (1993).

90. Women's Health Equity Act of 1993, H.R. 3075, 103rd Cong. (1993).

91. Gender Equity in Education Act of 1993, H.R. 1793, 103rd Cong. (1993).

92. Children's Electromagnetic Field Risk Reduction Act of 1993, H.R. 1494, 103rd Cong. (1993).

93. To Award Posthumously a Congressional Gold Medal to Addie Mae Collins, Denise McNair, Carole Robertson, and Cynthia Wesley to Commemorate the Lives They Lost 50 Years Ago in the Bombing of the Sixteen Street Baptist Church, Where These 4 Little Black girls' Ultimate Sacrifice Served as a Catalyst for the Civil Rights Movement, H.R. 360, 113th Cong. (2013), signed Mary 24, 2013, Public law No. 113-11.

94. Hidden Figures Congressional Gold Medal Act, H.R. 1396, 116th Cong. (2019), signed November 8, 2019, Public Law No. 116-68.

95. Expressing the Sense of Congress with Respect to the Establishment of an Appropriate Day for the Commemoration of the Women Suffragists Who Fought for and Won the Right of Women to Vote in the United States, H.J. Res. 59, 109th Cong. (2005), signed August 2, 2005, Public Law No. 109-49.

96. Designating March 1993 and March 1994 both as "Women's History Month," H.J. Res. 143, 103rd Cong. (1993).

97. Sally K. Ride Congressional Gold Medal Act of 2014, H.R. 2422, 113th Cong. (2013).

98. Congressional Tribute to Constance Baker Motley Act of 2013, H.R. 3097, 113th Cong. (2013).

99. Shirley Chisholm Congressional Gold Medal Act, H.R. 188, 109th Cong. (2005).

100. Aretha Franklin Congressional Gold Medal Act, H.R. 6681, 115th Cong. (2018).

101. Expressing the Sense of the Congress That a Postage Stamp Should Be Issued to Honor Zora Neale Hurston, H. Con. Res. 129, 105th Cong. (1997).

102. Honoring the life of Betty Shabazz, H. Res. 183, 105th Cong. (1997).

103. Authorizing the Remains of Rosa Parks to Lie in Honor in the Rotunda of the Capitol, H. Con. Res. 286, 109th Cong. (2005).

104. Honoring the Life and Accomplishments of Mrs. Coretta Scott King and Her Contributions as a Leader in the Struggle for Civil Rights, and Expressing Condolences to the King Family on Her Passing, H. Res. 655, 109th Cong. (2006), agreed to in House February 1, 2006.

105. Commending the State of Kuwait for Granting Women Certain Important Political Rights, H. Res. 343, 109th Cong. (2005), agreed to in House July 12, 2005.

106. Commending and Supporting Radio Al Mahabba, Iraq's First and Only Radio Station for Women, H. Res. 784, 109th Cong. (2006), agreed to in House July 18, 2006.

107. Tribute to a Great Texas Woman, 142 Cong. Rec. E432 (1996); Honoring the Work of Louise Ballerstedt Raggio, Mother of the Texas Family Code, 155 Cong. Rec. E1352 (2009); Remembering Louise Hilm Ballerstedt Raggio, 157 Cong. Rec. E99 (2011).

108. Women in Public Service, 142 Cong. Rec. H2662 (1996); Recognizing the Distinguished Career and Retirement of Demetris A. Sampson, 160 Cong. Rec. E1091 (2014); Women's History Month, 165 Cong. Rec. E347 (2019).

109. Women's History Month, 145 Cong. Rec. H1686 (1999).

110. Expressing the Sense of the Congress That All Workers Deserve Fair Treatment and Safe Working Conditions, and Honoring Dolores Huerta for Her Commitment to the Improvement of Working Conditions for Children, Women, and Farm Worker Families, H. Con. Res. 177, 107th Cong. (2001).

111. To Award a Congressional Gold Medal to Malala Yousufzai, in Recognition of Her Devoted Service to Education, Justice, and Equality in Pakistan, H.R. 6588, 112th Cong. (2012); To Award a Congressional Gold Medal to Malala Yousufzai, in Recognition of Her Devoted Service to Education, Justice, and Equality in Pakistan, H.R. 69, 113th Cong. (2013); To Award a Congressional Gold Medal to Malala Yousafzai, a Recipient of the Nobel Prize for Peace, in Recognition of Her Devoted Service to Education, Justice, and Equality in Pakistan, H.R. 69, 114th Cong. (2016).

112. Honoring Lindy Boggs on her 95th Birthday, 157 Cong. Rec. E1016 (2011); Honoring Ambassador Lindy Boggs, 159 Cong. Rec. E1164 (2013).

113. Supporting the Goals of International Women's Day, 153 Cong. Rec. H2178 (2007); Recognizing Ellen Johnson Sirleaf, President of Liberia, 163 Cong. Rec. E840 (2017).

114. Recognizing the Significant Achievement of Chief Justice Carolyn Wright, 163 Cong. Rec. E349 (2017).

115. Celebrating 90 years of Peacemaking, 151 Cong. Rec. E651 (2005).

116. Expressing the Sense of the Congress That Women Throughout the World Should Join Together for a Week of Workshops, Forums, and Other Events to Speak Up for World Peace, H.Con.Res. 107-290, 107th Cong. (2001).

117. Executive Order: Instituting a National Action Plan on Women, Peace, and Security, the White House, Office of the Press Secretary, December 19, 2011, https://obamawhitehouse.archives.gov/the-press-office/2011/12/19/executive-order-instituting-national-action-plan-women-peace-and-securit.

118. Women, Peace, and Security Act of 2017, S.1141, 115th Cong. (2017), signed October 6, 2017, Public Law No. 115-68.

Notes for Chapter 17

1. "Lucas Statement on Chairwoman Eddie Bernice Johnson's Retirement," *Committee on Science, Space, and Technology*, November 19, 2021, https://science.house.gov/2021/11/lucas-statement-chairwoman-eddie-bernice-johnson-s-retirement.

2. Retiring Women Members of Congress, 142 Cong. Rec. H11218 (1996).

Notes for Epilogue

1. Sam Roberts, "Eddie Bernice Johnson, Trailblazer in Congress and Beyond, Dies at 89," *New York Times*, January 3, 2024, https://www.nytimes.com/2024/01/03/us/politics/eddie-bernice-johnson-dead.html.

2. Harrison Smith, "Eddie Bernice Johnson, Trailblazing Texan in U.S. House Dies at 89," *Washington Post*, January 2, 2024, https://www.washingtonpost.com/obituaries/2024/01/02/eddie-bernice-johnson-dead/.

3. Colin McCullough, "Trailblazing Former Rep. Eddie Bernice Johnson, Who Served Nearly 30 Years in Congress, Dies at 88," *CNN*, January 1, 2024, https://www.cnn.com/2024/01/01/politics/eddie-bernice-johnson-death/index.html.

4. "Influential Former Texas US Rep. Eddie Bernice Johnson Dies at 89," *ABC News*, December 31, 2023, https://abcnews.go.com/US/wireStory/influential-former-texas-us-rep-eddie-bernice-johnson-106024237.

5. "Influential Former Texas US Rep. Eddie Bernice Johnson Dies at 89," *U.S. News and World Report*, Dec. 31, 2023, https://www.usnews.com/news/best-states/texas/articles/2023-12-31/influential-former-texas-us-rep-eddie-bernice-johnson-dies-at-88.

6. Statement from President Joe Biden on the Passing of Former Congresswoman Eddie Bernice Johnson, December 31, 2023, https://www.whitehouse.gov/briefing-room/statements-releases/2023/12/31/statement-from-president-joe-biden-on-the-passing-of-former-congresswoman-eddie-bernice-johnson/.

7. Statement by Vice President Kamala Harris on The Passing of Congresswoman Eddie Bernice Johnson, December 31, 2023, https://www.whitehouse.gov/briefing-room/statements-releases/2023/12/31/statement-by-vice-president-kamala-harris-on-the-passing-of-congresswoman-eddie-bernice-johnson/.

8. "Texas Democratic Party Mourns the Loss of Former Congresswoman Eddie Bernice Johnson," *Texas Democrats*, December 31, 2023, https://www.texasdemocrats.org/media/texas-democratic-party-mourns-the-loss-of-former-congresswoman-eddie-bernice-johnson.

9. "Opinion: Eddie Bernice Johnson's Wisdom, Optimism for America Will Be Missed: Her Steely Will and Gentle Graces Defined Her Rise in Texas Politics," *Dallas Morning News*, January 1, 2024, https://www.dallasnews.com/opinion/editorials/2024/01/01/eddie-bernice-johnsons-wisdom-optimism-for-america-will-be-missed/.

10. Danette Anthony Reed, international president and CEO of Alpha Kappa Alpha Sorority, "Eddie Bernice Johnson Funeral (Jan. 9. 2024)," WFAA, YouTube video, 1:36, https://www.youtube.com/watch?v=kX82vkgkZaM.

11. Ethel Issacs Williams, JD, national president, The Links, Inc., "Eddie Bernice Johnson Funeral," 1:41.

12. Dallas County judge Clay Jenkins, "Former Congresswoman Eddie Bernice Johnson's Wake at Concord Church in Dallas," WFAA, January 8, 2024, YouTube video, 12:46–16:12, https://www.youtube.com/watch?v=ka2SjV2kU7o.

13. Curtis King, founder, Texas Black Academy of Arts and Letters, "Eddie Bernice Johnson's Wake," 19:59–24:00.

14. Congresswoman Sheila Jackson Lee, "Eddie Bernice Johnson's Wake," 50:23–55:41.

15. Former congressman Gregory Meeks, "Eddie Bernice Johnson's Wake," 1:01:53–1:06:53.

16. Senior Pastor Bryan Carter, "Live: Eddie Bernice Johnson Funeral," WFAA, January 9, 2024, YouTube video, 20:47–22:17.

17. Vice President Kamala Harris, "Eddie Bernice Johnson Funeral," 35:05–36:28.

18. Former president William Jefferson Clinton, "Eddie Bernice Johnson Funeral," 36:29–38:47.

19. Secretary Marcia Fudge, "Eddie Bernice Johnson Funeral," 43:40–43:50.

20. Congressman Hakeem Jeffries, "Eddie Bernice Johnson Funeral," 47:04–49:23.

21. Congressman James Clyburn, "Live: Eddie Bernice Johnson Funeral," 52:37–54:49.

22. Dr. Stephanie S. Elizalde, superintendent, Dallas Independent School District, "Eddie Bernice Johnson Funeral," 1:30:46–1:30:50.

23. Luci Baines Johnson, daughter of President and Mrs. Lyndon Baines Johnson, "Eddie Bernice Johnson's Funeral," 1:53:55–1:54:32.

24. Ron Kirk, Royce West, Rodney Ellis, "Eddie Bernice Johnson Funeral," 1:06:26–1:14:51.

25. Dallas Mayor Eric Johnson, "Eddie Bernice Johnson Funeral," 1:22:00–1:24:54.

26. Kennedy Johnson and Lily Johnson, "Eddie Bernice Johnson Funeral," 2:30:24–2:31:12.

27. Kirk Johnson, "Eddie Bernice Johnson Funeral," 2:41:12–2:41:54.

Bibliography

Books and Reports

Goodwin, Ken, Scott Ainsworth, and Erik Goodwin. *Lobbying and Policy Making*: *The Public Pursuit of Private Interests*. Los Angeles: Sage Publications, 2013.

National Academies of Sciences, Engineering, and Medicine. *Sexual Harassment of Women*: *Climate, Culture, and Consequences in Academic Sciences, Engineering, and Medicine*. Washington, DC: National Academies Press, 2018.

Journals

Chamberlin, J. "Congressional Black Caucus Spring Health Braintrust Focuses on Universal Health Care." *American Psychological Association* 32, no. 7 (July/August 2001).

Johnson, Eddie Bernice, and Molly Galvin. "The More Inclusion We Have in Science, the Better Outcomes We'll Get." *Issues in Science and Technology* 39, no. 2 (Winter 2023): 27–30.

Newspapers

Austin American-Statesman
Charlotte Observer
Corpus Christi Caller
Corpus Christi Times
Dallas Morning News
Detroit Free Press
El Paso Times
Fort Worth Star-Telegram
Grand Prairie Daily News
Kilgore News Herald
Kinder Courier News
Longview News-Journal
Los Angeles Times
Lubbock Avalanche-Journal
New York Times
Odessa American

Paris News
South Bend Tribune
Tyler Morning Telegraph
Valley Morning Star
Victoria Advocate
Waco News-Tribune
Washington Post

Index

C

D